The Beginnings of Christianity

Andrew Welburn

The Beginnings of Christianity

Essene mystery, Gnostic revelation
and the Christian vision

Floris Books

First published in 1991 by Floris Books
Revised 2004
© 1991 Andrew Welburn

British Library CIP Data available

ISBN 0-86315-448-4

Printed by The Bath Press, Bath

For Sophia

*Christianity, in its abstract purity, became the exoteric expression of
the esoteric doctrines of the poetry and wisdom of antiquity*
Percy Bysshe Shelley

*The Cross on Golgotha is the Mystery cult of antiquity
epitomized in an historical fact*
Rudolf Steiner

Contents

Acknowledgements

Since I hope that the following book does most of what is necessary to explain itself, it remains by way of preface and acknowledgement rather to explain — very briefly — what it does not try to be. My indebtedness to various works of scholarship and spiritual insight is documented in many notes and references, and I can only ask for pardon where through neglect or forgetfulness I have omitted to cite the appropriate author. But more importantly still, I must admit to using much scholarly information in the quest for syntheses rather different from those which dominate the research efforts of the scholars in question. My aim has not at all been to present a consensus view, but quite deliberately to suggest that the results can better be put together in a novel way — at least in some significant respects. It is not unfair to characterize the reception of new ideas in Christian theological circles as, on the whole, an attempt to limit their impact on cherished traditional positions, or at best to assimilate them to those entrenched views with as little disruption as possible. A good deal of even the radical Protestant historical theology this century has been typically defensive: an effort to find room for traditional religious belief in the universe of modern science, even at the cost of jettisoning the 'myth' which clothed that belief in an earlier age.

The present book arose from a sense of the constriction inherent in such an approach, and the wish for a freer look. It seemed rather worthwhile to try to understand what the myths meant to the times which believed in them, and how they were affected by the history that overtook them, including the events underlying the New Testament. The possibility of such a book came out of the modern discoveries of early Christian and pre-Christian writings; on the one hand, broadening the range of our knowledge far beyond what was preserved and hardened into tradition of the Church; and on the other out of Rudolf Steiner's ideas concerning the history of human consciousness. Instead of trying to ask how we can continue to believe in some ancient notions while remaining inhabitants of the modem conceptual universe, Steiner introduced a genuinely historical dimension into science and knowledge generally. We can understand both myth and modem knowledge as corresponding to an evolution of consciousness that is not yet at a conclusion.

The note of defensiveness need not be the prevailing one; and the whole story may turn out to have a spiritual import none the less significant to Christian thought. But it may be as well to let these underlying thoughts emerge in the course of the various studies to come. I only make the point that much accepted information is here to be viewed in an altered context, and since it seemed inappropriate to indulge in the inevitably long arguments against rival interpretations, my conclusions might occasionally surprise the authors quoted to support them. At the same time, they may be surprised at the extent to which Rudolf Steiner — sometimes portrayed as an outsider to the mainstream of Christian tradition — effectively rehabilitated the grand themes of centrally Christian thinking. In this way, surprise on both sides may only be a prelude to the beginning of a reconciliation.

The book covers a wide field, and is not addressed to specialists. Where it relies on new interpretations of material discovered at Nag Hammadi or elsewhere, I have published more detailed scholarly accounts establishing my position. The material from the *Apocalypse of Adam* is analysed in my article published in W. Haase and H. Temporini (eds.), *Aufstieg und Niedergang der romischen Welt*, Part II, vol. 25.4, Berlin and New York 1988; the details of Gnostic cosmology are reconstructed in my articles in the journals *Vigiliae Christianae* (1978) and *Novum Testamentum* (1981); the background of the *Gospel of Philip* is the theme of another Contribution to *Aufstieg und Niedergang der romischen Welt*, the still forthcoming Part II, vol. 22. I have to thank for help and advice at various stages Robin Lane Fox, for encouraging me in my Gnostic studies; Mary Boyce for invaluable aid with Iranian materials; Sebastian Brock for his kind response to queries from a non-Syriac speaker; Rudolf Kohler for his positive assessment of the present work in its earliest form; Michael Tapp and Tony Brown for looking over a later version with theologians' and historians' eyes; Jonathan Westphal for his friendly philosophical perplexity over the Gnostic parts and sense of the important issues concealed in the whole; Jon Michael Ebersole for sending me his comments on the earlier chapters; Julia Wedgwood for enthusiastically reading and painstakingly correcting the typescript; Mona Bradley for typing it and for asking, at every stage, the right questions. I would also like to acknowledge the support, in the later stages of writing this book, from the Margaret Wilkinson Fund.

Although his name and work are infrequently cited below, the work of Oscar Cullmann occupies a much larger place in my view of the field than references to him could suggest. His sense of the setting of early Christianity in the world of the esoteric Jewish sects first encouraged me to think that a survey of the kind that has occupied me in this book could seriously be undertaken. I mention his achievement with a sense of gratitude and humility.

A.W.

Foreword to the New Edition

Every book is written to address a specific situation, and a new edition is a chance to remember that and reassess the relevance of a work to the situation that now prevails. Ten years or so ago, as I was finishing this book, it was apparent that the picture of Christian origins among scholars was under serious review. Nowadays anyone who strays into scholarly debates on the subject might be forgiven for feeling that everything is review, and very little picture remains at all! So many possible reconstructions have been mooted, and so many have been rejected and demolished once more. Yet I take a pleasure in this proliferation which is not, I think, a perverse pleasure. Part of the point of this book was to contest the notion that Christianity had been a successful propaganda campaign, in the course of which a small group of obscure sectarians promoted a Messiah through a simple message and spread their views by a mixture of persuasion and conquest throughout the known world. Christianity was a deep change in the way people experienced themselves, the world and God. Many different cultures and types of individual were desperately seeking something that ancient civilisation could no longer satisfy, even though at the same time Christianity was a radical shock to the foundations on which they were seeking it. Many different forms of earliest Christianity seized hold of the much-needed change of viewpoint in a particular aspect; many groups furnished essential ideas to Christian development, yet none of them is the whole truth of what was happening. I continue to think that the backgrounds of which I have written in this book were the main currents around which the 'Christian breakthrough' occurred, though of course there were others still worth exploring about which I have learned significantly and added some material in response. But even more important, the whole obsessive investigation of Christian origins will surely continue to throw up a welter of different elements, none of which can give 'the answer,' unless we find a connection to that larger change which makes sense of them all. In a very unperverse way, therefore, the current excitement and diversity has posed once again in a living way not just an academic-historical question but the very central question of Christianity itself.

People with whom I talk about these things recognise both the greater import and the openness of the search, and find it gripping in a way that the well-crafted selective version of events preserved by the Church's tradition failed fully to engage. I do not mean that they identify (apart from small bands of enthusiasts) with the specific forms: there is after all something highly artificial in the idea of trying to be a modern-day Essene, or a twenty-first-century Gnostic. Paradoxically, however, the picture of Christianity is under attack today, if one has to see it that way, not so much from the sceptics, who have long ago ceased to worry about skirmishing with religion, but from the side of spirituality. Among the many forms of 'alternative' and liberated spiritual activity, Christianity in its dogmatic sense has come to seem thoroughly antipathetic. The realisation that various approaches to spiritual life can find a common centre and sense of direction while remaining true to the diversity of seeking is surely just what Christianity needs if it is to find again that overwhelming power of change and renewal. Likewise, the many-headed hydra of spirituality can hardly do more than flounder in an alien, 'hi-tech,' manipulative world unless it can truly find the kind of selflessness or self-transforming which is the heart of the Christian answer to the vast potential of the evolution of the individual, the personal moral force that we still need to take us into a fulfilling future. Whatever its historical failings, Christianity showed that such a power can change the world.

The diversity of the modern situation only increases the relevance, I would therefore say, of the approach I tried to take. Before coming to some of the newer developments that seem most interesting, it might be as well to thank the reviewers of the first edition for their criticisms and comments. Diversity was the most striking feature here too, as viewpoints ranged from efforts to limit the validity of my approach to all the Mysteries, religions and philosophies of late antiquity but *not* to Christianity, to congratulating me on a showing Christianity as a sweeping synthesis of the kind I certainly did not mean, even if I had had the vast historical acumen to present it. Indeed I have tried to stress the lack of a schematic development above all, but rather the way that the presence of tensions and different approaches in earliest Christianity put the individual in the forefront, having to find meaning in his or her own history and background that turned out to lead, like others from other directions, to Christian recognition. Many right up to Augustine found the deeper significance of Christianity by this route — though it remains a profound irony that such leading figures came to deny to others the right of seeking personal answers by the path which they had found so full of divine calling and grace.

Other reviewers were worried by the appearance of Rudolf Steiner. In view of what I have said already about the spiritual potential of the situation today, I can only affirm the extraordinary interest of his ideas, while pointing out that he is a help in interpreting a subject which I have also explored with the aid of over a hundred explicitly cited other writers and experts. I have found him throughout my work a liberating and not an authority-figure. Some reviewers wanted to associate Steiner with narrow positions, for instance on oriental influence: perhaps I should just point out that Steiner's comments on the background of the gospels came years before Reitzenstein's grand, synthetic account of the 'Iranian Mystery of Redemption' — and that Reitzenstein, brilliant as he sometimes was in detail, is intent on formulating just the sort of historical synthesis that Steiner clearly avoids presenting as the 'essence of Christianity,' and which opened Reitzenstein subsequently to devastating critiques. Rather than going back to a past era of synthesis, we need to be open to many discoveries still being made, or still only half understood. Least of all should we try to draw strict boundaries in over-reaction against past errors. Links between Christian 'regeneration' and the Mysteries have met strong opposition, recently from Wagner among others. But I can only find strange the grounds on which a historian of the calibre of Martin Hengel, writing in 1997, should forcibly distance earliest Christian practices from aspects of the Mysteries. True, we need to be careful, since much of the evidence about such things as Mithraism stems from the 'later, Roman' Mysteries. Plutarch, he admits, speaks of the practice of Mithraic 'mystery-rites' earlier, just at the time Christianity was emerging: but then, *we do not know* how Mithraism evolved into its fully-fledged Roman form from earlier stages, and *therefore* (!?) the passage from Plutarch cannot be used in evidence. Surely the wish to avoid excesses has turned our ignorance into a curiously dogmatic and cavalier attitude to genuine information about a cult which arrived in the first century AD from the Middle East, like Christianity, in Nero's Rome? It is part of a historical picture about whose connection to other developments, one might think, we should at least keep an open mind? Meanwhile experts on the Mysteries such as Walter Burkert consider that the Roman features in the later cult are sometimes hardly more than veneer, the current language into which the religion was rendered, beneath which the Middle Eastern structures remain strongly visible.

As heated debate and research continue, much undoubtedly remains to be discovered and discerned, though in a Foreword like this I can do no more than indicate some of the fieldwork and the extent to which it supports or challenges the approach I adopt in the book. We may start with the Essenes, or better perhaps the 'Dead Sea Scrolls' — or perhaps better still the rediscovery of the various Judaisms which have been explored and tentatively assessed as the larger picture of Jewish religion at the time, so much broader than was realised, has so strikingly emerged. For the scrolls showed Jewish scholars above all that no one line led on to the later period of the Rabbis. Here too there was creative variety. Essenes, Pharisees, Sadducees and other smaller groups have come to life as a rich response to the life of the epoch. In light of the work of J.J. Collins, one might mention such circles as those around the alternative 'temple' in Egypt, in Leontopolis, whose ideas are preserved in sections of the extraordinary *Sibylline Oracles*. The Essenes themselves were rooted in that diversity of Jewish life and particularly the range of baptizing sects, and the interest in them as a special group has to some extent given way to the concern with features that they likely shared, for example, with wider circles before they took their decisive step and made a 'new covenant' in the land of Damascus. Their own distinctive divinely-revealed Law, for example, recorded as from the lips of God himself in the *Temple Scroll*, may in reality also be a key to ideas and practices in Jerusalem itself before the Hasmonaean reforms.

From the Qumran caves themselves more texts and fragments of texts have continued to be found. And technological advances mean that from time-corroded scraps words in black-on-black can now be deciphered. But if the writings fuelled new explorations in Judaism, there has been a long-running suspicion, even at times a strong whiff of scandal, about the way that conservative scholarship seemed to be trying, by dubious or political means to divorce Christianity from the discoveries being made. Publication was so slow that in effect some important texts simply sank without trace, with only designated scholars from particular projects having access for decades at a time. On a more subtle level, there has been a counter-reaction to the initial excitement of the 'Scrolls,' and a drive in certain circles to re-emphasise more traditional ideas of the setting of Christianity. But now the tide may be reversing once again, as the emergent picture of Jewish-Christianity in the early period, before the unifying of the Church and the influence of Paul on Christian theology, also takes ever more concrete shape. Traditions in the name of Jesus' brother James are increasingly identified as a specific force, and may have dominated in the Jerusalem of the apostles after Jesus' death: and he was remembered as 'just' in the exacting terms of a Jewish holy man, taking nothing away from the fulfilment of the Law. R. Eisenman took the initiative and published many of the land-logged Dead Sea texts, and drawn many lines from Essene theology to the Christianity of James and his followers, before publishing his very substantial book on this brother of Jesus whom many now see as increasingly important. What is significant is not so much the theory that this 'Righteous' man is the Righteous Teacher mentioned by the Scrolls, but the demonstration of the many continuing lines of development from the esoteric ideals of the Essenes to early Christians. Interestingly in this new context, Rudolf Steiner stressed the lack of any clear boundaries between Christianity and Judaism up to AD 70 and the new picture may, as we shall see, help to some extent in creating a plausible frame for the Jesus of history before he was taken over by the Church. One specific issue that appears to have been definitely resolved, at any rate, is the early dating of the passages in the *Book of Enoch* which relate to the 'Son of Man': though some scholars long doubted it, clearly they *were* extant by the time of Jesus; the Qumran evidence was finally forthcoming. Some have now wondered whether Jesus even knew these texts and meditated on them, as he must have known the ideas behind them. Certainly we need to draw on *Enoch* to understand some aspects of Jesus' words at his trial, for example, which cannot be fully comprehended through the usual cross-referencing to Daniel chapter 7. When Jesus confronts the Jewish authorities at his trial before the Sanhedrin with his revelatory 'I am,' and tells how they will see the Son of Man sitting at the right hand of the Power in heaven, he is presenting their actions, and his own significance, as the fulfilment of Enoch's prophecies in chapter 62: 'the governors, the high officials and the landlords shall see and recognise him — how he sits on the throne of his Glory ... They shall be fearful and downcast, and pain will take hold of them when they see that Son of Man...' And yet the authorities have rejected these and other prized traditions treasured among the Essenes, and they do not recognise what they see. His meaning here is once again a mystery, visible only to the initiated, and seeming to those outside a blasphemy.

The exploration of Jewish-Christian traditions takes us not only into the domain of the 'Scrolls,' however, but into Gnostic terrain and Nag Hammadi studies. In the *Secret Book of James* from the Nag Hammadi library we have not only traditions related to those just surveyed, but in all probability an independent witness to the words of Jesus, that has not gone through the channel of the orthodox Church. What may perturb the reader on first acquaintance, however, is the way his words are interpreted in a strange 'dualistic' way. The work stresses not the continuity of the revelation with the earthly Christ, but the way the meaning did *not* come through until its spiritual side was afterwards opened up. Of course, in the New Testament too we frequently have allusions to the disciples' failure to see until later, until after the resurrection, until Pentecost: but the disparity here seems to open a deeper fissure in what we must see as a Gnostic trend. Or to put it another way, those called Gnostics in the subsequent traditions were following on in a slightly different way from the earliest tendencies too, and were only later pushed out to form marginal, 'heretical' groups.

All this, and much else that has been uncovered in detail since I wrote, has confirmed for me the approach I adopted in this book, which argues that esoteric-Jewish and Gnostic ideas are not in any simple way to be opposed, but are two sides of a complex of problems essential to the origins of Christianity. Without pre-empting my presentation in detail, both were wrestling with tensions that were ever more powerfully being felt between the spiritual life as it had long been experienced through myth and rite, and earthly-historical reality which had come to assume for Judaism a special meaning as the dimension of God's special revelation, the special meaning of the 'chosen people' with a destiny to fulfil. Now, it is perfectly possible to resolve the problem one way or another, so long as one is prepared to lock oneself within a particular framework. One could belong to the Jewish sense of religious history and moral decision, which places the individual in a role of considerable responsibility, and at the same time offers very substantial communal support. Or one could preserve something of the value of belonging to the cosmos with its timeless patterns of renewal and revelation that could be ever retold in myths, or by Hellenistic times, increasingly rationalised as philosophy and science. For this culture, the Jewish claim to special destiny seemed strange and unintelligible. But supposing one wanted to bring the sense of history and individual responsibility to the wider world? Or supposing one wanted to add to the sense of one's uniqueness a philosophical and religious understanding of one's meaning in the cosmos? On a popular level, and even on a sophisticated one, all sorts of fudges are possible, and one can stay secure within one's own room, so to speak, while sweeping the contradictions under the carpet. But the 'esoteric' teaching of Essenes, Gnostics and others is 'set apart,' and its real importance lies, rather, in its refusal to stay within boxes, but to face up to the wider issues. All of their teachings deal directly with the crisis posed, though they differ in that some of them think that we can transcend the particular conditions of history in an act of inner regeneration and 'breakthrough' understanding — a meltdown in terms of thinking and consciousness; while others think that the world itself will have to change, even be catastrophically destroyed and literally come to an end — a meltdown in terms of society and nature that will allow the contradictions to cancel out and a new, harmonious and unified level of life to begin. Christianity drew on both these visions and, as I try to bring out, it offered a deeper vision still in which individual and social change are part of a deeper whole, and we are in a potentially creative relationship both to society and to the natural world around us. The sense of individual destiny, and of cosmic significance, are crucial to any version of Christianity that is worth taking forward in the crises of today, which can still be aptly described as both Gnostic ones of consciousness and inner contradiction, and apocalyptic ones of our relationship to the world around us that is dramatically changing either for disaster or renewal. At the same time, the certainty that neither can be solved separately has never been so clear.

Neither Gnosticism nor esoteric Judaism should be seen as separate new 'religions' however. On the contrary, the new picture has shown the Essenes despite their settlement at remote Qumran as very much part of the Judaism of their time; and the Gnosticism which shows itself in so many forms, both pagan and then Christian, was probably less like the organised movement with a set of distinctive ideas, the 'Gnostic religion' once imagined by Hans Jonas, than a tendency linking many of the loosely associated cults that were active in the Middle-Eastern and Mediterranean worlds. That does not mean it was just a splinter, a disintegrating breakaway ideology from Alexandrian Judaism, or that because we cannot construct a monolithic movement there can have been nothing but various protests and individual challenges to the perspective of whichever 'box' — so that Gnosticism in reality never existed, as one American scholar has seen fit to assert. That is to misunderstand the shared 'religiousness,' as R. Lane Fox has called it of the Hellenistic world, which enabled many different local cultic forms to collaborate and interact. Walter Burkert too has stressed how the Mystery-cults never broke with the pattern of small groups in scattered centres, yet maintained a web of interaction and nurtured important new developments in religion and thought. To look for a shared 'new faith' like that of emergent Christianity, which was a striking and unparalleled phenomenon, is to fall back into the error of many early Christian Fathers themselves. We have not yet freed ourselves sufficiently from our assumptions that other forms of 'religiousness' must all be organised along the lines of our own familiar forms. But Gnosticism arose as a coherent attitude and a profound response where cosmic and individual-historical perspectives clashed, and was elaborated in 'esoteric' centres like those of the Mystery-cults into a way of spiritual transcendence.

The pagan *thiasos* or cultic community like those of the Mysteries remains the obvious basis for a Gnostic cell, and the evidence of cultic activity either continuing or underlying Gnostic ideas is documented overwhelmingly in the Nag Hammadi writings and elsewhere, even if there was later often a move away from cultic ideas. In the ancient world, ideas spread through these networks in a rather living, creative way — being absorbed into local religious forms if they could be found to harmonise, or bringing an element of challenge and stimulating development to religious life. There is increasing evidence that earliest Christianity too spread through such networks. Helmut Koester thinks that the earliest Christians in Corinth, who were there before Paul arrived, were organised as a Mystery-community. Jesus was to them the great initiator, and since they specially valued his sayings they may have regarded them as a 'path' of wisdom; similar ideas are found in the 'esoteric theology,' as Koester calls it, of *The Gospel of Thomas*; and Jesus is regarded as founder and initiator in the Mystery-rites in the *Gospel of Philip*; our familiar Gospel of Mark may have had similar origins, if we accept the evidence of the 'secret Mark.' Subsequently, indeed, Christianity left behind these forms and obtained its startling power to unite people right across society and across the inhabited world by becoming a unified creed of a 'catholic' (universal) nature. But we may follow Rudolf Steiner in questioning whether it did not lose something essential to the full spiritual life, and also to understanding itself and its origins, in the process. He believed that in reality the universal message need not mean a break with the kind of immediacy and challenge that people experienced in the Mysteries, and that today too Christianity needs constantly to keep in touch with its esoteric roots if it is show itself the religion of the future. In fact, one might well characterise that as the essence of his message and the gist of his approach to Christianity in his incredibly productive and active teaching life.

Mention of the 'secret Gospel' of Mark brings us to the hub of the matter, where the ideas from wider sources most obviously push in upon familiar territory and challenge older views. Resistance remains strong, but the possibility that what many regard as our earliest source for Jesus' life may have issued from esoteric circles which baptized pupils into a 'mystery' has to be considered, and a number of influential voices are in favour. Those against mostly try to turn the fragment into a 'apocryphal' text. But one must be very careful here. For the passage quoted as 'secret' by Clement of Alexandria in his newly discovered *Letter to Theodore* only attests to a version of the Gospel that was longer than ours. There are many indications that the passage is genuine Mark, though argument continues to smoulder. Quite distinct as an issue, however, is the matter of Clement's theory of its composition. Only if we accept this do we find ourselves believing in a second work from Mark's hand with deeper esoteric materials ('thus he composed a more spiritual Gospel'). But this language echoes Clement's on another occasion, about the Gospel of John, and reflects his own most favourite approach — with which one might well suspect he is forcing the substance of his account to fit in. Moreover, Clement as we know from elsewhere was at the same time committed to the prevailing legend in the Church which connected Mark's Gospel with Rome, and the elaborate multi-stage theory rather obviously allows him to adhere to this while pursuing his favourite idea of a higher-level Christianity for the élite. But was the secret passage the product of these sorts of ideas in Clement's second-century world? The fact that it does not really fit with his views, so that he has to mention yet a third level since it seems to him that even now Mark has not included mention of those prized doctrines 'that are not to be spoken of,' suggests that actually it was not. The case based on Clement for an apocryphal, separate Gospel, the 'secret Mark,' at any rate, is actually most tenuous of all.

If traditions like those from Corinth, from *Thomas*, *Philip* and the longer Mark are genuine, it implies that Jesus must at the very least have been known in the esoteric baptizing sects as a teacher and initiator, as one of their own. Perhaps in this context one might mention something stemming from the increasing recognition of the Gospel of John as an historical source that stands close to Jesus. In contrast to the account in the synoptics (Matthew, Mark and Luke), John is now thought to be more authentic in connecting Jesus' earliest disciples with the circles of John the Baptist in Judaea, rather than pointing to Galilee. It is interesting, perhaps, that one of Rudolf Steiner's early followers, the oriental scholar Hermann Beckh, also arrived at this very conviction, that the calling of the disciples in Galilee is a spiritual-imaginative picture, and that John has preserved more of the historical events. The picture tells us a profound truth, since in the Gospels and in the experience of the early Christians Galilee is charged with theological significance as the place of the future, of the 'new age' as one Markan scholar has recently called it, in contrast to the past of Jerusalem and Judaea, and even of the wilderness whence John the Baptist proclaimed their end, and the axe laid to the root of the tree. 'He goes before you into Galilee.' Perhaps any earthly locality where one is called to the work of the future and of

Christ is rightly called Galilee. But my point here is that the link of Christian origins to the baptizing milieu is not at all limited to the Essenes, but to the network which included other kinds of spiritual attitudes, developing gradually into what we call Gnosticism as well as into Jewish Christianity. The kind of experiences which initiation into their vision afforded might in turn explain the 'spiritual-imaginative pictures': in the work of R. Malina, for instance, we have at last the exciting scholarly recognition that scenes like the 'walking on the water' reflect altered states of consciousness, spiritual experiences. The possibility of breaking free from the old dichotomy of literal miracles or stories dismissed as myths at last seems to be opening up.

How we accommodate Jesus in the historical setting of those spiritual movements is dependent, naturally, on how we evaluate the Gospels and understand their manner of expression. That in its turn is somewhat dependent on the problematic nature of documents originating some thousands of years ago about whose authors and their purposes we know fundamentally very little. But it is even more dependent upon the kind of presuppositions we bring to them as modern researchers. Nowhere have altering perspectives based on changing our methods and assumptions produced more dramatic results, in fact, than in recent Gospel studies. Nowhere, one might add, has it proved more difficult to shift intransigent methodological commitments that have effectively blinkered generations of scholars. When I wrote this book scarcely anyone, outside what would be dismissed as 'fundamentalist' circles, believed that one could see through the literary traditions of the Gospels to the historical reality of the events behind them at all. What one saw looking back through them was rather the complex literary process of their construction out of the many traditional units which were patched together from many sources of varying age and authenticity. Or, since the Gospels were all plainly more organised that this allowed, one could see through to the selection-procedures of a 'redactor' or editor-figure. And as a result, no-one bothered to ask many basic historical questions, either about the Gospels or their contents.

So unquestionably was it assumed that the Gospels were compiled from traditions presenting Jesus as a figure of religious proclamation, *kerygma*, that the question of what contemporary literary form might be relevant to their presentation was systematically excluded from consideration. The 'kerygmatic Gospels' of the New Testament told us nothing about the life of Jesus, but only about what people supposed that life to have meant for faith. So all-consuming to scholars were the fascinating details of the shared components or units of tradition among the several Gospels that they came to make up a 'synoptic' world of their own, which rather than touching upon external historical reality required the invention of fictional common source-documents such as 'Q' (from German *Quelle*, 'source'). A hypnotic logical game blossomed, so complex that Hermann Hesse's glass-bead game might be child's play in comparison, trying to account for the texts by conjuring up their origins from themselves. It is remarkable how easily people accepted that Matthew and Luke have some materials in common that are not in Mark, so they *must* have had a common source, Q. Scholars argued with curiously impassioned certainty that this inference was absolutely safe — indeed it was only putting into formal terms the evidence of the Gospel-texts themselves! Now, one might think that such an inference would require us to show that the common materials all show some similar attitude or characteristic, giving us an outside criterion to test the case, otherwise just putting the shared materials together actually amounts to nothing at all. (Unfortunately even this touch of history would be too much: Q is admitted to have no singular characteristic or viewpoint. But, say the devotees, it could be analysed into several stages ....) But in the end it is actually the whole logic that it questionable, for a celebrated rule of logic states that in explaining something, the number of explanatory factors should be kept to a minimum, should not be multiplied *beyond necessity*. And in fact Q is not at all a necessary assumption, still less an inescapable fact given by the texts. Indeed in all their logical speculation the scholars seem to have forgotten the most basic historical question of all. Why do we need to assume that the material Luke shares with Matthew once existed independently of both of them? What if Luke simply knew Matthew's text? Logically this requires fewer unwarranted assumptions than the Q-hypothesis. Historically, we are learning in ever more detail just how widely known and respected was Matthew's Gospel in the earliest Church; the possibility that it would be known to Luke is surely strong. Obsessive, but not very strong, logic for long held back the asking of an obvious factual question.

Such arguments have now been used by Michael Goulder to propose a new theory of the Gospels. Whether or not he proves to be correct, what matters more is the new openness to historical criteria which in other circles has also allowed scholars to ask, for instance, about the literary form of the Gospels from an outside perspective, not one defined in terms of themselves. And, to widespread amazement, a strong case emerged for the Gospels' being *biographies* of Jesus. R.A. Burridge and others who had studied Graeco-Roman lives of famous men were able to point out many conformities to type which make it certain that anyone reading the Gospels in their time of writing would have recognised their genre as biographical. They were telling us, in other words, about that 'life of Jesus' which the self-defining keryg-matic Gospels of theological theorising had so completely ruled out. True, their criteria were religious and not based on an interest in personality or in documentation of facts, like modern biographies; but then the ancient biographies of statesmen and philosophers were not based on our standards either. The writers of philosophers' lives were often their pupils who are out to spread their ideas by judiciously chosen episodes from their life-story or telling anecdotes. And the terminology for these techniques is just what we find in our earliest accounts of how the Gospels were written! So if the Gospels turn out to be biographies, we stand immediately in a cultural reality in the world of Hellenistic-Roman times. We stand in Greek cultural territory, for Jewish culture does not naturally treat its religious leaders, such as great Rabbis, as the subject of biography but remembers them for some sharp comment on the meaning of the Bible, or for exemplifying some special quality such as patience, or for their connection to some period in the history of the community. Rudolf Steiner rightly commented that the idea of the divine becoming a personality, about whom a biography could therefore be written, belongs to the Graeco-Roman 'cultural impulse.' Yet it is not ultimately surprising to find Jesus, or someone from the Jewish world becoming the subject of biography because more and more we are learning how Judaism and Hellenism were not monolithic warring entities but richly interacting aspects of culture for many people at the eastern end of the Mediterranean, both in Palestine and in Alexandria. The great Jewish theologian-philosopher Philo at around that very time even wrote a *Life of Moses*, presenting the Law-giver in a mode comprehensible to Greek-speaking culture, for whom the more original account of his significance in the destiny of Israel and as bearer of God's revelation in the Bible was largely impenetrable. New perspectives were thus arising, and the Gospels might be a related phenomenon bridging Judaic and Greek.

And so the Gospels might after all open the door to the history of the time in which Jesus takes his place. 'Jesus-studies' and other activities of the 'Jesus Seminar' have boomed accordingly. J.H. Charlesworth set the stage with his *Jesus within Judaism*. Since then book after book has been published to tell us of the rediscovery of the historical Jesus. But at this point I may as well confess to a certain scepticism. History we certainly need, but that is different from suggesting that Jesus' personality is the key to the rise of Christianity, or that his person can be found through the historical materials that we have. For one thing I need only survey the titles of some of them to realise that agreement on the historical reality behind the Gospel-figure is still in short supply. A figure of worldly significance or a religious fanatic? I find books on *The Charismatic Leader and his Followers*, and on *Jesus the Seer* and even *Jesus the Exorcist.* An ordinary man or someone claiming miraculous, divine powers? There are books on Jesus with subtitles like 'the life of a Mediterranean peasant,' jostling with *Jesus the Magician.* Part of the Jewish mainstream? I find a *Jesus the Pharisee* and *Jesus as A Marginal Jew.* Looking into them I find some unexpected conclusions which make me doubt whether we have enough solid history to escape from the assumptions of our own time, as when Ben Witherington comes up with a Jesus who recommends taking time off from a stressful life — though this is as unsurprising I suppose in its way as Milton's seventeenth-century Jesus who had studied the classics, enthused over Reason ('the stubborn only to subdue') and aspired to be something above 'the herd.' Others offer a new and *True Gospel of Jesus,* while others continue to write a *Life of Christ* as though nothing had changed since the time of Charles Dickens. But beyond this piecemeal scepticism of doubts about the detail, I wonder whether even the success of this type of historical approach is after all quite what we need to tell us how Jesus brought about the Christianity which sprang from his life and death? Certainly he existed within the parameters of his time, but if we had met him I wonder whether we could have stuck an historical label on him so easily. Certainly that kind of reduction is not what I mean by the importance of history. I wonder whether knowing what he was by way of origins and personal life-story would tell us what is essential, or rather after all tell us what he somehow sacrificed to a complex something that was greater than his own time? He seems to me not so much to have stamped himself on the movement we call Christianity as allowed all sorts of people, ideas and aspirations to find a common focus while retaining their own sense of individual fulfilment. And since that is the thought with which I began this book, it may make sense for the reader to turn to it now.

1. Wisdom Among the Initiated

What kind of religion is Christianity? It seems never too late to ask the question, though the answers are obviously likely to vary according to the standpoint of the answerer.

Christianity has been so many things in so many places and at so many times that one might be forgiven for supposing that no single response is possible. Jesus himself has been regarded so variously that, as Don Cupitt points out, he has been declared to be the exemplar for hermits, peasants, gentlemen, revolutionaries, pacifists, feudal lords, soldiers and others. There seem to be as many Christs as Christianities. But this is a shallow approach. There is more insight in Oscar Wilde's observation that in the presence of Jesus, portrayed in the Gospels, all people become themselves. Christianity has been involved throughout Western history in man's self-discovery, the evolution of that self-consciousness and individualism which marks off Christianity from the cosmic religions of the East. On the surface, Christianity has been a definable body of doctrine maintained by a Church. Yet there is some sense in which it has fostered Western man's development on quite a different level, leading him to become himself in the modem world.

Was this connected with the hints of a more 'esoteric,' even secret side of Christianity that meet us from the New Testament onward? Jesus gave parables to the multitude; but often he taught his disciples 'apart,' or referred to 'outsiders' and 'insiders' and the gulf between. Is it possible to say anything more definite on the subject of these esoteric teachings in early Christianity? I believe that it is. It is possible partly on the basis of a study of the New Testament itself, although it must be admitted from the start that we find there little more than tantalizing hints and veiled suggestions. This is no more than we should expect, since we are by definition involved in a search for teachings of a kind that go beyond what was spoken of openly — teachings which were in some sense, to adopt a phrase from Paul, a 'wisdom among the initiated.' In addition, we shall have to investigate certain important documents originating, like the New Testament writings, in early Christian circles, or in the immediate environment of early Christianity. For the twentieth century has witnessed a rich variety of archaeological discoveries which have put into our hands a whole range of illuminating writings from the early Christian period. We shall be examining some of them in the next chapter. With their help, a great many of the problems in understanding what the first Christians were like and how they thought are beginning to be solved. They furnish us too with not a few surprises about the inner secrets of the early Christian world. Perhaps as important, there have also been significant spiritual developments in the twentieth century, which have shed a new and unique light upon the Gospels and the historical Mystery which lies behind them. Thence too we can derive valuable material for our study. It will be the purpose of this book to sketch, in outline, a picture of Christianity and Christian origins which emerges from these developments — a picture in which, as we shall see, the element of esotericism in Christianity, not in any cliquish sense but as a level of profounder understanding, occupies a natural, indeed a highly significant place in the living heart of Christianity.

We must expect that the subject of esoteric Christianity will raise large and often perplexing issues. It will inevitably bring into focus certain crucial questions of Christian belief. If Christ came for all men, is it compatible with his gospel that higher teachings should be given to the initiated few? If certain individuals have been in possession of more spiritual interpretations or deeper knowledge of the Christian Mystery, what are we to think of the adequacy of the Christian faith as it has appeared in its succession of outward historical forms? Can the esoteric wisdom of Christianity become in principle more widely known? Could it become in short a Christianity for the future? These are fundamental issues which we must not dodge, nor lose sight of amongst the details of historical investigation. The answers we give to them will affect our understanding of history. Indeed, the ability to find a meaning in history is already a central part of the Christian vision of the world.

Among the passages in the New Testament which bear strikingly upon the theme of our study, there are several places in the Gospels where Jesus is described as instructing the disciples in a teaching withheld from the many — 'those outside,' as he calls them. Such passages appear to possess a special significance in the Gospel of Mark, and perhaps none is more notable or more disturbing than the following:

> And when he was alone, those who were around him with the Twelve asked for the parables.
>   And he said to them, 'To you is given the mystery of the kingdom of God; but to those outside all things are done in parables, so that seeing they may see, and not perceive; and hearing they may hear, and not understand; lest they should turn again and be forgiven.' (4:10–12)

Here Jesus asserts that he addresses the outsiders in parables whose full meaning is hidden from the profane and known only to the inner circle, to whom is given 'the mystery of the kingdom of God.' The latter part of Jesus' saying is an allusion to a passage from the prophet Isaiah, concerned with the sinful Israel no longer accounted worthy of God's favour. It seems therefore that Jesus speaks to the 'true Israel' who not only hear and see, but understand the spiritual meaning in the imagery of the parables. Jesus' words in Mark may be ranked among the most uncompromising statements of esotericism in the New Testament. The startling expression '*so that* seeing they may ... not perceive' actively and forcefully excludes those who would look on from outside, who would like to evaluate the mystery from without. The words express the demand for a leap from 'outside' to the 'inside' view, which alone reveals the true interpretation. There can be no in-between. To the outsiders all things happen in parables; 'but privately to his own disciples he expounded everything.' (4:34)

We can discover something of the character of the esotericism in the Gospel of Mark if we connect Jesus' difficult saying with the many instances in Mark where Jesus enjoins secrecy. Frequently when a healing has been performed, or some mystery revealed, Jesus imposes a solemn charge of silence, whether it be on his disciples, on the sick who have been healed, or on the demons who have been exorcized. Perhaps the supreme instance is that of Peter's confession, where he acknowledges Jesus as the Christ: Jesus' immediate response is to charge the disciples that they tell no one of him. Mark has been termed a Gospel of 'secret epiphanies.'[1]

We gradually come to understand as the Gospel proceeds that all the events of Jesus' life and his parables of the 'mystery of the kingdom of God' can only be comprehended in the light of his death and resurrection — in the light of his being the Christ. It was because they could begin to understand this that the disciples could find the meaning of the parables, while 'those outside' could not. In his death and resurrection, still unknown to those 'outside,' lies the key to all his earthly work. When we have understood this, we too can begin to comprehend the 'mystery.' We realize the prophetic significance of the parables, so hard to grasp even for the disciples before the event on Golgotha; and we realize why the teachings had to be secret so that the Messiah should suffer the fate and fulfil the destiny prepared for him.

Thus we have in Mark a good example of the way an 'esoteric' teaching can come in due course to be more widely spread and understood. When the events of death and resurrection have been described in the Gospel — albeit mysteriously and with strange omissions in the expected narrative, ending with fear and an empty tomb — every Christian reader is in possession of the key. He knows what beforehand was known to only a handful of men, Jesus' closest disciples.

Was there more to the secrecy than this? Are there perhaps further secrets embedded in the Gospel, which could in turn be understood by those who received still higher revelations? There may well be. In fact, we shall see later on that a recent discovery relating to the Gospel of Mark suggests that its Mystery-aspect is only just beginning to be fathomed. For the moment, however, let us stay purely within the sphere of the New Testament as it has come down to us.

Let us compare with the discrepancy between Jesus' teaching to 'those outside' and to his disciples another discrepancy: that between the kind of teaching Jesus gives in the so-called

Synoptic Gospels (Matthew, Mark and Luke) and the teaching he gives in the Gospel of John. It is difficult not to notice that in the first three Gospels Jesus teaches in brief parables, or in short, memorable sayings, while in the fourth Gospel we encounter long discourses of great theological profundity worked out in considerable detail. In the Gospel of John, Jesus also speaks with unprecedented directness of his divine origin and work:

> No man can come to me, unless the Father who sent me draws him: and I will raise him up in the Last Day. It is written in the prophets, 'And they shall all be taught by God.' Everyone who has heard from the Father, and has learned, comes to me. Not that any man has seen the Father, except he who is from God; he has seen the Father ... (6:44–46)

It was easy for hostile modern critics of the Bible to point to the disparity between the language of Jesus in the Gospel of John and in the Synoptics as a proof that John could not be an authentic eyewitness report of the events in Palestine. Indeed, quite early in the history of the Church certain objections had been raised against the Gospel of John precisely because it did not seem to fit with the character of the other three Gospels. As far back as the second century an attempt was made to attribute the Gospel of John to a heretic named Cerinthus, and so discredit its authority. The resemblance between John and some of the Gnostic teachings in particular has worried modem scholars, too. One has even gone so far as to describe the Gospel of John as 'frankly heretical.'[2]

A much more interesting line of enquiry opens up, however, when we consider the obvious possibility that Jesus may have taught in more than one way. In other words, we might have in the Gospel of John a record of Jesus' more esoteric teaching, given to the 'beloved disciple' and perhaps others. Hence the style in which he spoke would naturally be different from that in which he addressed the larger group of his followers, or even the Twelve. Several modem scholars have inclined toward a view of this sort — though they are uneasy about the possibility of it amounting to a 'secret teaching.'[3] Further plausibility is given to the idea by the occasional hint in the language of the Synoptic Gospels that Jesus did in fact sometimes speak in another fashion. A striking instance is the hymn of Jesus to the Father, which suddenly conjures up the language of the Gospel of John (a so-called 'Johannine thunderbolt') in the middle of the Gospels of Matthew and Luke. Matthew's version runs:

> All things have been delivered to me by my Father: and no-one knows the Son, except the Father; nor does anyone know the Father, except the Son, and he to whom the Son wills to reveal him.[4]

It is notable that just before this passage, Jesus remarks how God has concealed his wisdom from the supposedly 'wise and understanding' and revealed it to 'babes.' Thus it may well be that we overhear a fragment of the teaching given to those who must 'become as children,' be reborn in order to enter the kingdom of heaven.

Some of the most controversial examples of esoteric language in the New Testament, however, come not from the Gospels but from the letters of Paul. In certain cases there are expressions which, on the face of it, deal directly with matters of esotericism and theosophy ('wisdom of God'). This emerges all the more clearly if we translate them a little more forthrightly than did our Renaissance forefathers when they produced the Authorized Version:

> For we speak a wisdom among the initiated, a wisdom not of this aeon, nor of the world-rulers of this aeon who are passing away. We speak a wisdom of God in a mystery, an occult wisdom which God ordained before the aeons for our glory, and which none of the world-rulers of this aeon knows. (1 Cor 2:6–8)

The claim to esoteric knowledge is put, one might suppose, clearly enough!

Yet it is worthwhile attending to the arguments of modern New Testament research on this extraordinary passage. For the scholars justifiably emphasize the need to understand Paul in context. Probably everyone has at some time had the experience of hearing his own words taken up by someone, but used to mean exactly the opposite of what they originally meant; or even more likely, had his own words quoted back at him in an altered context with a resulting subtle shift in meaning or tone. It has been suggested that something like this lies behind the language of Paul here. He is writing, it is said, to a faction in Corinth which has turned Christianity into an exclusive Mystery for 'those who know' (*gnostikoi*, Gnostics). For the purposes of his argument with them, Paul adopts a 'mystery language' — telling them in effect that the Christian proclamation already includes everything they think they have to gain from an exclusive Mystery. We speak it, already, openly, in the Church.[5]

Now there is undoubtedly a considerable amount of truth in this interpretation, which helps explain the highly unusual vocabulary employed by Paul on a unique occasion. Yet the passage cannot be explained away. Paul still appears to be saying that Christianity does have its 'initiates,' does have a cosmic knowledge, a 'wisdom of God' that can stand in its own right against the wisdom of the pagans or the pagan-Christian mixture in Corinth, but which is yet not of the same exclusive, 'closed' kind. We shall understand more of his distinction after our further studies — the idea of a mystery that is shouted from the rooftops, a secret available to all.

The example also shows how careful we must be not to cut comers in our quest to find the nature of Christian esotericism. We must avoid the danger of turning Christianity into just another Mystery-religion like those which flourished around it in the pagan world of antiquity. Yet Paul certainly had mystical experiences, of a kind which he found only partially communicable to the uninitiated. For this is the Paul who wrote of himself in those same Corinthian letters:

> I know a man in Christ who fourteen years ago was
> caught up to the third heaven — whether in the body or
> out of the body I do not know, God knows. And I know
> that this man was caught up into Paradise — whether in
> the body or out of the body I do not know, God knows —

and he heard things that cannot be told, which man may
not utter.[6]

He does not boast of his experience or claim any special 'spiritual' status, as he accuses his opponents in Corinth of doing. He
does strongly make the point, however, that Christians can
expect to have direct experience of spiritual worlds and the
mysteries of the divine.

There are other 'esoteric' passages in the New Testament to
which we shall later refer. But those instances may suffice to
demonstrate the suggestive nature of the New Testament evidence
on the subject of esoteric teaching and the elusiveness of the subject itself. That is the way with esoteric knowledge: it is there for
the insider, but for those outside, things happen only in parables.

One way — paradoxically — in which we can try to penetrate to
the 'inside' view of Christian esotericism is to turn our attention
to the broad religious setting within which Christianity came
into being. For early Christianity, in its efforts to comprehend
the overwhelming and all-transforming Mystery of Christ, certainly drew to some extent upon the wisdom of earlier religious
traditions or made use of methods similar to theirs. And we find
that esotericism was an important feature of many religious
teachings in early Christian times.

In contemporary Judaism, for example, the Rabbis were
empowered to interpret openly most passages in the
Scriptures. There were two areas, however, which were
regarded as esoteric — and so were not allowed to be discussed in public. One was the material relating to the creation
of the world described in the opening chapters of Genesis. The
other was a section from the book of Ezekiel, where the
prophet relates a mystical vision of the Throne-Chariot
(*Merkavah*) of God and the Living Creatures attending it. This
vision and any material relating to it was regarded as highly
esoteric. The great compilation of Jewish law known as the
Mishnah lays it down that:

It is forbidden to discourse ... on the Creation of the World
in the presence of two, and on the *Merkavah* in the

presence of one, unless he is wise and able to understand of himself. [7]

Thus it appears that a Rabbi was permitted to expound the mysteries of creation only to a single pupil in private; and the exposition of Ezekiel's mystical vision of the Throne-Chariot was entirely forbidden in principle, although it could be discussed in strict privacy among those who of themselves had attained the degree of spiritual maturity requisite for understanding it. The Rabbinic literature stresses the psychic and physical dangers of meddling with these mysteries; some of them are spelled out in various cautionary tales. For instance, a Jew came from Galilee to Babylonia and was asked by the people there to discourse on the *Merkavah*. He did so, but was soon afflicted and died. Or there was the case of the young and inexperienced students who discoursed on the word *hashmal* (referring to a type of angel) which occurs in Ezekiel's vision. A fire came out and consumed them. Certain of the great Rabbis of the early period were renowned, however, for their spiritual powers and acknowledged fit by God and by their fellow men to enter into these secrets.

Hence it would not have been unusual, even from the standpoint of Judaism, for Jesus to have taught esoteric matters to his disciples in private. Moreover, the kinds of spiritual experience reported by the early mystics of Judaism resembled, at least in certain respects, Paul's ascension into Paradise in the heavenly spheres. It was a familiar idea that the Paradise which had originally been present on earth had, since the Fall, been withdrawn into the heavenly regions. There it could still be seen by the mystic in higher vision. The famous story of the four Rabbis who entered Paradise illustrates this conception, and again stresses the dangers inherent in the mystical enterprise. One of the Rabbis died; another went mad; another was drawn into heresy; and only the celebrated Rabbi Akiva ascended and returned in tranquility and peace of mind.[8]

Nevertheless there were also profound differences between the Judaism of the Rabbis and Christianity, and to understand the background to Christian esotericism more fully we must consider in addition the secret teachings of the ancient pagan world — an esotericism summed up in the institution of the Mysteries.

There have been Mysteries and rites of initiation from the very beginnings of the religious evolution of mankind. There have always been rites and methods of training, that is to say, whereby a man could be inwardly transformed and his consciousness raised to an experience of the divine. So drastic is the change these procedures induce, or have induced in the humanity of past ages, that the initiate was said to emerge from them a new person, reborn, or recreated in the image of the gods — just as 'Saul' emerged from his Damascus vision a new man, and became Paul, with his divine mission. Sometimes the techniques of initiation could be psychological and spiritual; sometimes they involved physical ordeals of courage and fearlessness; sometimes they appear to have employed dramatic scenes and representations of the central myth of the Mystery-cult, as in the ancient Greek case of the Mysteries of Eleusis, near Athens, where rites were performed from prehistoric times and on into the Christian era. The great myth which was there used to give new meaning and the hope of immortality to the initiated was the tale of the rape of Persephone by the god of Hades, the underworld; every spring, however, she was allowed to return to the upper world, and she gave birth to the cosmic Child who seems to have been identified with the god Dionysus. We know very little of the details of the rites, because at Eleusis as in all Mysteries a solemn vow of silence was exacted which very few of the initiates broke. To do so would have been a dangerous offence.

There were other Mysteries in the ancient Greek world, notably those of Orpheus, the legendary Thracian poet who descended into the underworld to rescue his beloved Eurydice. But we know little more from classical sources about these Orphic Mysteries than we do about those in Eleusis. Closely connected with the Orphic Mysteries, however, was the early philosopher Pythagoras, remembered for his mathematical theorem and his theories of cosmic harmony. He stands in the tradition of philosophy which later included the great Plato, who himself appears to have taught certain secret doctrines to his more intimate pupils. Later, among the followers of Plato who became known as Neoplatonists, esotericism became a central feature of philosophical teaching which was thoroughly pervaded by an atmosphere of mystic aspiration. Some of Plato's more mysterious teaching evidently related to the secrets of the creation of the world. On this subject he pointed to the importance of the thinker Timaeus, and in his dialogue of that name describes the formation of the lower world by a Demiurge or cosmic Craftsman after the pattern of the spiritual world of ideas, as well as the history of the continent of Atlantis and its disastrous end.

Subsequent philosophy in ancient Greece still generally retained an e;soteric character, as we can see from an incident relating to Aristotle and his most famous pupil, Alexander the Great. In his *Life of Alexander*, Plutarch (who himself became a priest of the Delphic Oracle and knew a good deal about such matters) remarks:

> It seems clear too that Alexander was instructed by his teacher not only in the principles of ethics and politics, but also in those secret and more esoteric studies which philosophers do not impart to the general run of students, but only by word of mouth to a select circle of the initiated. Some years later, when Alexander had crossed into Asia, he learned that Aristotle had published some treatises dealing with these esoteric matters, and he wrote to him in blunt language and took him to task for the sake of the prestige of philosophy.[9]

Aristotle replied that the works he referred to could be regarded as 'in a sense both published and not published' — that is, they were in such a form that they would still be understood only by those who knew the secret teaching.

As the empire of Alexander the Great expanded, the currents of Greek wisdom flowed together with the Mysteries of the ancient cultures of the East: the old Iranian Mysteries of Mithra or Mithras; the Egyptian traditions in the name of the 'thrice-greatest' Hermes or Thoth; the Asiatic Mysteries of the Great Mother Goddess. There were also the Egyptian Mysteries of Serapis, a kind of universal brotherhood whose character grew more and more vague as the ancient knowledge that had once filled it faded away; and the noble Mysteries of Isis, the greatest and most popular of the Egyptian goddesses. The Isis Mysteries are particularly interesting, since they provide one of the few literary accounts of initiation experience, albeit in riddling phrases which allow Apuleius, the initiate, to keep his conscience calm. He gives little away. Yet his description is of great interest to any student of the Mysteries:

> I entered the confines of death, and having crossed the threshold of Persephone I was caught rapt through all the elements; I saw the sun shining at midnight with a brilliant light; I beheld the upper and the lower gods, and drew near and adored.[10]

Through such experiences the Mysteries satisfied the religious needs of ancient man for thousands of years.

Was Christianity in some sense the heir to this esoteric wisdom of the Mysteries? That it may have been is suggested by what we have already encountered as the Gnostic literature, in which Jesus figures as a divine hierophant — that is, an initiator who can open to the apostles the mysteries of the Pleroma, the World of Fullness. This Gnostic literature has always been a thorn in the flesh of modern, rationalist biblical criticism. A book which has been known for some considerable time is the *Pistis Sophia* (literally Faith Wisdom, the name given to a divine being), which tells in detail of Jesus' initiatory activities after his resurrection. But it is obviously put together at a late date out of many and various traditions, some of which are evidently more reliable than others. Its interest has now been largely eclipsed by the discovery of many much earlier and coherent Gnostic texts. We shall be describing soon how this highly esoteric Gnostic literature came into being. For the present, however, let us simply remark that the writings of the Gnostics pose in the most direct and challenging way the question of Christianity's relation to the esoteric teaching of the Mysteries. At the same time, they illustrate once more the dangers which an esoteric connection could constitute to the integrity of the Christian Mystery itself. For it certainly seems to be true of many of the Gnostics that in their pursuit of esoteric enlightenment they lost their inner grip upon some of the central truths of Christian teaching, particularly on the subject of the earthly work and the historical ministry of the Christ.

Here we have, then, three streams of religious wisdom around the time of the origins of Christianity: Christianity itself, as we know it from the New Testament with its hints of esoteric teaching; Judaism as it was being developed by the Rabbis; the frankly esoteric world of the pagan Mysteries and the Gnostics. Yet until very recently it has seemed difficult to know how to fit these three together into a unified picture. The great breakthrough came with some new discoveries, together with a new look at some old documents — and, as I shall suggest, the picture might be completed through attention to the spiritual investigations of Rudolf Steiner.

Fig. 1. The Community Rule, one of the most important Essene writings from Qumran by the Dead Sea (part of the so-called Dead Sea Scrolls). Containing the regulations for life in the Essene centre and initiation into its esoteric teachings, the Rule has no parallel among Jewish writings, but its form and even its very words were used in early Christian manuals, pointing to the influence of Essenism in the earliest Jewish-Christian communities. (Manuscript now in the Shrine of the Book, Jerusalem.)

2. New Discoveries — New Perspectives

The Scroll and the Codex

To many researchers the question of the origins of Christianity has seemed like nothing so much as a jigsaw puzzle with many of the pieces missing. Some progress in filling in the gaps, however, began to be made during the first half of the twentieth century — partly through a series of rather spectacular archaelogical finds. A flood of new evidence became available that not only added to our information, but radically changed the previous perspective. The three separate realities (as they had seemed) of Judaism, early Christianity and the pagan Mysteries began in unexpected ways to give up their firm boundaries, and historically to blend and interact. Some scholars and historians had earlier made efforts to break through the apparent boundary-lines, but the results had been of little value. Eccentric nineteenth-century professors (they have had their successors in modern times too) had tried to argue away Christianity and turn it into pure mythology, suggesting that Christ never lived but was a 'dying god' like the oriental divinities Osiris, Attis, Adonis and so on. But for most it had seemed impossible that the influence of the Mysteries should have penetrated into the very heart of Palestine, the land of Judaism with its fierce insistence on the worship of one transcendent God alone. Surely, the conventional scholars argued, Christianity must in its origins have been much simpler than later on — and much more Jewish.

Then, inadvertently, a crucial step forward was taken by a Bedouin shepherd in 1947, when he stumbled upon a lonely cave in the steep cliffs at Qumran by the Dead Sea. The cave contained several jars, in which were found preserved a variety of ancient manuscripts — long scrolls, some of them twenty feet or more in length, containing biblical and other Hebrew texts. It took some time for the writings to filter through the hands of tradesmen, minor officials, Museums, professors of philology and translators. Then the world was told of the extraordinary significance of the 'Dead Sea Scrolls.'

The Qumran manuscripts turned out to be the library, or collected sacred literature, of a settlement of Jewish Essenes dating from the first and second centuries BC. Some of the texts were familiar books of the Old Testament, such as Isaiah and Habakkuk; but others were esoteric writings containing the special teachings of the Essene *illuminati*. A little had been known about the Essenes before the discovery at Qumran from ancient historical writers like Josephus and Pliny the Elder, and from the work of Philo Judaeus, a member of the Greek-speaking Jewish population in the greatest 'international' centre of learning in the late antiquity, Alexandria. These authors had made it known that there was a mystical, esoteric movement within Judaism in the last centuries BC and in early Christian times. Yet so obscure did it appear, and the statements about it so dubious, that it was hardly taken into account in views of Christian origins taken by scholarly investigators. The whole subject of the Essenes was scarcely more than a matter of loosely based conjectures about a small religious movement that had disappeared virtually without trace from the annals of history. The Dead Sea Scrolls altered all that.

Quite suddenly the Qumran discovery made it clear that in the Judean wilderness had lived a community of Essene initiates, perhaps a few hundred strong, who had studied the Old Testament and interpreted it in a mystical sense. They disagreed in their understanding of it from both the other major religious parties in Judaism, the Sadducees (the aristocratic priestly party) and Pharisees (the representatives of Rabbinic Judaism). They considered that there was a hidden, esoteric meaning in the older writings which could be understood by one who had been 'illumined,' that is, initiated. Several examples of such illumined interpretation survive in the Scrolls. Illumination, however, demanded a lengthy period of spiritual probation, followed by initiatory rites of baptism and instruction in secret knowledge. The baptism was not the token affair that is common in churches today, but real submersion, experienced as a dying and rebirth to a higher life. The initiate came to know himself as a 'son of Light' engaged in the cosmic war with the powers of Darkness, a war which had begun in primordial times and which would only end in the last days of the universe. The underlying principle of Essene esoteric interpretation of the Scriptures was the ability to see this cosmic struggle behind the events narrated there, or in the prophecies and psalms. Their library also included non-canonical literature, often of an 'apocalyptic' nature, such as the *Book of Enoch*, where the cosmic struggle is extensively described, together with visions of the heavenly spheres and the angelic worlds; it is also noteworthy that their calendar, a sun-calendar in contradistinction to the moon-calendar employed in regular Judaism, is identical with that described in Enoch and the *Book of Jubilees*, another Essene work offering an esoteric interpretation of Old Testament history. Essene initiation bestowed, in effect, a *gnosis* or divine knowledge. The Essenes' God was the 'God of Knowledge'; it was he who awakened the light of spiritual vision and understanding in the breast of the initiate. A hymn from the *Community Rule* expresses it well:

> For from the source of His righteousness
>   is my justification,
> and from His marvellous mysteries
>   is the light in my heart.
> My eyes have gazed
>   on that which is eternal
> on wisdom concealed from men,
>   on knowledge and wise design
>   (hidden) from the sons of men ...
> God had given them to His chosen ones
>   as an eternal possession,
> and has caused them to inherit
>   the lot of the Holy Ones.
> He has joined their assembly
>   to the Sons of Heaven
> to be a Council of the Community,
> a foundation of the Building of Holiness,
> an everlasting Plant throughout all ages to come.[1]

Admission to the 'Council of the Community' was evidently a further stage of initiation, and it conferred the right to attend the sacred Meal. This was understood by the Essenes as a ritual anticipation of the meal of bread and wine which would be held by the Messiah — or rather, the two Messiahs whom the Community expected. It was extremely holy, so that even many of the 'sons of Light' had to be excluded as not yet sufficiently pure in heart.

Here, then, in the Essenism revealed by the Dead Sea Scrolls was an astonishing phenomenon: a Mystery flourishing in the heartland of Judea, a *gnosis* with its own rites of initiation, a sacramental meal, and an esoteric understanding of the Jewish scriptures; it bestowed an experience of 'illumination' and vision of the eternal, taught a doctrine of cosmic spirits of Light and Darkness, and such esoteric topics as astrology and physiognomy. Any remnants of the notion that Palestine in the time of Jesus or immediately before was out of the sphere of influence of the Mysteries had to be abandoned.[2]

But if the writings from Qumran pointed strongly in the direction of the Mysteries on the one hand, they gestured on the other in the direction of Christianity. There is nothing in Jewish literature, for instance, resembling the Qumran *Community Rule*, which spells out the kind of life Essenes are expected to lead in various respects. Remarkably like it, however, is the early Christian document known as the *Didache* (Teaching of the Twelve Apostles). Connections (and differences) in terms of doctrine between the Essenes and early Christians will form a subject for discussion later in this book. Besides the *Community Rule* and the Bible texts and commentaries, the Qumran Library contained a *Damascus Rule*, which casts an interesting light on the history of the Essenes and the 'New Covenant,' which was evidently made 'in the land of Damascus.' There are also a *Messianic Rule* and a *War Rule* concerned with the events of the Last Days; a collection of Hymns and new psalms; the so-called *Angelic Liturgy*, describing divine worship in heaven and a vision of the Throne-Chariot or *Merkavah*; a *Messianic Anthology*, or collection of biblical texts taken to refer to the Messiahs; and a fragmentary work of *Melchizedek*, the angelic priest-king. Other fragmentary and miscellaneous writings bring the total number of texts recovered, if we include all the smallest, to nearly a hundred. Even the fullest collections are misleading, however, to the extent that they fail to reflect the prominence of familiar biblical texts — not only the beautiful *Isaiah-Scroll*, but now virtually the whole of the Hebrew Bible. Because of the way that older manuscripts were successively copied and then destroyed, moreover, this Hebrew text of the Bible is quite literally thousands of years older than those which have come down to the present day.

It would be hard to exaggerate the impact which the Dead Sea Scrolls have made on scholarship and on the awareness of the educated public. Less well-known, though perhaps just as significant for the study of early Christianity, is another archaeological find of almost the same time. In 1945, this time in Upper Egypt, two peasants digging out fertilizer made the discovery: they broke open an old jar to find the Coptic Gnostic Library from ancient Chenoboskion, the modern Nag Hammadi. Whereas the writings from Qumran date back to the first and second centuries BC, and are inscribed on the older type of manuscript, the long scroll, the Gnostic Library consisted of a codex — that is, books made up of separate sheets, in this case of papyrus. They date from the early centuries of the Christian era and amount in all to some fifteen hundred pages. Many of the writings are Christian, or more exactly emanate from that Gnostic world of thought where Christ was understood purely in terms of the ancient Mysteries and a hostile attitude was adopted towards Judaism and the Jewish Law. Or rather ... the case is somewhat more complex.

The writings contained in the Nag Hammadi Library seem to come from a variety of sources. Many are thoroughly Gnostic writings; others stem from the Egyptian magical religion of Hermes Trismegistus; there is a passage from Plato's *Republic*,' a collection of well-known ethical maxims, the *Sentences of Sextus*, popular in early Christian circles; and a number of works whose origin is uncertain or disputed. It has been suggested that the Library did not belong to a Gnostic group at all, but represents wide the range of interests of the monks in the nearby Monastery of St Pachomius (a founding father of Monasticism, who may himself have been none-too-orthodox!). However, what unites the works gathered together in the Library can be most plausibly explained as their relevance to Gnostic ideas. The Library may have had a chequered history but it seems fairly safe to assume that it was given its present form in a Gnostic setting.

There are, for instance, interesting minor additions and sub-tractions which we can sometimes detect. In the important trea-tise *On the Resurrection,* the hand of a Gnostic — more precisely, a Gnostic who followed the teacher Valentinus — has added a phrase explaining the text in a highly Gnostic way, which was not necessarily the way its author intended. And in the *Gospel of Thomas,* known previously only as a series of unidentified frag-ments, a phrase objectionable to Gnostic ears has been left out.[3]

Thus we see how the Library seems to have been slightly edited to make all the texts suitable for use in a Gnostic com-munity. Of all the Nag Hammadi Library books, the *Gospel of Thomas* has caused the greatest stir. It purports to be a collection of the 'secret sayings' of Jesus, communicated to the apostle Thomas and written down by Matthias. Its compiler evidently drew on a range of Gnostic and Jewish-Christian sources; some of the sayings are identical with utterances of Jesus in the New Testament Gospels, and others at the very least go a long way back in the Christian tradition and may be authentic. According to a prominent scholar of the New Testament writings, a 'com-parison of the sayings in the *Gospel of Thomas* with the parallels in the synoptic Gospels suggest that the sayings in the *Gospel of Thomas* either are present in a more primitive form, or are devel-opments of a more primitive form of such sayings.' Work in sorting out the layers of tradition in *Thomas* is still going on.[4]

Other important works in the Library include the *Secret Book of John,* a primary Gnostic cosmological treatise giving an account of the earliest, purely spiritual phases of world-evolu-tion, followed by the origin of the material world and the moulding of man's physical body. The cosmic-angelic powers which govern his life are described, as is the descent of the spir-itual Christ to redeem him. Similar material is treated in *The Nature of the World-Rulers* (or *Archons*) and the more exoteric book *On the Origin of the World.* All these works violently reject the biblical Creator of Jewish tradition.

Certain works represent the Gnostic thought specifically of the school of Valentinus. Above all one might mention *The Gospel of Truth,* a meditation on the deed of Christ from a standpoint which seems to assume a detailed knowledge of esoteric cosmology. Then, there is a *Gospel of Philip,* which represents a Mystery-form of Christianity deriving from Syria, with much to say about an elaborate system of sacraments. Valentinus and his followers seem to have been much influenced by this type of Mystery-Christianity. *The Gospel of Philip*, too, may contain older material, as in the case of *Thomas*, though probably to a lesser extent.

Among the oldest writings contained in the Nag Hammadi discovery must be reckoned the extremely interesting *Apocalypse of Adam*. This is a work which shares many features of Gnosticism, but is probably pre-Christian in origin. As we shall see later on, it may cast a good deal of light on the esoteric background of Gnosticism. In a similar context we shall find reason to discuss the *Sacred Book of the Invisible Spirit*.

Other books and fragments bring the total number of treatises in the Nag Hammadi Codex to fifty-two.

In the writings of the Gnostic Library, Christ and the apostles figure as representatives of. an esoteric tradition of knowledge like that of the Mysteries. We have mentioned that certain features of the tradition may genuinely reach back to the beginnings of Christianity; others betray the influence of special interests: the Christ as he was understood through the profound mysticism of the Gnosis predominating over the Christ who appeared on the stage of history in a human body. On the other hand, other documents like the *Apocalypse of Adam* seem to reach back into pre-Christian times.

The Essene scriptures from Qumran showed a *rapprochement* between Judaism and the Mysteries. Nag Hammadi shows a Mystery-oriented Christianity, but in violent opposition to Jewish spirituality. Still contradictions! The complete picture evidently requires a yet wider perspective.

Gold in the Mud

> *There is some gold to be found in the mud of aprocrypha.*
>
> Augustine

A *Gospel of Philip*, of *Thomas*, of the *Egyptians*, of *Truth*! But surely there are only four *real* Gospels: those of Matthew, Mark, Luke and John?

The proper distinction to be made here, which is a very

important one, is that Gospels like those from the Nag Hammadi find are so-called 'aprocryphal' Gospels, whilst the well-known four of the New Testament are the 'canonical' ones. As Christianity began to organize itself in the course of the first centuries and grew from a scattering of small communities into a large-scale movement, the Churches began to draw up an agreed 'canon' (literally, measuring rod) of books that were to be regarded as sacred. The result was our canonical New Testament. The process involved many disputes: we have already mentioned the fact that continuing efforts were made to exclude the Gospel of John by certain parties, and similar pressures were brought to bear against, for instance, the Apocalypse of John, the Acts of the Apostles, and sometimes other works. Conversely, books such as the *Apocalypse of Peter* and the *Epistle of Barnabas* were for a long time strong contenders for inclusion.

The time for these disputes is long past. I certainly do not wish to quarrel over the status of these early Christian books. In the case of the four canonical Gospels we can only be profoundly glad that these narratives, with their different but spiritually complementary points of view, were preserved and brought together in the New Testament setting. It is only that we must not allow overfamiliarity, with the famous four Gospels to make us forget that in the early Christian communities there were circulating many books — and traditions — from which our canon was gradually selected as representing the best and deepest accounts of the work of Christ. The New Testament writers even assumed familiarity with the background of traditions and written accounts. Thus Luke begins his Gospel by saying:

> Inasmuch as many people have undertaken to draw up a
> narration of those events which have been fulfilled
> amongst us ...

Profound though the canonical Gospels undoubtedly are, we have a wrong picture of the earliest Christianity unless we remember the living diversity of traditions and writings which preceded the formation of the canon, and expressed itself in those works which we now (since the formation of the canon)

call 'apocryphal.' Lack of awareness of the world in which the
New Testament evolved, Rudolf Steiner once said, led the theologians and historians of his day into all sorts of illusions. And
one of the main reasons for their myopia he located — as we can
now see, very perceptively — in 'the fact that the apocryphal
Gospels, that is, those not officially recognized by the Christian
Church, are very little known today and are virtually ignored,
especially by Christian theologians.'[5]

Some of the books used by particular groups and communities within the earliest Christianity were never intended for
public display; they were books for the circles of the initiated,
and their contents were intended to be preserved in secrecy. It is
to these that we owe the term aprocryphal, since *apocryphon* in
its original connotation means 'a secret book.' Gnostic literature
provides many instances — for example, the Nag Hammadi
Secret Book (apocryphon) of John. The *Gospel of Thomas* also contains secret teaching, as when Jesus takes Thomas on one side
and speaks to him three words:

> Now when Thomas came to his companions, they asked
> him: What did Jesus say unto thee? Thomas said to them:
> If I tell you one of the words which he said to me, you
> will take up stones and throw them at me; and a fire will
> come out of the stones and destroy you.[6]

The danger ascribed here to wrongful possession of esoteric
knowledge reminds us of the fate of those students who discoursed on *hashmal* in Ezekiel's vision of the *Merkavah*, and
points to a close link with Jewish esotericism.

Other books, however, were not intended to be secret documents. The term apocryphal was simply used, after a while, to
denote any gospel or similar work that did not become part of
the New Testament canon. Or perhaps we should say, of the biblical canon; for there are also in existence a number of books
associated with the Old Testament, and widely read especially
among the Greek-speaking Jews of the ancient world. For these
books there are no Hebrew originals. These non-Hebrew works
were rejected, quite naturally, from the canon of the Hebrew
Bible which was only fixed around the time of early Christianity,

and they are nowadays often omitted from Bibles in translation. When they are included, the Bible usually bears on the title-page the motto 'with Apocrypha.' These Old Testament apocrypha include the books of the Maccabees, Ecclesiasticus, Tobit, Wisdom of Solomon, and so on.

In addition to the Old Testament apocrypha, there were various writings which attached themselves to Old Testament characters or events, but whose authenticity was never so widely accepted. A further name had to be found for these, and scholarship hit upon the term 'pseudepigrapha' — literally, 'false writings.' They are at least as multitudinous as the New Testament apocrypha: they include the *Books of Adam and Eve*, literature such as the *Book of Enoch* and *Jubilees* which we now know to have had Essene connections, the remarkable books called the *Testaments of the Twelve Patriarchs*, and much more.[7]

A great part of the aprocryphal and pseudepigrapha literature, aside from some of the major works we have mentioned, is of small value from a religious and spiritual point of view. The books later in date among the New Testament apocrypha, in particular, frequently only represent the legendary reworking or expansion of episodes from the canonical Gospels. There is a whole genre of 'Infancy Gospels' which elaborate on the childhood and youth of Jesus, so tantalizingly left blank in the New Testament. Occasionally there are interesting conceptions to be met with here, but also much that is fanciful or inauthentic. Along rather similar lines there are also many accounts of the life, and more of the death, of the Virgin Mary — often mediaeval in feeling and designed to fill in the gaps of the Gospel histories with suitably edifying material, only rarely drawing upon genuinely early tradition.

But coming to the really interesting material from the sphere of the New Testament aprocrypha, we can distinguish several broad classes of writing. First of all, we must mention the enigmatic Jewish-Christian Gospels, discussed and sometimes quoted by several Church Fathers: the *Gospel of the Hebrews or Nazarenes*, and (what may be simply a later variant of the same basic work) the *Gospel of the Ebionites*. Of these and their intimate relationship to the canonical Gospel of Matthew we shall have more to say later. A second class of materials comprises Gnostic and other accounts of Christ's life, sayings, death and resurrection. Many were known even before the Nag Hammadi discovery, which has now vastly swelled their number. Unlike the canonical Gospels and the Jewish-Christian Gospels, these works were on the whole used by groups which came to be regarded by the evolving orthodox Church as 'heretical' although in many instances the distinctions were far from clear. We mentioned the titles of some of them in discussing the Nag Hammadi find; perhaps the only book we need single out here to add to the wider list is the fragment of the *Gospel of Peter,* since this constitutes our earliest account of the Passion that exists outside the canonical New Testament.

A third major division of the surviving New Testament apocrypha consists of traditions and legends in the name of the various individual apostles. In many ways, this body of material is the most interesting of all. For if it can be said that the modern study of the New Testament has established any fundamental principle of interpretation with regard to the earliest period of Christianity, it is that the earliest Christianity was a matter of living tradition before it was a matter of an authoritative book or books. 'It is now widely recognized,' writes C.H. Dodd, 'that the main factor in perpetuating and propagating the Christian faith and the Gospel story was oral tradition in its various forms.'[8] The traditions generally circulated in the name of an apostle, who brought the Gospel message to the community in question, and whose successors elaborated and preserved his teaching and spoke in his name. Traditions of this kind also lie behind the Gospels — both those in the New Testament and the earlier apocryphal Gospels such as those of Thomas and Philip. Now each of the apostles understood the unique and unfathomable Christ-event in his own way; each had his own experience, and each described the meaning of the profound change wrought by the Christ from his own special perspective. Later, when the traditions came to be written down, something of the diversity of standpoints was still preserved, as we see from reading the lengthy *Acts* which were compiled from them: the *Acts of John, Acts of Thomas, Acts of Andrew,* and so on. We have also valuable information from early Fathers of the Church who made a special study of the apostolic traditions. Papias, bishop of Hierapolis in Asia Minor in the second century, collected as many traditions as he could from anyone who had been a disciple of any of the apostles. His work has been lost, but the Church historian Eusebius later reported (with disapproval) on the esoteric character of many of the traditions. Papias quoted: 'certain strange parables of the Saviour and teachings of his, and some other things of a rather mythical character.'[9] A little later, Clement of Alexandria drew together many of the traditions he found circulating in the name of the apostles, and again the esoteric character of many of them is striking.

The diversity of points of view we encounter in the traditions of the apostles is no doubt partly due to the fact that they were handed down orally over long periods of time before getting committed to writing. But it also points to the original experience of the individual apostles and the different understandings of Christ at which they arrived through a lifetime's subsequent teaching and meditation. Although it is not safe to take later traditions without further ado as representative of the original teaching of an apostle, it is sometimes possible to be certain at least of some particulars. An example will make this clear — and also show why the Church had to hush some of them up. One feature of the traditions circulating under the name of John, in Gnostic literature and in the writings of Clement, is the mention of the physical nature of Jesus. He was not always present in a touchable body, according to John:

> For in the (esoteric) traditions it is reported that John
> touched the outward body (of Jesus) and put his hand
> deep inside and that the solidity of the flesh in no wise
> offered resistance but yielded to the disciple's hand.[10]

So writes Clement, and in the Secret Book of John, as well as in the *Acts of John*, we find similar ideas. John and his followers certainly will not have denied the physical incarnation of Christ because of these sorts of experience; for in the *Acts* John says that on other occasions 'when I wished to lay hold of him I encountered a material and solid body.' But one can appreciate how the Church could not afford to blur the issue in its massive propaganda campaign.

The study of the apostolic traditions contained in the apocryphal Acts, undertaken in depth as a result of the new discoveries, has done much to confirm Rudolf Steiner's characterization of the early Christian period. 'In those days,' he wrote, 'individual souls sought by very different paths to find the way from the ancient views to the Christian ones ... During the first centuries of Christianity the search for the divine path was a much more personal matter than it afterwards became.'[11] In the decades following Steiner's death, as if in belated recognition of this truth, several scholars came to similar conclusions on the basis of detailed historical investigation. The culmination was reached in the brilliant, and still controversial work of Walter Bauer: he attacked the whole notion — which goes back to the pioneers of Catholic orthodoxy like Irenaeus of Lyon — that the original teaching of Christianity had been simple and uniform ('orthodox'), and that all the variations and mystical interpretations were later perversions of the primal faith (that is, 'heresies'). Bauer came to the conclusion, like Steiner, that the earliest Christianity had contained an entire spectrum of attitudes and understandings of Christ, living in a more or less peaceable co-existence. The imposition of a standard, 'orthodox' belief came only later, with the concentration of authority in the hands of the Roman Church.[12] And we can in fact observe how the Church introduced its own literature, opposing the diversity of apostolic traditions with a colourless amalgam in the name of 'the Twelve Apostles.' This had two consequences: on the one hand it unified and strengthened the collective belief of the organized Church, and so helped the spread of Catholic Christianity; and on the other, it actually drove those who held to the older apostolic traditions outside the Church, ultimately turning them into 'heretics.'[13]

The crystallizing out of Catholic 'orthodoxy' and the consequent view of all other traditions as 'heresies' took a considerable time. In the second century, for instance, the great Gnostic teacher Valentinus was for long accepted in Christian circles and only later made a decisive break with the Church; in the third century, Origen, 'first of the orthodox and greatest of heretics' commanded widespread support among thinking Christians, and was only later declared to be theologically unacceptable, originating the paradox that the man who did so much to lay the foundations of orthodox theology on such matters as the Trinity should prove radically alien to the spirit of the Church. In the fourth century we witness the triumph of orthodoxy, when Augustine can declare roundly that he would not accept the truth of Christ and the Gospels at all, were it not that the Catholic Church informed him of the true belief. Or, as Cyprian had put it even slightly earlier; 'no one can have God for his Father unless he has the Church for his Mother.'

The foregoing pages will have achieved their purpose if they have given some fleeting impression of the wealth of ideas and traditions that were alive in the three worlds which met in ancient Palestine and together furnished mankind with a first understanding of the sublime event of Christ. There was the world of Judaism, including the pre-Christian esotericism of the Essenes which we can now study in the 'Dead Sea Scrolls' and to some extent in other Old Testament apocrypha and pseudepigrapha. There was the world of the oriental and pagan Mysteries, touching the spirit of the Essenes, and appearing powerfully within early Christianity in the esoteric literature of Gnosticism. And there was the world of emerging Christianity itself, a complex evolution of views drawing, as we can 'see from the New Testament and the early Christian aprocryphal literature, on an immense richness of ideas in its efforts to comprehend the Christ.

The diversity of all these sources may indeed seem baffling and labyrinthine at first. However, an additional and extraordinarily powerful light has been shed on the whole meaning and significance of the origins of Christianity from another source, which in conjunction with the study of literary testimonies can lead to important new insights into the history and very nature of Christianity.

The Spiritual Investigations of Rudolf Steiner

We have already found occasion to cite one or two remarks of Rudolf Steiner on the importance of the New Testament apocrypha and on the initial diversity of approaches in early Christianity to an understanding of the Christ. It would certainly be misleading, however, to see Steiner's remarks after the manner of scattered contributions to the study of early Christianity. Rather they form part of his astonishingly extensive 'spiritual investigations' in which Steiner presented a picture of the meaning and importance of Christianity against the backdrop of man's continually evolving consciousness — his changing relationship to the divine over historical time and his spiritual prospects or potential for the future.

Of course there have been others who have put forward visionary or mystical interpretations of Christianity, sometimes of considerable depth and insight. What is remarkable about the case of Steiner is the scientific exactness, and the profounder 'evolutionary' understanding of spiritual history which his researches unveiled. The extraordinary accuracy of his results emerges so strikingly in relation to the new textual and archaeological discoveries we have just considered, above all concerning the Essenes and Gnostics and, as we shall see, in the exact description of the Gospels of Mark and John as they were originally composed, that they can hardly any longer be ignored. It is only a pity that such efforts as have previously been made to assess Steiner's accuracy chose to focus rather on less clear, and indeed question-begging instances.[14]

It was part of Steiner's understanding of Christianity itself that it could not mean a retreat into a mysticism of nebulous feelings, or inchoate intuitions. Whatever else lies at the heart of Christianity, it contains at least the demand for deeper and more loving perception of the world around us as well as deeper insight into our own selves. So far, indeed, Steiner spoke in harmony with the feeling of the entire Christian tradition, so that it is very odd to find him presented by widely read works of reference as though he had virtually nothing in common with the theology and the forms of feeling moulded by the centuries of Christendom.[15] He did indeed demand a rigorous, philosophical critique of existing knowledge and existing faiths. He considered that nothing less would carry conviction in the modern age. The scope of the undertaking after all was the broadest conceivable. But it was precisely in the deeper implications of Christianity that he saw the principles which could make sense of man's modern consciousness, his evolving self. He saw that

Christianity had established a new relationship between the inner worlds of religious experience and the outer cosmos, the world of history. It was at once a Mystery and a fact.

Steiner's first major statement of his results came in 1902, with his book *Christianity as Mystical Fact*. Later he was to add to it many lecture-cycles, expanding upon and deepening what he had there to say. Not only were there courses on the Gospels, on the letters of Paul, and on the Apocalypse (Book of Revelation), but works with a wider sweep, such as the *Building Stones for an Understanding of the Mystery of Golgotha*, drawing sustained parallels between early Christian and modern thought, and the *Fifth Gospel* lectures. The last is not, as it is sometimes misrepresented, the 'Gospel according to Steiner,' but his version of the *evangelium eternum*, the 'spiritual gospel' whose revelation commenced at Pentecost and sent the apostles out into the world with a conviction of the spiritual reality and truth of what they had to proclaim. Such conviction can never be derived, though it may be fostered and helped by tradition, from anything but the response of man's spirit to the call of a higher truth than that handed down externally.

Steiner's investigations followed his spiritual method (and Steiner thoroughly discussed the methodological implications for those who wish to study them), but it would be a mistake to suppose that he rejected the endeavours of 'mere' historical research in so important a field. 'Historical research,' he once declared explicitly, 'will one day vindicate completely the evidence drawn from purely spiritual sources which forms the basis of my *Christianity as Mystical Fact*.'[16] He sometimes drew an analogy from mathematics: a researcher can arrive at the truth of certain propositions, and describe the conditions needed for their demonstration; but he will be only too happy to hear from the historian how they were first discovered and set forth in documentary form by Euclid or Pythagoras. Thus there is no contradiction between Steiner's researches and the historian's approach. The two should be complementary and mutually enriching.

To stave off another possible misunderstanding: Steiner did not imply that the events of history happen with a predictable logic, which can be grasped by some sort of inner mathematics, without reference to externals. His philosophy was opposed to that kind of metaphysical determinism. On the contrary, history was for Steiner the dimension of man's freedom, and so of man's growth. It has an organic, complex dynamic that like biological growth exhibits certain rhythms, but also new adaptations and varieties, new discoveries and new apprehensions of meaning in the past. One area in which his ideas have proved illuminating has been the study of language, seen as expressing man's changing consciousness and the meaning of his world. Owen Barfield, in the spirit of Steiner's anthroposophy (or 'wisdom of man'), dazzlingly extended his discoveries into a history of thought about the world around us, hoping thereby to dispel its tendency to erect idols of unalterable physical fact.[17] But it is not my point here to describe the many ways in which Steiner's ideas have proved fruitful. I wish simply to point to the evolutionary perspective he described, according to which the generations of human history do not simply follow each other, accumulating like discrete particles to make up the massive series of events. Each generation can only be understood by the whole history of what preceded it — just as the language we now speak can only be explained by going back to forms of speech developed many thousands of years ago, which evolved progressively into Sanskrit, Avestan, Greek, Latin, German and many other tongues. That history is a part of us whenever we speak. Hence it should not surprise us that if the past can be recovered at all it should be essentially by inward rather than external effort. All historical understanding, on whatever it is based, depends on the surprising ability we have to enter into the life-experience of an age remote from our own.

How then are we to make use of Steiner's insights here? Not, certainly, by an attempt to 'prove' everything that Steiner said. That would be to treat him as an 'intuitive,' a shrewd anticipator of more conventional methods and results — which is not at all the point. Steiner's investigations actually prove most valuable when used as a frame in which to interpret the facts, old and new, which come to meet them from texts and archaeology, nowhere more so than with the discoveries relating to Christian beginnings. The significance of the texts and of Steiner's vision are alike tested in a living process, a struggle to comprehend something of the Christian Mystery as well as the Gnostic Gospels. The value of both, I suggest, is confirmed and deepened.

Steiner's theological contemporaries generally failed to see the significance of his work, and it is interesting to consider for a moment why. Of course, let it be said immediately that there were honourable exceptions, men of the calibre of Rittelmeyer and Emil Bock. But for the most part theologians had oddly little sense of the spiritual history that lay behind Christian origins. Like many of their successors today they were obsessively analysing the New Testament or the Bible, treating it as a puzzle whose answers were all concealed in itself, abstracting it from its living context: the struggle of the first Christians to come to terms with the overwhelming experience that they had had of the Christ. Nowadays, at last, a different perspective is starting to be thrust upon them by the historical discoveries from the early Christian world. In this situation, Steiner's researches show themselves very illuminating indeed, as we shall discover in the rest of this book.

3. Esoteric History: Light from the East

With the aid of the aprocryphal literature (newly discovered or recently re-examined), the writings from Nag Hammadi, the Dead Sea Scrolls, and Steiner's spiritual researches — let us attempt to sketch the esoteric history that lies behind the origins of Christianity. Let us try to go back in imagination to the complicated world of secret teachings and rites among the Essenes, to move among the forerunners of the Gnostics, and even in the circles around Jesus himself and his disciples. Let us briefly sketch the profound historical process which leads, through that world, from the Mysteries to Christianity.

But first of all, let us glance back some one thousand years before the time of Christ for a prologue in the ancient Near East.

The Initiate Kings

It is the time of the first kings of Israel — Saul, David, Solomon, with their kingdom centred on the old Jebusite capital Salem, or Jerusalem as it now becomes known. And if we look to the powerful neighbouring cultures, we find that they, too, are ruled by kings. These were the great initiate-kings of Egypt and ancient Mesopotamia, whose dynasties had ruled 'since the time of the gods.'

The initiate-kings (or 'sacral kings' as they are more often known) were divine figures, the direct embodiments of the gods of their people and themselves filled with divine power. According to the ancient Sumerian 'king-list,' the kingship 'descended from heaven,' and the man who received it had therefore to be initiated into the secrets of the heavenly world. In Egypt, Sumeria, Babylon and Iran the royal ceremony of coronation was at the same time a rite of initiation, and although it took place publicly it was in the strictest sense a Mystery — an inner access to the divine world which was decisively closed to the profane multitude. For in those ancient times, it was the king alone who could be initiated into the presence of the gods; the king alone could be raised up to attain direct knowledge of the divine, and all his subjects received grace not through their personal religious experience, but through his manifestation of the holy. The rite was a Mystery in which the king alone had ultimate access to the world of the sacred — 'une forme privilégiée d'initiation,' as one modern scholar says.[1]

In Babylon the kingly initiation followed a pattern like that of the initiations which have been practised from archaic times: suffering, ritual humiliation, ordeals, a breaking down of any sense of the individual ego, all culminating in a sort of baptismal ordeal in which the king fought against the powers of 'the Deep,' had to precede the investiture and enthronement. Moreover, the rites were experienced as the focus of a vast mythological struggle, an event of the primordial past, yet an ever present reality, where the king was identified with the ruling god Marduk, and shared in the creative struggle against the chaos-monster Tiamat from whose dead corpse the world was made. The royal initiation rites were repeated every year at a great Festival, which was experienced as the recreation of the universe. When he was enthroned, the king was endowed with emblems of the seven planetary gods, since he was now no longer a mere man but had become the medium of cosmic powers. Yet every year the king had to be humiliated. The surviving 'Temple Programme for the New Year Festival at Babylon' tells how the priest was to 'take away the sceptre, the circle and the sword ... and strike the king's cheek. If, when he strikes the king's cheek, the tears flow, the god Bel-Marduk is friendly.'[2] The king protested that he had not failed in his office, had not offended against the gods. It is rather as if the all-toohuman had a way of beginning to creep back into the divinized king, and had to be purged away anew each year. The king atones through his suffering for his shortcomings, and is enthroned in divine glory once more. He becomes 'the king, son of his god,' and is often spoken of as god himself.

Similar rites and conceptions existed, often with their own peculiar forms and national character, in Egypt, Iran and many other ancient nations. The king was an initiate, a 'visionary seer,' even a god upon earth. In Tyre, the king was initiated and

*Fig. 2 The king-god Marduk ascending to his Father, the cosmic wisdomdi-
vinity Ea. In the Mystery-rites of Babylon, the earthly king was the representative of Marduk, enacting ritually both his descent into Hell (also
imagined as the belly of the chaos-monster Tiamat) and his victory over
death. The step-pyramid or ziqqurat up which he strides signifies the successive levels of cosmic ascension. Already we find mythical patterns that were
to be given new meaning in Christianity. (Cylinder-seal, Baghdad.)*

enthroned: he was hailed as the solar divinity, and appeared in
shining robes of epiphany like the first rays of dawn that rise
over the holy mountain. He walked among the 'stones of fire,'
the stars of heaven, as Baal-Shamem. He ruled the earth from
the 'holy mountain of God,' like the first-created Man in the
primeval Garden.

Indeed, through the ritual the people experienced anew the
conditions of harmony with the cosmos, the paradisal state of
human beginnings. Again there was a yearly ritual, which continued to be celebrated from the tenth century BC almost down to
New Testament times. In Iran, too, there was a great Festival at
which the king presided. His initiation was regarded as a 'second

birth,' and connected both with the beginning and the end of the world, which met at the moment of the new cycle, the new reign or the new year. The cosmic aspect of kingship was stressed even more than in Mesopotamia and Phoenicia, and the pattern of myth and ritual connected with the king can be traced back to remote times, before the Iranians had left their Indian kin behind to travel westward. One Iranian monarch proclaimed himself 'Shahpuhr, King of Kings, partner with the stars, brother of the Sun and Moon.' A strong experience in early Iranian times was the divine solar radiance which filled the aura of the king, making him too bright to look upon for ordinary mortals. The Greek historian Herodotus tells us that the Great King in Iran was 'invisible': he never appeared among his subjects except upon great ritual occasions, and his apartments were curtained off even at feasts. Sometimes his nobles were prepared and brought into his radiant presence, but even that was an exception. In later times this *khvarnah* or nimbus of light around the head or body was still experienced by the king, though it seems not always by the mass of people who participated in the New Year rites.

The picture is extremely similar when we examine the royal New Year festival in Israel at the time of the first kings. Once more it is clear that the king is initiated into his office, and in the Psalms recited on the occasion we catch the dimension of the Mystery that was being enacted. Psalm 110 preserves very ancient material proclaiming the mythical birth of the priest-king:

> In holy array step forth from the womb of Dawn, as Day
> have I begotten thee. '

If this or a similar translation of an admittedly difficult text is correct,' comments F. H. Borsch in his fascinating and wide-ranging study of those matters, 'we have a picture of the king being born and arising like the new sun. The day of his birth would not only be that of the festival; it would also be the day of creation.'[3] He adds that the Psalm declares the king to be a priest 'after the order of Melchizedek,' pointing to a continuity between the royal rites of the Israelite kings and the older Mystery-practices connected with Melchizedek, the ancestral king and priest of the Canaanite sun-god El-Elyon in Salem.

Other Davidic Psalms are based on the themes of initiatory ordeal, humiliation, struggle with the waters, followed by sun-like illumination and enthronement, recreation, and so on. These 'Mystery' Psalms are in fact our most authentic evidence of the time when Israel, like her Near Eastern neighbours, was ruled by initiate-kings who were looked on as all-but-divine. Solomon, the all-wise ruler whose name has been on the lips of kings, priests, prophets and magicians for centuries since, achieved a union between the best elements of Israel and Tyre, whence he brought the artisans of king Hiram to help build the Temple. Hence the later kings of Judah were initiated according to a slightly different pattern, of which strong traces can be located in other parts of the Old Testament. The Phoenician religion prac-tised in Tyre, as several historians of religion have noted, was more materially orientated than the transcendent spirituality of the Israelites. The Phoenician creator or demiurge is born from the dark Chaos, according to their mythology, rather than exist-ing on high from eternity like the Yahweh of the Israelites. It is no accident that the Phoenicians were esteemed in antiquity as inventors and propagators of culture, since their inner attitude led them toward involvement with and triumph over the condi-tions of the material world. In the fusion of Tyrian and Israelite forces in the building of the Temple and in the rites of kingly ini-tiation, one may rightly see a union of the more earthly, practical mysteries and the heavenly, transcendent tendency which always remained strong in Israel.[4] Rudolf Steiner has pointed out how important this fusion was for the religious evolution which eventually leads to Christianity, and which we shall attempt to trace below.

Nevertheless, even in the period of David and Solomon the Israelite conception of the king was somewhat modified in com-parison with the ideas in Iran, Egypt, or Babylon. The king was an initiate and a priest, but he could hardly be identified directly with Yahweh, the God of Abraham, the invisible God who made all things but who was not immediately present in any external form. The other peoples of the Near East lived in a mythological world where divine powers were still felt to be active every-where in the cosmos and in life, mediated by the king. But though the Israelite king was a godlike figure enthroned at the right hand of the divinity and a Melchizedekian priest, he was not worshipped as god on earth.

Here again the perspective offered by Rudolf Steiner provides an understanding, both of the kind of experience which lies behind the world-view of the ancient Near East and in which Israel at first largely shared, and of the unique direction taken by the subsequent evolution of Judaism, already beginning to be apparent in the differing attitude to the sacral king. Steiner's researches led him to conclude that human consciousness has changed and evolved over the millennia of cultural history, and that the type of individual self-awareness we take for granted today did not exist in ancient times. Each man did not feel himself to have a centre of being within him, an ego; rather he felt to be part of his people, could not even conceive of his existing at all except in terms of his place in the tribe or nation. In so far as he possessed anything like a centre of identity, an ego, it lay in the central figure of society — the king. It was only later that man became more individualized and demanded a spiritual autonomy, establishing his own personal relationship to the divine. In early times it was enough that the king was initiated into the divine secrets, for he was the identity of everyman. All this is clear when we grasp the different consciousness of those days, and it eliminates a whole series of fruitless arguments as to whether the myths spoke originally of a primordial Man who became a king, or whether the concept of the king gave rise to the idea of a First Man. As the king, he was also Man; not symbolically or by 'corporate representation,' but in the experience of his people.[5]

It is important to realize, too, that this meant a totally different experience of the outer cosmos: a mythological living-together with the deep rhythms of the natural world and its indwelling powers. Awareness was more at the level of vivid dream, rather than sharp awakening, but correspondingly in touch with the hidden depths of the soul.

Gradually men evolved toward a sense of greater individual consciousness. We can see it happening in various ways and in various parts of the ancient Near East. And with it comes the demand for a more personal spiritual experience. The techniques of initiation once reserved for the king alone are 'democ-

ratized,' though still reserved for the highly evolved, the esoteric few.

In Israel, however, matters took a different turn, leading to a
decisive break with the principle of initiation altogether. The
result was of crucial significance for the moral consciousness of
later humanity. We must examine what happened in more detail.

Towards Judaism

The religions of Egypt and Mesopotamia managed to adapt
themselves to the increasing individuality of human consciousness, in such a way that they could still succeed in initiating
men into an experience of the supra-personal, the spiritual.
They came to terms with changing conditions in cultural and
religious evolution, but in a manner that permitted them to
retain the old ideals essentially unchanged. The religion of
Israel, on the other hand, took the alternative course: it began
to look for the foundations of its spiritual values in individuality itself.

The consequences were immense, both for the inner life of
man and for his experience of the outer cosmos. In the first
place, the spiritual starts to be felt in a new way — as inwardness. For the mode of consciousness which now begins to
develop, God reveals himself in the inner dimension rather than
in cosmic-mythical patterns that were reactualized in a New
Year festival, when the world was recreated. The type of experience common to the older Mysteries, in which man was raised
above himself and felt part of the cosmic totality, is gradually
replaced by an inner apprehension of the presence of the divine.
Hence in the older sections of the Old Testament, Yahweh manifests himself in the power of storm and huge natural forces,
which to the seers of an earlier form of consciousness were
immediate revelations of spiritual energies. But in the later parts
he no longer shows himself in this way, but as a 'still small
voice' within.

'A man who is now called a 'prophet' was formerly called a
'seer' — so says the Book of Samuel. (1 Sam. 9:9) In fact the transition to the predominance in religious life of the 'prophet' (*nabi*)
was complicated; but the outcome was something entirely

suited to the new direction of consciousness in Israel. The prophet is not an initiate, but a man specially gifted by birth in spiritual matters, who hears the voice of Yahweh and proclaims to men what he hears. Evidently there were large numbers of prophets, as well as those whose utterances were included in the Scriptures. What they had in common was the sense of having been individually chosen as vehicles of the spirit of Yahweh — they had not been made seers through ritual participation or initiation, but elected directly by God. Thus Jeremiah:

> The word of Yahweh was addressed to me, saying 'Before I formed you in the womb I knew you; before you came to birth I consecrated you; I have appointed you as a prophet to the nations.'[6]

Such a sense of individual calling had simply not been possible for the pre-individualized consciousness of the surrounding ancient Near East.

The divine commands — the words of Yahweh uttered by the prophets — are addressed to an audience also consisting of individual consciousnesses. While the old myth-consciousness prevailed, people took part in the great collective rites and festivals; there was scarcely any demand made upon them in the way of individual response because the king acted for all: he was the centre of consciousness for each of his subjects. But now when the will of the spiritual world is no longer found in ritual participation, but is heard and spoken by the *nabi*, the people must make a moral response on the basis of a vastly expanded individual freedom. Personal freedom and moral responsibility emerge along with inwardness as the salient features of the new consciousness. Man no longer finds fulfilment of his nature in collective rituals, living out the great myths of creation and world-order year by year; he responds as a moral individual to the challenge of the divine. The great myths fade increasingly into the background. What man needs now is teaching — instruction on how to orientate himself in the world. And that is what we see coming to be in the period of the prophets in the Old Testament. 'All that had arisen in pictures in the Egyptian and Greek mythology,' says Rudolf Steiner, 'is to be found in the Old

Testament as actual doctrine, with the keynote of morality.'[7] The prophets become the conveyors of the moral teaching of Israelite religion.

Their task is also to rebuke the sinfulness of those who fall short of Yahweh's demands. And along with the increased scope of individual moral freedom comes the sense of guilt on a scale that could not be experienced in the framework of mythological consciousness. Indeed, confronted with the exalted demands of the spiritual world and with only his individual moral resources to draw upon, a man must inevitably suffer some degree of guilt at his shortcomings.

All this radically new development of consciousness is of paramount importance for understanding the life of today. It is in ancient Israel that we see humanity beginning to tread the long road that leads to our modern sense of freedom and our demand for autonomy as spiritual agents in the world. It is also where we see the great barrier of guilt beginning to be erected, which it is part of the meaning and mission of Christianity to overcome.

Not only the character of the inner life was changed by the new direction of consciousness: man's experience of the outer world was also considerably transformed.

Space under the old mythological consciousness had been a concrete dimension of spiritual revelation. Above all, the kingly rites of initiation had reactualized the primordial space — the space in which the gods acted to establish the order and harmony of the universe. Babylon became the universe, the centre of everything from which cosmic rule derived; and the same happened in Egypt and Iran, and ancient Israel too, for the Temple was regarded as standing at the centre of the cosmos, and even as holding down the waters of chaos and the Flood. Originally, then, space was an immediate channel of divine activity.

But as consciousness took a new course of evolution, man found himself in a very different type of universe. He could no longer give himself up to the experience of the cosmic myths: and he therefore had to start thinking of space from the standpoint of carrying out his individual moral purposes. The world spread out around him could no longer be felt to be permeated with the divine activity. It became more a fixed, inert stage on which the divine now enacted itself through the deeds of men. Hence arose the central idea of 'the Creation': God does not reveal himself in the world, but the world is linked to the divine by the relationship of 'createdness.' To mythological conscious- ness there had been no question of a 'created' world, but rather a 'cosmogony,' literally a 'birth of the cosmos.' In Babylon, for the instance, the Tiamat monster was on one level pictured as a vast foetus in the cosmic womb. Another occasion on which the New Year epic myth could be recited was to assist in cases of dif- ficult childbirth! To the Israelites, however, the world ceased to be the body of spiritual beings. It was the greatest sin — idola- try — to worship spiritual presences in any part of nature. Nevertheless, the world was to be admired as the finished work of the Creator. The doctrine of Creation became one of the cor- nerstones of the religion of Israel.

In a world that was no longer thronged with presences, man could find his own way forward with a new sense of freedom. But his freedom was bought at the expense of the mythical feel- ing for space as a dimension of immediate divine activity, in which the primordial acts of the gods were for ever being played out. In compensation, however, Hebraic man discovered a wholly new relationship to time.

Under the sway of mythological forces, ancient man had had little awareness of time and history. Rather, he saw the world perpetually renewed, reimmersed in the primordial time-space of the gods. There was little chance that man could carve out a personal history for himself or his people when time itself was not experienced as an onward flow, but was constantly brought back, so to speak, to the events of the beginning, the ever-pres- ent 'now' of the myth. When the great mythical realities began to fade from the consciousness of the Hebrews, however, they proceeded to make a staggering discovery: history. The Creation had happened — it was over; but the spirit could reveal mean- ing in the changing pattern of events that had occurred since. Not only could a man work out his own unique, individual biography through his moral deeds, but God himself was man- ifested in the large-scale history of the world and of the one peo- ple on earth able to grasp history, the people of Israel.

The events of myth were timelessly re-enactable; history happens only once. The Book of Genesis may be understood when we grasp that it is neither myth (for all its resemblances to the true creationmyths of Babylon, recited at New Year) nor 'scientific' cosmology: it sets out to be a 'history of Creation,' the beginning of divine revelation in time which continues into human history. Myth could be endlessly retold, unfolding different meanings and emphases with each speaker who told it in his own way. History demanded one definitive account: Israel began to gather its historical traditions into a sacred Book, whose every word had to be passed down to posterity unchanged, the authoritative account of God and man in their historical dealings with one another.

The culminating phase in the formation of Judaism out of the Near Eastern type of religion in archaic Israel was the magnificent achievement of Ezra, the 'scribe.' After the catastrophe of the Babylonian captivity, it was he who, like a new Moses, established among his people the study of the Scriptures containing the sacred history of Israel, the moral teaching of the Torah, and the doctrine of Creation which set the Jews religiously apart from their 'idolatrous' neighbours. Judaism had come into existence — and was to survive for millennia to come.

It had been a long process: the first kings of Israel reigned around 1000 BC; the mission of Ezra brings us to the fifth century BC. In the course of those centuries, the consciousness of a small part of humanity had evolved in a unique direction. A mode of spiritual awareness had been developed that broke with the ancient principle of initiation. Instead of raising man to the knowledge of his participation in the vast cosmic process, Judaism had impelled man to draw into himself to hear the word of truth. The world in space had been drained of its inherent divinity, coming to seem like the end-product of a long-discontinued creative activity of God. It had become a lonelier place, and many continued to long for the old myths. Indeed, the Old Testament is largely the story of how the prophets of individual moral awareness tried in vain to prevent the constant relapses of the people into the atavistic, mythological consciousness. But for those who accepted the burden as well as the exhilaration of individuality, a new dimension of freedom opened up. And like a great Father, Yahweh still cared for his people and their history, gave them his commandments and promised them a future end to their trials when all history would be fulfilled.

Yet what was to become of that human longing for spiritual vision like that of the ancient myths? Did it have to be sacrificed altogether for the sake of the inwardness and individual autonomy that Judaism had evolved?

At first sight it might appear that the Judaic evolution of self-conscious moral religion would lead to a decisive and perpetual break with the world of the Mysteries. That, however, turned out not to be the case.

The Rise of the Essenes

The history of the Jews through the period of the Old Testament is exciting and dramatic — inwardly as well as outwardly. The nation endured captivity and oppression under the rule of Assyrians, Babylonians, and Achaemenid kings of Iran; the new moral consciousness had many problems to face, many temptations to overcome in difficult times. Moreover, below the surface of religious history further changes were being prepared. Another step in the evolution of consciousness seems about to happen — at the very point when the Old Testament stops.

To watch that step in the making we must go to the Apocrypha, the books of the 'inter-testamental' period. In particular, we must go to the Books of the Maccabees which form, as Rudolf Steiner said, the significant dramatic climax of the Old Testament narrative.[8] Our story has now come down to the early second century BC. After having fallen to yet another empire-builder, Alexander the Great, Israel is under the rule of the Syrian-Greek armies of his successors, the Seleucids. But unrest soon spreads through the Jewish population when the Syrian king Antiochus IV 'Epiphanes' attempts to suppress the unintelligible religion he found among his subjects, so different from the mixed oriental and Greek paganism in which he had been reared. In 169 BC he visited Jerusalem and looted the Temple, irreverently entering the Holy of Holies where only the High Priests were permitted; and two years later he tried to outlaw

Judaism altogether. Armed revolt broke out, led by the Maccabees — the sons of the priest Mattathias. Their success was enormous. Not only did they manage to restore Judaism; they drove out the Seleucid forces completely and made Israel a sovereign state ruled by the Maccabees and their descendants, known as the Hasmonaeans after the grandfather of the Maccabee brothers, Hasmon. Priests and kings in one, the Hasmonaeans seemed to have restored a dream that had been barren since the days of Solomon. Initiates, sacral rulers sat once again on the throne of Israel.

The political reality was darker. Internal wrangling, quarrels and bloodshed turned out to be all too familiar a part of life under Hasmonaean rule. Yet a new direction in spiritual life had been inaugurated, imperfect though its realization might be. In the next two centuries the ideal of the 'king of the Jews' was to undergo a remarkable spiritual evolution.

Fascinating evidence of the kingly initiation practices of the Hasmonaeans can be found in a document called the *Testament of Levi* — one of the set of *Testaments of the Twelve Patriarchs*. Levi here stands for the archetypal priest; but, again with associations pointing to the figure of Melchizedek, he receives the insignia of kingship too. One passage in particular permits us to be present in imagination at a Hasmonaean initiation. Physical events of the rite and supersensory experiences are mingled in the description of the vision. Levi beholds seven figures clothed in white, who address him and perform several actions. They say:

> 'From henceforth become a priest of the Lord,
>   you and your seed for ever.'
> And the first anointed me with holy oil
>   and gave me the staff of judgment.
> And the second baptized me with pure water,
>   fed me with bread and holy wine,
>   and clad me with a holy and glorious robe.
> The third clothed me with a linen vestment like an ephod.
> The fourth put around me a girdle
>   like unto (royal) purple.
> The fifth gave me a branch of rich olive.

> The sixth placed a crown upon my head.
> The seventh placed on my head a priestly diadem
>   and filled my hands with incense,
>   that I might serve as a priest to the Lord God.[9]

The baptizing, investiture, coronation, and so on were no doubt physical happenings. But the seven white-robed figures recall the kingly initiations of the East: the seven planetary gods who presided over the Babylonian king and gifted him with cosmic power; or one may note an analogy with the Iranian king who is sometimes shown with his six chief nobles, an earthly reflection of the god Ohrmazd and the six other divine Amesha Spentas, the Bounteous Immortals.

What, then, was the source of the spiritual knowledge that lay behind the practices of the Hasmonaeans? And what was their link with the East?

An answer to the first question is extremely difficult, but is certainly to be found in some sort of connection with — the Essenes. The fact that the Essene library at Qumran contained copies of the *Testament of Levi* and certain of the other *Testaments* confirms that.[10] An answer to the second question again involves the Essenes, but also the more widespread phenomenon of which the Essenes were, from a certain point of view, a part: namely, the remarkable springing up of the esoteric baptizing sects particular in the Jordan valley of northern and eastern Israel.

We have mentioned the Essenes earlier, discussing briefly their baptismal rites, the experience of 'illumination' they conferred, and the further stages of initiation into the Mystery open to members of their community. We are now in a position to understand their appearance historically — as part of the return of the Mysteries to Palestine. Yet they offered something spiritually new, not just a return to the Mysteries of old. They did not offer a retreat from the moral responsibilities of Judaism, with its intense feeling of ethical individuality, into the comfort of archaic mythologies. They held with uncompromising strictness to the following of the Law. They worked toward a higher synthesis, a further development of Judaism, in the belief that apocalyptic changes were about to happen in the near future. Indeed, for the Essenes the initiated were already living in a new world.

In varying degrees and different ways, a similar spiritual step was being taken by many of the other esoteric sects. Like the Essenes, many of them had rites of initiation based upon the baptismal experience of death and regeneration. The ancient royal rites were 'democratized': in accordance with the post-Judaic consciousness of moral autonomy, each individual might now be made king and priest in his own unique relationship to God. Some sort of continuity with the ancient rites is clear. In particular, the experience of the auric radiance, the nimbus of divine light or *khvarnah* seems to have been cultivated. Even the later Neoplatonist Iamblichus had witnessed rites in which the candidate was united with a spiritual power, and, as he writes in his work *On the Mysteries*, the astral radiance, the 'form of fire':

> is seen by the recipient of the rite just before the actual receiving of the spirit into himself and sometimes, either when the God is descending or when he is withdrawing himself, it becomes visible to all the beholders.

Similar experiences are pointed to in the language of the baptizing sects. It is the case among the sect of the Mandaeans, for example, which persists to this day, curiously unchanged, in some regions of Iran and Iraq, that all the initiated received the visionary 'crown of light' and royal titles. The Essenes were also given the 'crown of glory' according to the *Community Rule*, and there are many further correspondences with what we know of the baptist sects and their Mandaean successors.[11]

During the two centuries following the liberation of Israel by the Maccabees we watch ever increasing activity among these esoteric sects on the fringes of Judaism and among the Essenes who penetrated into the deserts and cities of Judea. A new spiritual stream is evolving, based upon a kind of initiation which has a much higher respect for the individual ego — though still within the bounds of adherence to the paternal Law. We shall examine the Essene theology from this perspective in more detail in our next section. But we still have to explain why the increase in activity in the last two centuries BC should have been sustained so long and kept up so constantly. After all, the dream of the Hasmonaean priest-kings faded. Around 100 BC at the latest the Essenes had withdrawn their support, and in 63 BC the arrival of Pompey turned Palestine into a Roman province. Yet the impetus of the spiritual movement was maintained. Why?

The answer to this question also suggests a solution to that of the link of the Essenes and others to the East.

The Return of Zarathustra

The new discoveries at Qumran and Nag Hammadi have led many notable scholars to a conclusion already reached through spiritualscientific investigation by Rudolf Steiner, namely that in the esoteric baptizing sects we must discern an influence from the spiritual thought-world of Iran.[12] This was already explored in some detail in Steiner's lectures on *The Gospel of Matthew* (1910), decades before the archaeologists began to come up with surprising evidence to confirm his ideas. For a comparable insight into the motivating power of the Essene-baptist spiritual movements, we had to wait for the Nag Hammadi discovery. At many junctures in these writings, lurking just on or beneath the surface, we meet the expectation that Zarathustra, the great spiritual Master of Iran and founder of the Zoroastrian religion, will be reincarnated as a great 'Illuminator' in several nations in succession, and finally in Palestine.

The beginnings of the idea of the twelve incarnations are already to be found in Iranian tradition itself. Moreover, it was widely recognized that the Saoshyant or saviour who would come at the end of the world-age was in some sense a return of the founder, Zarathustra. In the works from the Nag Hammadi library we encounter further developments in esoteric thought. We find, as Jack Lindsay says, 'traditions of Zoroaster changing his appearance so as to be identified with the prophet Seth, son of Adam, and of ... Saoshyant becoming a form of Jesus.'[13] This Seth is an important figure among Essenes, Gnostics and early Christians, and is closely connected with such characters as Shem and Melchizedek as well as Jesus. He may provide, as we shall see, a vital clue to the secret history of Essenes and Gnostics in Palestine.

Most arresting of all the Nag Hammadi texts, from our present point of view, is undoubtedly the *Apocalypse of Adam*. Alexander Bohlig has shown that it is fundamentally a work deriving from a baptizing sect, somewhere on the Palestinian-Syrian borderlands and touched by the influence of Iranian spirituality.[14] The Apocalypse takes the form of a revelation to Adam, the primal man, related to his son Seth. The events of the flood figure prominently, and afterwards the earth is divided by Noah amongst his sons Shem, Ham and Japhet, whose descendants populate the world. We must remember, however, that there are in addition the spiritual descendants of Seth, who understand all these events through the revelation they have received; but their kingdom is not a worldly one. The descendants of Ham and Japhet flourish, and form twelve kingdoms spread over the face of the earth and worshipping the planetary spirits (the archons of later Gnosticism).

Adam reveals that the religion of the cosmic powers is not the highest to which man can aspire. He goes on to relate, prophetically, the work of the Illuminator among the several nations. Then, suddenly, the perspective is reversed: we hear instead what each of the kingdoms has to say about the Illuminator — Zarathustra — in his successive incarnations. They are the kinds of stories found in every religious tradition about initiates and holy men: miraculous birth, being nourished by birds or animals in the desert, protected by angels, and so on. Yet there is enough to make each embodiment recognisable, if we know which part of the world to look in for parallels. That is not always easy. Some of the incarnations are certainly Iranian, however. One would expect the First Kingdom to refer to Zarathustra himself — and so it does, though not to any detail of his earthly life. It points to his heavenly origin, in agreement with Zoroastrian tradition that the *fravashi* or pre-existent spirit of Zarathustra was created by Ohrmazd and 'nurtured in heaven' from primordial time. Then the Second Kingdom says of him:

> He originated from a great prophet. And a bird came,
> took the child who was born, and carried him to a high
> mountain. And he was nourished by the bird of heaven.

An angel came forth there and said to him, 'Rise up, God
has given you glory!'
He received glory and strength.
And thus he came upon the water.

There are several Iranian motifs here. In fact the story is that of
the hero Zal (or Dastan), who was brought up in the mountain
peaks of the Elburz by the mythical Simurgh bird, and afterwards by divine aid restored to the world of men where he performed great deeds. Or we may take the Eighth Kingdom:

A cloud came upon the earth and enveloped a rock. He
originated from it. The angels who were above the cloud
nourished him.
He received glory and power there.
And thus he came on the water.

This is the famous story of the birth of Mithra from the rock,
shown on many a relief in the Mithraic temples. As such it also
applies archetypally, we must remember, to every initiated
'Father' in the cult, who embodied the divine qualities of Mithra
himself. The legend, in fact, confirms the sources which point to
Zaratas, the reappearance of the prophet Zarathustra in Babylon
in the sixth century BC, as the founder of Mithraism. The Magi
who had migrated westward into Mesopotamia and Babylonia
were indeed especially devoted to Mithra, and it was certainly
thence that Mithraism spread into the Mediterranean world.

The fixed phrases of the 'refrain' depicting the birth of the
Illuminator are also revealing. Bohlig has pointed out that
they refer to the legend of the birth of the Saoshyants.
According to the legend, the spiritual seed of Zarathustra was
concealed in the Kasaoya Sea — physically Lake Hamun, on
the present-day frontier of Iran and Afghanistan. At the destined moments in the cycles of time, it was said, a virgin
would descend to bathe in the waters of the Sea, and emerge
having conceived the Saviour-child, the Saoshyant, who is
therefore said here to 'come upon the water' in fulfilment of
the prophetic pattern.

Some other identifications can be made. In the Fourth

Kingdom, the Illuminator appears as a contemporary of Solomon, who is shown as a great magician commanding an 'army of demons.' The story recounted is not known in exactly this form anywhere else, but is recognizably a version of the tale of the Queen of Sheba, the 'virgin' pursued by Solomon and bearer of his son in due course. The *Apocalypse* makes him not Solomon's literal but his spiritual son, and the son of the still virgin Queen, presumably on her return to Ethiopia whence she came. It is there that we must place the fourth incarnation. In the Ninth Kingdom we have a Greek incarnation:

> One of the nine Muses separated away. She came to a
> high mountain and spent some time dwelling there, so
> that she desired herself alone in order to become
> androgynous. She fulfilled her desire, and became
> pregnant from her desire. He was born. The angels who
> were over the desire nourished him.
> And he received glory there and power.
> And thus he came upon the water.

This incarnation was presumably spent in Orphic Mystery-circles: Orpheus was represented in Greek mythology as the son of the Muse Calliope. The doctrines of Orphism are extremely hard to recover from the little evidence that has come down to us, but the Pythagoreans were closely connected with them, developing their Mystery-teachings in a more 'philosophical' mode, and certainly among the Pythagoreans we find aspirations after the state of 'wholeness' that is psychically represented by 'androgyny.'

Another image of psychic wholeness is shown in the case of the Tenth Kingdom, which depicts an Egyptian incarnation:

> His god loved a cloud of desire. He begot him in his hand
> and cast some of the drop upon the cloud near him, and
> he was born.
> He received glory and power there.
> And thus he came upon the water.

The act of divine masturbation is not shocking in the context of oriental symbolism, which readily uses sexual imagery to refer to spiritual events. It symbolizes the self-sufficiency, the inherent creative power of the god Atum in Egyptian mythology, according to ideas which can be traced back to the Pyramid texts. Every Pharaoh was begotten, in priestly eyes, not by an act of human conception, but by such an autonomous divine sexual act.

And so the text runs through the twelve kingdoms and the twelve incarnations of the Illuminator. The prophecy does not end there, however. After the twelve kingdoms, the progeny of Ham and Japhet, have spoken, we hear from the thirteenth kingdom — which must mean the progeny of Shem, the Semites. In short, the *Apocalypse of Adam* adds to the ancient Iranian tradition of the twelve incarnations the new prophecy of a thirteenth incarnation in Judaea, among the Semitic people, the Jews. Unfortunately the language of the prophecy is obscure: but it has to do with the 'affirmation of the Word,' again the 'receiving of power and glory,' and the birth of the Illuminator-Zarathustra 'in order that the desire of the (cosmic) powers might be fulfilled.'

Even here the prophecy does not stop! We hear next and finally from the 'generation which has no king over it' (that is, who are all themselves 'kings'), which means the spiritual progeny of Seth, the receivers of this primordial revelation. Significantly, they do not make a fourteenth kingdom and a fourteenth incarnation: rather they add a view from the perspective of eternity, saying that 'God chose him from all the aeons,' and that through him (presumably in his final, thirteenth incarnation) God will 'cause a knowledge of the Undefiled One of Truth to come into being.' Here then we have a most remarkable prophecy concerning the mission of Zarathustra — contained in a document devoid of Christian influence and which in its original form probably goes back to an Iranian-Jewish baptizing sect!

In the light of expectations like these, the growing excitement and activity of the esoteric sects in the second and first centuries BC begins to make sense.

The Essenes and Zarathustra

The archaic wisdom of Zarathustra, preserved in the Zoroastrian religion, told of the primordial spirits of Light and Darkness, Good and Evil, Ohrmazd and Ahriman. According to some of Zarathustra's followers, there was a High God beyond Light and Darkness, whom they honoured under the name of Zervan; and it seems to have been the 'Zervanites' whose philosophy predominated in the centuries before Christ.[15] The Zoroastrian myth went on to relate how the present world came into being as a result of 'mixture' between the Light and Dark. The imperfection and restless struggle of existence originates from the unnatural mingling of the hostile cosmic principles. Every follower of Zarathustra places himself on the side of Light and Ohrmazd in the spiritual struggle that pervades all things.

'The body of Ohrmazd is Light and his spirit is Truth.' Ohrmazd is substantially present in light, and in everything that is clean and pure. The Zoroastrians revered in particular the pure elements of water and fire. The seven Amesha Spentas (often called 'archangels,' though they correspond more to the Exousiai, the creative spirits of Christian angelology) are also consubstantial with the being of Ohrmazd himself, and in all domains of the universe oppose the seven dark powers of Ahriman.

The Zoroastrian world-view arises out of a particular type of ancient oriental consciousness, in many ways more archaic even than the Babylonian perception of divine space-time. It stands in powerful contrast, therefore, to the Judaic understanding of the 'created world.' In so far as it can be apprehended as luminous, pure, and spiritually transparent or beautiful, the world is still experienced as an immediate revelation of indwelling Divinity. Its outwardness, its intractability, its imperviousness to spirit (all that seemed to the Jews to point to its createdness, its aspect of 'finished work') indicated to the Zoroastrian consciousness the presence of Ahriman, the impure power of darkness. Moreover, the Zoroastrian consciousness attributes no special significance to inwardness: the struggle of Light and Dark takes place in man as in the wide universe, but there is nothing to suggest that there is any particularly important role for man's ego. On the contrary, it is the cosmic dimension that is repeatedly stressed.

Rudolf Steiner linked the renewed expectations among the disciples of Zarathustra and their growing interest, and influence, in Palestine with a particular sect: the Essenes. This was remarkable, at least from an exoteric point of view, since in his day almost nothing was known about the Essenes from external sources. Since the discovery of the Dead Sea Scrolls at Qumran we know considerably more about them. We can see how they played a central role in the 'return of the Mysteries' to Palestine. Unlike the baptist groups on the fringes of Judaic territory, the Essenes penetrated the central religious life of the Jews, a third party alongside the Sadducees and Pharisees.

Most striking, however, was the realization that the writings from Qumran contained a teaching heavily influenced by a dualism of Light and Darkness, evidently identical with that which forms the core of the Zoroastrian myth! Parts of them might almost have been written by a Zervanite follower of Zarathustra:

> From the God of Knowledge comes all that is and happens ... He has created man to govern the world, and has appointed for him two Spirits in which to walk until the time of his visitation: the Spirit of Truth and the Spirit of Falsehood. Those born of Truth spring from a fountain of Light, but those born of falsehood spring from a source of Darkness. All the children of righteousness are ruled by the Prince of Light and walk in the ways of Light, but the children of falsehood are ruled by the Angel of Darkness and walk in the ways of Darkness.
>
> The Angel of Darkness leads all the children of righteousness astray, and until his end, all their sin, iniquities, wickedness, and all their unlawful deeds are caused by his dominion in accordance with the mysteries of God ...[16]

Here are many of the elements of Zoroastrian wisdom: the polarity of Light and Darkness, Truth and Falsity, the Two

Spirits. Moreover, the *Damascus Rule* also found at Qumran gives us a powerful clue to the origins of this esoteric teaching, since it relates that the body of members of the Essene movement at one stage spent a period of exile in Syria. Their great leader, the 'Teacher of Righteousness,' also apparently underwent a decisive religious experience there. Again, therefore, as with the baptizing sects, we find evidence of contact with the East and a strong interest in the esotericism stemming from Iran.

A close examination of passages like the one quoted above, however, soon reveals that the teaching of the Essenes was not merely a revived Zoroastrianism. The ancient initiation-knowledge has gone through a metamorphosis, and emerges in a more forwardlooking, individualistic guise. There is no reversion to an atavistic, mythological kind of consciousness: the Judaic sense of moral inwardness, of the 'creation,' and of history, remains uneroded; but there is an extension into the world of the Mysteries. The Iranian vision of the two principles, Ohrmazd and Ahriman, Light and Dark as cosmic realities, has been transformed into the teaching of 'two spirits in man,' shifting the scene of spiritual struggle from the great cosmos into the soul of man. Man in his ethical individuality is now felt as the crucial link in the chain.

No change could be more significant. It permits us to peer into the very heart of the process by which the Mysteries took on a new form, and pointed the way toward Christianity. The Essene initiate was no longer simply lifted out of himself in ecstasy and translated into the world of cosmic realities. He had to balance the forces of darkness by means of the light awakened in himself. He was an active moral agent, given by God the responsibility of 'governing' the earth. He was participating in an historical struggle, in accordance with 'the mysteries of God' until 'the time of his visitation,' that is, the advent of the Messiahs. His commitment to the forces of Light rather than Darkness was a moral decision which had to be continually renewed by an act of conscious decision, and on it depended his ability to penetrate into the spiritual world.

To help him distinguish Light from Darkness, the Essene initiate employed esoteric sciences, notably astrology and a type of occult physiognomy. The more recent finds at Qumran have brought us fragments of technical works on these subjects, and Essenes were famous in the ancient world for their powers of prophecy. Above all, they attempted to calculate astrologically the 'time of God's visitation': the nativity of the Messianic figures whom they expected.

We can see in Essenism the advance-guard of a highly significant transformation of religious consciousness: a Mystery fused with the sense of self that had evolved in Judaism; a kind of initiation that could be combined with a feeling for history as the revelation of 'the mysteries of God,' and a responsibility for the earth. The inner process begun in the days of the first Israelite kings, and the linking of Judaism with the initiatory wisdom of Mysteries like those of Tyre and the rest of the ancient Near East, comes to a head in the wisdom of the Essenes. And the mission of Zarathustra, already given universal scope in the conception of his twelve incarnations, finds further expression in a new and significant teaching.

Yet there are still obvious limitations. Essene theology man still measures himself against the dictates of the paternal Law, a code of conduct given from without. For most, this meant inevitable inadequacy. Essenism furnished a way of righteousness for the few, and left the many to carry the Judaic burden of irremovable guilt. Man, even in Essenism, still does not find the source of morality and spiritual life within.

The metamorphosis in man's changing historical relationship to the divine world had to be taken to a further stage yet — a stage that could not be attained from man's side alone.

4. Esoteric History: a Parting of the Ways

From Essenes to Christians

With the discovery of the Dead Sea Scrolls, some part of the veil shrouding the life of Jesus and the background of Christianity seemed to have been lifted. Some thought that Jesus might well have been brought up among Essenes — or even that the Scrolls were early Jewish-Christian writings. However, opinion now tends toward the view that although Jesus probably had a certain contact with the Essene movement, he was not actually a part of it. And here again the likely truth was a confirmation of the investigations carried out spiritually by Rudolf Steiner.

According to Steiner, the Essenes were so impressed by the reputation for wisdom which attached to the youthful Jesus that they were willing to enter into a sort of dialogue with him. 'The Essenes received him into their community — I do not say into the Order itself — as a kind of extern, or outside member,' Steiner asserts. 'In the Essene Order, Jesus of Nazareth heard far, far deeper teachings concerning the secret lore than he had ever heard from the scribes and doctors of the Law.' That would naturally be the case — though we should remember that Steiner also presents the young Jesus as an enthusiastic admirer of the Pharisee master Hillel. For the scriptures from Qumran have confirmed that the Essenes taught esoteric doctrines about those very matters where the Rabbis were severely limited: the interpretation of Ezekiel's *Merkavah*-mysticism, for example. We may recall that the Pharisees permitted discussion on this theme only with one 'who is able to understand of himself.' Evidently the Essenes had a similar rule concerning their 'wisdom among the initiated' — and were prepared to talk to Jesus as one clearly 'able to understand.' Jesus in turn learnt much from the life he encountered among the 'Essenes, and must have studied their secret writings. The influence of their literature on his own words can several times be detected. For instance, a Jewish hymn or prayer at that time, whether intended for use in the Temple or among the rabbis, began in a more or less standard way, 'Blessed be God ... ' The Essenes themselves occasionally use the formula. But they have their own preferred way of starting, which is 'I thank you ...' Indeed they had a whole collection of hymns and prayers making up what is now termed the *Thanksgiving Scroll*. It is a distinctive Essene feature. Now, when Jesus composes a hymn, how does it run?

> I thank you, Father, Lord of heaven and earth, because
> you have hidden these things from the wise and learned,
> and you have revealed them to little children. Yes, Father,
> for this was your good pleasure ...

'Not only the opening of Jesus' hymn but also the free rhythm of the poem and its content,' comments a Jewish scholar, 'show affinity with the Essene thanksgiving hymns ... both Jesus and the author of the *Thanksgiving Scroll* proclaim that they reveal to the simple divine things hidden from others. Thus it seems evident that Jesus knew the Essene thanksgiving hymns and used their form in order to express his own place in the divine economy, though he introduced into his own hymn the motif of his divine sonship, which is naturally absent from the *Thanksgiving Scroll*.'[1]

Much interest has been focused, of course, on Jesus' links with the world of the Qumran scrolls. But we have also seen that the Essenes were connected with a wider range of esoteric baptist movements in Syria and Palestine (and perhaps even Babylonia), and the most famous representative of these movements in the New Testament is a figure whom we must also examine here, namely John the Baptist. It has been pointed out that, though 'John may have moved around, the main centre of his preaching and baptismal ministry was almost certainly close to the fords of Jordan just south of Jericho, a point less than ten miles north of Qumran. It is impossible to suppose that John could be ignorant of the Essene/sectarian settlement existing within the very area in which he himself lived and worked.'[2] And knowing about them, he could hardly ignore them: the Essenes taught an initiatory baptism, perhaps similar to John's, and like him they expected the advent of the Messiah or Coming One.

Yet there were also differences. Above all, John worked publicly and, although his baptism was restricted to Jews, he accepted all who came without initiating them into a special sect or communal way of life. Very illuminating, therefore, are Steiner's conclusions based on esoteric research. He describes John the Baptist as one who had a temporary connection with the Essenes — 'but he too was not an Essene in the strict sense of the word.' He lived with the Essenes, and adopted certain of their customs, 'but he had never been able to exchange inwardly and completely the tenets of Judaism for those of the Essenes.'[3] He evidently stood somewhere between the transformed Mysteries of the Essenes proper and the mainstream Judaism of his time. Hence his emphasis on the individual moral decision that had to be taken by every person who wished to belong to the 'true Israel,' and the confining of his interest to the Jews. That was one side of his teaching of 'repentance' (*metanoia*): his stress on the unique moral consciousness that had evolved within Judaism. Yet at the same time his proclamation *Metanoeite* also suggests 'Change your attitude of mind.' In other words his baptism was associated with a feeling of inner awakening and a radical reorientation, something closely approaching to initiation like that of the Mysteries or the Essenes. According to Steiner, those baptized by John by immersion in the river Jordan experienced an inner shock, resembling even a near encounter with death, so that they saw their life spread out before their eyes, and returned to normal life to make a new beginning.

John's mission to baptize and proclaim publicly his message of *metanoia*, together with his expectation of the Coming One, meant that he could not stay with the Essenes, much as he had in common with them on many levels. Likewise Jesus went out of their monastic settlement to perform his ministry on the open stage of history, to teach and travel in Galilee and Samaria as well as in Judea, and to meet a death whose significance far outstripped that of any teaching: the death of the Cross. In a sense their departures signified a failure for the Essenes. Yet in another, far more important way, it was a triumph for the impulse which had brought Essenism into being. John the Baptist opened out for the Jewish people a road of approach to matters which had so far been understood by the initiated few, the Essenes who had managed to fuse the spiritual vision of the Mysteries with the inwardness of Judaic consciousness. And Jesus of Nazareth played his part in a Mystery, understood partly and prophetically by the Essene *illuminati*. The Mystery of Golgotha could not be contained by any movement or sect, however, but was in essence a Mystery for all mankind, a potent impulse in the transformation of man and his world whose power can hardly be exhausted. The Mystery for the few became an event accessible to all.

Many of the Essenes themselves soon recognized this event; though we do not know how long after the period of his connection with them they realized that Jesus was the one whom they had awaited. It is certain that a great many of them did recognize him — we shall see why in a moment. Perhaps they had their suspicions from the beginning, following their theories of occult physiognomy and the characteristics of the physical body of the Messiah, so stressed in some of the more esoteric works from Qumran; or from their astrological calculations, some of which have now been discovered, though they are unfortunately not well preserved.

We know that many Essenes did become Christians, because we can detect their hand in shaping to a greater or lesser degree many of the early Christian communities in Palestine and Syria. It was no doubt they who pioneered the social forms of the new movement, with their experience of building communities at Qumran and elsewhere. In fact, the Christian groups used handbooks very similar to the *Community Rule* of the Qumran Essenes: the best example is the *Didache* or *Teaching of the Lord*, which was widely used and its regulations repeated and paraphrased in letters to new communities. It commences with general information on 'the Two Ways' — of Light and Darkness, exactly as in the Essene manual we quoted in the last chapter. Indeed, to a surprisingly literal extent it reads as the *Community Rule* re-written in the light of the Sermon on the Mount! Compare with the Qumran teaching on the 'children of light,' the Angels of Light and Darkness, and so on, this version of the *Didache* appended to the *Epistle of Barnabas*:

> There are two Ways of teaching, and two wielders of power; one of light and the other of darkness. Between those two Ways there is a vast difference, because over the one are posted the light-bearing angels of God, and over the other the angels of Satan; and one of these two is the Lord from all eternity to all eternity, while the other stands paramount over this present age of iniquity ...[4]

The man who wrote this was almost certainly an Essene who had become a Christian; and there were many spreading the same ideas.

Nevertheless, the step from Essenism to Christianity was no small one, even if it was the Mystery-knowledge of the Essenes which provided much of the thought-life and social organization of the early Jewish Christians. The Essenes had lived by strict rules of purity — a spiritualized interpretation of the Torah. The Christian lives out of his experience and conviction of the Christ within. Qumran-style references to the punishment of transgressors had accordingly to be replaced in the *Didache* with Jesus' teaching about turning the other cheek. Yet the fact that so many Essenes made the transition is powerful testimony to the spiritual ideal they followed, which triumphed over the tendency toward rigid legalism and kept them open to the all-transforming significance of events, which happened only partially in the manner they had anticipated.

Following the discovery of the Dead Sea Scrolls, then, and making use of Steiner's results of spiritual investigation, it is thus possible to trace an evolution of man's religious life and consciousness from the time of the initiate-kings down to the beginnings of Christianity. The royal rites of initiation practised in the ancient Near East, including Israel, were gradually given a new form. Combined with the sense of inwardness and moral freedom that developed in Judaism, they led to a new fusion of spiritual vision and individual awareness in the

Essene movement, which prepared a way directly for the understanding of Christ. The ideal of the initiated 'King of Israel' is raised to a higher plane of significance, whose importance is extended to the whole of mankind. From the standpoint of spiritual history, we may say, the Essene and later the Christian Mystery cannot be understood only on the basis of the national hopes of Judaism. The Mysteries of other great worldreligions, especially those of Iran, played their part in the rise of the esoteric baptizing sects, as we can see from the *Apocalypse of Adam* and the thought of the Essenes.

Moreover, the history of these pre-Christian esoteric movements which brought together the wisdom of the East and the West may also furnish the key to understanding another spiritual phenomenon of the early Christian centuries: Gnosticism.

Essenes and Gnostics

It was when the modern biblical scholar R. M. Grant had been studying the writings from Qumran that it struck him, so he tells us, that 'nearly all the ingredients later found in Gnosticism were already present in the life and literature of these Essenes.'[5]

Let us accordingly retrace our steps a little: let us re-examine the trajectory we have traced, and see whether there is some important part of the story we might have missed. In particular we must consider that formative period when the Mysteries of the East were beginning to find a way back into the world of Judaism. For it is hardly to be imagined that the encounter between two very different spiritual streams would always proceed smoothly. The Essenes may have succeeded brilliantly in creating a synthesis, preserving the Judaic sense of history and man's responsibility for the earth alongside the visionary consciou,sness of the Mysteries of Iran — but let us look at it for a moment from the Eastern side: did all of those who belonged to the Mystery-stream automatically succeed in grasping this novel dimension? The Jewish consciousness of the 'finished creation,' of God's purpose in history and of human individuality was the product of a centuries-long evolution. Can we expect that all those who approached it from the oriental side would immediately be able to adjust?

Far more likely, we should expect that not all of those involved in the encounter would prove so forward-looking as the Essenes. Some would no doubt get a certain way, we might suppose, but remain ultimately unable to make the complete adjustment and fall back upon their Eastern ideas and attitudes. There was a great deal in the world-view of Judaism that caused problems for the oriental mind, which would naturally react with horror to the intensified self-consciousness, and the acceptance of the inert material creation as a 'work of God.' According to Zoroastrianism, we may remember, the material world was the work of Ahriman.

If on the one hand the encounter between Judaism and the oriental Mysteries could lead to a new fusion in the spirituality of Essenes and the baptizing sects, on the other it could lead to an opposite reaction: the shocked reiteration of the archaic-oriental point of view. And that is what we find in Gnosticism. Many of the strange doctrines we find in the Gnostic writings become intelligible when we realize that they originate from a reaffirmation of the oriental-archaic mode of vision, an emphatic reaffirmation made by men who have also to some extent entered into the alien experience of self-consciousness, and know something of the demythologized universe of the Judaic spirit. In place of the Essene synthesis, in the Gnostic writings two incompatible worlds, two modes of consciousness, glare across at each other unreconciled. Gnosticism develops in the form of a radical dualism — a conflict of opposite realities. For that is what we find in the Gnostic view of the world. The physical world, the material creation, is experienced as inert and 'finished,' 'out there' as it was for the Jews and as it is for most of modern humanity; at the same time the visionary world of Mystery-consciousness is strongly felt, in a way that cannot be reconciled with physical perception. The Gnostic cannot deny the 'reality' of either mode of awareness, for he has experienced both. And yet he cannot place himself as a moral agent between light and darkness as did the Essene: in so far as he has to accept the physical reality over against the spiritual, he feels himself pulled apart, split in two.

For the Gnostic, the aspect of the Divine which created the physical world cannot be held together in vision with the God of the spiritual world. It must rather be a 'fallen' divinity which fashioned the delusion, the *maya*, of the perceptible universe.

The Gnostic did not shrink from this recognition of a fallen God, or Demiurge, creator of the material universe. Before we dismiss the Gnostic world-view as a product of failure, or weakness, we must reflect upon the enormous inner strength needed to maintain a double vision, an acknowledgment of conflicting realities. How much more easy to lapse into materialism and deny the truth of the spiritual world — or to retreat from outer reality into some kind of quietism, turning away from difficulties without! The other Mysteries, in fact, had all fallen by early Christian times into a state of decadence precisely because they had refused to face the full truth of man's position, and his changing mode of consciousness. They had tried, in effect, to ignore the problem of changing spiritual conditions, which made man's contact with the spiritual world increasingly difficult as he developed a more earthly kind of consciousness. They had degenerated into more and more desperate attempts to induce any sort of visionary experience, in whatever crude way was necessary. The growing inefficacy of the traditional gods meanwhile led to the adoption of 'mixed' religions, in which individuals called on each and every known divinity, or identified them all with each other, so that the Mysteries turned into a mixture of objectionable and crude magic, or into colourless bodies teaching 'universal truths' of a general and unexciting nature.

By boldly 'bracketing off' the reality of the outer world and man's individual awareness, the Gnostic held back from this confusion. He was enabled by his defensive 'double vision' to preserve, in remarkably authentic form the visionary, archaic consciousness which formed the other side of the equation. Gnosticism encountered the more modern consciousness in its most advanced form — that of Judaism. But in the face of the experienced world of Jewish consciousness, Gnosticism held on to a mythological consciousness that could still make contact with the realities of the ancient world of the Mysteries, in a way that transcended that of the Essenes who after all had made many accommodations to the conditions of the Judaic world.

Here again Rudolf Steiner's descriptions of the Gnostics turned out to be startlingly accurate. He characterized them as the 'successors of the old initiates,' who preserved into later times the archaic attitudes of the Mysteries. As such they are to be distinguished, he said, from the forward-looking synthesis represented by the Essenes and their successors.[6] Above all, such a view of the Gnostics enables us to understand their paradoxically close involvement with, yet simultaneous hostility toward the spirit of Judaism. We must see the Gnostics as the 'other side' of the same development which produced the Essenes: the encounter between Judaism and the oriental consciousness. On the one hand, oriental Mystery-elements were absorbed into a new religion of individual moral awareness of the spiritual, among the Essenes. On the other, within the defensive framework of Gnostic dualism or double vision, an archaic mythological consciousness found a haven even inside the world of the new, alien awareness' (from the Eastern point of view) of the material creation.

Both sides of the development were to prove vital to the understanding of the 'Christian Mystery.'

In the course of the encounter, we should expect that there must have been many gradually developing differences of opinion, some groups inclining more to the oriental-Gnostic and others to the Essene attitude. There must surely have been many occasions for 'schisms' or 'secessions,' when part of an esoteric community took one side and part the other. There must in fact have been a range of in-between stations, a spectrum of views. It is possible that the new discovery at Nag Hammadi has actually brought us an obscurely narrated history of one such major split, when a part of the community branched off, one half being Essene and the other Gnostic — though probably the terms were not then in use. The record of their disagreement is contained in a book called *The Sacred Book of the Invisible Spirit.*

It is told from what became the Gnostic side; but the book stands in close relation to the older *Apocalypse of Adam*, though belonging to a later, Christian stage of the development. Its teaching in fact had much in common with that of the *Apocalypse of Adam*, and with other features of esoteric-baptist thought — for example, there is a spiritual being who presides over *Metanoia*. But the doctrine has inclined more particularly toward Gnosticism.

In order to understand the possible link with the Essenes before the, Gnostic inclination produced a schism, however, we need to consider two pieces of evidence.

The first is philological. For the name Qumran, coupled with the setting of the place in the low-lying region of the Dead Sea, has prompted modern investigators to speculate that 'Qumran' is a later spelling of the ancient place-name 'Gomorrha.' Some archaeological results point to remains of walls and stone constructions now under the waters of the Dead Sea, just below the site of present-day Qumran. Or it may simply have received the name in later times because it was then thought to have been the place of the older town. The coastal plain certainly used to be much more fertile: some salt-encrusted palm-trunks have been found; a luxurious civilization could once have flourished there, and even in historical times the Essenes probably lived mainly on dates from the rich groves, as indeed the ancient historian Pliny said. Moreover, despite the infamy of Sodom and Gomorrha in the Old Testament, by the early Christian era everything had changed. We know from the writer Synesius of Cyrene that both places were then famous for their piety, and above all for their colonies of Essenes.[7] Thus if we are to expect references to Qumran in early literature, it would certainly be with the older spelling 'Gomorrha.'

The evidence is thus plausible enough. Present 'Qumran' represents the name Gomorrha, whether or not accurately identified. And there, by the last century BC we should expect to find Essenes (that is, the Qumran community) and other religious groups. The earlier cities had of course long been destroyed by the time we are referring to — that tale is narrated in the Bible.

Secondly, we must know something about a figure who was important among Essenes and Gnostics alike: the 'great Seth,' son of Adam. We may recall that the *Apocalypse of Adam* presented itself as a revelation of Adam to his son Seth. Already in the *Book of Enoch*, which was read as scripture by the Essenes, Seth appears as the representative of a holy race, a 'spiritual seed' — not a physical race so much as a spiritual brotherhood, since the three archetypal figures Seth, Abel and Cain are represented after the Flood by the three sons of Noah: Shem, Ham and Japhet, the founders of the physical races. Closely connected with the idea of the 'spiritual seed' are ancient Near Eastern symbols of kingship-initiation. The king in his elevation to become the Man is the ruler in paradise, ritually recreated. His rod or sceptre is represented in early texts by the ideogram of the Tree of Life. These ideas are woven together in the legend that Seth received a rod from Adam, which was passed down to Moses; or that Seth was allowed back into paradise briefly to fetch seeds from the Tree of Life after the Fall. 'So, too, in Israel as elsewhere,' writes F. H. Borsch, 'the description of the ruler as a *shoot* or *branch* ultimately depends upon this symbolism. And it is from the tree of life that kings are said to be anointed, from which their garland crown is made, and from its branches the ritual hut is constructed.'[8] It is no accident that we find this symbolism employed by the Qumran community in a self-description from a Hymn we quoted earlier:

> He has joined their assembly
>   to the Sons of Heaven
> To be a Council of the Community,
> a foundation of the Building of Holiness,
> an everlasting Plant throughout all ages to come.[9]

Such language also occurs in the Nag Hammadi *Sacred Book*, to which we must now turn.

The Sacred Book describes Sodom and Gomorrha as holy places, and adds that 'the great Seth came and brought his seed ... to Sodom.' It further reveals that the history of this event was rather complicated. Evidently it involved a dispute between two parties ('Some say ... others say'), who disagreed on the interpretation of spiritual teaching — in other words, as to which party could properly be called the 'seed of Seth.'

> Some say that Sodom is the nurturing-place of the great
> Seth, which is Gomorrha. But others say that the great
> Seth took his plant out of Gomorrha and planted it in the
> second place to which he gave the name Sodom.

The course of events might be reconstructed as follows: a group who regarded themselves as the true 'plant' of Seth became involved in a disagreement with the other members of the original community at Gomorrha-Qumran. They finally withdrew to Sodom, where they organized their own esoteric establishment. Meanwhile the original community continued vehemently to deny that Sodom was a place of nurture of the great Seth, insisting that this was Gomorrha-Qumran.

Those who kept to the view that the nurturing-place of Seth was Gomorrha were, presumably, the Essenes who inhabited the place until the disturbances of the Jewish Revolt made it unsafe. Scholars such as Jean Doresse and Hans Jonas have pointed out that the others, who declared that Seth had removed his 'plant' and transferred it to Sodom, became the adherents of the teaching in the *Sacred Book* — that is to say, they developed in the Gnostic way of thought! Here then we have an historical instance of the parting of the ways: an esoteric group which could not finally accept the Essene teaching goes over to form the ranks of at least one school of Gnostics.

The view of the Gnostic party is clarified in another, highly symbolic yet clear passage. Gomorrha may have been the 'spring' of the teaching of the great Seth; but 'Sodom ... is the fruit of the spring of Gomorrha.'[10]

The Essenes, of course, continued to disagree.

The Pagan Gnostics

The difference of opinion recorded in the *Sacred Book* took place, it seems probable, in pre-Christian times. Certainly there is evidence of the spread of the new ideas, the offspring of the encounter between Judaic consciousness and the East, from various parts of the pre-Christian world — Syria, Samaria, Mesopotamia. And the evidence suggests that in these other places too the results tended both in an Essene and in a Gnostic direction.

In Egypt, for example, we hear of a group called the Therapeutae, who sound extremely like Egyptian Essenes. We have to remember that there were many Jews in Egypt at this period, especially in Alexandria.

But a good deal more attention was attracted by a group which took up the ideas in the Gnostic form, namely, the followers of Hermes Trismegistus, to whom were attributed the famous writings of the 'Hermetic Corpus' which have had such an enormous influence on esoteric thought ever since. Hermes was the Greek name for the god whom the Egyptians called Thoth or Tehuti, the heavenly scribe and master of wisdom; the title 'Trismegistus' means thrice-greatest, and goes back to old Egyptian honorific practice in addressing the gods. Esoteric astrological traditions in the name of Hermes-Thoth can be traced back to 150 BC, and doubtless the earlier priests guarded secrets before that. At some stage in the time leading up to the Christian era, however, the followers of Hermes evidently felt the need to bring the older Egyptian wisdom up to date: possibly this was around the time of Ptolemy II, when the great task of translating the Old Testament into Greek was also undertaken in Egypt.[11] The Hermetists reformulated their wisdom, drawing on many ideas from Greek philosophy, especially Platonism, but above all on the concepts and practices of the new Jewish-Iranian esotericism. Their results were finally given definitive form in the body of writings which have come down to us as the *Corpus Hermeticum*, the final written version dating from the early centuries AD. Its teachings are of extraordinary interest in themselves. It has also long been recognized that the *Corpus Hermeticum* is able to cast a powerful sidelight on the background of at least parts of the New Testament.

The Hermetic Gnostics practised a kind of baptism, and their teaching included a call for *metanoia*, the transformation of one's consciousness. The baptism and the special terminology point to circles close to the Essenes and indeed to John the Baptist as the source from which the Egyptian Mysteries were updated. (Remember that the *Apocalypse of Adam* also points to one or more Egyptian incarnations!) But until recently there was a baffling lack of evidence about the actual rites that the Hermetists performed. Once again it was the Nag Hammadi discovery which brought more detail. A fascinating document called *On the Eighth and the Ninth* (*Levels of Consciousness*) gives us an intimation of the powerful ritual process by means of which the neophyte was raised in consciousness through the levels corresponding to the planetary spheres — and beyond.

Hermes Trismegistus figures as the hierophant, the 'Father,' and the neophyte is the 'son.' There is a 'rebirth' which is at the same time an energy awakening in the spirit which overflows like a fountain. There is an experience of Light. There is also a strong impression of the inadequacy of language, and a sense of meaning conveyed in silence which yet has the force of hymn or prayer, uttered supersensibly by the angelic powers of the eighth and ninth levels. The pupil is taken to the very limits of mortal vision: more he cannot attain until the body has been laid aside completely at death.

The recovery, at least in part, of Hermetic ritual practice has revealed a further problem. For just as clear as the practice itself is the evidence that Hermetism gradually abandoned rituals, and emphasized more purely inward methods — meditation and silent prayer. When we find influence from Hermetism on early Christianity, notably on the *Gospel of Thomas* and its tradition, it has the effect of steering Christianity away from outer enactments and sacraments toward a mystery of 'interpretation': inner discovery through finding the meaning of Jesus' words. But the precise stages of the change, or perhaps the emergence of different trends within Hermeticism, cannot yet be perceived in any depth.[12]

On the Eighth and Ninth gives us a glimpse of Hermetic religious experience. But what of the cosmic vision that underlies it? For this we must turn to the previously known writings. In the first book or tractate of the *Corpus Hermeticum*, which has the title *Poimandres* (sometimes wrongly given to the whole *Corpus*), the author has a vision. In it we recognize many features known also from Essene teaching on the Light and Darkness, the Two Ways, and so on. But here the underlying attitude to the world is distinctively Gnostic. According to the vision, man belongs essentially to the realm of Light and is a stranger here on earth. The material world was formed by a Demiurge, or lower God, who cannot be the God of the exalted regions which are man's original spiritual home. After the creation of the cosmic system, the stars and planets, which happens in accordance with the Jewish Genesis-account, it is related that the supra-celestial Man, who existed archetypally, looked down through the spheres and saw his image reflected in the deep. Nature, who here represents the 'downwardtending' power of material creation, fell in love with the divine Man; he likewise fell in love narcissistically with his material image in Nature and was thenceforth trapped in the perishable material body, subjected to the astrological forces of the spheres:

> And that is why man, unlike all other living creatures upon earth, is twofold. He is mortal by reason of his body; he is immortal by reason of the Man of eternal substance. He is immortal, and has all things in his power; yet he suffers the lot of a mortal, being subject to Destiny. He is above the Harmony (of the Spheres); yet he is born a slave. He is bisexual, as his Father is bisexual, and sleepless, as his Father is sleepless; yet he is mastered by carnal desire and by oblivion.[13]

The aim of Hermetic *gnosis* is to liberate man from his subjection on earth, and allow him to reascend to the realms where he originally belonged.

Despite certain similarities with Essene teaching, the different emphasis is clear. The Essenes showed how man, through a moral struggle to serve the Light in the historical process of overcoming the Darkness, could act as an individual agent, with a responsibility for his fellow men and for the earth itself. For the Gnostic, man does not belong on earth; his individuality is an illusion, caused by the subjection of the archetypal Man to the 'downward-tending' powers of Nature and the multiplication of physical bodies in which he is 'trapped'; the goal of man is to recognize himself as belonging to Life and Light, so that he can leave the Darkness behind. For there is here no historical struggle: Darkness cannot be overcome, but exists eternally as a second Principle alongside the Light. Having left the Darkness behind, man will ultimately merge his identity into the infinite Light.

The Samaritan Gnostics

The Hermetists drew upon the Jewish-Iranian esotericism to reinterpret their own ancient wisdom, giving it a distinctively Gnostic form — though as we have seen there were probably

Essene-type settlements in their environment too. Other territories on the fringe of Judea also fostered developments of a similar nature. In Samaria, for example, we hear of the celebrated adept Simon, known as the Magus.

There seems to be direct links once more with the Essenes. It is likely that the Teacher of Righteousness, the Essene leader, was drawn to Damascus where he had one of his most important experiences, because of a particular connection. Damascus was one of the cities supposed to have been founded by the sons of Seth, and we have seen how important a figure Seth was in Jewish esotericism. The Teacher was probably trying to contact other 'Sethites.' Whether or not he was successful, his ideas appear to have affected a Samaritan teacher who is referred to as Dositheus, or Dostai in the Jewish sources: he went on to found an esoteric movement within Samaritanism, and among his most important pupils was Simon. However, the movement soon ceased to represent Essene attitudes and became thoroughly Gnostic, under the further direct influence of Eastern ideas.

The scholar Jean Daniélou has pieced together some details of the obscure and fascinating story. According to the Jewish chroniclers, he points out, Dostai came from Kokaba, which he identifies with the town of 'Kokaba near Damascus, the site of an Essene community.' It was there, thinks Daniélou, 'that Simon, a disciple of Dositheus, was converted to dualism by Zoroastrian magi (hence Simon is 'Magus').'[14]

In the secret teaching of the Samaritan Gnostics we can immediately identify familiar elements: the reappearing prophet like the Illuminator (Zarathustra) of the *Apocalypse of Adam*, for instance, is a prominent doctrine, and there are baptismal rites of initiation. Simon himself later became a figure of legend, a prototype of the medieval Faust; hence it is extremely difficult to untangle fantasy and fact about his actual life and teaching, now seen through the haze of medieval romance. But we do know that he spoke in the name of 'the Great Power,' which is a circumlocution for God. In doing so he was not claiming to be God, nor, as many later Christian writers thought, setting himself up as a rival to Christ. He was speaking in the oriental manner out of a consciousness which transcended individuality —

in which individual awareness was abandoned and a universal power could speak out of the depths of the soul. Simon appears to have taught that anyone could discover that power within himself.

Simon's universalist doctrines are set out in a remarkable document called the *Great Annunciation*, of which passages have been preserved, and wi!ich was probably written in his name by his disciples at an early stage in the tradition. According to Simon, the basic energy-substance of the universe is Fire, and this exists in two forms, one 'manifest' and the other 'hidden' or occult. Further forms are distinguished in turn on the basis of the primal polarity, totalling six modes of cosmic power visible and invisible. But the real interest centres on the Seventh Power: for this is not yet unfolded, but lies dormant in unawakened mankind, and it subsumes into itself the working of all the other six powers. Hence the man who knows how to awaken the Seventh Power within himself, knows himself as a microcosm, a 'lesser world' in which all the cosmic powers are united. In fact, the Seventh Power restores the original unity and co-operation of the Godhead which is lost and divided in its cosmic manifestations, so that in reality according to Simon's system it is the Godhead, the Great Power which awakens to full self-knowledge in man.

Behind Simon's pattern of thought lies a mythology: a myth of a Godhead which, in some primeval, pre-cosmic catastrophe lost its essential unity and was scattered in the form of illusory individual selves through the lower world. In some of the legendary accounts of Simon, it is said that he recognized the fallen First Thought of the Godhead, who had existed before the world was made, sunk through a series of incarnations to become a prostitute living in a brothel in Tyre. Earlier she had been Helen of Troy, for whose beauty men had fought the Trojan War. But probably these are embroideries on the original myth. The important point was that for Simon, the process of redemption was the self-finding of the Godhead:

> This is the meaning of the saying, 'I and thou are one,
> thou art before me, I am after thee.' This is the One
> Power, divided as being above and below, self-generating,

self-increasing, self-seeking, self-finding, its own mother, its own father ... unity, the root of all.[15]

Here, as for all Gnostic thought, man is caught up in a divine process which has meaning not only for him but for the whole universe and God himself. In later Gnostic myth this is expressed as the self-redeeming of the Redeemer, the story of the divine Man who comes to rescue his own lost Self.

The figure of the divine Man and his original glory, related to the idea of cosmic kingship, no doubt came to Simon from his Zoroastrian teachers, and could be combined with already existing ideas about Adam from Jewish esotericism. In Iranian myth the Light-God Ohrmazd sometimes appears as-an Archetypal Man, and the idea of the Seven Powers may reflect the teaching that Ohrmazd manifests himself with his six Creator Spirits (Amesha Spentas), himself being the Seventh yet also being the totality — a profound idea we shall meet again.

The teaching about the creation of the material cosmos is clearly based, however, on Judaism and the Genesis account in particular. Simon's attitude is essentially Gnostic: the created world reveals only the divided, separated Powers; the original unity, rediscovered in the Seventh Power, awakens on a purely spiritual level. Moreover, in order to participate as a 'knower,' a Gnostic, in the divine process, man must put aside his delusive individuality. The real Man existed at the beginning, and can be found again through spiritual awakening, as the universal, the totality of the Powers; the selfhood, the moral individuality, for Simon, is an illusion.

Nevertheless, the myth behind Simon's Gnostic teaching perhaps expressed a truth which could be interpreted from a Christian perspective. For it spoke of a divine-cosmic process in which man was centrally involved as well as God: transposed on to the plane of history, the myth might embody a truth more universal than the meaning Simon, or any other of the Gnostics, was able to give it.

Gnostic Cosmology: the Ophite Diagram

One group who present Gnostic teaching, and its emphasis on the split nature of man's being, in particularly radical form, and who ' therefore probably split off fairly early, were the so-called Ophites. In Greek *ophis* means a snake: the sect derived their name from the fact that they pictured the World-Soul in the form of the Leviathan or cosmic snake biting his own tail, a symbol of the endless cycles of becoming.

A main feature of the Ophite *gnosis* was the insistence that the act of creation described in Genesis was not the very beginning of things. In fact it was a relatively late stage in the world-process. The formation of the physical world was preceded by three spiritual and psychic phases of existence. Moreover, Man originated as an archetypal being in those earlier worlds, and not in the material creation. Hence the Ophites regarded the-world-creator of Judaic tradition, whom they referred to by the esoteric name Ialdabaoth, as a lowly being, whose material creation contrasted unfavourably with the spiritual worlds which had existed before him. He had formed a world of sufferings and estrangement, without precedent from the higher worlds. He and his angels fashioned the body of man (Adam): but it remained unable to stand, until through the providence of the heavenly Sophia, the divine spark of spirit and thought was breathed into it. Then Adam stood upright, 'and he at once gave thanks to the First Man, forsaking his (material) creators.' It is the spark of spirit and thought in man which can be saved — through the knowledge that man essentially belongs to the higher worlds, and not to the material earth.

Here we have an uncompromising interpretation of physical-material creation from the standpoint of the archaic, oriental mind! The Ophites were familiar with the Jewish history of creation, and so far belonged to the Judaic mode of consciousness as to admit that it was in some sense 'true': yet their evaluation of the physical world, and of its creator, was diametrically opposed to that of orthodox Judaism. Far more important seemed to them the spiritual worlds which pre-existed the physical, and in which man finds the ground of his being, the archetype of his humanity. Again, the teachings about those worlds came from the Iranian mysteries. The Ophites represented the fourfold world-process in a Diagram, a proto-version of the kabbalistic Tree of Life.[16]

The Ophites probably began as a Jewish-Iranian esoteric sect in pre-Christian times. But their radical ideas about the separateness of spirit and matter clearly soon made an appeal in

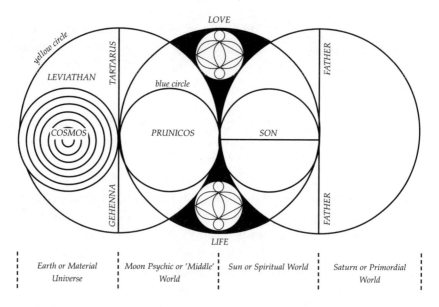

Fig. 3 The Ophite Diagram: Gnostic' cosmology.
A kind of mandala, the Diagram was meditated upon by the Gnostics and they experienced through it the cosmic powers and relations which have shaped our fallen or material world. Basically, read from right to left, it reveals the four-fold world-process through the stages traditionally called Saturn, Sun, Moon and Earth, although the physical ('archontic') planetary bodies of those names belong only to the fourth or Earth stage.

In meditation, the Gnostic could ascend through the knowledge represented by the various spheres and numerical relationships of the Diagram to the attainment of supersensible states of consciousness.

Prunicos, in the intermediate sphere, is an aspect of the divine Sophia, God's primal wisdom, here in her lower form manifested as the 'desire' which brings about birth and death — not known in the primal spiritual stages of the world.

The three large circles represent the Principles of all existence: God, Spirit, Darkness; these and the whole Diagram, recall ancient Iranian ideas as well as anticipating the Kabbalistic 'Tree of Life. '

some early Christian circles, among those who understood that Christ had come to save man from the 'fall into matter' and lead him back to a purely spiritual level of existence. Paul found that ideas very close to those of the Ophites, if not identical with them, had taken hold in the Christian community at Corinth, and had to argue against them, giving his own ideas about esotericism, about such matters as the First Man, the nature of the physical body, and so on, which he did in his letters to the Corinthian community, two of which are still extant in the New Testament.[17]

We are now in a position to clarify at least some of the difficulties which beset us when we surveyed the new discoveries from Qumran and Nag Hammadi. The confusing presence of Jewish and anti-Jewish features in the documents, the ambiguous attitude to the Mysteries — these make sense in relation to early Christianity once we understand that there had already been a complex evolution before Christianity began: the Mysteries and Judaism were no longer pure, isolated and opposed religious movements, but had made contact and produced the profound teaching of the Essenes, as well as the mythological 'double vision' of the Gnostics. There was already an Essene Mystery of man's moral individuality in his caring role for the earth. There was also a Gnostic revelation of Man and his cosmic significance for realms beyond the earth.

Against this rich spiritual background it is time to turn to some of the writings from the New Testament itself.

5. Jesus and Zarathustra, or
the Hebrew Gospel

The Gospel of Matthew

The Gospel of Matthew has always been recognized as the most Jewish of the canonical four. It is not just that it is full of references to the Old Testament, especially to the words of the prophets which have been fulfilled by Jesus, the Messiah. Many of the discussions between Jesus and the disciples which Matthew records centre on issues of life and religion which were also prominent topics of dispute among contemporary Jews. Hence, as Rudolf Steiner points out, the Gospel could itself be cited on occasion by Jewish experts on a particular problem in the interpretation of the Torah — as in the story of Rabbi Gamaliel. A complex tangle over the question of the continuing validity of the Jewish Law was resolved by a judge when he cited the words of the Gospel to the effect that Christ 'did not come into the world to destroy the Law but to fulfil it.'[1]

Other features of the Gospel, too, point to a strongly Jewish background, as we shall see. Yet the exact nature of the circles: from which the Gospel of Matthew originated remained, at least until recently, obscure. The learned detail and the sheer abundance of references to the Old Testament and Jewish lore made it seem that no one individual could have shaped the tradition of 'prophetic' interpretation out of which it grew. Moreover, the Gospel shows a strong interest in community (it is the only Gospel to refer explicity to *ekklesia*, the community), again prompting the thought that behind it lay some kind of organized movement.

Having seen how the successors of the Essenes took a firm

hand in organizing the Jewish-Christian communities which sprang up in Syria and Palestine, we may feel that it is no longer difficult to know in which direction to look. And in fact since the discovery of the Scrolls at Qumran and in spite of the strong resistance to the idea generated in some quarters, it has seemed fairly obvious to many scholars that in Matthew we have in effect 'the Gospel of the Essenes.'[2] In many passages of the Gospel, for instance in what are known as the 'community discourses' of Jesus in chapters 10 and 18, we hear exactly the sort of ordinances for a spiritually vital society that figured so prominently in the Qumran *Community Rule*. In some cases, we can see that Matthew presents Jesus as giving out, almost word for word, the advanced social philosophy of the Essene order. Here for example is a passage from the *Community Rule:*

> They shall rebuke one another in truth, humility and charity. Let no man address his companion in anger, or ill-temper, or obduracy, or with envy prompted by the spirit of wickedness. Let him not hate him (because of his unregenerate heart), but let him rebuke him on the very same day lest he incur guilt because of him. And furthermore, let no man accuse his companion before the Community without having first admonished him in the presence of witnesses.[3]

And here is Jesus in the Gospel of Matthew:

> If your brother sins against you, go, tell him his fault, between you and him in private. If he listens to you — you have gained your brother. If he does not listen, take one or two other people with you, so that 'at the mouth of two witnesses or three every word may be established' [Deut. 19:15]. If he refuses to listen to them, tell it to the Community: if he refuses to listen to the Community too, then let him be for you like the gentile and the publican. (18:15–17)

It appears that in portraying what seemed to him the essential aspects of Jesus' mission and teaching, the writer of Matthew has assembled those aspects which actually recall the Essene interest in spiritual and social organization. Perhaps we hear sounding through these passages echoes from the time of Jesus' own sojourn with the Essenes discussing their 'new age' teachings.

On a certain level, then, the Gospel of Matthew is a Christian *Community Rule*, like the *Didache* written by later Christian Essenes, but with the added dimension that the Gospel is grounded in a far more comprehensive way in the life and teachings of Jesus. Many other parallels between the Gospel and the Qumran Scrolls can easily be assembled. But it is perhaps worth noting at this juncture that even when Jesus is seen reproducing the Essene spiritual teaching word-for-word, he cannot be described simply as an Essene preacher. There is a significant change of context. It was one thing for an esoterically minded group of people to separate themselves from Jewish society in order to live by a higher spiritual ideal: they could organize their own 'alternative,' a religious order where property was held in common, and welfare services were provided for the sick and the elderly, and the Essenes were in fact the only known religious group to do just that. But it was quite another thing for Jesus to proclaim these ideas to 'all Israel,' and even be willing to traffic with Gentiles! That must have been highly disturbing both to many Essenes and to the leaders of traditional Jewish society, tightly knit as it was; Jesus was attacking the ultimate weapon of society against the individual, the threat of exclusion for the refusal to conform.

Furthermore, Jesus' discourses in the Gospel of Matthew are by no means free from well-directed criticism of certain aspects of older Essenism. When Jesus says:

> You have heard that it was said, 'You shall love your
> neighbour and hate your enemy,' but I say to you, love
> your enemies and pray for those who persecute you, so
> that you may be sons of your Father who is in heaven ...

he must be referring to the Essene division of men into 'sons of Light' and 'sons of Darkness,' and the teaching that we must love those of Light and hate those of Darkness. This is said explicitly in the Qumran writings, though it appears nowhere in the Old Testament. The Essene dualism suited a moment in history, a moment of decision and the awaiting of a new revelation, the moment of apocalypse: but in the longer perspective it is the teaching of love which must predominate.[4] The Essene teachings had to be taken a stage further into universalism, which is what Matthew portrays in his Gospel.

The Essene background, however, remains strongly felt. The rather stereotyped description of Jerusalem as the place where God's prophets are rejected and their words are not heeded, for example, has its roots in Essene experience. Historically their Teacher of Righteousness had been forced to split with the Jerusalem Temple, and his 'new covenant' had been one preached in the wilderness. Matthew evidently sees Jerusalem and the High Priest's rejection of Jesus as the culminating instance in an established negative pattern.

The way in which Matthew interprets Old Testament sayings has also been studied in the light of the elaborate techniques of esoteric 'illumined' interpretation evolved by the Essenes. We can see the same process of selection and 'spiritual' interpretation that Matthew uses being pioneered, for example, in the Qumran *Commentary on Habakkuk*. The Essenes, too, were especially interested in those texts which seemed to promise the coming of a Messiah, or a great priestly interpreter of the Torah who would make all things clear. All of which is seen in a particularly fascinating light in view of the fact that already by the year 1910 Rudolf Steiner had discovered from his spiritual researches that the Gospel of Matthew drew heavily on Essene traditions, and even went into some detail concerning the particular points of contact between the Essenes and the Gospel, in a way that has been remarkably borne out by the archaeological finds of the Dead Sea Scrolls.

Steiner pointed specifically to the first chapters of Matthew — the infancy chapters — and asserted that these belonged almost wholly to the sphere of Essenism and its expectations of the Messiah. His remarks have found confirmation through the Scrolls, since they solve the riddle about the 'prophecies' fulfilled by Jesus' miraculous birth. Matthew regards this as a 'proof' of Jesus' Messianic dignity, which is odd, because the

Jewish expectation of the Messiah contained nothing to suggest a miraculously born being. However, the Qumran library was found to contain an apocryphal expansion of the Old Testament passages about the birth of the patriarchs (the so-called *Genesis Apocryphon*). Noah is born in a miraculous fashion, causing Lamech his father to be wrongly suspicious; there are prophetic dreams and appearances of God in visions to announce his intentions. Some of this seems to have been developed from the *Book of Jubilees*. But much more interesting is the comparison with Matthew's fulfilment stories. Scholars have pointed out that Matthew is portraying a birth exactly like one of these Essene legends. He shows Jesus as a new Noah or Melchizedek. Nor is this all that serves to confirm Steiner's perspective.

Steiner explained, for instance, that the Essenes had been particularly interested in the physical descent of the Christ — naturally we can see this in the Gospel through the long genealogical tables placed' at the beginning, tracing Jesus' ancestry back to Abraham, father of the Jews. That this concern with the physical descent and the predicted physical appearance of the Messiah was Essene has been proved by the physiognomical and astrological fragments at Qumran. It transpires that the aim of many of the astrological studies and study of physiognomy from an occult viewpoint among the Essenes had as its aim precisely the prediction of the birth and physical characteristics of the expected Messiah. The more recent cave discoveries have even brought us the horoscope of a royal Messiah, which is worth quoting here, although it is rather damaged and fragmentary:

> ... of his hand: two ... a birthmark. And his hair will be red. And there will be lentils on ... and small birthmarks on his thigh. (After two years) he will know how to distinguish one thing from another. In his youth he shall be like ... (like a) man who knows nothing until the time when he knows the three Books.
>
> And then he will acquire wisdom and learn understanding ... vision will come to him on his knees. And with his father and his ancester's ... life and old age. Counsel and prudence will be with him, and he will know

the secrets of man. His wisdom will reach all the peoples,
and he will know the secrets of all the living. And all their
designs against him will come to nothing, and his rule
over all the living will be great. His designs (will succeed)
for .. he is the Elect of God. His birth and the breath of his
spirit ... and his design shall be for ever ...[5]

Astrological calculations and physiognomical suitability were
also evidently taken into account when candidates were considered for membership of the order.

Other pronouncements made by Steiner not only anticipated.
the archaeological evidence, but ran directly counter to the
assumptions of historians and biblical critics in his day. He said,
for example, that the Gospel of Matthew was originally composed in Hebrew — like the Qumran scriptures, and as one
would expect of a work with an esoteric Jewish (Essene) background. The Greek version, the oldest that has actually come
down to us and which forms the basis of all subsequent versions, was a translation of the original. In the opinion of scholars in Steiner's time, and still of many today, on the other hand,
the Greek version of Matthew is the original: they suppose it to
be partly based on the Greek text of the Gospel of Mark, with
which it has much material in common, and partly on other traditions.

These scholars have had to deal somehow with a variety of
evidences, however, from early Christian writers, which support something much more like Steiner's account. The early
writer Papias, whom we have met before and may remember as
a collector of numerous 'esoteric' or 'mythical' traditions of the
Lord, reported that the author of Matthew collected the sayings
of the Lord 'in the Hebrew tongue.' Even as late as Jerome (c. AD
390) the Gospel was palpably still accessible in its original
Hebrew edition. Jerome writes:

Matthew in Judea was the first to compose the gospel of
Christ in the Hebrew character and speech for the sake of
those who came over to the faith from Judaism. Who he
was who later translated it into Greek is no longer known
with certainty. Further the Hebrew text itself is still

preserved in the library at Caesarea ... The Nazaraeans in
Beroea, a city of Syria, who use this book, also permitted
me to copy it. In it it is to be noted that wherever the
evangelist adduces testimonies from the Old Testament —
be this done by himself or by our Lord and Saviour — he
follows not the (Greek) Septuagint translation, but the
Hebrew original text.[6]

Elsewhere Jerome claims that he has 'translated' this Semitic
Gospel; but here unfortunately his own testimony is full of con-
tradictions, like that of some other early writers who refer to it.
One other significant piece of information we glean from
Jerome, however, is that in its original guise the book was usu-
ally known as *The Gospel of the Hebrews*.

The inconsistencies in the evidence of Jerome and others led
modern scholarship basically to ignore it altogether, especially
since it contradicted their favourite theories about the text of the
Greek Gospels.

Now however a Hebrew scholar from Jerusalem, David
Flusser, has sought to put the study of the Gospel of Matthew on
a more, solid historical foundation, taking into account the new
evidence about the Jewish background. One stumbling-block in
the minds of scholars to accepting a Hebrew original Matthew
was the rather obvious objection that Aramaic and Greek were
the spoken languages of Palestine at the time of Jesus, not
Hebrew. Even some of the later parts of the Old Testament are
composed in Aramaic. But Flusser has demonstrated that the
language in which Matthew wrote was the scholarly Hebrew
which continued to be used by the Rabbis as a learned tongue
(rather as Latin was used in Europe until quite recently as a
scholarly language). This would fit well with Steiner's comment, expanding on a remark of Jerome, that Matthew was written in the Hebrew script 'though its language was not the
customary Hebrew of the time' (that is, it was not Aramaic).
Further evidence from writings and inscriptions has also lent
support to the idea that, at least in religious matters, Hebrew
continued to be used in the later period: Thus once more
Steiner's researches seem to have uncannily predicted the lines
of future interpretation.

The difficulties still remaining have come a step nearer resolution through the most recent discovery to be made in this area
by G. Howard.[7] He took a shrewd look at one of the Hebrew
versions of Matthew used for polemical purposes against the
Christians by mediaeval Jews. The work *Even Bohan* by Shem-
Tov ben-Isaac ben Shaprut gives the whole Gospel in Hebrew,
with a verse by verse commentary showing how the words can
be turned against Christianity and made to support Judaism. 'In
this way glory will come to the Jew who debates with them
whenever he captures them in their own pit.' The Gospel's sympathetic closeness to the spirit of Judaism which we noted earlier is here dragged down into the bitter persecutions and
rivalries of a later time. But Howard was interested in the text of
the Hebrew Matthew itself, embedded in the polemicist's manual. It had always been assumed to be a translation from the
Greek used by the Christians, and indeed follows the Greek in
most readings. But there were odd signs that in order to make it
do so the polemical Jew had made small alterations, and there
remained a number of features in which the Hebrew seemed
independent. After careful examination, Howard decided that it
was not a translation after all, but derived from a 'primitive
Hebrew text': from the Hebrew original of the Gospel of
Matthew.

There were, for instance, many cases of word echoes, where a
sharp difference of meaning is brought out by using Hebrew
terms which look or sound similar but mean opposite things (a
favoured device in some Hebrew literature). Could this clever
verbal play really have been made by translating the Greek?
And why should the hostile translator have bothered to make
the Christian Gospel into a brilliant literary work; It seemed
more likely that the Greek had been unable to reproduce the full
effect of the Hebrew, the original text. And then there were facts
about the Hebrew which simply could not be derived from the
Greek. For example, the tantalizing information that the form of
the name Jesus (which can be Yeshua or Yeheshua in Hebrew) is
different in the infancy chapters from that used in the account of
the mature ministry. There is no difference in the Greek Gospel.
Why should the translator into Hebrew introduce such a difference? Here again it seemed more likely that the two forms of the

name were a feature belonging to an original Hebrew text. It is one more mystery which was evidently glossed over when the Gospel came to be rendered into Greek.

The Hebrew text is obviously important in many ways for Christian scholarship, not least because it brings us, if it is genuine, considerably closer to the words Jesus actually spoke. Interestingly, its version of some sayings — like the one in chapter 12 about sinning against the Father and the Son — agrees with the *Gospel of Thomas* rather than with the canonical Greek Matthew. The saying about the continuing validity of the Law which was cited by Rabbi Gamaliel is also given in an unfamiliar form, which may nevertheless have a strong claim to priority. According to Hebrew Matthew 5:17–18, Christ came 'neither to take away nor to add to the Law of Moses' — a form more subtle and ambiguous than the Greek reference to fulfilment. Howard suggests that the latter may have come in as a misunderstanding of the Semitic terms: the word 'to add' could easily be misread as 'to end,' so bringing in the notion of bringing to an end and its antithesis of affirmation or fulfilment. It is notable that the passage in the Talmud concerning Gamaliel which was cited by Rudolf Steiner also gives the saying in this same wording. The Christian principle would thus enable the Rabbi to affirm that the Law held good over the matters belonging to the Mosaic dispensation — but the saying at the same time opens the door to matters that do not fall under the Law, the r,ealms which are especially the Christian province. Once again, it is more likely that a complex and original statement should be later modified to make it straightforwardly positive about the Law for Jewish Christians than the reverse. The Hebrew form is more likely authentic.

There are a great many significant variants in the Hebrew Matthew we possess embedded in *Even Bohan*, or rather now extracted from it by scholarly diligence. There will be much to learn from them about the meaning of the Gospel. In other respects, however, it appears that we are still liable to be cheated in our hopes of possessing the text as originally circulated. For Howard also noted the evidence that in many ways the Hebrew text has (already been modified to bring it closer to the Greek than it may at first have been. We can understand the motive. What would be the use of quoting to the Christian out of his own book in defence of Judaism, if the version quoted were not the one he recognized as authoritative? Minor variations would be useful, but any larger departures from the canonical Matthew would merely have led to charges of falsifying. In other words, we cannot get at any of the more major differences which there may well have been in the first instance between the 'Gospel of the Hebrews' and the Church's Matthew. For the latter has certainly exerted considerable influence over our surviving text of the former, despite the variants we have noted. The alarmed tone of Jerome's remarks is only part of the evidence that bigger discrepancies separated the original Hebrew from the ecclesiastically acceptable Greek than have come to light in *Even Bohan*.

But if, in spite of everything, the original form of the Hebrew Gospel of Matthew is lost to us, we do fortunately still possess many quotations from it made by ancient and medieval writers to whom it was still available. We soon discern the reasons for Jerome's disquietude, and his evident decision not to publish the contents of the *Gospel of the Hebrews* after all. For it is clear that the original version of Matthew contained 'esoteric' passages, relating to mysteries that had been understood by the Essenes but which were not regarded as suitable for the uninitiated. These passages had therefore been omitted from the Greek (as later from Jerome's Latin) translation.

Some of them related to Jesus' inner experiences at the time of the Temptation in the wilderness; they also reveal an esoteric conception of the Christ. In our Greek-derived Matthew it says that 'Jesus was led by the Spirit up into the wilderness.' But in the Hebrew original Jesus apparently said:

> Even so did my mother, the Holy Spirit, take me by one of
> my hairs, and carry me away to the great mountain
> Tabor.[8]

Being caught up by the hair is an expression known in mystical circles for inner rapture — it is used for example by Ezekiel — and the understanding of the Holy Spirit as feminine and the true 'mother' of Jesus reflects esoteric teaching known in

Jewish-Christian as well as Gnostic circles. The mention of Mount Tabor is also extremely important: it is, with its extraordinary rounded form, a numinous and solemn place, which had been a centre of mysteries and religious experience from archaic times, making it one of the most significant spiritual sites in Israel.

The Gospel of the Hebrews contained in addition sayings of Jesus concerning the stages of inner awareness, including a celebrated saying about 'wonder' which also turned up in the *Gospel of Thomas*. Since it is known from several different sources there is a good probability that it genuinely goes back to a saying of Jesus, and it is therefore quite reasonable to suppose that it did stand in the original version of Matthew. Indeed it represents an extension of certain aspects of Jesus' teaching already known there. In our familiar Gospel of Matthew, Jesus says:

> Ask, and it shall be given you;
> seek, and you will find ...

It was already evident that this formed part of a more extensive, deeper instruction: a little later in the Gospel there is a further passage in which Jesus discourses on the theme of 'seeking' and 'finding rest.' It is part of that section in Matthew where Jesus speaks with unprecedented directness of himself as the Son in relation to the heavenly Father. As in parts of the Gospel of John, we hear the tones of Jesus speaking to his closest disciples in a language of mysteries:

> Come to me, all you who labour and are heavily laden,
> and I will give you rest. Take my yoke upon you, and
> learn of me ... and you will find rest for your souls.

In the *Gospel of the Hebrews*, we are told, Jesus developed his teaching in fuller terms:

> He that seeks will not rest until he finds; but he that has
> found shall wonder; and he that has wondered shall reign;
> and he that has reigned shall rest.[9]

Similar stages are described in the Hermetic *gnosis*, which as we have noted drew on the new concepts of the Jewish-Iranian esotericism of the baptizing sects, related to the Essenes. Here therefore Jesus seems once more to be taking up and developing ideas from the esoteric world of Syria and Palestine. On the path of inner awareness, a phase of increased 'openness' to cosmic reality, of wonder, is followed by a regaining of psychic equilibrium, 'self-sovereignty' and mystical 'rest.'

Once more, however, the older mystical ideas are given a new dimension in the teaching of Jesus, and the concept of 'rest,' denoting the highest stage of vision, possessed a special significance among the users of the *Hebrew Gospel*: of which we shall have more to say shortly.

Faced with esoteric matters such as these, which apparently neither he nor his congregation could comprehend, Jerome evidently decided to steer clear of difficulties and perpetuate the shorter, strictly exoteric version of Matthew. 'In the first place,' says Steiner, 'he thought it would be dangerous to translate this Gospel of Matthew as it was, because there were things in it which those who up to then had possessed it as their sacred writing wished to keep from the profane world. He thought that this Gospel, if it were translated complete, would cause disturbance rather than edification ...'[10]

The Coming of the Magi

> At the time when Jesus was born in Bethlehem of Judea, when Herod was king, behold, there came Magi from the East, saying: 'Where is the one who is born King of the Jews? For we have observed his star in the ascendant, and have come to worship him.' (Matthew 2:1–2)

The term Magi derives from the old Iranian word *magu*, meaning 'priest,' and the men to whom it referred were a priestly tribe or caste in Zoroastrian Iran. They had to be present for any ritual of the ancient Iranian religion to be valid; and they were the guardians of the spiritual knowledge as well as the ritual procedures which belonged to the 'Good Religion,' and they brought with them, when they spread westward into Syria and

Asia Minor from their native Iran, the great symbols and mythological images of Zarathustra's teaching. Hence they were well-known figures in the ancient world, and they impressed pagan and Christian alike with their extreme veneration of the pure elements of fire and water, and their knowledge of the stars. Several Greek philosophers of early times — notably Pythagoras, but also Democritus, the founder of atomism — had undertaken long pilgrimages in order to sit at their feet.

Their rather unexpected presence in the New Testament posed a riddle, above all to earlier translators, who hardly knew what to make of them. The Authorized Version solved the riddle by translating them away into inoffensive and unproblematic 'wise men.' But with the aid of modern discoveries we can now do a little better, and especially with the help of Rudolf Steiner's insights we can at least confront directly the question as to what these Zoroastrian priests are doing in the Gospel of Matthew.

The riddle has gradually begun to yield a profound and interesting sense. To begin with we find associated with the Magi in Christian tradition a number of legends and ideas that cast an additional light on their journey to Bethlehem, even though it must be admitted that these are known to us only in forms dating from some centuries after the composition of the Gospel of Matthew. There are, for example, the remarkable stories told in the ancient Syriac *Chronicle of Zuqnin*. And in close connection with these, there are the traditions to be found in a fascinating *Homily on the Gospel of Matthew* wrongly attributed to John Chrysostom (and therefore known, in scholarly parlance, as the pseudo-Chrysostom). In these traditions we again meet a mythical figure from the very beginnings of human history: Seth, the son of Adam and founder of a spiritual 'race.'

In the pseudo-Chrysostom we find that one important idea is that Seth wrote down the prophetic knowledge, entrusted to him by Adam himself, the founder of the human race, in the form of certain books. This took place long before the Flood. The books were then concealed on a high mountain — called the *Mons Victorialis* or 'Mount of Triumph,' and supposed to be somewhere in Iran. Very similar things are asserted in the *Chronicle of Zuqnin*, and hints along similar lines appear in various old Testament pseudepigrapha. In his study of the figure of Seth, A. F. J. Klijn draws attention to several Jewish and Samaritan sources containing related conceptions. According to the Apocryphal *Life of Adam and Eve*, he points out, Seth 'possessed information about the time before Adam's expulsion from paradise and had to write it down on tablets. According to Josephus, Seth and the Sethites were experts in astrology and this knowledge also had to be preserved for a later generation.'[11]

The books on the *Mons Victorialis* were found by the ancestors of the Magi, continues the tradition, after the Flood. They were found to contain prophecies of the coming of the Christ at the end of the age; and it was on the basis of these prophecies that the Magi calculated astrologically the time of the birth and made their way to Judea.

According to the *Chronicle of Zuqnin*, the Magi of ancient times used to make an annual pilgrimage to the Mountain. They expected that, in fulfilment of their prophecies, a star would one day descend from the skies, enter the holy cave on the mountain top, and take the form of a royal child. After generations of waiting, the Magi eventually saw a great column of light and at its top a radiant star, which descended to the mountain peak. It did not, however, enter the cave — but led the Magi on their long pilgrimage to Bethlehem, where they found the child born in a cave and gave him their gifts.

Research into the background of these legends, beautiful and evocative as they are, showed that they do indeed contain many genuine Iranian features. Above all, there were in ancient Iran a number of traditions about a prince who would appear from the heights of heaven at the end of the age, and descend in the guise of a star. These have been studied by the brilliant specialist on Jewish and Iranian religion (a rare combination!), Geo Widengren. Often, he points out, it was said that the 'Messianic' prince would be born when a star fell to earth, as a meteor or a lightning-flash. Stories about such events were told in connection with a number of Iranian kings, who, as we may recall, were themselves 'divine' saviours of their people. But the prophecies were connected above all with the end-time, and the saviour-prince was expected to appear from the summit of a sacred mountain: the spectacular Mount Hukhairya in the Elburz range, south of the Caspian sea. Widengren is strongly inclined to identify the Elburz with the *Mons Victorialis* of the Christian traditions. Birth in a cave, too, corresponds to the myths of Iran about the future saviour.[12]

The saviour-prince was to be born from the seed of Zarathustra. In esoteric circles, he was frequently understood to be a reincarnation of the primordial prophet. As if to emphasize their inner identity, identical stories about a birth from a flash of lightning and a falling star are told about the original Zarathustra too; but at the same time, the prince would embody something greater than the prophet, for he would be an *avatar* or embodiment of the sun-god Mithra.

The legends of the pseudo-Chrysostom and the *Chronicle of Zuqnin* were regarded hitherto as too late in date to provide decisive evidence about the background of the New Testament. Now however, we are able for the first time to bring them into connection with documents and ideas from much earlier stages of the tradition. For in the stories of the descending star and the birth of the child in the mountain cave we can recognize further versions of the prophecies which circulated concerning the reincarnations of Zarathustra, who is to appear as the Saoshyant at the end of time. We know of these prophecies in some detail now from the *Apocalypse of Adam* — a pre-Christian document used by some Jewish-Iranian baptizing sect, related somehow or other to the Essenes. In fact we have already seen from several different angles how Iranian Mystery-concepts flowed into the world of Jewish esotericism, in the last centuries before the Christian era. Already there the prophecy of the final, thirteenth incarnation, in which Zarathustra was to be vessel of some greater being, had looked westward to Judea. In the Chronicle of Zuqnin we have a working out in the beautiful images of Iranian mythology a truth about the birth of the Illuminator in Judaea which had already been expressed in pre-Christian times by the author of the strange *Apocalypse*; and in the pseudo-Chrysostom only a slight variant, according to which it was the prophetic books which the Magi found on the mountain, not the divine child himself or the radiant star.

Striking confirmation of the continuity between the traditions is to be found when we consider the form taken by the *Apocalypse of Adam*: it is a book of wisdom prophesied to Seth by his father Adam before the Flood, exactly as in the later tales! Moreover, closely connected with the *Apocalypse*, though somewhat later, is another Nag Hammadi document, the *Sacred Book of the Invisible Great Spirit*, which also serves to confirm the antiquity of the Iranian traditions that lie behind the New Testament scene of the coming of the Magi. There again, Seth and his knowledge occupied a prominent place, and the *Sacred Book* seems strongly to imply that the prophecies of the *Apocalypse of Adam* have been fulfilled in Jesus. *The Sacred Book* ends as follows:

> The great Seth wrote this book with letters in one
> hundred and thirty years. He placed it in the mountain
> that is called Charaxio, in order that, at the end of the
> times and eras, by the will of the divine Self-Begotten and
> the whole fullness (of the spiritual world), through the
> gift of the untraceable, unthinkable, fatherly love, it may
> come forth and reveal the incorruptible holy race of the
> great Saviour ...[13]

The 'mountain that is called Charaxio' may well be an attempt to transcribe the name of the sacred peak Hukhairya, which we too may thus identify with the Christian *Mons Victorialis*. Here we have all the elements preserved in the legends: the book of Seth left on the mountain-top, prophesying the coming of the Saviour is language derived from ancient Iran. In view of the fact that these writings contain so much that is authentically Iranian, we may consider it actually quite probable that such prophecies were found on mountain peaks in Iran: they were not, of course, left there before the Flood by Seth, son of Adam, but they were books of prophecy that come out of the great encounter we have been describing between the world of Judaism and the Mysteries of ancient Zoroastrianism. They were believed to contain knowledge already revealed to Seth in primordial times, foretelling the twelve incarnations of the Illuminator, and a climactic thirteenth incarnation. They were books resembling, if not identical with, the *Apocalypse of Adam* or similar forerunners of the *Sacred Book*. And they did indeed contain prophecies of the rebirth of Zarathustra as the Saoshyant in Palestine, there to become the vessel of 'the Undefiled One of Truth' or 'the great Saviour.'

For in the esoteric encounter between Judaism and the Mysteries, the spread of new prophetic knowledge was hardly a strictly oneway affair, and cannot have failed to have considerable consequences inside Iran itself. In fact it seems fairly certain that we can identify more exactly the circles in Iran which were most interested in the new prophecies.

The Gospel of the Hebrews, as quoted by a later writer, contained a longer version of the coming of the Magi, painting a vivid picture of their arrival at the cave, narrated by Joseph. He sees a crowd approaching, and says to a companion:

> It seems to me as if those coming were soothsayers, for every moment they look up to heaven and confer with one another. But they seem also to be strangers, for their appearance differs from ours. Their dress is very rich and their complexion quite dark. They have caps on their heads, and their garments seem to be silky — and they have breeches on their legs![14]

Trousers had been a feature of Iranian dress from early times. They formed a part of Iranian priestly vestments. But they caused openmouthed amazement in the Mediterranean world, devoted as it was to the toga and tunic! (The disciples of Mani were later to meet a similar gaping reception in the West because of their baggy trousers.) The caps, howeyer, are an interesting additional feature. For they identify the soothsayers more precisely as servants of a particular god from the Iranian pantheon: Mithra, the Mediator and genius of Light. His cult was to become popular in the West, especially among the Roman armies, and in its older form must be accounted one of the religious movements which prepared the way for Christianity. It possessed a series of sacraments, like those of Christianity to such an extent that the orthodox Fathers had to invent the theory that the Devil had parodied Christianity in advance so as to fight it with pagan rites. On more enlightened levels, however, there must certainly have been more intelligent contacts between Christians and Mithraists, particularly between esotericists on both sides. And even before that, it may well have been among the Magian followers of Mithra that the startling prophecies, about the rebirth of Zarathustra, first found open ears. For it was as a glorious manifestation of Mithra that the Magi expected to see their star-born prince descend from the sacred mountain, an *avatar* of the power of Light itself. Their way finally brought them, after a long journey, far from the holy peaks of Iran, to see such a glorious manifestation in a cave in Palestine. The original Gospel of Matthew, with its deep roots in the Jewish-Iranian esotericism of the Essenes and similar groups, still preserved in startling clarity the identity of the oriental priests who travelled so far to see the birth of one 'born to be king.'[15]

The Ebionim

Once we know the original esoteric character of the Gospel of Matthew, says Rudolf Steiner, we can understand why it should not have been communicated to all and sundry without further preparation. 'Those who were originally in possession of these communications, the Ebionites, did not impart them because, if received by unripe persons, they would have been so distorted that they must have led to what Jerome meant when he said that they would not serve for edification but destruction.'[16]

Who are these 'Ebionites'? And how does their possession of the original Matthew square with its Essene background? We seem to have run into contradictions.

The Church Fathers describe the Ebionites as a heretical sect — which they certainly were not, or at least were not until the later Church thrust that role upon them. They were a movement among the Jewish Christians, who called themselves the *ebionim*, that is, 'the poor ones,' the 'beggars of the spirit' described in the Beatitude. It is a name also adopted by the writer of the Epistle of James, written in the name of Jesus' brother James who became head of the Jerusalem community and was counted in the *Gospel of the Hebrews* as a prime witness of the resurrection.[17] But if we enquire into the nature and special beliefs of the *Ebionim*, there is a dearth of information. Almost our only solid knowledge comes from a later expert on heresies, Epiphanius. He says:

> Besides a daily ritual bath, they have a baptism of initiation and each year they celebrate certain mysteries resembling those of the Christian Church (that is, the sacraments of Catholicism). In these mysteries they use unleavened bread and, for the other part, pure water. They say that God has established two beings, Christ and the Devil. To the former has been committed the power of the world to come, and to the other the power of this world. They say that Jesus was begotten of human seed, and chosen, and thus called by election Son of God, Christ having come upon him from on high in the form of a dove. They say that he was not begotten by God the Father, but that he was created — like one of the archangels, but greater than they.

Also noteworthy is the following:

> And they too receive the Gospel of Matthew, and this they use ... to the exclusion of all others. But they call it the Gospel 'according to the Hebrews' — for, to speak truthfully, Matthew alone of New Testament writers presents and proclaims the gospel in Hebrew and in the Hebrew script.[18]

Thus the *Ebionim* used the original version of Matthew. As for their teaching, we hardly need the comment of Jean Daniélou: 'Many features in this passage recall Essenism. It is known, for instance, that the ritual bath was an essential Essene rite ... .The second part of the passage exhibits pure Essene doctrine. God has established from the beginning the two worlds, the present world which belongs to the devil, and the future world which belongs to Christ is also Essene.'[19] To this we may add that the designation *ebionim*, 'poor ones,' has also been found to be used by the Essenes at Qumran.

In the *Ebionim* we therefore recognize an Essene-derived movement which appears to have dominated much of Jewish-

Christian thought, and which used the esoteric version of the Gospel of Matthew — indeed, used it exclusively, as their authority on the life and teachings of Jesus. Their conception of Jesus was that of a prophet, on whom the Christ, an Angelic being of a high order, descended at the time of the baptism. In later Ebionite literature Jesus is known as the 'True Prophet,' and in the description of his many incarnations we hear a last echo of the esoteric tradition relating to Zarathustra. Oscar Cullmann summarizes the conception: 'Since the creation of the world, the True Prophet hastens through the centuries, changing his name and form of appearance. He incarnated himself again and again ... Jesus is the true incarnation of this Prophet.'[20] Only in his final incarnation as Jesus does the 'true Prophet' receive the full revelation of the Godhead.'

In the *Gospel of the Hebrews* the account of the baptism pointed the contrast between earlier prophets, the *nabiim* who had spoken in the Holy Spirit about the coming of the Messiah, and the fulfilment now achieved:

> And it happened that when the Lord had come up out of the water, the whole fount of the Holy Spirit descended upon him and rested upon him, and said to him: 'My Son, in all the prophets I was waiting for you to come, so that I might rest in you. For you are my rest. You are my first-begotten Son, who reigns for ever.'[21]

From that moment, the Prophet became the embodiment, the incarnation, of the Christ, and was addressed by the title Son of God.[22] We now understand more deeply the saying, quoted earlier, about wonder and rests and stages of higher vision. The rest referred to is the perfection which leads to the union of human and divine: it was first revealed in its highest form by the Christ at his baptism, ushering in a new stage of human history.

Jesus and Zarathustra

The story in our canonical Gospel of Matthew of the coming of the Magi stands almost symbolically for a profound truth about the nature of Christianity, a truth that was originally understood

Fig. 4 Huge cisterns at the Essene centre of Qumran on the Dead Sea. Cisterns such as this were used to provide 'living water' for the Essene baptismal rites and daily lustrations of the Essenes. In many ways the esoteric Jewish rites point forward directly to Christian baptism, especially among the Jewish-Christian Ebionim.

in concrete detail in esoteric circles like those of the *Ebionim*. The Iranian sages carrying their gifts into the heart of Judea embody the truth that Christianity came not only as the fulfilment of the spirit and the hopes of ancient Judaism, but also in fulfilment of the wisdom of oriental religion, more especially the ancient wisdom of Zarathustra. Indeed, as an 'initiate-king' on a higher 1nore universal plane of significance, Christ revealed a new truth in one of the key conceptions of ancient oriental thought: the idea of an archetypal Man. 'The result is,' writes one modern scholar, 'that Jesus reunites all aspects of the idea of Primeval Man and Primeval King in his own person, and so the entire mythology of the Ancient East is reinstated.'[23] As Rudolf Steiner made so clear from his spiritual researches, and the new writings from Qumran and Nag Hammadi help to confirm, Jesus could be understood as fulfilling the prophecies of ancient Iran, a reborn Zarathustra. 'It was out of a Judaism enriched by five centuries of contact with Zoroastrianism,' writes another modern authority, 'that Christianity arose in the Parthian period, a new religion with roots thus in two ancient faiths, one Semitic, the other Iranian. Doctrines taught perhaps a millennium and a half earlier by Zoroaster began in this way to reach fresh hearers.'[24] In the quest today for understanding among the different religions of East and West, this realization should be a source of reconciliation. It should help us burst the bounds of a narrow faith and, whilst remaining faithful to history, arrive at a Christian vision of the truth contained in the religious experience of oriental religions as well as in the religion of the Old Testament. It should enable us to understand the history of religions as an expression of the evolution of man's religious consciousness, his changing relationship to God in the past and in the future, of which the birth of Christianity marks a crucial phase.

As a matter of history, the seed of universal understanding we find in the esoteric circles of early Christianity did not take root as it might have done. It was not taken up by the developing Church, which needed a simplified teaching in order to carry on its own programme of spreading Christianity. Moreover, the Essene Christianity we have examined among the Ebionim has certain intrinsic shortcomings as a fully adequate interpretation of the Christian Mystery. We have seen that Jesus criticized the narrower aspects of Essenism in the Sermon on the Mount, and that those features of Essene esotericism which belonged to a specific moment of history had to be transcended in the greater universalism of the Christian message. In its figure of the 'True Prophet,' Ebionite Christianity summed up the wisdom and inner expectations of man throughout his former history; and with its teaching on the high Angelic being which descended upon Jesus it expressed an openness to a new dimension of the divine. Yet it rejected the further insights into that dimension which were taken up in the other Gospels, clinging exclusively to the Gospel of Matthew. Even more vehemently did it reject the pioneering spirit of the apostle Paul.

If we are to penetrate further into the many-sided, complex reality behind the events of Palestine we must be prepared to look to a still wider range of conceptions. We need to know more of what lay behind the all-important experience of baptism, for the initiates of antiquity and for Jesus himself. The *Ebionim* focused primarily on the historical preparation for the advent of the Christ: but we need to understand how the early Christians saw his coming as bound up with changes even on the cosmic scale. We must go beyond their particular viewpoint and look further afield — even if it means coming closer to Gnosticism.

6. Christian and Gnostic Initiation

The Baptist's Whirlpool

It is difficult to remember when we witness the baptismal sprinkling performed by most of the major churches today that baptism was in the ancient Church a vastly different affair. For one thing, it was mainly performed for adults rather than infants — although infant baptism seems to have been allowed from the beginning, too — and it was in its essential structure a rite of initiation. Extensive preparation was made through spiritual exercises and instruction in the Christian teachings, fasting, and so on, in the hope that the experience would be a real *metanoia*, the breakthrough to a new level of life. So daunting in fact was the undertaking that at certain periods of the early Church individuals would often postpone their initiation until they felt inwardly ready for so serious a step, sometimes until the very end of their lives.

Baptism-initiation was also placed in a highly significant relationship to the central mystery of Easter. It was frequently performed as part of the community's observance of Easter, with a special paschal vigil leading to the climax of initiation into Christ's death and resurrection. Moreover, baptism itself was a complex ritual process: it involved actual immersion, rather than a token sprinkling; there were connected with it further rites of anointing, 'sealing' in the sign of Christ, investiture in white robes, and even enthronement. We have already seen that many of these elements in the ritual go back to ancient Mystery practices, transmitted in one line of their development through the Essenes and other esoteric baptizing sects which had flourished on the Judaean borderlands. Sometimes early Christian writings even specify that baptism must be performed in 'living,' that is running water exactly as in many of the secret baptizing groups.[1]

The influence of the Essenes can be seen especially strongly in the heritage of the Jewish Christians, of Palestine and Syria. The Jewish Christians, in the years following the death on the cross, took as their representative James, the brother of Jesus who became head of the Jerusalem community. Some fragments of apostolic teaching were subsequently handed down in his name — although on the whole the later church suppressed them in the interests of what it had made into 'orthodoxy.' The discovery of the Nag Hammadi library has brought further aspects of James and his traditions to light, however — and it is especially noteworthy that much of it is close to the teachings preserved in the known fragments of the *Gospel of the Hebrews*. This tradition evidently taught that through baptism one became a 'son of the Holy Spirit': this was a powerful experience about whose nature we can in fact glean a little more information.[2]

The *Dialogue of the Saviour* is another Nag Hammadi work, presenting ideas of a markedly esoteric kind. It is in part based around the mystical sequence of seeking, finding, wondering, reigning and resting taught by Jesus in the *Gospel of the Hebrews* and in the *Gospel of Thomas*: the disciples ask questions about the several stages and are led gradually from understanding (seeking and finding) to actual visions (wondering), and look forward to the achievement of higher stages (reigning, rest). The transition involves an initiation — which is to say, a baptismal rite which brings about an inner death and rebirth. The disciples must face the power of 'fear,' which threatens to 'swallow them up,' but if they can summon the required inner strength they will pass through without dissolution. This is undertaken by three elect disciples, Judas Thomas, Matthew and Mariam, and their experience is described in the remainder of the work. Evidently it attests the kind of experiences undergone by those who were initiated in this particular stream of Christian initiation.

The disciples are immersed and, upon re-emerging there follows a laying on of hands. The result is that the disciples immediately behold cosmic visions — 'the whole of heaven and earth.' And here lies at least one source of the danger to the soul stressed in this passage about fear. The ordinary limits of the personality are dissolved, swept away in the cosmic scope of the visions, and unless inwardly prepared for the conditions of the visionary state the soul could lose its coherence, its centre of identity. It would then disintegrate into unconsciousness, the 'power of darkness' which lies at the root of the 'fear.'[3] The dangers to the psyche are terrible, and only those who have followed the path of seeking and finding come to these experiences in readiness.

For those who are ready follow the cosmic visions: they enter 'the place of life,' the spiritual realm where they behold the 'One Who is Forever.' They have the inner strength to control the tremendous energies released through their baptismal initiation, and they achieve a deeper integration of the soul, including much that for the ordinary man is hidden in the unconscious depths.

Other descriptions of baptism also mention these psychic energies. The *Gospel of the Hebrews* mentioned cosmic disturbances and light-phenomena at the baptism of Jesus, for example, the latter recalling the aura or 'crown of light' which shone forth from the ancient Essene initiate, and, originally, the initiate-king. But the descriptions are even more striking when we turn from the type of esotericism represented by the Essenes and their Christian successors to those which stem from Gnostic circles.

Whereas the Essenes had been concerned to develop a strong inner consciousness, giving man a sense of historical identity as well as a cosmic mission, among the Gnostics it was the cosmic aspiration which predominated. The Gnostics drew their sense of strength not from an inner 'I' or centre of identity, but from their vision of man in his cosmic nature. As we might expect, therefore, the experience of the personality dissolving and of being whirled away into the macrocosm by the awakened psychic energies is even more powerfully portrayed in the Gnostic writings. Surviving accounts tell of how the placidly flowing river in which the candidate was immersed seemed to grow disturbed, swirling and turbulent — seemed to become a whirlpool in which the candidate had to struggle against elemental disruptive powers. Most dramatic is the Saviour's description of his baptism in the Gnostic treatise called the *Paraphrase of Shem*, expressed in the form of vision and prophecy:

Then shall I come down ... to the water. And whirlpools of water and flames of fire will rise up against me. Then I shall come up from the water, having put on the light of Faith and the unquenchable (= spiritual) fire, in order that through my help the power of the Spirit may cross over ...[4]

Characteristically for a Gnostic writing, the Saviour establishes the pattern of a cosmic initiation. The initiate here is the one who can cross over, that is, come through toe ordeal by uniting himself with the cosmic mission of the Saviour.

A group of Gnostics who called themselves 'Crossers-Over' (Peratae, since *peras* in Greek means 'over' or 'beyond') carried on these ideas, describing an initiatory 'rebirth' into union with the cosmic Father. They stress the superearthly origin of man, and how through initiation man can ascend once more to his cosmic origins. They also emphasize once more the dangers involved:

For they say that if anyone of those here below has the strength even to comprehend that he is an 'imprint' of the Father brought down from above and put into a body in this world, then he becomes ... essentially the same in all respects with the Father in heaven, and he ascends to that place. But if he does not gain this teaching, nor recognize the necessity of generation, then he is born like an abortion in the night, and in the night shall he perish.[5]

Fig. 5 Gnostic baptism among the Mandaeans, who have survived as a small group into the twentieth century in parts of Iran and Iraq. Baptism is a rite practised in a variety of forms, all of which are held to communicate visionary knowledge (manda) and experience of the 'crown of light' around the head of the initiate. It involves total immersion, ritual handshakes and extensive spiritual preparation.

The accounts of the arousal of powerful, and sometimes dangerous psychic forces, connected with themes of rebirth and cosmic visions, show how such experiences continued among Jewish Christian mystics and Gnostic visionaries in the early centuries. The Jewish Christians laid more weight on the strengthening of the 'ego,' the spiritual centre in man. The Gnostics, on the other hand, preserved the old cosmic orientation and aimed to unite themselves with the archetypal Father, to whose realm they made their initiatory ascent into cosmic spheres beyond the earth.

This Gnostic dimension too was a necessary factor in the full unfolding of the Christian Mystery, for through it was revealed the cosmic scope of Christ's mission which the Essenes could understand primarily in its human and social significance. It found a place even in early Christian thought — as we can see if we turn our attention to a much better known visionary document from early Christian times, namely the Gospel of Mark. Interesting conclusions concerning the Gospel were reached by Rudolf Steiner through his spiritual investigations, and these in turn have been strikingly illuminated by yet another modern discovery.

Secrets of the Gospel of Mark

In order to grasp the importance of the new perspective, we must pause briefly to consider the more traditional view of the Gospels, and Mark in particular.

Scholars noticed, around the beginning of the nineteenth century, that the Gospels of Mark, Matthew and Luke had a good deal in common. Often they resembled each other right down to verbal detail, agreeing work for word. Then came a second observation: though there were differences between Matthew and Luke, the material which they did have in common — so it seemed to the textual critics — was to a large extent the exact material contained in Mark. From their observations, the scholars concluded that the three Gospels were closely related, and called them 'synoptic' — 'seeing from the same point of view' — and they said that Matthew and Luke had both used Mark as the basis of their own accounts of the Gospel message. This is the idea of the 'Synoptic Tradition' still taught today. Of course it soon emerged that the theory did not quite work. Not all the material common to Matthew and Luke is actually to be found in Mark. But rather than scrap the theory, scholars started the game of inventing hypothetical documents which were supposed to have been available to Matthew and Luke in addition to the Gospel of Mark. However, the ensuing complexities are no part of the point we have to make here: rather we are concerned with the resulting attitude to Mark.[6]

The Gospel of Mark was now seen to be the original Gospel, and it was widely assumed to be therefore the most authentic. Matthew and Luke were naturally swayed by the problems and interests of the evolving Church of their day and filtered their presentation of Jesus and his teaching accordingly, but Mark, it was supposed, presented the plain case. Scholars concurred that Mark was the 'simplest,' 'least theological' of the Gospels, and thus the most historically accurate. One can therefore hardly imagine what would have been the response for academic theologians if they had chanced to read Steiner's very different views expounded in his lectures of 1912!

For Steiner, the Gospels each represent different traditions and divergent, yet essentially true, ways of understanding the Event of Golgotha together with aspects of the life and teaching of Christ. Mark, he said, had not had direct access to the historical events, but had been a pupil of the disciple Peter. 'The so-called Gospel of Mark was originally compiled by such a pupil of Peter, and it was given out by him, though at first only by word of mouth ... After a period as the pupil of Peter, Mark travelled to a place that provided an environment and outward setting suitable for the special colouring which his Gospel required ... He went to Alexandria. There he resided, at a time when the theosophical and philosophical teaching of Judaism had reached a climax in its development. And there too he absorbed the best aspects of pagan Gnosticism, from which he gained the prevalent ideas concerning the descent of man from spiritual spheres.'[7] Mysteries based on the Gnostic-Hermetic wisdom were indeed flourishing in Alexandria, and it was in this atmosphere that Mark wrote his Gospel.

It might fairly be said that at the time Steiner spoke there was no external evidence to support his claim.[8] It is true, as we have already seen that ideas from Gnosticism and the Jewish-Iranian esoteric sects had been taken up by followers of Hermes Trismegistus in cosmopolitan Egypt; and it is also perfectly true that such ideas had led to a mystical and theosophical interpretation of Judaism — notably in the allegorical and mystical works of Philo of Alexandria (often known as Philo Judaeus). But this seemed the least likely setting for Mark, the 'simplest' and 'least theological' of the Gospels!

The situation did not change until 1958. Then, an American researcher working at a monastery in the Judean desert discovered part of a letter by Clement, one of the Fathers of the Alexandrian church, which discussed the secret history of the Gospel of Mark. Clement was known to have been diligent and highly intelligent in his study of apostolic traditions, an expert on the subject in fact: his letter therefore demanded to be treated seriously. The revelations turned out to be astonishing in many ways, and not least remarkable is the tale it tells of the Gospel's origin. Clement's letter relates it as follows:

> Mark, then, during Peter's stay in Rome, wrote an account of the deeds of the Lord, not however declaring all of them, nor yet hinting at the secret ones, but selecting those he thought most useful for increasing the faith of those who were being instructed. But when Peter died as a martyr, Mark came over to Alexandria, bringing both his own notes and those of Peter, from which he transferred to his former book the things suitable to whatever makes for progress towards knowledge (*gnosis*). Thus he composed a more spiritual Gospel for the use of those who were being initiated ... When he died, he left his composition to the church in Alexandria, where it is even yet most carefully guarded, being read only to those who are being initiated into the great Mysteries.[9]

The letter also contained extracts from the 'secret Gospel,' including a story resembling that of the raising of Lazarus.

Here then was a discovery which began to make some sense in terms of Steiner's spiritual results. Not only did the story of the Gospel's origins substantially agree with Steiner's, but the character of the Gospel itself was clarified by the realization that, rather as with Matthew and the *Gospel of the Hebrews*, certain passages of the original Gospel of Mark had been regarded as esoteric. The publicly circulated version of Mark did not contain the 'secret' deeds of the Lord, since the full 'Gnostic' version of the Gospel was 'carefully guarded' and read only to those being initiated into the 'great Mysteries.'

But what are the 'great Mysteries'? The decisive step forward in the understanding of the new fragment was made by the scholar Cyril Richardson. Initiation of course took the form of baptism, and the 'great Mysteries,' he said, were the rites of the paschal vigil in the Alexandrian church — the solemn Easter festival at which initiations were performed.[10] The esoteric passages in the Gospel were read as part of the instruction of the new initiates. Several features of the document now begin to fall into place; and we can also begin to relate them to our earlier studies of the meaning and character of Christian initiation, especially the Gnostic trends which form a part of its background. To this the 'secret Gospel' fragment furnishes additional evidence, and enables us, if we are willing, to see several aspects of the Gospel of Mark in a new light.

Unlike the Gospels of Matthew and Luke, for instance, which give us infancy stories and genealogies, background history and human information, the Gospel of Mark commences in a uniquely commanding way:

> The beginning of the Gospel of Jesus Christ, the Son of God ...

Immediately there follows — the baptism by John. The heavens open and the Spirit descends like a great bird; a heavenly voice declares the oracle of Sonship. This is very different from Matthew's careful preparation of the chosen prophet, acknowledged at birth by the Magi, or Luke's scenes in the Temple. The 'beginning of the Gospel' erupts from the heavenly world, the Spirit descends and the Son of God stands before us.

Now if there is anywhere in early Christian literature where we find something similar, it is in the thought of Basilides: an

Alexandrian Gnostic. Although he works them out in elaborate detail typical of the great Gnostic systems of the second century, his basic concepts are the same, namely: the Gospel, a cosmic power which descends out of heaven; Sonship, which must be revealed in the earthly world and which leads to the cosmic restoration. Now clearly these ideas may well have formed part of the Gnostic heritage in Alexandria, and Mark too might have drawn upon them at an earlier stage.

Basilides presents them very graphically. The Gospel origi-nates in the higher cosmic regions and descends, like a burning source of light, through the lower spheres:

> So from the sphere of the Seven (that is, the planetary spheres) the light ... descended upon Jesus the Son of Mary, and he was illuminated and kindled by the light that shone upon him.[11]

The moment at which this occurred, we gather, was the baptism by John, and we know that Basilides' followers celebrated Epiphany (January 6) as the festival of the descent of the Son of God upon 'Jesus the Son of Mary.' It is hardly accidental that this date was also celebrated in ancient Alexandria as the birth of the Aion, god of the cosmic totality or of the completed cycle of Time. The background of his teachings thus lies in the *gnosis* and the Mysteries of Alexandria. But it is especially important to note that Basilides acknowledged another source for the specif-ically Christian part of his teaching. He had been instructed by one Glaucias, an 'interpreter of Peter' — that is to say, someone who taught orally on the basis of apostolic traditions handed down from Peter, someone who was therefore in a very similar position to Mark!

It would thus appear that for early Alexandrian Christianity, it is baptism which stands at the 'beginning of the Gospel,' and that baptism still has strong Gnostic over-tones of a cosmic initiation. The picture of a strongly Gnostic form of Christianity developing there only becomes more con-vincing when one adds to it the total failure of the 'orthodox' Christian historians to find anything in early Alexandrian Christianity that they could chronicle with approval, so that they had to leave an embarrassing blank in the records.[12] Thus it seems that as early as the time of Mark, one stream of Christianity had absorbed powerful Gnostic Mystery-elements. And further confirmation of this view may also be drawn from the scanty information on Alexandria which is to be found in the New Testament in the book of Acts, which come from the same writer as the Gospel of Luke. There we meet 'a Jew named Apollos, a native of Alexandria.' Oddly contradictory things are said concerning him. He had a thorough knowledge of the Old Testament (as one would expect of an educated Alexandrian Jew), and he had also 'been instructed in the way of the Lord, and he spoke with great fervour and taught about Jesus accurately' — yet 'he knew only the baptism of John.' What can this mean?

It cannot mean that he was a disciple of John the Baptist, since he knows 'accurately' about Jesus and 'the Way.' It seems rather to be Luke's way of pointing out an inadequacy, from his own standpoint when writing the Acts, in Apollos' under-standing. He appears to be saying in effect that Apollos' Christianity has got stuck at the stage of Jesus' baptism by John, and has not gone forward to take in the significance of the later events — the crucifixion and the resurrection. In another passage of Acts, Paul immediately clarifies the situation when he interviews a group of disciples who hold the same idea. They have received 'John's baptism,' as did Jesus himself. For Paul, however, a new era began after Christ's resurrection and ascension, for then the Holy Spirit was given, and in Paul's type of baptism this post-resurrection element of the giving of the Holy Spirit plays a central role. This side of Christian initiation, as we have seen, had its roots more in the Essene-derived stream of Christianity. The group of disciples have never heard of this at all, and 'know nothing of a Holy Spirit.' For the Alexandrian Gnostics, we remember, the Spirit which descended at the baptism was seen as the cosmic Christ-being coming down upon the man Jesus.

Apollos and the group of disciples encountered by Paul thus seem to confirm that Alexandria fostered a 'Gnostic' line of Christianity where the prime mystery was baptism: the epiphany of the cosmic Christ. [13]

The Youth in the Linen Cloth

The stress on baptism in the newly recovered 'secret Gospel' fragment fits well, therefore, with Clement's and Rudolf Steiner's assertion that Mark's Gospel was composed in Alexandria. It accords with the prominence given to the baptism of Jesus at the opening of the Gospel, with the vestiges of teaching we find connected with Apollos, the shadowy Glaucias, and their later elaboration by Basilides.

Quite as astonishing as the evidence about Jesus' baptism by John, however, was the information in the 'secret Gospel' about Jesus' own baptismal practice. Clement regards all this as highly esoteric, not under any circumstances to be divulged to the uninitiated but read only to those who are instructed in the 'great Mysteries,' the paschal vigil when initiation took place. Only there is it revealed to them that just as Christ was 'baptized' into his cosmic mission of manifesting the Kingdom of Heaven, so he instituted the initiatory rites of baptism which they now undergo. Nowhere in the rest of the New Testament is it said that Jesus baptized, although the texts on the subject do look very much tampered with, and at one point the insertion of an explicit denial sticks out like a sore thumb.[14]

Once again the comments of Rudolf Steiner on certain episodes in the Gospel of Mark will help to form a clear picture, especially when taken in conjunction with the esoteric material from the 'secret Gospel' fragment. Above all, new light is cast on the perplexing story of the Youth in the linen cloth.

The Youth makes his appearance at the tragic moment of Jesus' betrayal and arrest in the garden of Gethsemane. There is the calm and dignified response from Jesus, then confusion and flight as he is seized, sudden chaos and desertion. And then a strange apparition:

> A young man, wearing nothing but a linen garment, was following Jesus. But when they seized him, he fled away naked, leaving his garment behind. (Mark 14:51–2)

So Jesus goes to his death, but the curious youthful figure slips away unharmed leaving his linen garment behind. Are we here on the place of outer, physical events — or is the apparition of the Youth a mystical element, a truth of the scene on a higher level? Steiner suggested the latter. He pointed out that we meet the same Youth again later in the Gospel, when the women go to the tomb:

> And entering the sepulchre they saw a young man clothed in a white garment, sitting on the right-hand side ... [15]

The Youth announces to them the resurrection of Christ and his future work.

Steiner described the Youth as an 'Imagination': not a symbol but an imaginative form which was a real experience for those who went through the ordeals and processes of initiation, or for those who through other circumstances had become open to spiritual events. The Youth is an Imagination of the 'cosmic impulse' of the Christ. The youthful cosmic impulse appears alongside the Son of Man who goes to his death on the Cross. But it cannot be grasped by his earthly persecutors, it slips away. This vision is unique to Mark. 'No other Gospel tells us that in the moment when men, through their failure to comprehend, lay human hands on the Son of Man, the cosmic element eludes them, the youthful cosmic element which from that decisive point onwards is united with earthly evolution.' [16] It reappears, now clothed in shining white, in the glory of the resurrection, at the end of the Gospel, when the Youth announces the onward working of the Christ. 'He goes before you into Galilee!' .

Such a description does much to explain the mystifying appearance of the unexplained Youth. But it remains to ask why the Imagination should assume the precise form of a Youth in a linen cloth or a white garment. After all, the figure of a Youth is not an obvious manifestation of a 'cosmic impulse.' Here the 'secret Gospel' enables us to close a gap in interpretation.

First, however, we may observe that the figure of the Youth appearing in a mystical and cosmic connection is not unique to Mark and his tradition. Nor does it belong solely to the Gnostic end of the spiritual spectrum of early Christianity. There is something similar in a work that has come down to us, and that seems to, have its roots in the Essene-Ebionite wing of Christianity, with many familiar teachings about the Two Spirits, the coming new aeon, and so on. Its title however is *The Shepherd of Hermas* — which, in conjunction with a number of scenes in the book that recall episodes in the Gnostic-Hermetic writings, has prompted some to suppose that the author is also in touch with such pagan traditions of *gnosis* and is bringing them into Christian form. Anyone who had read in the Hermetic scriptures the opening revelation of Poimandres ('Man-Shepherd') to the Egyptian sage would certainly have found much to approve in the 'Shepherd of Saint Hermes.' In the course of a series of *Visions*, Hermas is shown tremendous scenes of cosmic creation: but he cannot understand the stupendous works of the angelic hierarchies, and is left bewildered by his vision. It is then that a Young Man appears to him, and begins to guide him toward cosmic under-standing. It is only gradually that Hermas also learns to recog-nize this Young Man. He is the 'Angel of *metanoia*' (repentance, 'transformation of mind').[17]

In the *Shepherd of Hermas*, then, a Youth also appears as a cos-mic guide and 'instructor to the seer. And he turns out to be the Angel of initiatory transformation, *metanoia*, which here as in early Christianity generally, means: baptism. It is through bap-tismal regeneration that the seer finds his way into cosmic real-ity, guided by the visionary Youth.

The esoteric section of the Gospel of Mark quoted in Clement's letter brings all these same themes together. It has a home in the original Gospel after the passage in chapter 10:34 where Jesus predicts his death and resurrection:

> And they come into Bethany, and a certain woman, whose brother had died, was there. And, coming, she prostrated herself before Jesus and says to him, 'Son of David, have mercy on me.' But the disciples rebuked her. And Jesus, being angered, went off with her into the garden where the tomb was, and straightaway a great cry was heard from the tomb. And straightaway, going in where the youth was, he stretched forth his hand and raised him, seizing his hand. But the youth, looking upon him, loved him and began to beseech him that he might be with him.

The story is very like that of Lazarus — indeed it is almost certainly the same story. What is especially interesting, however, is that the 'secret Gospel' shows it to be part of a process of initiation. For after six days of further preparation, Jesus goes on to instruct the man who has been raised from the dead in the secrets of the 'Kingdom.'

> And after six days Jesus told him what to do, and in the evening the youth came to him, wearing a linen cloth over his naked body. And he remained with him that night, for Jesus taught him the mystery of the Kingdom of God.[18]

Morton Smith, the discoverer of the fragment, saw that the rite performed by Jesus was evidently a baptism; hence the pupil arrives in the linen garment ready for immersion. He rightly adds that the 'mystery of the Kingdom' most probably refers to a Gnostic kind of ascent into heaven. 'The kingdom of God *par excellence* was the heavens, where God himself was, and his throne and paradise and the angels and the souls of the blest, where his will was done and his peace maintained. From ancient times there had circulated through the near east and Greece stories of men who had ascended into the heavens and thereby secured secret knowledge ... Stories about such ascents had been common in the pious literature of Palestine for at least a century before Jesus' time.'[19] After his initiatory death and resurrection, then, the candidate is to be united with the heavenly, cosmic powers. The evidence of the 'secret Gospel' seems to prove that, at least once in his life, Jesus initiated one of his pupils by means of a baptismal rite. And that moment was recalled for the initiates of the Alexandrian community when the esoteric passage from the Gospel was read to them during the celebration of the 'great Mysteries.'

In the original, esoteric version of Mark we thus find the primary appearance of the Youth in the linen cloth. He is the young man who is being baptized into the cosmic mysteries by Jesus, wearing only his baptismal robe. He reappears later before the visionary eye of the evangelist, as the representative of that cosmic Mystery revealed by the Christ. First we see him again in the half-light of the Garden of Gethsemane, then clad in white in the splendour of the resurrection. And he appears again in early Christian mysticism as the Angel of Baptism, the Young Man who unfolds to Hermas the meaning of his cosmic visions.

The fact that baptism, the rite of cosmic initiation, goes back to Jesus himself explains why it was taken up by all the different streams of early Christianity. In the Gnostic stream it assumed a position of absolute centrality: we see this reflected in the Gospel of Mark, written in the Gnostic atmosphere of Alexandria, and in the later development of the same fundamental ideas by the Gnostic Basilides. We see it in slightly different form in the *Shepherd of Hermas*, for there too we have an influence from the pagan Hermetic Gnosticism of Alexandria. Baptism and 'transformation' had been important to the Hermetists already in pre-Christian times. Thus it is natural that in Alexandria these aspects of Christianity should have been taken up and flourished, to leave their traces especially in the Gospel of Mark.

Later, Paul evolved a new kind of baptism — still an initiatory rite, but drawing its significance from the death and resurrection of Christ in conjunction with the sending of the Holy Spirit. It became inevitable that the older forms of esotericism should disappear when Paul's ideas were absorbed into 'orthodoxy.' And those who like Basilides continued to develop along other lines soon acquired a standard name: heretics.

A Gnostic Gospel?

It would be easy to go on and Interpret many other features of the Gospel of Mark in terms of the Alexandrian Gnostic milieu. The dominant theme of the whole first part of the Gospel, depicting the world in the grip of demonic powers whom Jesus has come to exorcize, immediately suggests the Gnostic vision of the evil worldrulers whom the heavenly Revealer descends to overthrow. The very technique of the writer, with his sudden changes of direction, apparently inconsequential breaks in the flow of the narrative, his frequent use of 'suddenly,' 'immediately,' recalls the Gnostic fragmentation of time: rather than employing narrative to build up the sense of a continuous reality in the flow of time, the Gnostics sought to reveal the illusion of our ordinary 'sequential' experience, and through its fragmentation tried to convey a mystical reality out-of-time. The Gospel of Mark also undermines our sense of time by a similar method, hinting at something more real though hidden from our gaze, and ends quite literally trembling on the edge of an unimaginable revelation.[20]

Yet it would be a mistake to conclude that Mark simply adopted the Gnostic world-view of Alexandria and conformed his understanding of the Christian Mystery to older, Gnostic traditions. He found in them something which could not be so readily found in the Essene-derived practices and teachings which inspiled the author of Matthew: namely the dimension of cosmic myth which is intangibly present throughout Mark's Gospel, and which we have explored in this chapter from certain points of view, necessarily limited. The cosmic background gives the Gospel of Mark its 'unique quality. But Mark also found that he had to reinterpret, to redirect the cosmic wisdom of Alexandria if it was truly to become an instrument for understanding the Christ. It had somehow to come to terms also with the dark reality of the crucifixion.

One of the ways in which the Gnostics described the process of initiatory awakening was as the response to a 'Call.' It is an illusion, they taught, that a man decides in his ordinary consciousness to dedicate himself to the spiritual or the earthly: it is the spiritual which sends out a cry which, if he hears it, the earthly man may answer. In the moment when he hears the call, which comes from the divine being who is himself 'Knowledge of Life,' all earthly glory is darkened for a man and he turns instead to the spiritual:

> A cry rang out over the whole world, the splendour
> departed from every city. Knowledge of Life revealed
> himself to all the children of men and redeemed them
> from darkness into the light.[21]

Wolfgang Schenk, in an important article, recognized that a similar Gnostic scene lay behind Mark's interpretation of the death of Jesus. Darkness falls over the face of the whole land, and

Jesus 'cried out with a loud voice' from the Cross. Nor does his cry go unheard:

> And when the centurion, who stood there in front of
> Jesus, heard his cry and saw how he died, he said, 'Surely
> this man was the Son of God!'

The veil of the Temple is torn in two — another symbol much used by the Gnostics, for whom the 'veil' represents the threshold dividing the physical from the cosmic-spiritual realms, which is torn in the instant of inner awakening to a higher truth. The centurion, in fact, voices in response to Jesus' cry the central truth of Mark's Gospel: the realization that 'this man was the Son of God.'

Schenk points out, however, that Mark has not just taken over a Gnostic scene, but has given it a new meaning. It was inconceivable for any thoroughgoing Gnostic that the Revealer — the essence, the *gnosis* of Life itself, could have been born in the material sense, let alone die on a shameful cross! Yet that is precisely what Mark describes, though using the Gnostics' own terms against them. The evangelist presents as the fulfilment of the Gnostic Mystery something which no Gnostic as such could accept: the death of Jesus on Golgotha.[22] Although he retains the cosmic and mythical resonance of the Gnostic vision, Mark brings it in anew, Christian way into relationship with the earthly world. For the pure Gnostic, the earthly world is sheer negativity. But Mark makes an earthly event — a death under circumstances when all but a basic human dignity has been stripped away — the fulfilment of the cosmic archetype. He goes beyond Gnosticism whilst making use of it to establish the possibility, the impending revelation, of a new link between the earthly and the divine.

7. Buddha and Christ

The World of the Greeks

The Christian vision cannot be fully understood by considering
only the world of the ancient Near East and Palestine, whose
religious and esoteric currents we have so far been examining.
The rise of Christianity as a transforming factor in the life of the
late antique world, its startling diffusion over large stretches of
the globe which seemed even to the early Christian writers
themselves a 'miraculous' achievement, demands that we turn
to the other great civilization of the Mediterranean — the
Greeks.

By the beginning of the Christian era, however, Greek civilization had little to do with the 'classical' culture of the old city-
states of Athens and Sparta, the world which had produced the
great tragic poets, the sculptors and artists who gave birth to our
modern concept of beauty, or the first philosophers, brightly
exploring the new dominion of thought. The centre of power
had long before swung north to Macedon, and the democratic
structure of the city-states had been swept away by the formation of the greatest Empire the world had known. Alexander of
Macedon — Alexander the Great, as he came to be known —
subdued Greece, Egypt, Iran and finally even India in his amazing sequence of conquests. Greek language and Greek culture
went wherever he did, creating a vast network of trading and
cultural links; men in the Far East and in the western
Mediterranean found themselves speaking a common language,
beginning to think in similar ways, above all beginning to consider themselves 'citizens of the world' rather than as belonging
to a local or tribal community. Greek became the language not
just of Greece, but the *koine*, the common tongue of the inhabited
world then known to men.

In the process of expansion, Greek speech and thought were inevitably altered in their turn by the world they had created. Especially after Alexander's death, when the huge Empire fell apart into several quarrelling factions, the conquered Orient began to use the culture and ideas of the Greeks in its own way, to tinge Hellenic values with its own exotic colours, absorbing back into archaic Eastern forms of life the invader's novel concepts so as to express them once again in something like its ancient fashion. In the centuries before the time of Christ, it was again the East which had gained the upper hand, and using the international network of Greek civilization for its own purposes was bringing oriental notions and attitudes, especially in religion, flooding back into the West. Historians no longer use the terms 'Greek' or 'Hellenic' to refer to this later phase of civilization: they call it 'Hellenistic,' which usually means in effect 'Graeco-Oriental,' the fusion of Greek with Eastern attitudes or styles.

Adopting this larger world-perspective, our previous studies can be placed in a still broader spiritual context. The 'return of the Mysteries' to Palestine, which we traced in an earlier chapter, was only part of a larger process, whereby the archaically powerful Mysteries of the East returned to join with what had developed in the West. The individual moral consciousness of Israel, the rational thought and art of Greece, encountered once more the primal spirituality of Egypt, Iran and India. We have seen that exciting new religious developments sprang from that meeting: advanced groups like the Essenes took what was best from both for their pioneering situation, others like the Gnostics clung on to what was old, adopting a defensive attitude to the consciousness of the West. In the larger Greek world, the flooding back of the oriental world brought the spread of the oriental Mysteries into the rational and increasingly secular culture of the Greeks. Gods like Osiris, Isis, Mithra and the Great Mother came to be worshipped throughout the Hellenistic world, and later were known throughout the Roman Empire which sprang up in its wake.[1] And Christianity was to emerge, not only with a synthesis of myth and history, of cosmic experience and rational consciousness — but as the seed of a world that would far outlive the disruptions of the age in which it came into being.

Adopting such a wider perspective, we can set the Christian

Mystery against a vaster backdrop, still deeper than that we have adopted before. Not only was the Greek expansion a precondition for the ultimate spread of the Christian message: it also opened up the possibility of spiritual communication between West and East, even India, which enables us to appreciate another dimension of the universal role in which the Christ appears.

Alexander had paved the way. Syrian merchants — the great go-betweens of antiquity — had established trade-routes to India across the difficult terrain. In the first century BC trading was increased with the discovery of the pattern of the monsoon, which facilitated sailing from the south-west and returning from the north-east in the course of the season, bringing India within range of profitable shipping. Religious and philosophical encounters were also enriched: early Christian writers know something of the naked *yogis* of the Brahminical religion; above all, Buddhist missionaries begin to appear in the West, notably in cosmopolitan Alexandria, but no doubt also at other religious centres. The Gnostic discoveries at Nag Hammadi have raised in some minds the question of Far Eastern influence. And there are other traditions in apocryphal and canonical writings which are equally suggestive of Buddhist or Hindu interests.

The literature that has come down to us linked with the name of Thomas is particularly rich in oriental features. It is not only that the apostle is supposed to have travelled to India (where the 'Thomas Christians' still exist today, though they have long been brought under the wing of orthodoxy). In the *Gospel of Thomas* found at Nag Hammadi, for instance, Jesus figures more as a *guru* than as a Saviour in the later Christian sense:

> Jesus said to his disciples: 'Make a comparison to me, and tell me whom I am like ...'
>
> Thomas said to him, 'Master, my mouth will not suffer that I say whom thou art like.'
>
> Jesus said: 'I am not thy Master. Because thou hast drunk, thou hast become intoxicated from the bubbling spring which I have measured out.'

Thomas has attained 'liberation'; he has grasped the truth, and Jesus no longer needs to be his teacher and guide. 'Some scholars have suggested that if the names were changed, the 'living Buddha' appropriately could say what the *Gospel of Thomas* attributes to the living Jesus. Could Hindu or Buddhist tradition have influenced gnosticism?'[2] The answer to the question appears to be 'yes.' The collection of legends and teachings called the *Acts of Thomas*, preserved in Syria, for example, contains genuine historical information about Gundaphorus, a king of Hellenistic India, and some of the legends reflect Indian mythology. And we also possess in the name of Thomas an *Infancy Gospel*. In fact, it is in the legends of Jesus' childhood that the oriental and Indian features are most markedly developed.[3]

The Childhood of Buddha and Jesus

The first-century Indian poet Ashvaghosha, in his *Buddhacarita*, thus describes the birth of the Bodhisattva who had been destined to gain Enlightenment under the bodhi-tree, some five centuries earlier:

> There lived once upon a time a king of the Shakyas, a scion of the solar race, whose name was Shuddhodana. He was pure in conduct, and beloved of the Shakyas like the autumn moon. He had a wife, splendid, beautiful, and steadfast, who was called the Great Maya, from her resemblance to Maya the Goddess. These two tasted of love's delights, and one day she conceived the fruit of her womb, but without any defilement, in the same way that knowledge joined to trance bears fruit. Just before her conception she had a dream. A white king elephant seemed to enter her body, but without causing her any pain. So Maya, queen of that godlike king, bore in her womb the glory of his dynasty. But she remained free from the fatigues, depressions, and fancies which usually accompany pregnancies ... When the queen noticed that the time of her delivery was approaching, she went to a couch overspread with an awning, thousands of waiting-women looking on in joy from their hearts. The propitious constellation of Pushya shone brightly when a

son was born to the queen, for the weal of the world. He
came out of his mother's side, without causing her pain
or injury. His birth was as miraculous as that of Aurva,
Prithu, Mandhatri, and Kakshivat, heroes of old who
were born respectively from the thigh, from the hand, the
head or the armpit. So he issued from the womb as befits
a Buddha. He did not enter the world in the usual
manner, and he appeared like one descended from the
sky. And since he had for many aeons been engaged in
the practice of meditation, he was now born in full
awareness, and not thoughtless and bewildered as other
people are. When born, he was so lustrous and steadfast
that it appeared as if the young sun had come down to
earth. And yet, when people gazed at his dazzling
brilliance, he held their eyes like' the moon. His limbs
shone with the radiant hue of precious gold and lit up
the space all around. Instantly he walked seven steps,
firmly and with long strides. In that he was like the
constellation of the Seven Seers. With the bearing of a
lion he surveyed the four quarters, and spoke these
words full of meaning for the future: 'For enlightenment
I was born, for the good of all that lives. This is the last
time that I have been born into this world of becoming.'[4]

In many ways this birth-legend is full of Indian extravagance:
no Christian account of Jesus imagines the child being born with
thousands of attendants looking on, nor has the child announce
immediately his religious goal. But for all that we recognize
many similar themes to those even in the canonical gospels —
the prophetic dream, the undefiled conception. And when we
turn to the apocrypha we find many more.

Probably the earliest 'infancy gospel' is the so-called
Protevangelium. Its traditions are of very mixed quality, but some
are significant; its most famous passage is the description of the
miraculous stillness which fell over the world at the time of
Jesus' birth. The birth itself is scarcely that of an ordinary child.
Joseph goes to fetch a midwife — though in the event she is to
be a witness rather than to give practical aid. Joseph tells her to
'come and see':

> And he went to the place of the cave, and behold a bright
> cloud overshadowed the cave. And the midwife said, 'My
> soul is magnified today, for my eyes have seen wonderful
> things; for salvation is born to Israel.'
>
> And immediately the cloud disappeared from the cave,
> and a great light appeared, so that their eyes could not
> bear it. A short time afterwards that light withdrew until
> the child appeared, and it went and took the breast of its
> mother, Mary.[5]

Jesus is here born in a manner befitting a divine child. No more
than the Buddha did he enter the world in the usual manner, but
appears more 'like one descended from the sky.' The same heavenly brilliance which surrounded the birth of Buddha hovers
over him, too. One might even be tempted to suppose that for
the author of the *Protevangelium* the appearance of the child was
not a birth but a miraculous epiphany. The detailed investigations by the midwife and Salome, however, serve to establish
that, although a virgin, Mary has definitely brought forth the
fruit of the womb.

When we come to the *Infancy Gospel of Thomas*, the atmosphere is even more startling. The childhood incidents involving
Jesus are recounted with great circumstantiality, but 'if the
"child" or "boy" were not actually called Jesus, no one would
guess that the tales of this playful divine boy were intended to
supplement the tradition about him. Numerous parallels can be
cited from the legends of Krishna and Buddha ...'[6] The infant
Jesus toys with his fellow children as well as with adults in ways
which playfully reveal him already as a supernatural being
among men, while he yet stays charmingly human. The attrac-
tion of the *Infancy Gospel* lies in the truly imaginative mixture of
innocence, childishness and the supernatural in Jesus — exactly
as in the stories of Krishna among the shepherds and the village
girls, or in some of the tales connected with the Buddha.

In the Thomas-tradition stories as a whole, however, there is
certainly a danger that the oriental pattern will usurp the meaning of the whole Christian story, rather than leading to a deeper
insight into Jesus and his ministry. They do serve to show that
Jesus could be seen, in the first centuries, through the eyes of

oriental expectation and ideas — as someone destined from his childhood to fulfil the role of an enlightened being or a Buddha. But it is far from clear when we read them how this understanding of Jesus could be brought constructively within the sphere of the Christian vision.

For that, we must turn to the documents which stand closer to the mainstream of unfolding Christian life. And of the writings included in the New Testament the one which undeniably has an affinity with the oriental spirit and miraculous tale-telling of Thomas is — the Gospel of Luke.

Clairvoyant Witness: the Gospel of Luke

The language of the Gospels of Matthew and Mark echoed the special religious traditions from which they drew: Matthew was rendered into Greek from a Semitic original, Mark was expressed in the Gnostic style with its disjunctions and sudden insights. With the language of the Gospel of Luke we are immediately at home in the cosmopolitan world of Hellenistic times. The smoothly constructed sentences and the stream of well-chosen *mots justes* will satisfy the stylistic demands of the most educated reader. The formal Dedication, which opens the book in the way educated readers would expect, makes it clear that the writer is to be taken seriously, and is not addressing only a small minority of the committed but a wide circle, including men of the calibre of the 'most excellent Theophilus.' More than the other Gospels, that of Luke speaks to the larger Hellenistic community who do not have a Jewish background or come from the intense religious atmosphere of Alexandria. His message is for all men. Following on from his Gospel, Luke traces the spread of Christianity further in his Acts of the Apostles, expanding his vision progressively from Palestine out into the world and extending salvation-history forward in time with reference to historical events and persons well known to all.

It is not. surprising, therefore, that many of Luke's characteristics are those of the age to which he belonged. No more than the other evangelists is he an objective chronicler or a scientific historian presenting mere facts. His vision is shaped by the Gentile Christianity to which he belonged, and his Gospel reveals the special insights of that Christianity. Some of its characteristics can easily be noted.

Luke is not much interested in the geography and chronology of Jesus' life — having once established the historical setting, that is, with his reference to the census and the Emperor Augustus. He presents all of Jesus' life as a pilgrimage to Jerusalem, so that the powerful imaginative picture of the 'way of the cross' predominates over the detail of Jesus' earthly wanderings back and forth. In fact, Luke has a distinct tendency to shape his material into vivid and moving scenes of a pictorial quality, summing up an aspect of the Gospel and evoking a strong emotional response. When Jesus has been arrested, for example, and Peter has three times denied any connection with him to the servants of the High Priest, it is Luke alone who tells us:

> The Lord turned and looked straight at Peter. Then Peter
> remembered the word the Lord had spoken to him:
> 'Before the cock crows today, you will disown me three
> times.' And he went outside and wept bitterly. [7]

With that single look, Luke has created an unforgettable 'Imagination' of the event, which can rise ever and again before the inner eye.

This brilliant 'imaginative' quality of Luke's Gospel is undoubtedly connected with his fascination, by comparison with the other Gospels, with the world of dream and visions. He — and his readers — accept without explanation the common Hellenistic view that dreams and visions are a normal channel of communication between man and the divine. The Gospel begins with a vision in the Temple; there is the apparition of the angel to Mary, still in Chapter 1. In the Acts of the Apostles there is the vision of Ananias, making known Saul's conversion and transformation to Paul, and it is said that Paul had a corresponding vision of Ananias. Paul's vision on the road to Damascus is recounted in vivid detail no less than three times. Many other instances can easily be located.[8] The Hellenistic mind had still not evolved so far in the direction of severely rational consciousness such as we have today. The conscious world was still open to communication from deeper psychic levels — especially in the form of 'images' which would rise up before the waking soul or persist vividly from dream.

We today have largely lost this openness to the psychic depths: but in Hellenistic times such 'images' were still a language, not yet atrophied into the inconsequential dreams of modern man, a means of communication exploiting faculties not under conscious control. It was used by pagans and Christians alike, and in the Hellenistic tradition (contrary to the Jewish) it was visual 'imaginations' which were especially valued as manifestations of the divine, rather than written or verbal revelations. One way of finding a solution to one's problems in life was to go to a holy place and sleep there: in the dream an answer would be revealed, or a vision would make it known. Among the pagans, the shrines of the healer god Asclepius were favourite sites for this practice (called 'incubation'); among the Christians, tombs of early martyrs were generally frequented.

In the Mystery religions, the 'visionary faculty' was intensified by psychological and sometimes physiological practices. Similar things were done in Christian circles too, where indeed ascetic procedures were carried to far greater lengths. Undoubtedly many early Christian prophets (just like the Desert Fathers a little later) saw visions of the life and teaching of Jesus, or his post-resurrection teaching to the disciples; or saw the Risen One and heard a saying from his lips, either confirming the tradition or adding some new utterance to it. Modern scholarship is only beginning to wake up to the fact that in some measure the Gospel tradition is based on visionary revelations as well as on historical records. Paul himself had received 'words of the Lord' in vision, and talks of seers and prophets as well-known persons in his communities. A study of the phenomenon in Christianity reveals 'the presence of features in the Gospels, says one scholar, 'which cannot be considered as distortions of the original or as literary falsifications, or as emanating from discussions with the Jews or from controversies within the community, but which must be considered as utterances of men who spoke "in the name," that is, at the command and with the authority of the exalted Lord, and whose words were heard and honoured as words of the exalted Lord himself, and were repeated in the accounts of his earthly life as words of the earthly Lord.'[9]

Modern scholarship has thus come by its own route to something oddly like the view of Rudolf Steiner: that the scenes in the Gospels are partly based upon tradition but also upon 'clairvoyant' visions. The Gospel of Luke in particular suggests that the tradition has been transfigured in the process of devoted meditation into a sequence of 'images'; the prominence of visions and dreams in Luke's world makes it highly likely that many of them were actually 'seen' by the evangelist or his immediate predecessors. Whereas it is clear that Luke had not physically known Jesus or any of the other characters in the Gospel, he makes it evident that he had diligently researched his sources; yet it is striking that these do not include anything in the way of written documents, letters, and so on. He speaks rather of 'the things that have been fulfilled among us,' and bases himself on what has been handed down by 'those who were from the beginning *autoptai* and ministers of the word.' One might well suppose that those who spoke 'in the name' of the exalted Lord are precisely the ones who regarded themselves as 'ministers of the word'; and the term *autoptes* (literally, 'self-seer') also has a Mystery connotation.[9b]

Rudolf Steiner pointed out that in certain of the Hellenistic Mysteries the pupils were brought to a stage where they experienced the visionary 'Imaginations,' but did not attain to the higher achievements of initiation. Such an 'imaginative' seer was called an *autoptes*. His observation is confirmed by the late Greek writer Psellus, who noted the distinction of two levels in the Mystery experience — especially perhaps in later times — corresponding to the terms *autoptes* and *epoptes* ('super-seer'). *Epopteia* is in fact the familiar term in ancient sources for the highest level of initiation into the Mysteries, for standing in the actual presence of the god. The *autoptes*, on the other hand, saw images and visions, and his experience may have been characteristic of the more contemplative cults, as opposed to the ones which offered, by means of dramatic and harrowing events, to raise the initiate up to the very level of the gods. It suited the contemplative and philosophical Hermetists, for example, who aimed to see the Godhead revealed through the visual splendour of the heavenly configurations of the stars. After describing the starry heavens, Hermes in one of the fragments is made to say:

> He who is not ignorant of these things can apprehend
> God precisely. Indeed, to speak boldly, he may become an
> *autoptes* and behold him (in vision); and beholding, he
> may be blessed.[10]

Seeing images in the stars, in fact, is one of the oldest exercises of the 'visionary faculty,' which had a long history both in Greece and in ancient Egypt.

By Luke's time, the Christian *autoptai* and 'ministers of the word' had already been at work, helping to shape the traditions and images of Jesus' life. With his powerful visual sense and his delight in the visionary and miraculous, Luke stands in the same line, and the work he produced was extremely satisfying in terms of the spiritual expectations shared by his Hellenistic audience. The visionary quality of the Gospel of Luke made it especially dear to some of the Gnostics who, as we have seen, were spreading oriental ideas through the same medium of Hellenistic cultural life. In fact, there are in the Gospel a number of indications that certain forms of Gnosticism were flourishing in the area where Luke worked, and that these helped to shape his awareness of the Christian message. A little after Luke's time the great theologian from Pontus called Marcion, who may be described as a theoretical (rather than a practising) Gnostic, adopted the Gospel of Luke with enthusiasm. It was, together with a critically edited collection of the letters of Paul, the sole New Testament book he regarded as inspired and authoritative. The Church Fathers further report that Valentinus — the most brilliant of the Christian Gnostics in Alexandria and subsequently in Rome — set enormous store by the Gospel of Luke. And Origen remarks in passing that 'all sorts of heretics ... base themselves on the Gospel of Luke.'[11]

What interests us now, however, is the fact that the 'visionary' author of the Gospel seems to have displayed an openness to those oriental, even Indian conceptions of Jesus and his work which we have examined in the more apocryphal sources.

The Vehicles of Glory

No canonical Gospel is so concerned with the childhood of Jesus as is the Gospel of Luke. And no chapters in the Gospel are so full of dreams, visions and signs as the infancy stories, where we recognize, albeit in somewhat more sober guise, the dazzling *Wunderkind* from the legends of Thomas.

Most striking of all, however, is the attestation of Luke's Jesus in the Temple by the aged seer Simeon. It has been revealed to Simeon that he will not die until he has seen the Messiah. He now recognizes the 'glory of Israel' and the 'revelation to the Gentiles' in the boy Jesus, and utters the famous verse which became known in the Latin church as the 'Nunc dimittis' ('Sovereign Lord, as you have promised, you now dismiss your servant in peace ... '). Rudolf Steiner pointed out that these happenings are like a reenactment of events which took place at the birth of the Buddha, with the coming of the sage Asita. Let us return to the poet Ashvaghosha and his account in the *Buddhacarita*:

> Then Asita, the great seer, came to the palace of the ruler of the Shakyas, thirsting for the true Dharma. He knew of the birth of him who would put at end to birth, for in his trance he had perceived the miraculous signs which had attended it. In wonderment he looked upon the wondrous royal babe ... Lying on his nurse's lap the child seemed to Asita to be like Skanda, son of Agni, on the lap of his divine mother. With tears flickering on his eyelashes the seer sighed, and looked up to the highest heaven. He then explained his agitation to the king in these words: 'It is not for him that I am perturbed, but I am alarmed because disappointed for myself. For the time has come when I must pass away, just when he is born who shall discover the extinction of birth, which is so hard to win. Uninterested in wordly affairs he will give up his kingdom. By strenuous efforts he will win that which is truly real. His gnosis will blaze forth like the sun, and remove the darkness of delusion from this world ...

Through my proficiency in the trances I can take up my
abode in the highest heaven. But even that I must regard
as a misfortune, since I shall not be able to hear this
Dharma.'[12]

The similarity between the two scenes, Christian and Buddhist,
is indeed startling. Nevertheless, Steiner also stressed the
important differences which show that Luke has remained
firmly within the Christian sphere even whilst recreating an
extraordinarily 'oriental' Imagination. The danger, evident in
the Thomas-tradition, of yielding to a wholly oriental standpoint, has been successfully resisted.

The Indian sage is left frustrated and disappointed. The
Boddhisattva has been born in order to show men how to escape
the dreary 'wheel of rebirths'; he has come to reveal a light that
will dispel the 'illusion' of this world. But Asita remains trapped
in the system from which even his trance-abilities cannot rescue
him. For him, illusory history will go on and his opportunity has
been missed. The prophet Simeon, on the other hand, is able to
die in peace. The birth of the Messiah has set in motion a train
of events in history which will glorify Israel and be a revelation
to the other nations. Here history itself has become the fulfilment of God's promise. Simeon can rest contented. It is as
though in Luke's 'Imagination' of the scene the frustration and
sense of defeat in the oriental legend has been taken up and
assuaged in the message of Christian hope.

Other elements that we recall from the apocryphal legends
occur in the story of the annunciation to the shepherds. For like
Krishna and Buddha, Luke's Messiah is not an imposing royal
figure, but a Saviour of the humble and the poor, a companion
of herdsmen and shepherds. Luke's shepherds, too, see the aura
of light or 'glory' which figured so prominently in the
Protevangelium, and hear an angel announcing the birth of the
saviour-child. In Buddhist tradition, this 'vehicle of glory' which
invests the Buddha with an atmosphere of light is referred to as
the *Nirmanakaya*. It is one of the several 'vehicles' which may be
utilized by a Buddha for the purposes of his cosmic or earthly
manifestation. Three are usually described and discussed in
Buddhist writings, and the Buddhist scholar Edward Conze has

noted that very similar conceptions are found in Christian Gnosticism, though they are there used to describe the 'vestures' which were put on by the cosmic Christ in his descent to earth and his appearance among men.[13]

The important Alexandrian Gnostic whom we have already mentioned, Valentinus, seems to have been a case in point, at least so far as we can judge from the reports of his pupils. One of these expounded a teaching which distinguished three main manifestations of the cosmic Christ. The first is the transcendental Christ, the 'fruit of all the aeons,' in the purely spiritual regions. It is he who undertakes the vast cosmic work of redemption, which includes all beings in the universe as well as men, the 'psychic' as well as the 'spiritual' — in short, all sentient beings. This corresponds, as Conze observes, to the *Dharmakaya* of Buddhist thought: it is the manifestation which works down from the spiritual world and impels the bearer on toward Enlightenment, *Nirvana*. One who wears it has become identical in his inmost being with the cosmic principle which is also the *Dharma*, the Teaching or the Way of Buddhism.

The descending Christ, secondly, put on the 'psychic Christ' who had been seen in visions and foretold by the prophets. The psychic Jesus belongs to the world of change and suffering, though he still belongs to cosmic rather than earthly realms: he is the 'suffering Jesus' of Manichaean *gnosis*, involved in the redemption of the scattered sparks of Light. He is 'still invisible' and can only manifest himself on earth through a special body, 'woven for him out of invisible, psychic substance' and rendered perceptible by 'ineffable art.' This figure, says Conze, 'is not at all dissimilar to the Buddha's intermediary body (*Sambhogakaya*) in its more cosmic interpretations.' The *Sambhogakaya* expresses the individual nature of the Enlightened being more than the transcendent 'body of Dharma.'

Finally, in the *Nirmanakaya* a Buddha appears on earth in what seems like a physical body, but is really a supernatural manifestation, an 'astral' body which can appear in various states of splendour, since it belongs to one who has passed through the stage of perfection, but voluntarily returns to teach Enlightenment to mankind. Corresponding to this, the Gnostics taught that the Christ had appeared historically and had gone through the Passion only in a *Nirmanakaya*, a 'body of transformation' or 'illusion.' In Luke such an exaggerated over-emphasis is avoided: yet it is notable that he also vividly represents the light-manifestations and heavenly glory of a supernatural being hovering about the newly-appeared child.[14] Luke's messianic infant takes on to the full the human condition, in its historical reality and its ultimate end in death. There is not for him an 'escape' from the cycle of incarnations, but an affirmation of the meaningfulness of the earth and human life. But he does come trailing those clouds of glory which had signalled Enlightenment to men in past ages, whose hopes could now be given new direction — not beyond the earth, but in the future of the earth itself.

In absorbing oriental ideas and spiritual aspirations, then, the Gospel of Luke also gives them a new Christian significance. The same conclusion meets us in a comparison of the subsequent moment in the life of Jesus which reminds us most forcefully of Buddha: the moment of the Transfiguration. Again the similarities serve to show the new meaning which has been given to archaic patterns of religious experience.

When he reached Enlightenment, under the bodhi-tree by the river Hiranya, the Buddha was transfigured. Before the eyes of Ananda and others of his disciples, the Enlightened one's body began to glow with brilliant light. His spirit moves with consummate mastery through the mystic sequence of the trance states, until he attains ultimate *gnosis*, the peace of *Nirvana*. He dies pronouncing the maxim of the unreality of all that changes, and leaves behind the illusion of his physical body which is all that remains visible to those left behind on earth. He had shown men the way of compassion, the recognition of suffering and the path of transcendence of suffering; his work was therefore complete.

When Jesus ascends the mountain with his close disciples, Peter, John and James, something similar occurs. The disciples are in an intermediate state of consciousness, struggling to carry wakefulness over into the normally unconscious areas of the psyche. When they become 'fully awake' within their trance, they see Jesus: his face is changed, he shines with light like a lightning flash, and he is in the company of the great forerunners Moses and Elijah, the lawgiver and the returning prophet. They speak of the work still to be completed, which will take Jesus to Jerusalem. A cloud of light — like the one at his birth according to the *Protevangelium* — appears and envelops Jesus. A heavenly voice proclaims him the chosen one. Then, suddenly, Jesus is alone.

At this juncture in the story of Buddha, the Enlightened one is taken beyond the sphere of ordinary humanity for ever, and his body alone remains on earth. Yet though Jesus now certainly enters upon the supernatural dimension of his work, in the presence of Moses and Elijah, at the end of the scene he still stands firmly on the earth.

Later, before his arrest and betrayal, he asks the disciples once more to stay awake while he prays to the Father that the cup of suffering may be taken from him. But they still cannot follow him to the full extent of his mission, any more than the disciples of Buddha could follow him into *Nirvana*. They lapse into exhausted sleep.

Jesus, however, does not leave the disciples then to take his own way beyond the realms of earth and earthly happenings. As Rudolf Steiner points out, 'Buddha's earthly life ends at this point, but it is here that the most important part of the life of Jesus begins — his suffering, death, and resurrection. The difference between Buddha and Christ lies in the necessity that required the life of Christ to continue beyond that of Buddha.'[15] The further deeds of Christ will not point, like the teaching of Buddha, to a transcendent archetype, a super-earthly pattern which each man must try to fulfil. They will be inscribed into the very history of the earth.

A reading of the Gospel of Luke, the visionary Gospel which approaches most nearly the oriental teaching of love and compassion of which the Buddha was an *avatar* or embodiment, shows us once more that Christian origins can only be understood against the widest spiritual background. Forms of religious experience which had been living forces of inner illumination in the East appear also in Christianity. Yet they are given a new level of significance by a spirituality that had developed in the West: a spirituality sufficiently powerful to enter into the domain of action, event and history; which gave to man the fruits of his inner development without depriving him of his earthly identity and moral individuality.

The different Gospels record different traditions about Jesus and his life. Matthew and Luke relate stories of his childhood which hardly seem to refer to the same child at all; Mark has nothing to say of the infant Jesus, but commences his Gospel with the baptism and descent of the Spirit. Taken one-sidedly, the different traditions could give rise to extreme understandings and misunderstandings of Christ's work, either divorcing him from history entirely in an oriental way, or losing the 'mythical' dimension and reducing cosmically significant happenings to the acts of an 'inspired man.' In each of the canonical Gospels, however, different themes and traditions like those we find separately in many of the apocryphal writings are woven together around a central thread. In real history as in real myth, there is never a simple either/or: complex events can be illuminated from multiple perspectives and only gain in richness and fidelity. It is time to see how some of the themes we have sounded come together in the Mystery of a myth that had taken root in the happenings of time, a mystical event that had strangely become a 'fact.'

8. The Two Messiahs

Priest, King and Messiah

The Greek-educated public of Hellenistic times constituted a world of mutual understanding. Greeks and Romans felt that they could talk to Egyptians, Syrians, even Indians, and make their viewpoint known. In matters of religion it was an age of tolerance: one could worship any god in the world, so long as the cult did not imperil state security or public morals, and everyone had a definite right to carry on ancestral customs. But there was one religion the Greeks found almost totally baffling. They could not understand the God of Judaism's claim to be worshipped to the exclusion of all others. The refusal of Jews and subsequently Christians to accept the religious festivals of the state meant that they were even branded 'atheists.' Greek writers swung between extreme evaluations of the Jews as a 'race of philosophers' and as a grossly superstitious, highly troublesome ethnic minority who needed severely bringing up to date. Their scriptures were impenetrable and Greek incomprehension almost total: a late Greek historian, Alexander Polyhistor, bit so determinedly on the wrong end of the stick that he thought Moses was a woman. The concepts of individual 'election,' of 'salvation in history,' of the 'Creation,' were so alien to Greek thought that a writer such as Luke, when he came to tell the story of Christ's appearance in Judaea, had no easy task to make the Jewish background intelligible to his readership.

There was one aspect of Judaism, however, which was immediately comprehensible. One thing that everyone could understand was a Temple and a priesthood. It is no accident that Luke is particularly interested in this aspect of Judaism, and that it strongly colours his presentation of the nature and work of the Christ. Whereas many of the other concepts applied to

Christ, such as the fulfilment of prophecies, of being a 'true prophet,' or being 'the Messiah,' seemed specially focussed on the heritage of Jews, the ideal of the Priest was finely suited to describe the universal saving activity whose unfolding Luke sets out to narrate.

The image of Temple worship establishes a frame for the whole Gospel of Luke. It begins with the 'priest named Zechariah' serving in the Temple according to the rota, the well-organized 'custom of the priesthood,' and his prophetic vision introducing the events which will set the history of salvation in motion. It ends, quite unlike the other Gospels, with the command of the risen Christ to the disciples to return to Jerusalem:

> And they returned to Jerusalem with great joy, and were continually in the Temple blessing God.

Other important incidents in the Gospel show Jesus 'in his Father's house,' that is, the Temple, to be circumcized and acknowledged by the aged prophet Simeon and the prophetess Anna, then at the age of twelve to become a 'son of the Law' — and to instruct the instructors. When he arrives again in Jerusalem in his maturity, after his long pilgrimage, Jesus is again said to be 'teaching every day in the Temple ... . Early in the morning all the people came to him in the Temple to hear him.'[1] In the Acts of the Apostles, Luke shows a marked tendency to present Christianity as the 'true Judaism,' implying that the communion with the true God which was formerly conducted in God's Temple at Jerusalem could henceforth be achieved all over the world through Christ. This means in effect that Christ is the new and universal High Priest, interceding with God on behalf of all mankind.

Precisely such a concept of Christ as the new High Priest is worked out in great detail in the New Testament in the Letter to the Hebrews, which came to be included with the letters of Paul. There we meet again the old Jebusite priest-king Melchizedek, who was so important to the Essenes and Gnostics, and whose name seems to be linked with the thread of sun-symbolism which runs, often in a hidden and esoteric manner, through the predominantly lunar religion of Judaism. Through him, in the

Letter to the Hebrews, the concept of Priesthood is elevated to metaphysical heights, for he appears, not as an ordinary priest belonging to the earthly lineage of Levi like the priests of the Jerusalem Temple, but a 'heavenly being.' We meet the idea of a spiritual priesthood transcending the significance of the local, physical priesthood on earth. In some mystical way he merges with the figure of the Christ — something now graphically represented in the Gnostic book *Melchizedek* from Nag Hammadi — and thus takes on a Messianic meaning.

But equally important, he is a manifestation of the archetypal Man who was in the beginning. Behind the visage of the mystic High Priest we also discern the image of primal, innocent Man in Paradise, in his true relation to God. 'In certain speculations about Adam,' writes a New Testament scholar, 'the priest-king assumes also the characteristics of Adam conceived as the ideal man'; and this is a matter also investigated, with extremely interesting results, as we shall see, by Rudolf Steiner.[2] It is notable that Luke provides his Jesus with a genealogy reaching back to 'Adam, the son of God' — suggesting that his Messianic ideal has little in common with the warlike King of traditional Jewish expectation, who will smash the power of the Gentiles. He seems instead to see Jesus bringing back man's paradisal state of 'sonship,' restoring his lost innocence and spreading peace over the earth. Indeed we may easily have the impression, (above all when we also read the Letter to the Hebrews,) that the image of the cosmic High Priest has become a complete Christology, expressing the themes of creation, salvation and the apocalyptic future in terms entirely independent of the other traditional ideas of Christ.

We seem to be in a different world from that occupied by the Jesus of Matthew's Gospel. Of course, it is also the spiritual dimension of kingship which we find in Matthew's vision of Christ, just as it is a spiritualized ideal of priesthood which we find in Luke. But Matthew's Jesus is undoubtedly much closer to the conventional royal Messiah of Jewish prophecy. In the *Gospel of the Hebrews*, according to Jerome, the heavenly voice at Jesus' baptism announced:

Thou art my beloved Son who reigns for ever.

This recalls those well-attested variant readings in the texts of the Gospels which quote at that juncture the kingship oracle from the time of the Israelite initiated rulers:

> Thou art my beloved Son; this day I have begotten thee.[3]

Those who had spiritual 'ears to hear' perceived in the event of Christ's baptism a recreation of something that was realized in ancient rites when a divinely illumined King was consecrated. It was in a kingly Messiah that Matthew was primarily interested, and in a Messiah who had come out of Israel. Even the title of his Gospel makes this clear: 'The book of the genealogy of Jesus the Messiah, the son of David, the son of Abraham.' He makes no effort to trace Jesus' descent back to the ideal innocent Man, as does Luke. He goes back no further than Abraham, the progenitor of the Jews, and he especially stresses the great King David, to whom God made the promise of eternal kingship for Israel.

Luke, on the other hand, seems to be working out of a completely different background. How then does his expectation fit together with the other conceptions of the Messiah? That turns out to be a fascinating story in its own right.

Mashiah is the Hebrew word meaning 'anointed.' It was applied originally and above all to the initiate rulers who were ritually anointed into their office; but it was also used in connection with priests and sometimes with prophets. The Greeks got their tongues round it as best they could and came out with *Messias*; we have followed suit in English and speak of the Messiah. But the Greeks also used their own Greek word for 'anointed,' namely *Christos*; and we in turn speak of the Christ. By the beginning of our era, the expectation of the coming of a Messiah was widespread, and figures in all the Gospels. Nevertheless we seem to have such radically different images of the Messiah, notably in the contrast between the Gospel of Matthew and the Gospel of Luke, that we must be in the presence of separate traditions. One seems to anticipate the coming of a 'priestly Messiah,' while the other expects a royal or 'kingly Messiah.'[4] That polarity turns out once more to have been grounded in the esoteric wisdom of pre-Christian religious groups, most notably the Essenes — as we can see when we examine some of the texts from the Dead Sea Scrolls and the extraordinary *Testaments of the Patriarchs*.

The Messiah of Aaron and the Messiah of Israel

The collection of short documents called the *Testaments of the Twelve Patriarchs* is an Essene work, though it was probably written somewhat earlier than most of the texts that have come down to us from Qumran, perhaps during the reign of John Hyrcanus in the latter half of the second century BC. It belongs to the phase of Essene history when the Hasmonaean rulers still seemed to offer the hope of a spiritually restored Israel. (What appear to be later insertions show a contrasting disillusionment with the priesthood existing on earth.) The *Testaments* probably originated in Syria. Fragments of them have been found in Aramaic at the Essene settlement at Qumran.

They take the form of dying speeches by each of the twelve sons of Jacob (also called Israel) to their sons and descendants the twelve tribes of Israel, counselling good behaviour, reflecting on life's vicissitudes and prophesying the future. At numerous points they mention the coming of a Messiah: but so difficult and obscure is the language they use in regard to his nature that they were only understood properly when the discovery of the later Qumran Scrolls had made the Essene doctrine explicit. It then transpired that the Essenes had expected not one, but two Messiahs.

The text of the *Testaments* can now be read with greater confidence, and the confusions brought in by copyists (and perhaps by a later Christian editor) can be removed. It reveals that a Messiah is to arise from the seed of two of Israel's sons:

> For the Lord will raise up from Levi a High Priest, and
> from Judah a King, who will save all the gentiles and the
> tribe of Israel.[5]

Levi was the ancestor of all the priestly clans of Israel (the Levites); likewise Judah was associated with the line of the monarchy of Israel. The early Essenes thus expected that the spiritual and temporal jurisdiction of God's chosen nation would be extended in the end-time to cover all the earth. Particularly interesting is a dream of one of the other patriarchs, Naphtali, in which he sees Levi, the Priest, reach out and grasp the sun; Judah, the King, grasps hold of the moon. Now Judaism regulated its calendar and its outward festivals by the moon, while the Essenes used the Enochian sun-calendar: hence the meaning of the dream seems to be that the King Messiah will be a more exoteric figure, whose domain is the extemal life of the nations, while the Priest Messiah is linked with that secret 'sun'-strain which comes to the surface now and again in Judaism, as in the case of the heavenly priest Melchizedek.[6] Both of them, however, are decidedly cosmic figures.

The kingly Messiah's coming is described fairly briefly. He is the 'star' which shall arise out of Jacob. He is the 'scion' or 'shoot' of the plant of God, the 'fountain of life for all humanity' and the 'rod of righteousness for the nations.' The advent of the priestly Messiah, on the other hand, occasions a long hymnic celebration:

> Then the Lord will raise up a new Priest
> to whom all the words of the Lord will be revealed.
> He shall effect the judgment of truth over the
>   earth for many days.
> And his star shall rise in heaven like a king;
> kindling the light of knowledge as day is
>   illumed by the sun.
> And he shall be extolled by the whole inhabited world.
> This one will shine forth like the sun in the earth;
> he shall take away all darkness from under heaven,
> and there shall be peace in all the earth.
> The heavens shall greatly rejoice in his days
> and the earth shall be glad;
> the clouds will be filled with joy
> and the knowledge of the Lord will be poured out on
>   the earth like the water of the seas.
> And the angels of glory of the Lord's presence
>   will be made glad by him.

Also prominent is the theme of Adamic restoration, the removal of the 'fiery sword' which after the Fall barred man's way back into Paradise:

> In his priesthood sin shall cease
> and lawless men shall rest from their evil deeds,
> and righteous men shall find rest in him.
> And he shall open the gates of Paradise;
> he shall remove the sword that has threatened since Adam,
> and he will grant to the saints to eat of the Tree of Life.
> The spirit of holiness shall be upon them.[7]

Plainly, for the Essenes it was the priestly Messiah whose work stood on the higher plane. The kingly Messiah would hardly do more than prepare the way.

The Essene evaluation is confirmed by the Qumran Scrolls. It would appear that the teaching about two Messiahs belonged to the esoteric knowledge of the sect, since the *Damascus Document* intended for the lay members scattered through the towns and villages of Palestine makes no mention of it. In the other documents, however, the two Messiahs are always distinguished. The kingly Messiah is again 'the shoot of David,' and pre-eminently 'the Messiah of Israel' who will bring death to the ungodly and establish 'the Kingdom of his people.' More important, however, is the priestly Messiah: he is the 'Messiah of Aaron' — Aaron having been a priest and companion of Moses — and thus 'the Priest,' and 'the Interpreter of the Law.' He will 'teach righteousness at the end of days.' The kingly Messiah is to defer to his judgment, and the judgment of the priesthood in general, in all matters of the Law. The so-called *Messianic Anthology* in the Dead Sea Scrolls refers to various Old Testament proof-texts from which the Essenes derived scriptural support for their dual teaching.[8]

The discovery of the Essene expectation of two Messiahs throws considerable light on the background of the Gospels. It helps explain how the Gospel writers came to utilize such different traditions and created such divergent images of Jesus while agreeing that he was the Messiah. For originally these traditions actually referred to different figures. Startling as it may at first seem, the religious groups who like the Essenes created and guarded the traditions about the coming of a Messianic Priest and a King Messiah expected them to be fulfilled by separate individuals. Before the discovery of the Dead Sea Scrolls, the only clear statement of this double expectation was in the writings and lectures based on Rudolf Steiner's researches.

Hardly has this Mystery been established, however, before we begin to hear about a deeper secret. For it is hinted that, after all, the two roles of Priest and King must merge into one.

Already in some of the *Testaments of the Patriarchs* we find a teaching of a single agent of redemption 'from Levi and Judah,' priest and king in one. We saw in an earlier chapter that certain of the Hasmonaeans attempted to realize in their own persons this dream of restoring the union of king and priest presumed to have existed in primordial times. The signal failure of the Hasmonaean rulers to raise their conception of the role to a sufficiently high spiritual plane perhaps explains why in the later Essene texts, which we know from Qumran, the hope of a single embodiment of priesthood and kingship seems to have receded. We do not find the hope explicitly again until we read it expressed in a Christian writer, Hippolytus, who evidently knew the Essene secret teaching and saw it fulfilled in Jesus. He interpreted the different genealogies of Jesus advanced in the Gospels to signify the coming together of two lineages, each with its prophetic justification.

In his commentary *On the Benedictions of Isaac, Jacob and Moses* Hippolytus writes:

> (It was prophesied) that the Christ would be born,
> according to his bodily descent, from the tribe of Levi,
> from the priestly order, from the house of Aaron ...

Yet the usual tradition makes the Messiah a royal figure, descended from Judah! Hippolytus, however, is in possession of prophecies which he believes can reconcile the two versions:

> For we have found it written that the Christ must also
> appear from the tribe of Levi, as a priest of the Father,

from a commingling of the tribe of Judah with the tribe of
Levi, so that the Son of God should be made known from
both as King and as Priest.[9]

The scriptural derivation of the dual promise from the blessings
uttered by Moses in the book of Deuteronomy is exactly that
employed in the Essene *Messianic Anthology*. It is therefore a virtually definite assumption that the Essene teaching has been
handed down within Christianity, and is being made known by
Hippolytus. We know too that the *Testaments of the Patriarchs*
were prepared for use by Christians. And after Hippolytus'
time, the idea was accepted and taken up by the highly influential Ambrose in his book *On the Patriarchs*. We are therefore in
the presence of a line of Essene secret teaching which continued
within Christian circles.

Despite the efforts of Essenes and Christians to uncover the
germ of their Messianic hopes in the earlier parts of the Old
Testament, on the other hand, history shows that the notion of a
priestly advent was actually a relatively late development in
Judaism. The prophetic oracle promising that 'the Lord whom
you seek will suddenly come to his Temple' (Mal.3:1) was
among the latest to be added to the Old Testament canon of
scripture. And the teaching about the fusion of the roles of King
and Priest, like so much else in Essenism, was inspired by ideas
emanating from Iran.

An old Iranian legend relates that Ohrmazd approached the
first man Jamshid, and offered to him the total revelation of the
divine, including all that was later to be made known through
Zarathustra as 'the Good Religion.' But Jamshid refused the revelation of the Religion, and accepted only that part which was
the sacred Kingship. Ohrmazd granted him the Kingship, and in
fact had known through his omniscience that Jamshid would
refuse the Religion destined for the prophet Zarathustra. But his
offer had established an ideal: the eventual unity of the
Kingship and the Religion; though Ohrmazd knew that the long
struggle against Ahriman, the Destructive Spirit, was still to be
fought, and that the union of the two forces for good would only
come after long ages and would mean the end of Ahriman.
Therefore the Zoroastrians still teach:

The thing against which the Destructive Spirit struggles most violently is the coming together in full force of the dignities of Kingship and the Good Religion in one person, because such a conjunction must destroy him.

Here the word for 'dignity' is the same as for the aura of light, the 'glory' (*khvarnah*) seen around a sacred person. The text goes on:

For if the highest power of the dignity of Kingship had been joined to the highest power of the dignity of the Good Religion in Jamshid, or if the highest power of the dignity of Kingship as it existed in Jamshid had been joined to the highest dignity of the Good Religion in Zarathustra, then the Destructive Spirit would have met with swift destruction, creation would have escaped from the Aggressor, and the desired Rehabilitation would have been brought about in the two worlds ... When these two dignities meet in one man, then will the Aggressor be completely vanquished and creation saved and purged; from this the final Rehabilitation proceeds. The Good Religion reveals that these two dignities will meet together in the Saoshyant.[10]

Thus it is in the Zoroastrian 'Saviour' that the unity of Priesthood and Kingship will be accomplished. A pattern was established which deeply influenced the esoteric thought of the Essenes concerning the Messiahs, the Priest and King, and the union of both in a single overwhelming figure.

It is fascinating to read Rudolf Steiner's description of how the twin ideals came together, as a matter of historical occurrence, in the development of Jesus of Nazareth from his childhood to the point where he accepted the astonishing responsibility of his mission.[11] His account has only gained in force and relevance with the modern discoveries which have confirmed so much of what he had to say. For there survive, from the world of Gnosticism and early Christianity, several fragmentary 'Imaginations' of the process whereby, in the words of the apocryphal *Gospel of the Egyptians*, 'the two shall become one' and bring about the coming of the Kingdom.[12]

'When Two Become One'

Our first Imagination comes from the remnants of an early Gnostic book attributed to one Justin. The reports of it are rather garbled, despite the fact that we have a series of direct quotations from it, and we know that the title of it was *Baruch*.

Fundamentally it concerns itself with a now familiar theme, the twelve incarnations of the Illuminator, who is here described as an 'angelic' being and who bears the name Baruch. 'What has happened is that Baruch has been identified, in a Jewish-Gnostic circle, with Zarathustra and has been viewed as the Emissary and son of God.'[13] Now 'Baruch' is in fact nothing more than a title, meaning 'the Blessed,' which has been applied honorifically to Zarathustra as the returning 'true Prophet,' the Illuminator. There is in the fragments of Justin no trace of the confusion which crept into the tradition, based on the unfortunate coincidence that the friend and scribe of Jeremiah in the Bible bore the name Baruch. In Jewish and Syriac apocryphal writings this caused havoc when the esoteric ideas of the *Baruch*-mysticism were not properly grasped. It even led, for example, to the bizarre notion that Baruch the Scribe had apostasized from Judaism and had written the Iranian scriptures known as the *Avesta*! In the long-continued tradition which saw in Zarathustra a prophet of Christianity, as often as not Zarathustra was identified with this scribe Baruch.

From all this nonsense Justin's *gnosis* was entirely free. His book was clearly a description of the twelve appearances on earth of the Blessed One, the true Prophet. He was an 'angelic' being (cf. 'nurtured in the heavens,' his origin according to the *Apocalypse of Adam*) who came to bring enlightenment to men. (In order to make the significance of his twelve incarnations clear to pagan readers, however, at some stage a comparison was made with the mythological 'twelve labours of Hercules': this too seems to have been misunderstood in subsequent reports on Justin's book.)

Of particular interest to us here, on the other hand, is again the incarnation which follows the last of the twelve 'labours' — that is, the thirteenth, when the Blessed One was again dispatched by

Elohim, which for Justin is a name for the world-creator God, who in his turn points toward the highest nature of the Godhead, called simply 'the Good.' For:

> Last of all, 'in the days of Herod the king,' Baruch was once more sent down as an emissary of Elohim. When he came to Nazareth, he found Jesus the son of Joseph and Mary, as a twelve-year-old boy tending sheep. And he proclaimed to him all that had happened from the beginning of the world ... and what was to happen in the future.
>
> And he said, 'All the prophets before you allowed themselves to be led astray (by the powers of the world). Take heed, Jesus, Son of Man, and do not allow yourself to be led astray, but proclaim this word to men, and tell them what concerns God and the Good, and ascend to the Good and enthrone yourself there by the side of Elohim, the Father of us all.'
>
> And Jesus obeyed the angel and said, 'Lord, all this will I do,' and he preached.[14]

In so remarkable a Gnostic 'Imagination' several features stand out and demand comment. For in the first place, we have something here quite different from the birth-legends of the Illuminator, culminating in his birth as Jesus, found in the *Apocalypse of Adam*. No mention is made of his being born. Moreover, the Jesus described here is plainly not the royal child of Matthew's tradition, to whom the Iranian Magi came to bear witness. His peaceful occupation tending sheep in the hills above Nazareth, and the specific quotation 'in the days of Herod the king,' make it plain that this is Luke's Jesus, the friend of the lowly who on those very hills was proclaimed to the shepherds. Moreover, the scene is exactly prefigured by Jesus' priestly ancestor and prototype Levi in the *Testaments of the Patriarchs*:

> I was a youth, about twenty years old ... As I was tending sheep in Abel-Meholah, a spirit of understanding from the Lord came upon me ... and behold, the heavens were

opened, and an angel of the Lord spoke to me: 'Levi, Levi, enter!'[15]

It is in the course of his visions that Levi received his divine commission to be a priest.

The Jesus of our Gnostic 'Imagination' is already twelve years old when he feels the presence of Zarathustra steal upon him on the lonely hills. The age must certainly be significant: it is the age at which Jesus must be taken to the Temple to be made a 'son of the Law,' but when he reveals himself to be enlightened already beyond the understanding of the teachers. The incident forms the climax of the *Infancy Gospel of Thomas*, and is of course included in the Gospel of Luke. It seems that we are expected to see in that well-documented event the point at which Jesus began to preach in obedience to the angelic Illuminator now present within him. It must reflect the moment, in other words, when 'the two became one.'[16]

The other Imagination preserved for us in Gnostic sources comes from that late Gnostic miscellany called the *Pistis Sophia*. Once more it describes an incident from Jesus' childhood, put into the mouth of Mary. She narrates it in order to explain the fulfilment of the saying, 'Mercy and truth are met together, righteousness and peace have kissed each other; truth has flourished on the earth, and righteousness has looked down from heaven':

> When you were small, before the Spirit had come upon you, while you were with Joseph in one of the vineyards, the Spirit came from on high and came to me in my house, looking like you, and I did not recognize him, and I thought that it was you. And the Spirit said to me, 'Where is Jesus, my brother, that I may meet him?' When he said this to me, I was perplexed and thought that it was a ghost come to tempt me. And I seized him and bound him to the foot of the bed which is in my house, until I went out to you both, to you and Joseph in the field and found you in the vineyard, while Joseph was fencing-in the vineyard.
>
> Now it happened that you heard what I said to Joseph, and when you understood you were glad, and said,

'Where is he, that I may see him? for I await him in this place.' And it happened that, when Joseph heard you say these words, he was perplexed, and we went up together, entered the house, and found the Spirit bound to the bed. And we looked at you, and at him, and found that you resembled him. And when he who was bound to the bed was freed, he embraced you and kissed you, and you kissed him, and you both became one.[17]

In these somewhat anecdotal reflections on the part of the mother of Jesus, it yet may be that we possess a refraction of esoteric and Gnostic traditions concerning what happened to Jesus at the age of twelve.

More important, we can see how behind these 'images' of Jesus stand whole traditions. They are 'Imaginations' which grew out of and summed up currents of both popular and esoteric religious thought in the centuries before Christ: ideas about a miraculous 'divine child,' about a Messianic Priest, about a 'true Prophet' or angelic Illuminator, about a Kingly Messiah, about an Enlightened Being, about an earthly agent who would reveal God's power in history. The amazing thing is the way these 'images' formed themselves around the figure of Jesus of Nazareth, who seems to stand as at the centre of a vortex of ideas and hopes.

Against this backcloth of myth and history it is time to return to our question about Jesus himself. What was his own vision? How did he relate to the many roles envisaged for him by Essenes and other seers? Who is this Jesus, Son of Man?

9. Christianity and Consciousness: the Son of Man

Strange though it might appear, the task of reconstructing the teaching of Jesus and his spiritual development, which might seem an obvious and, on the basis of the Gospels, a straightforward task, has scarcely been addressed until very recent times — and almost always raises more problems than it solves. We have seen that the evangelist set out to interpret Christ's saving work against a variety of cultural and religious backgrounds — for instance, Jewish, Essene, Hellenistic-Oriental — and to show his life and utterances as a part of his mission. None of them makes the attempt to epitomize his teaching as such.

On the other hand, there certainly are many passages in the Gospels which repeat traditions of the words of Jesus. In fact, we know that collections of 'Sayings of the Lord' constituted the earliest prototypes of the Gospel form. The type is itself preserved in the Nag Hammadi *Gospel of Thomas,* consisting of sayings attributed to Jesus with very little in the way of narrative indications, for most sayings none at all, and this together with other evidence has prompted the view that the *Gospel* contains authentic and early materials. Many of *Thomas'* sayings were already known from the canonical Gospels, which in turn agree upon a large number of utterances which they ascribe to Jesus. Hence, unless we are determined to adopt an extreme position of scepticism with regard to all the records, we do seem to have at our disposal some corroborated evidence by which to infer, at least to some extent, how the utterer of the sayings saw himself — in contradistinction to how the evangelists saw him.

Moreover, on the basis of the Gospel traditions, we can in principle point to a series of decisive spiritual experiences which appear to have shaped Jesus' awareness of himself and his role.

Of Jesus' childhood we have mentioned a number of stories, differing in plausibility and to be found in apocryphal gospels as well as in those of Matthew and Luke. Their real importance is that they express the hopes and religious conceptions of the society in which Jesus grew up: they point to the world of the Essenes, linked mysteriously to the visionary universe of Zoroastrianism and the Magi; or to the expectations of a divine 'wonder-child' like those of oriental mythology. But there is obviously no way of telling how Jesus responded to such ideas. All we can say is that, quite early on, they found a place in the traditions of Christianity and indeed in the New Testament canon.

When it comes to the ideals of 'kingship' and 'priesthood,' we reach firmer ground. From the words and deeds of the mature Jesus we know that these conceptions had formed part of his own self-awareness. There are many places in which Jesus points to himself as a kingly Messiah — although he always tends to shift its meaning, indicating the spiritual essence of kingship, rather than the political hero of popular Jewish messianism. His is a kingdom 'not of this world.'[1] Jesus inherits the spiritual dimension of the cosmic kingship which belonged to the initiate-rulers of the ancient Near East, and lifts it to a new level of universalism. When he made his triumphal entry into Jerusalem riding 'on an ass and on a colt, the foal of an ass,' he certainly knew that he was fulfilling the kingly oracle of Zechariah (9:9). So did the people who strewed palms before him and hailed the Davidic royal Messiah ('Hosanna to the Son of David'). There was no doubt in the minds of the Jewish officials when they brought him to be tried before Pilate that Jesus had claimed to be 'the King of the Jews,' and that is what, according to the tradition, was inscribed in three languages on the Cross.

But there is evidence that in Jesus' mind his kingly and Messianic role was modified by the ideal of the 'High Priest.' Oscar Cullmann has shown that the Melchizedekian priest of Psalm 110 is interpreted by Jesus in reference to himself. Thus we have to reckon with the strong probability that 'the idea was not foreign to Jesus that he had also to fulfil the office of the true high priesthood ... Is it not significant that Jesus applies to himself a saying about the eternal High Priest precisely when he stands before the Jewish high priest and is questioned by him concerning his claim to be the Messiah? He says in effect that his messiahship is not that of an earthly Messiah ... but that he is the heavenly Son of Man and the heavenly High Priest. This saying is thus parallel to that in the Gospel of John in which Jesus tells Pilate that his kingship is not of this world (John 18:36). He tells the earthly ruler that his government is not earthly; he tells the earthly high priest that his priesthood is not earthly.'[2] Instead, he claims to embody the essence of Priesthood, freed from its external forms.

In this case, then, Jesus' self-consciousness seems itself to have been moulded by the images and ideas we have seen presented by the different evangelists in earlier chapters. He presents himself as the fulfilment of the great twin ideals of ancient religious life, 'kingship' and 'priesthood,' both of them having a profound dimension of archaic myth and experience as well as a long history in Israel and the ancient East. And since it figures in several lines of tradition, including the canonical Gospel of Luke, there is no real reason to reject the account of Jesus' remarkable 'awakening' at around the age of twelve when, in the terms of our last chapter, 'the two became one' and the future role that he was to play began to be focussed in Jesus' mind: so much so that he could say memorable things to those whom he found in 'his Father's house,' the Temple.

The impetus to go out and begin his ministry came, however, after some further time. Jesus, as it now appears, was in touch during the intervening time with the Essenes and their teachings. But it was his baptism by John which evidently opened up a new depth to Jesus' calling. From the original *Gospel of the Hebrews* we gather that the event was somehow a royal proclamation, of Jesus' spiritual kingship. All accounts agree that it was a revelation of Jesus' heavenly origin: the Spirit descended upon him at that moment, as is impressively related at the beginning of the Gospel of Mark. After it, according to the *Gospel of the Hebrews*, Jesus referred to 'my mother the Holy Spirit.' But with this revelation that he is henceforth the bearer of the Christ, and thus the full scope of his mission, came also the experience of the Temptation. The accession of a new level of consciousness also brings with it new problems, new burdens and new dangers. He goes out into the wilderness, there to struggle with the hostile powers.

Beyond Judaism: Consciousness and Temptation

> At once the Spirit sent him out into the desert; and he was
> in the desert for forty days, being tempted by Satan. He
> was with the wild animals, and angels attended him.[3]

In terms of mainstream Judaism, the forces against which Jesus
has to struggle in the wilderness are aspects of 'Satan,' the Devil
— the power of evil which succeeded in enticing the first man
Adam, to sin. Since the time of Adam's fall, all men had been
born already under the sway of these forces (the doctrine later
called 'original sin').

In the more esoteric and apocalyptic literature of Judaism,
'this world' into which we are born is regarded in a much more
thoroughgoing way as being presently under the sway of evil
powers; only in the future 'world to come' will God's rule be
manifested here below. The full development of these apocalyptic ideas came about under the influence of Iran and its mythi-
calcosmological dualism. We have seen how this shaped the
Essene thought-world. Judaism had always had a myth of the
tempter, Lucifer as he was later called, who destroys man's
proper relationship to God by inflating him in pride and sensu-
ality. Alongside this idea in Essene and apocalyptic writings,
however, is a demonology enriched by the notion of a power
like that of Ahriman, the Zoroastrian daemon of darkness and
alienation, another aspect of 'Satan,' and the vision of a world
governed by 'spiritual forces of evil in the heavenly spaces' as
well as in the soul of man.

The spiritual currents of Iran and Judaism again flowed
together in the nightmare vision of evil powers. The import of
Jesus' struggle therefore only becomes clear when set against
the history of consciousness. For the 'hostile powers' represent
the dangers and temptations inherent in man's evolviong sense
of individuality. We sketched at the outset of this book some
aspects of the development of Judaism — the religion which
records most profoundly man's discovery of the individual
moral self, emerging out of the mythic participation in a divine
order experienced by the ancient East. In Judaism man entered

into a more individualized relationship to the divine, responding to the ethical challenge of the prophets, who spoke
Yahweh's commandments, and helping to shape the historical
destiny of Yahweh's people. But the sense of greater individuality brought with it the temptation to value the self too highly, to
lapse into self-centredness or even self-worship ('You shall be as
God ...' promises the Tempter). That temptation always forms
one pole of the Jewish consciousness in its most characteristic
manifestations.

Its polar opposite, and counterpart, is the sense of guilt: for
just as the self can assert itself too much, aggrandize itself into
God, so it can also be tortured by the sense of its shortcomings
in the face of the exalted demands of the Father. The individuality of man in Judaism is measured against the scale of 'righteousness,' an absolute scale against which every man must
ultimately fall short and therefore experience the pangs of guilt.
The myth of the 'original sin' of Adam and so of all men who
have followed him embodies the important truth that these two
poles, of guilt and pride, are inherent in the very condition of
becoming individual. No man who develops that sense of moral
identity which was cultivated in Judaism can live without the
temptation to the one and the inevitable acknowledgement of
the other.

But being individual in the Jewish way had other consequences. For it did not only affect man's inner being, but also his
experience of the cosmos. To ancient man, the cosmos around
him had been a fullness of divine activity, the domain of timeless myths which were ever being re-enacted. Man experienced
his own being in that process, and conceived of himself only in
relation to the spiritual totality of what he still experienced in
the mythical cosmos. But when Judaic man began to find himself and his God in the 'still small voice' of inwardness, things
changed: the outer cosmos was drained of its indwelling mythical powers and was perceived as a 'finished work,' the end-
product of creative activity that was now inert, fixed, no longer
full of the divine. The ancient East, and the Iranians in particular, had dreaded that kind of experience of the world above all
else. They attributed the sense of the inertness and otherness of
things to the malignant spirit of Darkness, Ahriman, and they

did everything possible to preserve their original perception of the divine fullness associated with Ohrmazd and his angels of Light, the Bounteous Immortals. It was Ahriman who estranged man from the participation he originally knew in the cosmic whole, and imprisoned him in the loneliness of himself.

The Jews coped with the sense of alienation and loneliness in a quite different way. We saw in an earlier chapter how they evolved the doctrine of Creation: in short, they were taught never to look at the material world, inert and finished as it was, without remembering that it was linked to the divine by that relation of 'createdness,' that it was the sublime product of a Being whose unfathomable greatness it only served to throw into relief. Magnificent and great as the creation was, it pointed to One still higher and greater. The sense of Yahweh as Father and Creator thus effectively shielded the Jews from having to face the full consequences of alienation. They did not have to confront a universe experienced as fully Ahrimanic, because they derived an inner strength and reassurance from their awe of the Creator. Their inner gaze was diverted from the fact of the outwardness and inertness of mere things as such, and was turned instead to the transcendent, paternal figure of Yahweh.

The Jewish consciousness of individuality, in essence, could emerge historically because the religious forms of Judaism provided a suitable 'shelter' in which it could be cultivated. Man could begin to foster the sense of individual consciousness in Judaism without having to bear the full burden of alienation, the vision of the Ahrimanic, which was still carried for him by the paternal deity. Part of the price of individuality in this form, however, was that man was left with a sense of inadequacy and guilt: his proper relationship to God could not be achieved in the present, but was awaited at the end of history when the Messiah would be victorious and the forces of Adam's 'original sin' would no longer have power over men. Jewish eschatology, that is, its teaching about the end of time, of history, thus also arises inevitably out of the Jewish consciousness. At the end of time the present framework of things would be broken, and a more integral state succeed.

In the large-scale and historical evolution of consciousness it is the same as in individual development. Evolution cannot be held back. A person cannot remain for ever under fatherly protection, but reaches a stage where he wishes — even demands — to make his own way and solve his own problems. It is the same in regard to the larger context where humanity faces the ultimate problems of existence and shapes forms of life, of culture and belief. Judaism had fostered a degree of individual consciousness unprecedented in the history of the ancient world, albeit its individualism was still limited by the paternal concept of Yahweh and the resulting solidarity of all the 'children of Abraham,' and the greater part of the burden of individual awareness in regard to the outer cosmos was still borne by the Creator. It was inevitable, that on the basis of Judaism a demand would arise for a further step in egohood, by which the individual would resolve to shoulder those very burdens of which Judaism relieved him. For if that could be done, man would no longer need to measure himself against an external rule and atone in guilt. He would overcome the limitations and inherent problems of Judaic consciousness at the same time as he took upon himself the burdens which the God of Judaism had carried for his children. Man would be able to achieve his proper relationship to the world and the spirit here and now, and live out of his deepest truth.

Such a further step on consciousness would be a momentous event. Yet there is evidence that by the time of Christian origins a portion of humanity had reached the stage of demanding it. Naturally enough they were mainly Jews — although it is true that parallel developments of consciousness had also taken place in different ways elsewhere, for example on the basis of Greek rationalism.[4] If, however, they were to take the further step in awareness which we have suggested, it is obvious that they would need resources beyond those offered by ordinary Jewish tradition.

Judaism had long wrestled with the problems of man's inner being, with the themes of pride and temptation; conceivably an extension of Jewish thought pure and simple could therefore have brought a new solution to one side of the problem. What was needed was a means by which man could break through to the deeper layers of his own being: for it is by acting out of his deepest, most authentic nature, resisting the superficial distortions of his being which always tend to influence him, that man attains the essential autonomy and egohood we have described. And in fact what developed was a new, a Jewish form of initiation. We have already spoken at length about the new form of initiation: it was the form evolved by the Essenes. For the Essene Mystery, as we remarked, placed the individual spirit as a moral agent between the Two Spirits, the light and the dark. It did not overwhelm man's identity in an oriental 'cosmic consciousness' but allowed man to discover and act out of his deepest individual being. Although inspired by initiation-practices from further East, this 'individualism' of the Essene initiation was the uniquely Jewish contribution to the Mystery and could only have come into being on Jewish soil.

Yet in stepping forward from the limited individualism of traditional Jewish spirituality, man did not only have to deal with the difficulties of the inner self. He had also to accept the burden of alienation in the outer cosmos which had formerly been lifted for him by the paternal God of the creation. And here he needed resources from quite outside the Jewish tradition. For it was rather in Iran that the sages had evolved spiritual ways of defending man from the terrifying experience of the Ahrimanic, of the loneliness and estrangement which the individual knows when he faces the full reality of his 'separateness.' That terror of alienation could be fought, the Iranian sages had found, by means of the forces awakened in the soul through a cosmic initiation. By bringing man into contact with the psychic powers that had governed man in the stage of his mythological consciousness, giving him a sense of cosmic participation, they could liberate man again from the overwhelming fear of the Ahrimanic. In Judaism, the doctrine of Creation had eliminated the necessity for a cosmic initiation; but when man attempted to go beyond the framework of Judaism and shoulder his own existential burdens it was inevitable that he should need to call upon powers like those of the ancient cosmic initiations once more. A new form of 'mythological' consciousness had to be developed. We can therefore begin to see why Iranian thought proved so valuable to those who were involved in the awakening of a new consciousness going beyond Judaism. For it was there that they could find the spiritual resources for the outer, cosmic side of that evolution in awareness. We have seen that it was the Gnostics who did most, historically speaking, to preserve the Mystery of Cosmic Man into the time of which we are speaking. It was among the Gnostics that the cosmic, mythical dimension of human experience was continued, still inspired by the spirit of ancient Iranian thought.

Two streams of development thus come before us, both immensely significant for the history of consciousness: the Essene Mystery of the individual moral spirit and the Gnostic revelation of the cosmic dimension of man's experience. But neither of them is yet sufficient for the tremendous further step into egohood.

The Essene Mystery allowed man to discover himself as a moral agent, but still held to the Jewish framework of the Creation and the sinfulness of guilty man when he did not live up to the Essene code of righteousness. The Gnostic revelation still succeeded in overcoming the Ahrimanic only by eliminating the sense of self in man, regarding consciousness as a 'counterfeit' of the spirit and the objective universe as the product of a false God, a Demiurge. The Essenes were too much confined to history and inwardness to break through to the dimension of myth. The Gnostics were too absorbed in the myth to come to a positive understanding of objective consciousness and history. What was needed was a fusion of myth with history: and that was to come about for the first time in Christianity. There for the first time we encounter historical events with the scope and resonance of myth, and with the power of myth to work within and to transform. And it is in Jesus that we witness the discovery of the new consciousness.

The description in the Gospel traditions of Jesus' struggle with the powers of evil and temptation can be understood as the story of a consciousness struggling with the new dangers and tendencies that fully achieved egohood brings with it. He does indeed have to wrestle with powers which have kept a hold on man from the moment he began to assume individual awareness within the framework of Judaism, and with the Ahrimanic estrangement which was known in the Mysteries of Iran and overcome through a cosmic — initiation. Now it has to be overcome by one who does not thereby give up his individuality.

And this indeed is what Jesus undertakes after his baptism, which is thus in the fullest sense an initiation into a higher mode of being and awareness. Alone in the wilderness of alienation (in Greek it is literally 'the solitude'), Jesus also resists the temptation to inner pride and triumphs through the strength of his new Christ-Self.

It is part of the central importance of Rudolf Steiner's spiritual description of the evolution of consciousness that he has brought before us the importance of the discovery of this Self in Christianity, and its consequences even for our future history. The old ideal of the initiate-king has been raised to a new and more inward level, that of the individual spiritual Self, and no longer looks back to an atavistic loss of identity. The 'Kingdom of Heaven' is to be achieved, not through outward action, but by a breakthrough in consciousness.

What, asks Steiner, was the result of Jesus' experience and his struggle in the wilderness? 'The natural result was the preaching of the Kingdom. The Gospel of Matthew therefore relates the Temptation first and then proceeds to describe the stages of the ascent of the Self, the 'I,' that henceforth will be able consciously to experience in itself the spiritual world. The secret of the 'I' that, in accordance with the mode of consciousness prevailing in the external world, rises into the spiritual world — this secret... was now to be unveiled through the Christ Being during the time following the Temptation.'[5] That, says Steiner, is the meaning of the teaching of the Kingdom.

Since Steiner's day, it has come to be widely accepted that the teaching of the Kingdom did indeed stand at the centre of Jesus' teaching. Rudolf Bultmann particularly emphasized it, and in his 'phenomenological' paraphrase of the New Testament concept he went far in understanding the immense demand upon self-consciousness which is made in this aspect of Christ's teaching.[6] It is to be regretted that in other respects Bultmann pushed his critical approach to unrealistic extremes in the interpretation of Jesus' own role, and that he failed to understand the significance of 'myth' in any but a negative sense. But in regard to this, the exoteric teaching of Jesus, the preaching of the Kingdom, he brought the force of his insight to bear in a fruitful and valuable way.

In order to understand more fully Jesus' relation to the Kingdom, however, and the way he spoke of himself in connection with its coming, we must turn to another central idea: the Son of Man.

The Son of Man

When we study the New Testament it soon becomes apparent that in this riddling phrase, the Son of Man, is hidden a key to Jesus' own vision of his task, its sources and its aims. Although he accepted elements of a Kingly and a Priestly messianic role, it is notable how often in the Gospels when questioned about himself Jesus replies with a saying about 'the Son of Man.' The fact is thrown into relief by the equally striking discovery that the phrase is hardly used by anyone else in the New Testament — or for that matter in other early Christian literature. The Church Fathers make no use of it in their theologies, any more than do the evangelists who employ it solely when reporting Jesus' own words. Not surprisingly, modern scholarship has responded to these mysterious silences with enthusiastic speculation and critical research.[7]

Now Jesus of course spoke, not in Greek but in Aramaic: the researchers have therefore quite rightly pointed to the corresponding phrase in the Semitic tongue of which 'Son of Man' is a slavish equivalent, namely *bar nasha* (corresponding in turn to the older Hebrew form *ben Adam*). The words mean quite literally 'son of man,' that is, a man, in accordance with a particular kind of idiom much used in Semitic languages, as for example a liar would be a 'son of lying' or a wicked man a 'son of wickedness.' The phrase therefore denotes in the widest sense a man as such — and indeed there are places where *bar nasha* seems to have been translated into Greek simply as 'Man,' rather than by the unidiomatic foreign phrase.

Specialists in these matters have also established that the phrase was used in a particular way in the language of Jesus' time, namely as a way of saying 'I' — somewhat as we can refer to ourselves on occasion as 'number one' for instance: so an Aramaic speaker could under certain conditions refer to himself by saying 'the Son of Man,' This was especially so when what one said about oneself was generally applicable to men as such, implying not only that I could do it but so could any man. One or two extremists have gone on to conclude that 'the Son of Man' is of no interest from the point of view of religious thought, since it was simply Jesus' Aramaic way of sometimes saying 'I.' However, a wider look at the problem soon suggests that this solution is too simple. The very fact that the phrase was transmitted in early tradition in a very literal rendering surely means that a special significance was accorded to it. And there are scholars who point to a very different background from that immediately suggested by linguistic considerations.

We have seen in earlier chapters of this book that there were ancient Near Eastern religions, Mysteries, centred on the figure of a cosmic Man. The king, who was so to speak the Man on earth, might often be referred to as his Son. The royal initiation rites can thus be seen, from one perspective, as a ritual enactment in which the Man confers power and glory upon his earthly Son. Such language was certainly used of the earthly representative, the Son of the heavenly Man, and we have seen that connected with Luke's presentation of the ideal High Priest, for example, are themes linking the Christ to the First Man, as in the genealogy tracing back Jesus' ancestry to Adam, son of God. It thus seems possible that Jesus himself was using language drawn from the Mysteries of the First Man, and that this lies behind the strange emphasis which he gives to the phrase *bar nasha* in his words about himself.

Arguments between the opposing schools of thought go on. Both can marshal considerable evidence for their points of view. But more interesting is the fact that Rudolf Steiner, independently of philological research and drawing on his usual spiritual methods of investigation, advanced an interpretation of the 'Son of Man' which to a surprising extent makes sense of both parties' views.

According to Rudolf Steiner, the 'Son of Man' does refer to man's individuality, his personality, his 'I' In this respect, what he says is perfectly consistent with what we know about the idiomatic use of the phrase when talking about oneself, or oneself as an individual among individuals. But in particular circles, asserts Steiner — and we shall see later what circles they were — the phrase was a *terminus technicus* in a sort of esoteric psychology. It was used to refer to man's individuality, and implied a cosmological vision of man's origins and earthly development which looks back to the Mysteries of the cosmic Man, the Son of God. Man, in this cosmology, was regarded as a divinely originated being: but that was in his archetypal nature. What we are aware of as our 'I,' our individuality, is not Man in his cosmic essence. Our 'I' is the offspring, the earthly echo, the child, of the original heavenly Archetype, and as such was designated the Son of Man.[8]

We can detect behind such a cosmology and psychology patterns deriving from the Near Eastern rites we have mentioned, where originally the King stood as the 'I' of his community. He too, as the scholars have pointed out, was the Son of the Heavenly Man, his offspring on earth. In a later, more individualized age, among the Jews, everyone could lay claim to such an individuality for himself.

When Jesus used the phrase 'Son of Man,' therefore, on the surface level he was employing something which referred in a wellknown, idiomatic way to man's individual 'I.' But for those with ears to hear, the phrase would have pointed to a deeper understanding of this 'I' against the background of an esoteric psychology and cosmology. In this added dimension which was present for 'those inside' we seem to have a key to Jesus' special emphasis. Here was a language which was widely understandable in its basic connotation, but which could be radically deepened for those who understood it in terms of a more esoteric vision, a background of Mystery.

Could such a background have made itself felt in Palestine at the time of Christ? That was one of the difficult questions for those who suggested the influence of ancient Near Eastern rites: but the new discoveries from Nag Hammadi, and the revival of interest in Gnosticism deriving from their publication, has once more brought to light something highly significant. We noticed that the phrase 'the Son of Man' is employed in early Christian literature almost exclusively by Jesus, and immediately disappears from the thought of the Church. We are in quite a different position, however, when we turn to Gnostic literature! There we find the phrase employed in a rich variety of contexts, some of them to do with Jesus, some of them apparently looking back more directly to ancient practices and not derived from the New Testament use of the title at all.

If we subtract all those which are based on New Testament passages, as F. H. Borsch, a noted expert on this material, has shown, we still have a number of uses of 'Son of Man' which suggest older rites. Often they are in the setting of a cosmogony of mythical-divine anthropogeny. Thus we can establish that the title 'Son of Man' was indeed being actively employed among the Gnostics. And the conclusion to be drawn from this, as Borsch himself concludes, is an extremely significant one: the Gnostics have preserved a part of the background to Jesus' teaching and world of ideas which rapidly vanished from the more orthodox Church. In the Gnostic writings we gain access to part of Jesus' own background which has otherwise disappeared from Christian tradition.

That is not to say that Jesus was a Gnostic — any more than was the evangelist Mark, who drew upon the Gnostic thought-world of Alexandria but gave the Gnostic Mystery a new, historical meaning through the Mystery of Golgotha. We know from our earlier studies in this book that the Gnostics emerged as one wing of a widespread esoteric movement which also included, at the Jewish end of the spectrum, groups such as the Essenes with whom Jesus was certainly in contact. F. H. Borsch suggests that we look at Jesus' teaching against the broader backdrop of this 'Syrian-Palestinian baptist movement under Iranian and Jewish influence,'[9] including that section of it which evolved into radical Gnosticism, as well as to the strongly Jewish Essene wing.

In this way we shall also be able to appreciate the origins of Jesus' criticism of Judaism and the Law, and those elements in his consciousness which undoubtedly go 'beyond Judaism.' In particular, we shall be able to grasp his teaching of the Son of Man.

It was the Gnostics who especially preserved from older Mysteries the vision of the cosmic Man. We met this divine Man in the gnosis of the Ophites, and he appears in many other Gnostic world-views. Among certain successors of the Ophite Gnostics — a group called the Naassenes — we also encounter a striking description of the Son of Man. The Naassene cosmology, like that of their Ophite forerunners, described the cosmic origination of Man, who existed long before this physical.,material world was fashioned. Only at a comparatively late stage of his development did the spiritual Man come to be formed in matter — or, as the Naassenes put it, taking very literally a phrase in Genesis, was this archetypal man 'imprinted' into matter. The cosmic Prototype was known as the Unimprinted Man, or Logos; and of the individualized, earthly men who are 'generated' below, the Naassenes said that:

> in all that have been generated is the imprinted Son of
> Man from the Unimprinted Logos (above).[10]

The Gnostic Son of Man thus sounds very like the usage characterized by Steiner.

The Naassenes belong to a somewhat later time than Jesus' own age: but they look back to the Ophites, originally pre-Christian, and no doubt to other sources now obscure. Their description of the cosmological process whereby individual men are 'imprinted' below as children of the Man, the macrocosmic original, is modelled after older Mysteries, and some versions of it might certainly have been current among the esoteric baptizers of a Gnostic leaning in Palestine at the time of Christ.

Steiner's account of the Son of Man is further supported by the discovery among the Gnostics of an additional application of the same principle which produced the phrase. The Son of Man came into being from the heavenly Man through his earthly descent, his fragmentation, according to the Gnostic view, into scattered individual sparks here below. If there is a further step in his development, leading toward a reunification, the 'collecting' of the Archetype out of his fragmentation once more — then that further development would be a 'son of the Son of Man': and in fact we do find this expression, used in such a sense, in several of the new Gnostic writings. The cosmic Self which is awakened in the Gnostic initiate is born as the 'son of the Son of Man,' an event which, in the Gnostic fashion, was also experienced as a cosmic reality and as a reunion with the original macrocosmic Man.[11]

It seems likely, then, that an understanding of the Son of Man existed among the esoteric baptizing sects of Jesus' time, in the sense of a *terminus technicus* of the Mysteries as described by Steiner. Yet from a certain point of view, this discovery only makes Jesus' use of the term harder to understand. For in the Near Eastern Mysteries and among the Gnostics the individuality of the 'imprinted' man is of little importance. It is not the Son of Man who stands at the centre of Gnostic hopes, but the cosmic Man above 'in the spiritual world. (The passages in Gnostic literature where the Son of Man appears as a Saviour figure must certainly be traced to the influence of the New Testament.)

The further back we trace the Son of Man in the ancient Mysteries the clearer does this become: we may recall in the Babylonian kingly initiation how the King was chastised, humiliated, so that the all-too-human part of him could be purged away and he should be the mirror of the supra-individual cosmic Man. As an individual, he was considered the lowly deputy of the spiritual Archetype, and honoured only in so far as the macrocosmic spirit of Man shone through him. How did it come about, then, that Jesus should give the place of honour in his teaching to the Son of Man?

The value placed on the individuality of man points to the sphere of Judaism where, as we have seen, man came to place a religious and moral significance on individuality itself, a personal relationship with God. Moreover, we have seen that Gnosticism, with its peculiar 'double vision' or sharp antithesis between spiritual and material, was shaped by the encounter between the Mystery-consciousness of the ancient East and the individualized consciousness of Judaism. One reaction to that encounter was the Gnostic dualism: but another was a fusion of old and new, among groups such as the Essenes, and it is to these that we must now look for the shadowy, pre-history of the glorified Son of Man. It is in the esoteric Jewish literature such as the *Book of Enoch*, or the biblical book of Daniel (written at the time of the Maccabees), that we first find it intimated that the Son of Man may one day be heir to a special glory of his own.

The scene depicted in the vision of Daniel still recalls directly the royal initiations of the Near East. God is seen like an Old Man in white garments on a flaming throne; his title is the

Ancient of Days, a phrase which really means Antecedent of Time, the Eternal:

> And in my vision at night I looked, and there was before me one like the Son of Man, coming with the clouds of heaven. He approached the Ancient of Days and was led into his presence. He was given authority, glory and sovereign power; all peoples, nations and men of every language worshipped him. His dominion is an everlasting dominion that will not pass away, and his kingdom is one that will never be destroyed. (7:13–14)

The Son of Man here hardly plays any special role: he receives cosmic dominion from the Fatherly figure, the Antecedent of Time, like the kings of Babylonia or ancient Iran. He is the representative of the enthroned Divine Ruler, and his kingship is of a cosmic nature that extends in principle over the whole world; but the Son of Man simply has his kingship conferred on him from above.

A further development has taken place in the *Book of Enoch*. The Antecedent of Time and the Son of Man again appear, and I God also receives his characteristic Enochian name of the Lord of the Spirits. There is no conferring of kingship as in the Book of Daniel, but reference is made to the fact that God has chosen the Son of Man, prior to the creation of the world, to reveal his righteousness and glory at the end of days. He has done so, however, in a secret manner: this is expressed by saying that before the world began God gave a name to the Son of Man, but no one knows the name until the time of his coming; the secret is hidden with God. Thus the Son of Man has become the Elect One, a Messianic figure:

> For this purpose he became the Chosen One; he was concealed in the presence of the Lord of the Spirits prior to the creation of the world, and for eternity. And he has revealed the wisdom of the Lord of the Spirits to the righteous and holy ones ... because they will be saved in his name and it is his good pleasure that they have life.

A more esoteric conception of the Son of Man finds its place here with the idea of a wisdom and promise revealed to the few. And the content of the promise also goes beyond what we find in Daniel. For the Son of Man in *Enoch* is not a passive figure receiving kingship from on high; he plays a vital, active role in the events of the last days as the Elect One or Messiah, when the dead shall be raised:

> For the Lord of the Spirits has said ... : in those days, the Elect One shall sit on my throne, and from the conscience of his mouth shall come out all the secrets of wisdom, for the Lord of the Spirits has given them to him and glorified him. (1 *Enoch* 50–51)

At the climax of the vision, then, Enoch envisages the Son of Man actually placed on the throne of God.

Such a conception of the future glorification of the Son of Man was too radical to find inclusion in external Judaism, and remained the expectation of esoteric circles who produced and read *Enoch* in the century or so before Christ. From the discoveries at Qumran we know that it was read by Essenes, though copies of the passages relating to the Son of Man have unfortunately not yet been found. And even in Essene and esoteric circles, the inherent structure of the Jewish consciousness means that this glorification must be thrown forward to the farthest verge of foreseeable history, to the eschatological margin of time.

For the enthronement of the Son of Man on the divine throne breaks the framework of the Judaic world-conception apart: man is seen in Judaism in his creaturely dependence, his finiteness, his limited consciousness before a paternal God. In order for the Son of Man to be seated on God's throne, man's fallen state and even his creaturely dependence on a higher divinity must have been transcended absolutely, in a way that external Judaism could not conceive — and in a way which can be grasped by esoteric Judaism only as the terminus, the ultimate boundary of prophetic vision.

Jesus, by speaking of himself as the Son of Man, thus fulfils the promises for the future of the human individuality which were heard and fostered in esoteric circles of Judaism. At the same time, he goes beyond Judaism in claiming to have attained in his own consciousness something prophesied for the end of time and the overturning of the whole created order. The claim was still possible for the Gnostic, in his atavistic way: he could claim to have transcended the created order together with the moral Law and found his way to the higher world, but in order to do so he had to leave behind his sense of personal identity. Jesus' claim goes beyond Gnosticism and Judaism alike to assert a new form of consciousness, the present glorification of the Son of Man.

The whole structure of the world mapped out by Judaism is thereby brought to an end, just as the exaltation of the Son of Man is 'on another level the eschatological fulfilment and thus the transcendence of 'saving history' as conceived by Judaism. This puts Jesus at the very least in the position of a new Moses, announcing a new consciousness beyond Judaism just as Moses had announced the Law and the historical covenant of God with his people:

> No-one has ever gone up to heaven except the one who came from heaven — the Son of Man. Just as Moses lifted up the serpent in the wilderness, so the Son of Man must be exalted, that everyone who believes in him may have eternal life. (John 3:13–15)

More than a new Moses, Jesus can claim to be the Son of Man, concealed in heaven from the beginning and destined to be exalted in the last days of the universe.

The language Jesus employed concerning the Son of Man is thus his way of describing the Christ-consciousness which he attained through the baptism and the experiences of the Temptation. For the Jew, the exaltation of the Son of Man denotes the end of the world, overturning the entire order of things. From the standpoint of the evolutionary view of man which we have adopted in this book we can comprehend the reality which lies behind this: for the breakthrough in con-sciousness achieved by Jesus dissolves and overthrows the whole world-view which expressed the Jewish mode of consciousness. In a quite genuine sense a world, a world-experience which had lasted for centuries, came to an end for Jesus and will do so for all who follow him into a new order, the world 'apprehended in a new way.

Expressed in a more imaginative and mythological guise, this breakthrough in the relationship of man to his world was embodied in the stories of Jesus' struggle with the cosmic powers at the Temptation. As prophesied by Enoch, the Lord of Spirits has given the secrets of wisdom and righteousness to the Son of Man, exalting him to a position formerly reserved for the super-human, for the Divine itself. And, if we may also paraphrase in somewhat less pictorial language the teaching of the *Book of Enoch* concerning the 'secret' and the name given before the foundation of the world: we are to see in the exaltation of man's individuality, the Son of Man, the real meaning of all man's evolution, implicit in his whole development from the beginning of time.

The Messianic Secret

A definite milestone in Jesus' teaching seems to be reached with Peter's confession:

> Jesus and his disciples went on to the villages around Caesarea Philippi. On the way he asked them, 'Who do people say that I am?' They replied, 'Some say John the Baptist; others say Elijah; and still others, one of the prophets.'
>
> 'But what about you?' he asked. 'Who do you say I am?' Peter answered, 'You are the Christ.'
>
> Jesus warned them not to tell anyone about him. And he began to teach them concerning the Son of Man ... (Mark 8:27–31)[12]

It is well known to all the readers of the Gospels that the scene is one of the great turning-points in the events of Jesus' life. It also marks a change in the character of Jesus' instruction of the disciples. Before this time there has been virtually no mention of the Son of Man, but henceforth the teaching recurs again and again. The typical pattern found in Jesus' treatment of the figure is also first clearly laid out: the disciples, headed by Peter, see him as the Christ, the Messiah — but Jesus shifts the ground of the discussion to the more esoteric Son of Man, and without denying his Messianic role fundamentally reinterprets its significance. Particularly in Mark, too, we encounter the injunction to secrecy which we have mentioned before under the name of the 'Messianic secret.' The phrase could also be translated by 'the Christ Mystery.' In the light of our studies we may now be in a position to probe a little more deeply into its content.

In the Gnostic and Jewish esoteric traditions which describe the Son of Man, and prophesy his future glory, we are on markedly 'secret' territory. The Son of Man has the potential to burst the framework of Judaism wide open, and to give an entirely new meaning to the Gnostic transcendence of the creation and the moral Law, a meaning that did not necessitate the abnegation of personality that had been required in the archaic Mysteries. In order to proclaim his teaching of the Son of Man to the people, Jesus could appeal to the passage in the Book of Daniel (which we know that he did); but there the doctrine was not expressed in its esoteric form. Beyond that it must have been necessary to proceed with great caution — even secrecy. Not everyone was sufficiently prepared to face the consequences of so profound a discovery.[13]

In short, it may be that the question of the Son of Man, the 'Messianic Secret' and the esoteric teaching of Jesus converge upon a single point. For the teaching of the Son of Man now emerges as the esoteric side of Jesus' preaching of the Kingdom, the coming world-order based on the rule of the Divine. It describes the step in consciousness which is needed for the Kingdom to be realized in man's earthly experience. The individual essence of man, according to the teaching of Jesus, can take upon itself the burdens of moral existence, can be placed upon the throne of the paternal God as foretold by the *Book of Enoch*, 'and from the conscience of his mouth shall come out all. the secrets of wisdom, for the Lord of Spirits has given them to him and glorified him.' Since his baptism and the struggles of the Temptation, Jesus has become the incarnation of that Son of Man. And from the point where Peter and the disciples acknowledge him as the Messiah, he gradually reveals himself to them, showing them that the glorification of the Son of Man is indeed coming about.[14]

Something of tremendous depth thus stands behind the simple phrase 'the Son of Man' with which Jesus increasingly identifies himself in his teaching as it stands in the Gospels. It conceals something that drew upon a background of Mystery and esotericism, but essentially marked the revelation of a new form of consciousness transcending both Judaism and ancient Gnosis. The discovery of that consciousness stands at the heart of Christianity: it was to alter man's fundamental evaluation of himself along with his world. It was this discovery which was taken up by the profoundest exponents of the Christian vision in the first age of Christianity, Paul and the evangelist John. But the astonishing step was taken by Jesus, and fulfilled in the events of his life and death.

The question of the 'collective' and 'individual' aspects of the Son of Man has in fact vexed scholars from the beginning of their investigations. Neither in Daniel, *Enoch* or other sources is it entirely clear whether the Son of Man is a single Messianic hero or whether he 'stands for' a community of the redeemed. In reality he is neither. Here again Steiner's conclusion concerning the meaning of 'Son of Man' enables us to bring the issue a stage nearer solution, and at the same time to give an answer to the problem of 'esotericism' and its frequently questioned compatibility with the Christian spirit. For in Steiner's results of spiritual research it emerged that in the context of an esoteric psychology 'Son of Man' denoted what we should nowadays call a 'principle' which can be realized within every individual. Nevertheless it has not yet been 'glorified' in most people's spiritual development. That principle must be incarnated first of all in a single personality, who shows the way toward what can ultimately be achieved by all mankind. The early Christians had several ways of describing Jesus as one who had developed so far that he could accept that breakthrough as his destiny: he was a reborn Zarathustra who had gathered together the wisdom of all the nations; he was a union of the Kingly and Priestly virtues. Jesus himself taught that he was the embodiment of the exalted Son of Man, and he called upon men to follow the way he had prepared.

The teaching of the Son of Man is therefore 'esoteric' only in a qualified sense. It cannot ultimately be kept from anyone, above all else should not be kept from anyone, because it relates to what already exists potentially in each individual. Yet each individual must be educated gradually toward the responsibilities of freedom: he must first learn the immense moral demands of the Kingdom. Individuality means development, so that each man must come to the awakening of his free spiritual consciousness by his own route and in his own time. Until the right moment for his awakening comes, determined by his own unique destiny, the potentiality and the burden of his freedom must slumber in well-protected secrecy.

The call to inner freedom, the glorification of the Son of Man, cannot be thrust upon anyone; it must arise out of his life's experience and the maturing of his own soul. Hence the paradox of the Gospel from beginning to end: it is a truth known only to 'those inside'; yet it is a message shouted from the rooftops to the limits of the inhabited world.

Consciousness and 'Salvation'

The evidence is that a number of people at the time of Christ had developed so far in their consciousness as to be able to receive the message of the Son of Man. Although many of Jesus' followers deserted at the very point where he began to reveal the full implications of his teaching — the period commencing with Peter's so-called confession — others came forward to hear him; and some, such as Paul, came over to his message after his death. Perhaps in the violent loyalties which swayed Paul's soul both before his conversion and afterwards we should see the sign of a desperate longing, for something which had not yet been articulated but which, when discovered, was capable of absorbing all those energies that had formerly been expended on savage persecution. At any rate, after the crisis of his Damascus experience, Paul more than anyone else lived the new Christian consciousness to the very depths of his exceptional nature.

Yet the number of souls who were thus on the brink of a step in awareness can only have been small. If Christianity had been the religion of them alone it would have remained certainly an esoteric hot-house for the few. Yet Christianity spread phenomenally through the ancient world. And its appeal was not simply to those who felt ready for a higher development, but to the large masses of those who were much more dimly groping their way toward individualization. To them the Christian awakening was not felt as achievement, but as rescue, as redemption from the perils of the soul. The new consciousness was experienced above all as *salvation*.

Nevertheless, we must understand their experience, too, as a part of the same evolutionary process in man's spiritual life which we have all along tried to elucidate. Indeed it will be an important outcome of our investigations that the distinction, raised to a level of absolute significance by some schools of theology, between the concept of the spiritual life as development or maturation and the idea of grace freely given beyond man's desert, or salvation, is by no means an ultimate one. The two aspects may rather be different facets of a single evolution, and can be understood together.

We must return to consider the broadest aspect of the process we have traced behind the emergence of Christianity: the encounter and confluence of East and West. We have watched this in the return of the Mysteries into Jewish Palestine; in the origins of Gnostic dualism; on a still wider scale in the spread of oriental religion into the Hellenistic world. The consciousness of the Greeks, pioneers of 'reason' and clear-headed wakefulness, was undermined in Hellenistic times by the cults of dream and ecstasy, the Eastern Mysteries which found their way into even the hearts of the practical, hard-headed Romans — and yet, from a further perspective, they also prepared the way for the Christian synthesis in which Graeco-Oriental spirituality was to be subsumed and transfigured. From the fusion of East and West a new quality of consciousness was created, with a deeper sense of individuality and with a vision of cosmic significance. What must we assume to be the fate, however, of those in the Hellenistic world who did not take the leap to the new level?

The question has recently been answered, from an interesting psychological viewpoint, by a researcher into dreams and psychic disturbances. Speaking of the oriental Mystery-cults and their atavistic methods, she says: 'the spread of cults using techniques for diminishing self-consciousness rendered their participants susceptible to irrational influences capable of dominating the personality. Thus arose states of consciousness in which men felt themselves "possessed" by demons, and demonic possession became a widespread phenomenon in the Hellenistic world.'[15]

Another form of 'domination' of the personality by psychic forces was to be seen in the pervasive religion of deterministic Astrology, almost universally accepted among Hellenistic pagans. Here the personality felt itself helpless before powers experienced as connected with the starpatterns and the 'wandering stars' (the planets). Astrological 'fate' was not a theory, but a description of the actual experience of many in the Graeco-Roman world. Hence we may say that the infiltration of the Western 'realistic' consciousness by the dreams and myths of the East posed a formidable challenge as well as holding out the possibility of a higher fusion. For if a man did not find a way of coming to terms with the forces at work on him, the psychic pressures both within and without, he could be dominated by deep compulsions beyond his control, or lose his grip on reality altogether. Indeed, we see the late Hellenistic consciousness struggling with these problems urgently in the attempted solutions of philosophers to the riddle of man's destiny, as well as among the practices of healer-priests and astrologers.

The Stoic philosophy, the most popular in the Hellenistic era, made all of life into role-playing: all the world's a stage, and often the events there seem to take on a dream-like inconsequentiality, or look only half-real. To the Stoic emperor Marcus Aurelius his huge wars, involving thousands of lives and deaths, seemed at moments but a minor disturbance on the face of the earth — 'like puppies scrapping over a bone.' Elsewhere he terms the whole of our conscious life 'a dream and a delirium.'

From the time of Marcus Aurelius until that of the triumph of Christianity in the Empire there was 'an age of anxiety': consciousness was suspended in a kind of tension between dreamlike unreality threatened at one pole, and the sense of compulsion, of being 'puppets jerking on a string' (Marcus again) on the other.[16] In a previous time, when man's individuality was not so far evolved, people had found immense satisfaction in living out of the cosmic rhythms of the psyche and of nature. It was out of such pre-individualized experience that Babylonian star-religion had originated. But the personal self, the 'I' of later times now experienced these deeper-lying forces as a constant danger and threat — or as an overwhelming tide in which the personal ego was simply swept away. Stoicism enabled many to come to terms with their situation in an interim way: it taught that one should embrace one's fate and play out one's role to the end. Only in Christianity was a profounder resolution achieved. Only in Christianity did the personality find a way of drawing upon its own inner resources, thereby achieving balance and freedom of action within the configuration of pressures, anxieties and psychic dangers of the late Antique world.

One theme in early Christian literature is precisely this freedom. Approaching from the background of Judaism, it was a freedom from 'sin' and guilt which 'enslaved' man before; from the standpoint of the larger Hellenistic world, it was freedom from enslavement to psychic forces of demonic 'possession' and especially those of the 'stars.' Paul taught that:

> Even so we, when we were children, were in bondage
> under the elements of the world.

Now, as Christians, we are 'free.'[17] Justin — not the Gnostic but a notable martyr — takes up his theme: 'No longer are we children, under compulsion from the stars.' Christ has set us free, and the horoscope is no longer valid.

Christian individuation, then, gave man a freedom and authority within this world. And there is extraordinary significance in that 'within.' For it brings into focus the difference between the Christian resolution and certain other radical attempts to solve the crisis and allay the anxiety of man's consciousness. We turn yet again to Gnosticism. Even more than Stoicism, the Gnostic dualism allowed man to live in the world without feeling wholly a part of it. Its ultimate aim was to show the illusion of the material half of its double equation, and restore man to the sense of his spiritual origin. The material world, with its seeming solidity and its inescapable laws was therefore before man's gaze; but the Gnostic could ascend beyond it, transcend its mock-reality and find his way of escape. That too could be experienced as 'salvation,' and even described in semi-Christian terms. Yet the difference is clear. The Gnostic finds 'freedom,' 'salvation,' outside the cosmos, in the 'beyond.' He has somehow managed to suggest away the immediate world of matter and laws of necessity that confronts him, and has brought back a kind of consciousness deeper than and prior to our modern kind of objective awareness. The Christian, on the other hand, by maintaining and deepening his personality and his vision, has attained freedom within the cosmos, within the complex world which confronts him and in which he lives with his fellow men.

It was inevitable that the old kind of 'liberation,' the sense of union with the spiritual world, as mankind in general evolved toward a greater degree of individuality, should become increasingly difficult to achieve. Once a spontaneous expression of man's consciousness, it could later be brought about, even in the East, through elaborate practices of yoga or esoteric rites of a highly dramatic nature. It becomes more and more marginal, in terms of the immediate reality confronting man's consciousness. In Gnosticism, we reach the stage where unspiritual reality fills the whole of consciousness of man, so that there need to be actually two consciousnesses, two standards of reality, a double vision; salvation or liberation can no longer be described in any terms deriving from natural reality, but is opposed to it absolutely, explicable in negative terms, or in contradictions, paradoxes. Buddhism presents many parallels, and was perhaps in contact with Gnosticism, as we have seen. Thus in the East, too, the consciousness of more individualized man came to be filled more and more with the world of material law, the cycles of birth and death, and he lost his natural atavistic awareness of a deeper identity with the whole. He felt himself trapped in cycles of fate and locked in illusion. Salvation or liberation was 'outside' this system, as in Gnosis it could be described only negatively or through the mind-demolishing paradoxes which were increasingly cultivated, for instance, by the Zen school.

Even for Eastern consciousness, then, salvation became more and more marginal. A feeling of despair could easily take root, since the system of fate, birth and death, seemed inexorable and, to the unawakened, seemed to be everything. We may recall the sage Asita, in the Buddhist legend, and contrast his frustration, the difficulty of extricating himself from the tangle of rebirths, with the Christian consciousness in the metamorphosis of the tale in the Gospel of Luke. The Christian consciousness brought freedom to man within the system of the cosmos itself: an ability to move, we might say, in the constantly changing balance and interplay of spiritual and physical reality.

The Christian resolution demanded an effort of unprecedented self-knowledge and a corresponding power of commitment. Yet many came to it and grasped it as 'salvation' because it was the only way they could see forward. It was the only way to withstand the spiritual and material pressures of their age and survive as an individuality; it was, therefore, a struggle and yet also a relief and a rescue. It made the material and spiritual environment once more a sphere of shared activity, historical action illuminated by the inner dimension of 'myth' that came-from the depth of their Christian experience. The archaic religions based on atavistic vision, or even the incipient personalization of Jewish and Greek thought, were no longer adequate to man's consciousness. The personality itself became a divine power to work on earth, and a new kind of society gradually began to arise.

The historian Peter Brown sees this as the greatest change brought about by Christianity, contrasting the new religion with the classical gods. Christianity brought the rise of the 'holy man,' the individual who was himself charged with divine power. 'Ancient religion had revolved round great temples, against whose ancient stones even the most impressive priest had paled into insignificance; the gods had spoken impersonally at their oracle sites; their ceremonies assumed a life in which the community, the city, dwarfed the individual ... the emergence of the holy man at the expense of the temple marks the end of the classical world.'[18] The emergence of the new society on a large scale would take us on into the fourth and fifth centuries. But the revolution which lay behind it has its roots in the Christian Mystery of the new consciousness, the freedom and power granted to the Son of Man. In the Gospel form, the biography of a personality walking the earth had been made the highest revelation of the Divine; in the Christian Mystery, the greatest turning-point in the history of man's consciousness had been passed, and the way ahead stretched forward with infinite possibilities.

To the Jewish seer, the glorification of the Son of Man betokened the end of the world. In fact, it turned out to be a beginning too. For the Christian, the world was made anew. Was this only a subjective experience? We have suggested that it had deep roots in man's evolution over long ages of time. For the first and only time in this book we must confront directly 'metaphysical' questions — questions about the real nature of the underlying change in human consciousness which we have described historically, concentrating on the emergence of a new individual awareness in connection with Christianity but also sketching in some of its further perspectives. We must ask a question now about consciousness as such.

We have observed that changes in consciousness are bound up with changing relationships between man and his perceived world, and man and his society. Some thinkers regard the social dimension as all-important and determinative of man's relation to nature or perceived reality; but this is at best a dqgmatic assumption, often contradicted by the historical facts.[19] The real problem lies in the notion of consciousness which we have inherited, all too uncritically, from the eighteenth century. That notion was worked out in the excitement of discovering the *camera obscura*, the image projected onto a blank screen: and in popular, even in scientific thought, this basic idea has remained with us. The conscious mind is supposed to be like a screen on which copies of the 'objective' world are thrown.

Over many years the *camera obscura* picture of the mind has been progressively outmoded by the evidences of developmental psychology, perceptual research, physiology, and not least by the arguments of philosophy. Among the critically informed, it is certainly acknowledged that the conception of consciousness as a 'mirror' reflecting the forms of objects simply cannot be correct, but that man's life of conscious ideas and perceptions emerges out of a highly complex interaction with the world —

much of it at an unconscious level. The problem has been, how-ever, that it is difficult to root out the vestiges of the eighteenth-century notion in their entirety, because they linger in the assumptions of so many disciplines, and any alternative requires a daring commitment to rethinking on a range of different fronts.

Part of the inherent difficulty in the copy-making idea of consciousness is that, since the copy is all that we have to go on, it is impossible to know what the image is a copy of, or whether it is accurate or not in reflecting what supposedly lies behind the copy. Philosophers have therefore been driven more and more, beginning in the late eighteenth century itself with Kant, to stress that human consciousness is partly the maker of what it sees; they have studied man's 'participation,' to adopt the term given new currency by Owen Barfield, in the construction of the conscious world-order he cognizes. Not all of them have followed the thought through so thoroughly as Barfield. Yet at least there is a growing appreciation of the scale of the problem. Professor Stephen R. L. Clark, discussing the issue of consciousness and evolution, comes up against the tangled difficulties of the copy-making or image-making theory. He has to consider the problem of the infinite recess involved in the copy-theory, and the objection that man knows himself consciously, according to the theory, as a copy-in-consciousness, so that the image seems ultimately to be making itself. 'But it is hardly likely,' he says, 'that the copy itself is adequate to the task of producing itself — unless we take a rather different attitude to the field of consciousness, and accept Rudolf Steiner's account of evolution.'[20]

Professor Clark, it should perhaps be added, is uncertain how far to take the 'rather different attitude'; but he deeply appreciates the motive behind it. From our historical perspective, we have even more need of Steiner's account. For we have come face to face with the issue of what really happened when man's consciousness changed with the impulse of Christianity. Could man, by changing his consciousness, effectively change the world around him? Or, if the world had not changed, how could it yet become something to which man stood in wholly new relationship, when his consciousness is a *camera obscura*?

The foundation of Rudolf Steiner's account of consciousness

is a thought that permits us to get away from both these one-sided alternatives. Briefly, the differentiation of the world into objects on the one hand and images, ideas-in-consciousness on the other, according to Steiner, is not a primary truth of the universe, but arises only as a result of man's constitution as a knowing mind. Thus Steiner cuts through the traditional dichotomy of the theory of knowledge, and is enabled to regard the so-called 'objective' world and the 'inner' world of consciousness as two sides of a unitary process. Reality is certainly greater than simply that which can be brought to conscious representation: Steiner escapes the absurd notion that simply by looking at things differently reality would be changed. But a change in consciousness is an expression of a process which extends beyond consciousness, and is part of an evolution of reality as well as mind. The two aspects only come before us separately because of the limitations of our human constitution.[21]

Such at any rate is a very brief and sketchy account of an approach to the theory of knowledge and the evolution of consciousness which Rudolf Steiner develops in manifold and frequently fascinating ways. Part of its importance is that it opens a road to the understanding of the historical dimension in epistemology, the theory of knowledge, and links it with a 'different attitude' to evolution. And it is especially vital for us to make some effort toward such a view of evolution if we are to understand the ways in which the early Christians regarded Jesus. They understood something, at any rate, of the change in consciousness that had come about through him, and employed the esoteric vocabulary of the 'Son of Man' to express its consequences for the human individuality. In the Gospel of John we also find the unique use of the 'I AM' in certain discourses to indicate one aspect of this, and in Paul we hear of 'the New Man' and similar things. But the early Christians grasped too that a change in consciousness was a transformation of the world. They did not grasp it abstractly or conceptually so much as pictorially, imaginatively; but they did not suppose that a great metamorphosis of things could have been brought about simply by man learning to see things differently. They saw behind it a change at deeper levels in the nature of reality itself. Accordingly they attributed the change that had been effected through Jesus to powers of a cosmic order. The origin of the new consciousness was not to be found simply on the human level but lay in the forces driving world-evolution; in the depths of being, not only in the human ego. Using ancient terms, they spoke about 'angelic,' cosmically active beings who acted through Jesus — we have already mentioned passages where angels are closely linked with the Son of Man. Ultimately they regarded the change as originating from the most comprehensive Ground of world-development that can be conceived, from the root-reality behind mind and world alike: they described Jesus as God.

It may seem a large step, from the radical transformation of consciousness achieved by a man in Judea to speaking of that man as an incarnate God. Yet the Christian thinkers were following through, in their profoundly imaginative way, truths which we too can begin to grasp if we strive seriously for an authentic account of consciousness, not as a mirror or a copy on a screen but as one pole of a continuously evolving reality.

10. The Mystery Gospels of Philip and Thomas

The Lord has done everything in a Mystery.
Gospel of Philip (Saying 68)

Our investigations have led to the view that the Christian Mystery expresses a transformation of consciousness, achieved at a point in history which thus acquires the significance of a turning-point. It is a change that must ultimately be considered in the widest terms: as the crux of history; and even as a change in the nature of things, consciousness and reality being in the last analysis elements of a deeper whole. And in that sense it was rightly experienced by the early Christians as a new self-revelation of God, a change originating in the deepest foundations of Being itself.

Our researches have also brought us close to answering the question from which we set out — that of the 'esoteric' teaching of Jesus to the inner circle of his disciples. An understanding of the different qualities of the different Gospels has enabled us to see the converging of spiritual traditions (of the Mysteries, the Essenes and Gnostics). Out of that convergence emerged the possibility of something radically new in Christianity itself, in which the cosmic orientation of the Mysteries and Gnosticism could be carried forward as could the historical and prophetic vision of the Essenes and Judaism. The recent discovery of the secret *Mark* fragment, coupled with Rudolf Steiner's insights, pointed to an original link between the baptismal Mystery of Christian baptism and Jesus' own experience and practice. We shall also be tracing the implications of that perspective through the New Testament writings of Paul and the Fourth Gospel. But in addition we must now consider the import of two 'new'

212 • *The Beginnings of Christianity*

Gospels, or rather two very early Gospels newly brought to light and made available to the world in the Nag Hammadi library.

These Gospels also provide extraordinary insight into the origins of the Christian Mystery. They do so in two ways: both as regards the background and the nature of Jesus' own inner teaching and ritual practice; and as regards the continuing activity of Mystery streams in early Christianity, taking that practice as the foundation for their development. In what follows we can look both ways at the new material — though of course it is the possibility of drawing closer to the practice and teaching of Jesus which stands as our especial goal.

The new Gospels come to us in the form of traditions, in large part sayings of Jesus, but also other matter. They were handed down in the names of the disciples Philip and Thomas. Scholarly examinations of their style and content have confirmed their antiquity, and indeed have increasingly tended to ascribe them to an early stage of the Christian tradition. Thus, for example, we know that collections of Jesus' sayings were the first stage in what evolved into the Gospel-form. The *Gospel of Thomas* preserves this primal type, and so must have been fixed at a point prior to the addition of biographical and theological material such as we find in the New Testament Gospels. (This is not strictly a matter of date, since obviously the Thomas-tradition could have retained its primitive character after certain traditions had further evolved in the Gospels of Matthew, Mark, and so on; but whenever it was fixed into its present literary shape, it preserves the very early traditions relatively unaltered, and therein lies its importance.) The *Gospel of Philip* likewise takes the form of a collection of sayings, together with other short paragraphs of a similar kind. It, too, is evidently early. Both Gospels have many links with material in the New Testament; but neither seems to be aware of anything like the 'canon,' the definitive grouping of Gospels, letters, and so on, regarded as authoritative by the Church, reinforcing the sense that they come from a time when Christianity still consisted of traditions handed on by the apostles and their immediate pupils. Both Gospels — *Thomas* and *Philip* — contain Mystery-elements, 'secret sayings,' teachings about the 'Son of

Man,' and so on. There are also strong contrasts between them, reflecting the different leanings of the two apostles and their followers.

Both documents were preserved by the Gnostics: a fact which perhaps calls for some explanation. Neither of them expresses a Gnostic 'system,' though they do have a Gnostic element to some lesser degree, especially *Philip*. But we know that various esoteric writings and teachings were preserved by the Gnostics after they had fallen from favour among the orthodox. We saw in the last chapter that the teaching of the Son of Man was preserved by the Gnostics in this way, whilst it disappeared from the Church's thinking. In the case of the *Gospel of Thomas*, we have very clear evidence that the work was not originally connected with a narrowly Gnostic group, but rather with the fusion of spiritual currents which originally happened around Jesus. For we can see at one point how the later Gnostics, in order to make use of the *Gospel of Thomas*, actually had to suppress part of the text.

Saying 5 in *Thomas* reads:

> Jesus said: Know what is before thy face, and what is hidden will be revealed. For nothing is hidden which will not be made manifest.

Now, as it happens, this saying and a few of its neighbours were already known in a collected form in Greek before the discovery of the Gnostic library. The title and extent of the collection was not formerly known, since some few fragments alone were extant. But the exact agreement of the (Greek) fragments with the order and words of the *Gospel of Thomas* in the (Coptic) Gnostic collection makes it plain that it is indeed the same work. There is, however, one notable change. In the Greek text, or version otherwise parallel to the Saying in the *Gospel* used by the Gnostics at Nag Hammadi, we read:

> Jesus says: ... before thine eye, and ... will be revealed ... nothing is hidden which will not (be) made manifest, nor buried that (will) not be raised up.[1]

Hence we see that the saying in the *Gospel of Thomas* originally contained a reference to the resurrection of the body. The strict Gnostics came to reject this part of the text, since their basic dualism did not allow of any such conception as bodily resurrection. But originally, for all its esoteric character and Gnostic affinities, the *Gospel of Thomas* embodies the thought-world of a Christian tradition where the idea of resurrection was held.

We must examine carefully the nature of these two Mystery Gospels and see whether their early character enables us to project ourselves into the world of Jesus' own disciples.

The Mystery of Paradise

> *Paradise is the place where they will say to me: Man, eat this or do not eat according to your desire. It is the place where I shall eat all things, because there is the Tree of Knowledge.*
>
> Gospel of Philip (Saying 94)

When describing the literary form of the early Gospels it is as well to resist describing them as 'simple.' They may lack the narrative interweaving of materials and themes we know from the New Testament writings, but the *Gospel of Philip* in particular demonstrates that an organization of considerable complexity can lie behind an assembly of short paragraphs. Themes are raised and abandoned, then taken up again deepened by connection with ideas that have intervened. Scholars have spoken of a 'spiralling' complexity, a constant enriching of themes as they rotate and disappear before our gaze in the course of the *Gospel*. The result is initially confusing: but this is probably deliberate. The *Gospel* begins to make sense when we see that it is actually organized around certain sacramental experiences, rather than around narrative events. To account for the first-person form of some of the sayings, such as Saying 94, the likeliest view is that the *Gospel of Philip* provided study-material for those who were to be initiated into Christianity. Its full meaning would only emerge in the light of their subsequent baptism and admission to the eucharistic meal. Probably the book itself was made available to them (rather than to their teacher) only after initiation.

The community from which the book comes is to be located in Syria. Though the book was originally in Greek it shows a knowledge of Syriac words, and almost certainly comes from the area of Antioch, one of the first important centres of Christianity. According to the Acts of the Apostles it was there that 'the disciples were first called Christians.' The meaning of 'becoming a Christian' is much discussed in the *Gospel*.[2]

'Becoming a Christian' is achieved by a ritual initiation with five degrees. To complete the quotation at the head of this chapter:

> The Lord has done everything in a Mystery, a baptism
> and an anointing and a eucharist and a redemption and a
> marriage-chamber.

The beginning of the process was baptism. As the rite of awakening to a higher life, it was much more dramatic than modern rites — like the Gnostic baptisms at Alexandria. We have seen that initiation was practised there as the 'Great Mysteries' at Easter. At Antioch, too, there was a distinct 'going down' into the waters, a descent into the underworld, yet 'not unto death.'[3] When the candidate came up out of the water, he said, 'I am a Christian' — that is, if he had 'received something.' Candidates are sternly warned against the danger of claiming the title merely after going through the externals of the rite: thoseowho do so 'take a name on loan,' and it is ominously added that repayment will be required of them. The successful aspirant, however, was rewarded with a sense of renewal or rejuvenation, an expansion of consciousness. He seemed to lose his awareness of bodily restrictions, and the waters, which had been waters of death, were felt as a living or flowing ethereal body which the initiate 'put on.' He also experienced a world of living 'images,' a visionary world through contact with which he was 'reborn.'[4]

The archetype of the baptized dying-and-reborn initiate was Christ himself, and the occasion of initiation in Syria too was certainly Easter. But behind the celebration of Easter suggested by the *Gospel of Philip* we detect the much older pattern of a Near Eastern spring festival of initiation, such as the ancient Babylonian royal rites. The death-and-rebirth of the candidate is experienced in parallel with the regeneration of nature as winter gives place to spring. The 'spirit' (or 'breath') which awakens in him is parallel to the 'breath' (or 'wind') which blows to disperse the winter drought. Rudolf Steiner regarded the early Christian Easter celebrations as a transformation of such older Mysteries, and certainly in the *Gospel of Philip* we witness one stage in the Christianizing process.[5] Some of the esoteric symbolism found in the Gospel was in fact already discussed by Steiner and related to a Mystery-background.

In ancient Mesopotamia ritual lustrations or baptisms were already well known. The priests of Ea, god of wisdom, guarded the springs where 'sweet water' was believed to well up from the *Apsu* or abyss. The function of the washings was especially to prepare the initiate to re-enter paradise. This was achieved by a ritual in the Temple precinct; but mythologically Paradise was represented as a 'Garden of Life' on a high mountain difficult of access. Ultimately the 'seven-story mountain' was an image of the cosmos itself, as was the Temple, and the initiate-ruler who ascended its different levels received cosmic power. Several scholars who have studied the *Gospel of Philip* were struck by the centrality of just such a spiritual ascension in its vision of things, and the closely related theme of regaining the condition of Paradise: something that does not belong to the biblical tradition at all.

The evolution of individual moral awareness in Judaism meant for the Jews the renunciation of Paradise, and their hope lay not in a way back but in a way forward to the celestial city, the heavenly Jerusalem already prefigured to Ezekiel and Zechariah. The Mystery-tradition of the Near East had not so severed its link with the 'Paradise'-intuition of man's beginnings, on the other hand, and it resurfaces here in the Syrian Mystery Gospel. Man is able by initiation to re-enter Paradise, and indeed to eat of the Tree of Knowledge. This is spiritual freedom. The ban on the famous 'forbidden fruit' will not hold. The whole perspective is subtly different from that of the Bible, even though it describes the same events of temptation and Fall. The *Gospel* relates that the Fall came about when Adam misunderstood his situation, when he took as Law what should have been freedom. Through Christ, who is the Tree in Paradise, freedom is regained. Once again we are in the presence of very old Mystery-themes. We need only recall the haunting early *Epic of Gilgamesh* and its hero's quest for 'the Plant of Life' in ancient Mesopotamia — a quest which we may see fulfilled by Christ in the *Gospel of Philip*. In another ancient myth, that of Adapa (compare Adam), man was offered the immortalizing food and drink of the gods, but rejected it as a trick. Thus it was that man became mortal. For the Christians of our *Gospel of Philip*, we might say, the offer was renewed through Christ.[6]

The perfecting of initiation (or spiritual freedom), however, demands further stages of ritual enactment. The anointing or chrism which follows baptism in the system of sacraments completes the return to life and 'Paradise.' According to the *Gospel of Philip* Saying 92, it originates from the Tree itself:

> The Tree of Life is in the midst of Paradise — the olive tree from which the anointing originated. Through it came the resurrection.

There are echoes here of Seth and his quest for the oil of life according to Jewish legends, which say that he fetched it from Paradise. Jewish-Christian writings from the circles of the *Ebionim* also knew the idea of being anointed with oil from the Tree of Life, and some Gnostics later preserved it into later times, when they still spoke of 'being anointed with light-oil from the Tree of Life.' At Antioch the anointing also seems to have been closely associated with light. At this point in their initiation, the candidates probably emerged from their dark baptismal 'death,' were clothed in 'heavenly' white garments and brought into the presence of light. Almost certainly they will have carried a lit taper, symbol of awakened consciousness. An important transition has been made in the Christian rite, however. In the pagan Mysteries there was usually a Lightbearer: in the Christian Mysteries each candidate bore his own flame of life and light.

After being anointed, the candidates were full Christians and could be admitted to the eucharist, the feast which is recognized by the Gospel as its third sacrament. The 'true bread' eaten by the initiate in Paradise is the 'food of life,' brought into the world by Christ. Rudolf Steiner already discussed the meaning of this Mystery in early Christianity, and the way it recalled the language of the older Eastern Mysteries. When a man eats in ordinary life, according to their ancient conceptions, 'he knows that whatever he is eating and drinking ... . that these things were at one time outside me, at another within me. And thus he stands in connection with earthly forces.' As an initiate, however, he was said to become an 'eater of spiritual things,' a bearer of cosmic powers as before he was a bearer of earthly ones. Steiner connected this with the teaching of a sort of spiritual 'chemistry.' The discovery of the *Gospel of Philip* has strikingly confirmed his insight into the connections between Mystery-rites and Christianity, especially with regard to Easter. For here in these rites of Christian initiation we find the symbolic language of 'eaters of dead things' (that is, earthly food) and 'eaters of living things' (that is, spiritual ones), and thereby of becoming a bearer of Christ, the Perfect Man. And at several points the *Gospel* makes reference to the spiritual significance of alchemy, treating baptism and regeneration as 'chemical' transformations to a new state of life. The material body is like a 'dead' vessel of clay; the reborn initiate is a 'vessel of life,' like the alchemists' 'living vessels' of glass which 'come into being from a breath (or spirit).' Baptism is likened to dyeing, and Christ is the heavenly dyer. [7]

Perhaps the first three stages of initiation form a distinct group, since all of them seem to be necessary to the Christian life. So in the Mysteries the early grades were preliminary to the candidate's admittance to the cultic meal of the initiates — notably to Mithraism. The other two sacraments may be higher grades, open to some who had already passed through the lower stages, but not required of all. One is that of 'the Marriage Chamber'; the other is called the 'redemption.'

The Marriage Chamber again recalls the archaic celebrations of the ancient Near East. Mythology tells of the sacred marriage or *hieros gamos* performed by the divine Father and Mother in the garden of Paradise. Sexuality is perceived as an intimation of a primal wholeness, not only uniting man and woman, but harmonizing man and world. In terms of the *Gospel of Philip*, the Marriage Chamber reintegrates the divided sexuality of fallen man into its primal wholeness 'when Eve was in Adam.' That state is also man's original, lost immortality. By his initiatory death and resurrection, the higher Christian is even enabled to approach this condition and so overcome what is divided and mortal in man.

> In the days when Eve was in Adam, there was no death. When she had separated from him, death arose. If he again unites with her, and takes death to himself, there shall be no death.

That is precisely what is declared to happen in the Marriage Chamber.[8]

Indeed, the pattern closely parallels the implied mythology of the Fall according to which Adam misinterpreted the gift of knowledge, taking as Law what should have been freedom. Man thereby failed to assume the stature of his full humanity. Likewise Eve is said not to have been united to Adam in a full initiatory integration of man, the Marriage Chamber; and precisely because the initiation was incomplete, man became sexually divided and subject to death and birth.

The initiate now re-enacts the mystery of union. He is reborn to primal wholeness and already shares in the life of his immortal self. The model for the union was again Christ: indeed, if we ask who begets and who is born of the union we can answer either that it is the Christ who is born within the soul of the initiate, or that the initiate himself is born — in a mystical way gives birth to himself, his eternal and spiritual part. Such a one has transcended the opposites (symbolized by right and left, life and death, male and female), and even the limitations of personal identity. 'For this one is no longer a Christian but a Christ.'

Here the *Gospel of Philip* takes its boldest step in applying the language of the Mysteries, many of which claimed to unite their adepts intimately to the life and being of the god. The Mystery instructors spoke of man 'becoming Adonis,' 'Attis,' or 'Mithras.' But the use of such Mystery concepts in Christianity is almost unparalleled in such radical form, though there are passages in the letters of Paul which go nearly as far. Man is reborn, but no longer as imperfect man, rather as Christ who is Perfect Man, the human-divine archetype. When we are also told, therefore, that Christ was born in Paradise, or in the Marriage Chamber, of the 'virgin earth' and the divine Spirit, we see the continuity with age-old religious rites involving the 'mother' earth and the heavenly powers, from whose union man (and the rest of the world) was born.

I say the rest of the world, too, because the Marriage Chamber myth of primordial division and reintegration is not limited in significance to man's soul. It encompasses the whole world of man's enhanced perception and spiritual activity. Like a Mithraic temple, the Marriage Chamber is an earthly representation of 'the All,' an image of the cosmos. When it comes to develop its teaching about 'works,' 'images' and 'children,' three different planes of spiritual life, the *Gospel* moves in its later sayings toward the unfolding of both human and macrocosmic events.

'Works' originate from the exercise of power and activity. An example would be the earthenware pots which the *Gospel* uses as a metaphor of the body. 'Works' can thus express a condition of the created world, but are also a description of the human condition which demands the exertion of man's energies for things outside himself, subjecting him to the 'dead things' of which he is an eater. In contrast, man 'begets' his children. He does not make them by his labour, but begets them out of his 'rest.' Begetting his children, man is not subjected to external objects, but produces something living out of his own being. In the *Gospel* this is a metaphor for the spiritually creative life, and 'rest' is the oneness of the spirit with its own highest nature. Between comes 'the image-like man,' that is, that part of man which lives in the contemplation of 'types and images.' For:

> Truth did not come into the world naked, but it came in
> types and images. (The world) will not receive it in any

other way. There is a rebirth, and an image of rebirth. It is truly fitting to be reborn through the image.

The world of images is a middle realm, through which the soul can ultimately reach rebirth when image becomes reality.

To achieve this, it seems, the candidate had to find within the image-world he experienced after his baptismal awakening one particular form: his own image. It was through finding this fulcrum of knowledge, where image and reality coincide in his own being, that he was further able to 'penetrate through the image into the truth.' We are thus able to understand the higher initiation of the Christians who made use of the *Gospel of Philip* as further stages in the transformation of consciousness. The first phases culminate in the reattaining of a 'Paradisal' awareness of harmony, and the bringing into consciousness of the sacramental life-processes. The higher ones lead to deeper self-knowledge, awareness of a world of creative images and of 'rest' as a higher creative faculty. Deeper levels of man's connection are uncovered in the process: for it is of the world itself that the *Gospel* says that 'it will not be able to receive incorruptibility unless it becomes a child.'[9]

For higher perception, then, the world can be released from the condition of 'works' and be reborn in the consciousness of the seer as a 'child,' as something that is no longer 'dead' but in which the spirit is active and alive. Thus the inert 'creation' is not the terminus of the *Gospel's* thought about the world, and this brings into focus the question of the book's connection with Gnostic teachings.

Now, in Gnosticism such a realm of spiritual activity was certainly known — and there are many tendencies toward Gnostic ideas in the *Gospel*. But Gnosticism stressed the radical gap, the abyss, between the world of living spirit and the inert world of things, objects. The *Gospel of Philip* on the other hand follows through a profound sequence of thought which appears rather to stress that the material world itself is or can become the locus of spiritual activity. Thus the holy man does not achieve the sanctity of his inner life in opposition to his body: 'the holy man is altogether holy, including his body.' For the vision of one who has 'already received the truth in the images,' the world and the eternal realm or Aeon are not radically opposed, but have become the same in the fullness (*pleroma*) of spiritual life.[10] The Gnostic view, which would have stressed the existential 'leap' needed to cross from material into the spiritual, rather than their continuity, would necessarily have displaced human consciousness from its place at the centre, holding together different levels of being. In the *Gospel of Philip*, however, that centrality is maintained through the teaching of 'the Son of Man' who actively joins together the whole:

> The Son of Man received from God the power to create. It is also his to beget.[11]

The child of his activity is a 'son of the Son of Man.'

The world-vision of the *Gospel of Philip* and its concept of the work of Christ, then, points to a new stirring of the divine-spiritual activity reaching to the material realm. Despite the evident Gnostic-baptizing background of the religionists who used it, the new and uniquely Christian conception of man's consciousness and his role in the world has asserted itself. And the remarkable fact is that the practices it suggests or describes show that its users stood in the mainstream, or were even the pioneers of early Christian liturgical development; their influence extended not only to Syria but to the rest of the Christian world including the Roman sphere. (Before this kind of liturgy reached Rome, Christians had had to use the older, Jewish prayers, as we can see from the *Letter* of Clement of Rome.) Much can be paralleled especially in the liturgy of the Syrian church, in the *Mystery-Instruction for those to be Baptized* (or *Mystagogical Catecheses*) of the fourth-century Cyril of Jerusalem, and in the *Apostolic Tradition* of the Roman bishop Hippolytus.[12] In our *Gospel*, however, they are associated more pervasively with esoteric teaching — more even than in Cyril's *disciplina arcani* or secret instruction. At the same time, the powerful Gnostic tendencies that were clearly still at work within the Christian church seem to be caught in the process of being transformed, to be taken up in the mature synthesis of Christianity. Through them its spiritual atmosphere still harks back strongly to the older Mysteries.

Can we identify a particular Mystery-stream as the background of the *Gospel of Philip*? An answer to this question would obviously be of considerable importance for our whole understanding of early Christianity, showing which Mystery-traditions remained a vital force and went on to work within the Christian evolution.

In fact we can identify a particular group with some certainty. Certain passages from the *Gospel of Philip* are indeed virtual quotations from the secret teachings of the Mandaeans: a Gnostic baptizing group who survive today in areas of Iraq and Iran, but who dwelled in former times in Palestine and the Jordan valley. Baptismal water is still for them today conceived as the 'Jordan.' They are still a non-Christian *gnosis*, although ideas have collected around legends of John the Baptist, causing them to be known locally by the odd name of 'Christians of St John.' Persecution has made them, in some respects, anti-Christian despite their clear connection with Christian beginnings. (Christ now figures in their teaching as a Luciferic Mercury-being who led many of their faithful astray.) At any rate, scholars of their rich mythological and liturgical texts have noticed the similarity between the *Gospel of Philip* 's sacraments and Mandaean rites. The dualism of the *Gospel*, or that part of its teaching which looks back to Gnostic thought, is summed up in a Saying which actually quotes a Mandaean 'secret scroll.' Thus the *Gospel*:

> Light and darkness, life and death, right and left, are
> brothers of one another. It is impossible that they separate
> one from another ...

And thus the Mandaean *Thousand and Twelve Questions*:

> Observe, that light and darkness are brothers, emanating
> from one mystery ...

They are related, the Mandaean text goes on to explain at length, as right and left in the body of the macrocosmic Adam.[13] And there are other significant allusions. For example, the idea of the 'true' name of Jesus being the 'Nasoraean'/

'Nazarene' in Saying 47 also points to Mandaean secret circles: 'Nasoraeans' is the self-designation of their higher initiates.

Still more interesting is the light shed by Mandaeism upon the *Gospel's* remaining cultic act — the 'redemption.' It seems to occupy a place between the first three stages and the highest rebirth in the Marriage Chamber, and perhaps formed the transition to that higher life. After studying the sacraments of the *Gospel of Philip*, H. G. Gaffron concluded that the 'redemption' was a rite like the Mandaean *masikta*, performed for the dead to ensure the redemption of the soul, in which the priest accompanies the departed, so to speak, through the realms of the other world. Lady Drower, who pioneered modern contacts with the Mandaeans and was initiated into their teachings, records the extensive preparations required to perform it. Its symbolism consists in 'the creation of the Secret Adam, the cosmic Adam, limb by limb in the primeval vastness of the cosmic womb, the Mother.' A second part of the rite includes the Mysteries of the Father, once more reproducing the archaic mystery of the 'sacred marriage' and, as in the *Gospel of Philip*, pointing to fulfilment in the Marriage-Chamber and the initiatory rebirth. The rite is so holy, continues Lady Drower, 'that lay eyes may not witness it, so sacredly dangerous that the least slip, the least omission, must be expiated by baptisms and ... may disqualify a priest for life.' The celebrant must hold a high office in the Mandaean priesthood; he and his assistants represent cosmic beings of the 'Great Ether' and the cosmic Word, Mahzian.

Evidently the rite is powerful not only for the redemption of the departed soul, but also for the celebrant. He too is taken up and shaped by cosmic forces. And perhaps because of this it came to be performed for reasons other than helping the departed, and became in early Christianity a stage of higher initiation. There seems to be some connection, too, with the later Gnostic rite of the *consolamentum*, a sacrament for the dying which could be performed earlier in the case of an advanced soul (an Elect, or Perfect). Those who had undergone the rite lived already in the spiritual world while yet alive.[14] The *Gospel of Philip* enables us to trace these developments back to the earliest phases of Christian sacramentalism.

Behind the sacraments of *Philip*, then, stands Mandaean ritualism. We see Gnostic practices and ideas being absorbed and
transformed into a Christian vision. In an earlier chapter it was
suggested that Gnosticism came into being as a response to the
meeting of East and West: oriental Mysteries came into contact
with the consciousness of Judaism and its world-view, producing both new syntheses such as Essenism and the defensive
reaction of Gnostic dualism. Can we then point to the Mystery-
tradition behind the Mandaean *gnosis* and its ritual practice? We
have already mentioned several points of similarity with
Mithraism, such as the idea of the initiation-chamber as *imago
mundi*, the concept of becoming one with the Mystery-god,
especially through a ritual meal, and so on. And in fact much
more can be paralleled in the detail of the rites. In Mithraism we
have a Mystery in several stages, through which the initiate is
successively admitted to the sacred meal, then to more esoteric
celebrations and teachings. The stages are experienced in close
connection to the cosmic spheres of the planets, sun and moon,
so that the whole progress of the initiate can be conceived in
terms of cosmic ascension, vividly represented in the 'cosmic
ladder' or staircase-constructions shown on Mithraic monu-
ments; elsewhere there were seven gates to be traversed as in
ancient Near Eastern temples. The early grades of initiation consisted of baptism, among other things, and to this was added, in
a manner strikingly akin to the *Gospel of Philip*, a light-symbol-
ism suggestive of an inner 'illumination.' That was for the grade
of *Nymphus* (Bride), referring to the stage of sacred marriage.
The grades were also linked to the different elements, and there
are similarities with the 'alchemical' imagery of the *Gospel of
Philip*. Many more particulars could be mentioned. The symbol
of the god as the Tree (in Paradise) is also known in Mithraism,
for instance. The common background of Mithraism and
Mandaeism can be seen in many of their cosmological ideas.
And both carried on the use of an archaic Iranian ritual gesture:
the clasping of the right hand of the initiate, signifying redemption. Strangely, perhaps, this ritual vanished from Christianity
although it appears again and is of central importance in
Manichaeism.[15]

In short, the interconnection of Mithraic Mysteries,

Mandaean *gnosis* and early Christian ritual sheds light on one of the previously baffling phenomena of religious history: the startling similarity between the Christian eucharist and the pagan feast of Mithras, between pagan initiations and Christian sacraments generally. The later Fathers were perplexed and appalled, but could not deny it, embarrassing to their 'orthodoxy' though it might be. In context we need not be so surprised. We saw in an earlier chapter that the Magi, and specifically the Magian priests of Mithra, had an interest in Christian beginnings, since they saw in Jesus the fulfilment of their own prophechies. As the Saoshyant he was the Saviour and a rebirth of the prophet, a Zarathustra *redivivus*. To understand the relevance of Mithraism, we simply need to see how the worship of Mithra had already spread to circles outside Zoroastrianism, and assumed the form of the Mithras Mysteries, known from Latin sources and the ruins of their temples.

Mithra was a very ancient god of the Indians and Iranians, and was honoured with special rites, the *Mithrakana*. It seems to have been the Magi of Babylonia, however, who gradually transformed these rites into the basis of a secret society. They apparently felt that spiritual conditions had changed so that the presence of the light-god was no longer perceptible in the ordinary world and by ordinary men. To share in the inner light of the god now required a special development — indeed several stages of development — and could be shared only by the few. They also anticipated, however, a glorious manifestation of Mithra in the time to come as a 'Great King,' like certain of the 'Sun'-kings of the legendary age of the Iranian past, but outshining them all. He may even have been equated in some prophecies with the promised Saoshyant. The inner structure of the Mysteries they adopted from the wisdom of the Babylonians, along with much cosmology and teaching about the creation. Hence we find the ancient Mesopotamian ideas, some of them going back to Gilgamesh and his quest for the Plant of Life, the ideas about Paradise as the Garden of the cosmic mount, and so on, woven into the religion of Mithra, as well as re-emerging in our *Gospel of Philip*.

Mithraism preserved a continuity with the very archaic rites of Mithra, whilst adapting itself to later conditions and availing itself of subsequent ideas. In the last century or so before Christ it constitutes a religious Mystery-tradition of extraordinary importance, spreading from Babylonia into Syria and Asia Minor (modern Turkey) where there were already established Zoroastrian communities. Subsequently we can see its influence in the Gnostic ritualism of the Mandaeans. In its pagan form it spread into Armenia and thence was brought to Rome: it acquired a powerfully military character, drawing many devotees from the Roman armies, and its rites became ever more extravagant. By the fourth century AD they had become bloody ordeals, culminating in the famous slaughter of the bull, whose blood dripped down on the initiate through a grill into a pit beneath the altar. We now know that the Mithraists had adopted this sacrifice from the crude and violent native religions of Asia Minor — a far cry from the cult of light and trustfulness from early Iran! In its purer form, on the other hand, the Mystery lived on in other ways. In the light of the *Gospel of Philip* indeed it is scarcely an exaggeration to say that the Mystery survived and developed as Christian sacramentalism.[16]

Thus the 'new' *Gospel* provides for the first time clear evidence of the contact between early Christianity and the Mysteries. It reveals how in their Gnostic form the Mysteries worked on in Christianity, shaping the prototype of Christian ritual life. But there is, of course, the remaining side of the question still to be discussed: for the *Gospel of Philip* makes the further claim that its Mysteries received the direct stamp of Jesus' own ritual acts.

That Jesus performed some kind of initiatory baptism is asserted also by the fragment of the secret *Mark*, the early tradition of the Alexandrian church. Complementary testimony from Syria is strong evidence, therefore. Scholars, notably Rudolf Bultmann, have sometimes made much of Mandaean evidence. And Lady Drower pointed out that several sayings of Jesus sound to Mandaeans like quotations from their sacred books. But we must beware of forcing the picture. For Jesus is not the only authority acknowledged in the *Gospel of Philip*; actual Sayings of the Lord make up only a minority of the entries. Hence, without discounting its tradition that 'the Lord did everything in a Mystery,' we must be prepared to suspect that the truth of the matter was a little more complex. It appears that Philip (or his disciples and successors) took an element that was genuinely a part of Jesus' own background and practice. But in establishing this form of Christianity in Syria, they evidently allowed the Mandaean Gnostic background to reassert itself very substantially, partly reabsorbing the new Christian message into older forms once more. The Christian spirit has transformed parts of the teaching in the *Gospel of Philip*, notably in the un-Gnostic approach to matter and the potential holiness even of the body. Yet in other ways the uniquely Christian balance has been disturbed, Christ is understood as a timeless Gnostic Mystery-god, and the relationship to history is at least partly lacking.[17] Before we can evaluate the *Gospel's* evidence of Jesus' own place in the Mystery-tradition, and in order to come closer to the actual circle of Jesus and his disciples, we must turn to yet another gospel. This time its traditions take the form almost completely of Sayings of Jesus. What kind of picture do they give?

The Mystery of 'Interpretation'

The *Gospel of Thomas* was one of the first documents from the Gnostic library to find its way into the public eye. A 'Gnostic gospel' was presented to a wide readership as a foretaste of further Gnostic revelations, to follow when the texts were released by the wrangling authorities. The earlier studies examined the book for evidence of Gnostic theology — and they found it. But gradually attention began to be paid to other aspects. The closeness, often the identity of Jesus' Sayings in the *Gospel of Thomas* with those in the canonical New Testament was noted. Discrepancies between the Nag Hammadi versions and the fragments known earlier revealed that the Gnostics had dropped certain elements from their edition, suggesting that the *Gospel* came into being at a stage in the tradition before 'orthodox' and 'Gnostic' schools had begun to go their separate ways, and predated the development of fully Gnosticized Christianity. In fact, analysis of the Sayings tended to show that they were earlier forms of the oral tradition than the 'literary' versions in the canonical Gospels. Scholars learned to take seriously the admonition of the *Gospel of Thomas* to 'find the interpretation.' It started to become clear that behind the 'Gnostic gospel' picture was a much more significant reality: a very early collection of Jesus' teachings and a tradition about their meaning.

Like the *Gospel of Philip*, the *Gospel of Thomas* represents a Christian tradition preserved in Syria. Legends of the apostle Thomas and evidence from the *Gospel* itself point, however, not to Antioch but to the more northerly centre of Edessa. An important trading city on the caravan routes between east and west, Edessa was a culturally rich 'Athens of the Orient' and also an early cradle of Christianity. The more intriguing of the legends concerning the coming of Christian teachers relate that Thaddaeus or Addai, one of the seventy-two disciples of Jesus mentioned by Luke, came to evangelize the city during the reign of its king Abgar V (known as 'the Black'). The details of the story are largely fanciful — especially the notion that there had been a preceding correspondence between Abgar and Jesus. These apocryphal letters are preserved, but are rather mediocre forgeries. Indeed the inclusion of the king in the events is wishful thinking altogether, since the first Christian king of Edessa was Abgar IX in the late second century. Nevertheless, the story preserves the significant knowledge that Christianity came to the city directly from Palestine, rather than from any of the Greek-speaking communities or from Antioch, and at an early date. The discovery of the *Gospel* confirms the basic assertion of the legends, and enables us to see what particular form of Christianity it was that 'Addai' (if that was the name of the earliest *teaching* in Edessa) brought: Christianity in the name of the apostle Thomas. Later on, by the third century, there was a flourishing literature about Thomas. It told of his spreading of the gospel in the East, including India, and most of it seems to have been written in Edessa. It is most likely therefore that Thomas-traditions were in truth the first form of Christianity to arrive there, and that it developed in connection with ideas from the East. Some of the legends in the so-called *Infancy Gospel of Thomas*, we have already seen have an authentically Indian flavour.

The background of the *Gospel of Thomas* has much in common

with the teaching of the *Ebionim*, deriving from the former Jewish esotericism of the Essenes. Of the Sayings which can be paralleled in the canonical Gospels, the largest number coincide with those in Matthew, the Jewish-Christian gospel.[18] Moreover, ancient writers quote some of the Sayings known to us now from *Thomas* as having been in the *Gospel of the Hebrews*: so it is possible that *Thomas* includes some of the more esoteric teaching which was later suppressed and omitted by the editors of the orthodox Gospel of Matthew. In addition, however, Thomas has developed his understanding of the Christ-event in his own unique way. If the legends of his travels in the East contain any truth, they would help explain the emphasis of his *Gospel* on a kind of Eastern 'illumination.'

Thomas is presented in the short introductory Saying of the *Gospel* as a typical 'minister of the word':

> These are the secret words which Jesus the Living spoke,
> and Didymus Judas Thomas wrote them down.

Thus the words are not presented as reports from a historical witness, but are the result of visions and auditions of the 'Living,' that is, the resurrected, Jesus. In the context of the *Gospel*, the Sayings are rarely referred to a situation in Jesus' life at all. Rather they constitute a path of meditation, the aim of which is to awaken knowledge of man's eternal and immortal self. In short, Jesus' words are not 'interpreted' by being placed in relation to his earthly mission, but to man's inner awakening. Hence:

> Whoever finds the interpretation of these words shall not
> taste death.

For he will have discovered his undying higher self. Behind this idea stands the teaching of the 'Son of Man,' first actualized in Jesus but potentially present in every man, as we learn later in the *Gospel*. Unity with the deeper self is achieved by that overcoming of dualities in the soul which is so central to the *Gospel of Philip*, and is again connected with man's power to assert his power over, to transform the earth:

Jesus said: When you make the two one, you shall become Sons of Man, and when you say 'Mountain, be moved,' it shall be moved.

This becoming a 'Son of Man' is mystically equivalent to the disciple's discovery of Christ in the inner depths; for as Jesus also says, 'I myself will become he, and the hidden things shall be revealed to him.'[19]

For Thomas, however, the achievement of the Christ-consciousness is not the outcome of a ritual initiation and sacramental devotion. It is the result of an austere course of meditation. Traditional ways of life, mainly Jewish, involving ritual food-laws, circumcision, observing fast-days, and so on, are all declared to be irrelevant in so far as they are practised outwardly: complete inner integrity is alone important. If circumcision were profitable, children would be born already circumcised, argues Jesus. The point is not for man to change himself outwardly, but spiritually.

The *Gospel of Thomas* is therefore set out as a series of meditative Sayings on 'the Way.' They are grouped, not around outer events but around their common spiritual goal. Prominent among them are the Parables of the Kingdom — many of which we know from Jesus' teaching in the New Testament. Familiar parables are the Sower (Saying 9), the Grain of Mustard-Seed (Saying 20), the Rich Man who died in the night and lost all his treasured possessions (63), the Wedding Guest (64), the Vineyard (65), the Pearl (76), the Leaven (96), the Lost Sheep (107) and the Hidden Treasure (109).[20] But there are also some unfamiliar parables, such as the one of the Fisherman (8):

And he said: Man is like a wise fisherman, who cast his net into the sea and drew it up from the sea full of small fish. Among them the wise fisherman found a large good fish. He threw down all the small fish into the sea; he chose the large fish without hesitation. He who has ears to hear, let him hear!

Interestingly, the object of the parable in this case is not described in terms of the Kingdom, but simply 'Man.' The para-

ble turns our attention inward to the source of spiritual commitment, our real self, and seems to warn us against being dis-
tracted by the myriad 'small fish' on our way.

Another parable unattested in the familiar Gospels focuses on
awareness/unawareness:

> Jesus said: The Kingdom of the Father is like a woman
> carrying a jar full of meal and walking a long way. The
> handle of the jar broke; the meal poured out behind her
> on the road. She was unaware, she did not know of her
> loss. When she came into her house, she put down the jar
> (and) found it empty.[21]

Those who are spiritually unaware believe that they possess just
as much of the truth, and see the whole of reality as do those
who are 'aware.' But on reaching the goal, the difference
emerges. Only those who are awake find the Kingdom. Indeed
the theme of awareness runs through the *Gospel* and illuminates
the parables in particular.

The parables of Jesus, both the familiar stories and the
authentic-sounding additions from the *Gospel of Thomas*, constitute an extraordinary case in the history of biblical studies.
On the face of it, they have all of them rather obvious meanings and because of their narrative simplicity we are able to
form a clear moral judgment about the characters sketched in
them: the Good Samaritan, the — Widow who gave her last
mite, the Servant who buried his treasure. Yet, as the scholar
T. W. Manson put it, we have the paradox that 'whole volumes have been written in exposition of compositions whose
meaning is supposed to be obvious.' Manson was led to investigate the background of 'parable,' the term used both by the
evangelists and by Jesus. He found it in the Hebrew term
mashal — which, however, had a somewhat wider meaning in
ancient Judaism than we have come to associate with the
word parable today. A *mashal* could be any condensed formulation of wisdom, for example in a brief gnomic verse, or a
proverb. Or it could refer to a vivid simile or instance which
becomes a byword for the point being made. This broader use
of the term appears in the New Testament too: thus the saying

'Physician, heal thyself' is called a 'parable' in Luke. Probably all the Sayings in the *Gospel of Thomas* could broadly have been classed as *mashal*.

The parables which take the form of stories, then, are not a special case to be set against the statements and discourses. Above all, neither in *Thomas* nor the New Testament are they 'helpful illustrations' of Jesus' teaching, but an integral part of it. They are 'Imaginations' in the sense of the term we have used earlier, embodying in pictorial form the same meaning that is served by the ministry of the word. The full force of Jesus' teaching is present in them, so that it is not so surprising to find that, as Rudolf Steiner commented, what is presented as parable in one gospel is presented in another as event. The episode of the Fig-Tree in the Gospel of Mark, for example, appears within a parable in Luke.[22] It would be entirely mistaken to see here a process whereby stories told by Jesus became part of the legend of his life. What is important to grasp is the process whereby the events of his life attain the power of parable, a hidden dimension grasped by 'those inside,' comparable to the transforming potency of the great myths of the ancient Mysteries, while 'those outside' see only the bizarre phenomenon of a crucified teacher and miracle-worker. Hence the sense of a 'gap' between the straightforward understanding and the sense of a deeper dimension is really the same as we find more generally in the content of Christianity.

Perhaps we can now return to the famous difficult summation given in Jesus' words according to Mark, where he says to the disciples:

> To you is given the secret of the Kingdom of God; but to those outside all things happen in parables.[23]

Thomas' doctrine of 'interpretation' derives in essence from this 'parabolic' method of Jesus' teaching. It is easy to comprehend that the woman with the jar of meal was lacking in awareness. But to grasp the crucial quality of awareness as a way to the Kingdom, as referring to man's own deepest reality or immortal self — that is something further, characterizing 'those inside.' By this stage in our studies it will, I think, be obvious that there is here no arbitrary privilege conferred. It is every man himself who either takes the step to a different way of seeing, or does not; he places himself in one category or the other according to his response to the teaching. This is the true esotericism, whether or not there is an element of outward secrecy. And it is in this sense that, while the object of the parables is the Kingdom, it is also 'Man,' as in the *Gospel of Thomas*, Saying 8.

In the Gospels that came down to us as part of the New Testament, the Kingdom to which sayings and parables point often seems bafflingly obscure, making the surface transparency of the parables all the more tantalizing. It is hard to see whether it is something to be actualized through apocalyptic events, something that takes place in a kind of moral reformation, a personal commitment to God here and now — or in what it consists! According to Mark's tradition, it belonged to the inner-circle teaching of Jesus, so that we shall hardly expect to see it explained at large there. Ultimately however, it must be contained in the mystery of the resurrection to which Mark so dramatically points, but once more does not make explicit. In the evangelists' own thought, we recall, the concept of the 'Son of Man' is no longer invoked. Hence the centre of the 'mystery of the Kingdom' is displaced, becomes elusive. What is striking about the *Gospel of Thomas*, on the other hand, is that the mystery of the Kingdom is intimately wedded to the broader surface-themes of the teaching in a highly centred manner: themes of seeking and finding, interpretation, hidden and manifest, rebirth, and above all the transformation of consciousness. We have a sense of coherence that suggests a closeness to the source of the ideas. In one Saying Jesus addresses the 'insiders' (the 'single ones' and the 'chosen') and tells them that the Kingdom is their own primal being:

> for you came forth from thence, and you shall go there once again.[24]

Thus the Kingdom is not discovering something that has not previously existed. But it requires a change of consciousness:

His disciples said to him: On what day will the Kingdom come? Jesus said: It does not come with looking. No-one will say, Lo it is here! or, Lo it is there! But the Kingdom of the Father is spread out upon the earth, and men do not see it.[25]

Learning to see 'what is before one's face' is also to see 'what is hidden.'

The location of the Kingdom in the world we actually know and see does not mean that Jesus' teaching could not have had an apocalyptic aspect. According to another Saying:

Jesus said: The heavens shall be rolled up and the earth before your face, and he who lives in the Living One shall neither see death nor fear; because Jesus says: He who shall find himself, of him the world is not worthy. [26]

After all, in Jewish tradition one important form of vision seen by those who have undergone a change of consciousness is the vision of impending crisis, or the last events. The Essenes had a highly apocalyptic world-view, yet they believed that they themselves were already living in the new order of things — and even that the new order could be entered through ritual such as baptism and their sacred meal.

Nevertheless, the strictly apocalyptic sense of an ending is absent from *Thomas*, despite its affinities with certain streams of Jewish esotericism. The end of the Jewish consciousness and its worldview turned out, for Christianity, also to be a beginning. This is reflected in the feeling for continuity which appears here. Yet another aspect of the importance of the *Gospel of Thomas* is that it helps confirm a trend of modern research, suggesting that Jesus' teaching was less apocalyptic than many theologians have supposed. Recently Christopher Rowland, for instance, has concluded of Jesus that 'there is an absence of the distinctive features of apocalyptic from his message. The message of the kingdom stresses the fact that the age to come has already made its start in his own ministry ... .' Yet: 'there is evidence to suggest that on certain occasions Jesus did receive visions which resemble the visions of apocalyptic.'[27] The teaching according to the

Gospel of Thomas fits well with the insight that for Jesus the 'apocalypse' was a change of consciousness, an 'End' but also the dawning of new awareness. There is the sense of an unveiling, but it is a revelation not so much of the secrets of heaven as of earth.

In its teaching of self-knowledge, of finding the Kingdom which is even now spread out on the physical earth through changed consciousness, the *Gospel of Thomas* expresses a Christian not a Gnostic vision. Yet it represents a form of Christianity which has much more in common with Gnosticism than any of the versions later tolerated by the Church, notably in its strong sense of secrecy, its stress on interpretation, its criticism of the Law. Does this represent Jesus' own drawing upon the teachings of the more Gnostic baptizing sects? The fact that it is mixed with features of Jewish-Christianity of Ebionite type does not detract from the authenticity of the picture, since we know of Jesus' contacts with the Essene background. And yet there are other Sayings which perhaps appear too purely Gnostic. Were these later insertions?

It seems rather that the *Gospel of Thomas* bears witness to the activity of another Mystery-school in the early stages of Christian evolution. Just as the *Gospel of Philip* shows how a ritual and sacramental tradition took a new direction from aspects of Jesus' teachings and practice, so the *Gospel of Thomas* illustrates the presence of another tradition rooted in the Mysteries. This group steered their form of Christianity away from ritualism, however, under the authority of Thomas the apostle, and developed techniques of enlightenment through sayings and parables. And once again it is possible to identify them through the spiritual language and symbolism they employed in the *Gospel* as it took literary form. For we know of a pagan Mystery which just at the time of Christian beginnings achieved an extensive literary expression, and which was moving radically away from rites and sacrifices like those of the temples. It demanded a 'spiritual sacrifice' and a 'baptism in mind.' For the root-problem of man was diagnosed in inner, psychological terms rather than by pointing to his position in the world: man was as if drunk, unaware, in a stupor as regards his higher self. That is the teaching of the Hermetic Mysteries:

> You men, where are you rushing in your drunkenness,
> you who have drained the undiluted doctrine of
> ignorance ... Be sober and stop, look up with the eyes of
> your heart!

And that is the language attributed to the Saviour in the *Gospel of Thomas*:

> Jesus said: I stood in the midst of the world, and I
> appeared to them in flesh. I found them all drunk, I found
> none among them thirsting; and my soul was afflicted for
> the sons of men, for they are blind in their heart and they
> do not see.

The scholar G. Quispel has seen this Hermetic influence as further evidence for the *Gospel's* origin in Edessa, where we know such Mysteries were prominent.[28] It also explains much about the character of the *Gospel*: its turning away from ritual, its austere emphasis on solitary meditation and the quest for truth. It shows that from the very beginning Mystery-circles were involved in Christianity. In fact, we have seen that Hermetism drew upon the Jewish-Iranian mysticism that lies also behind the Essenes and the early Christian *Ebionim*. They formerly practised a 'baptism of *metanoia*' like many of the esoteric sects, before adopting a purely 'spiritual' approach to the inner life. The ancient prophet Hermes — originally the Egyptian god of wisdom, Thoth — was later honoured by some Christians as a forerunner of Christ.

At the same time, it is obvious that Jesus' own words and teaching figure much more largely in the *Gospel of Thomas* than anything else. Yet, like the *Gospel of Philip*, it seems to have developed on the basis of a special tradition, and the delicate new synthesis of Christian vision is not fully achieved. Overall in the *Gospel of Thomas* we have a certain oriental sternness which seems inappropriate to the message of Jesus. Those critics who simply deny the presence of a doctrine of

love in it are, I think, wrong. The awakener who comes to rescue humanity from its ignorant stupor is moved to do so by
love. And if there are Buddhistic parallels, we should remember that Buddhism is the great religion of compassion. But one
is inclined to wonder if the *Gospel of Thomas* does not give
somewhat a one-sided version of Jesus' teachings, concen-
trated on intellectual illumination.

We stand once more, then, in a tantalizing position. Both
our Mystery Gospels derive from circles immediately around
Jesus and seem to contain authentic knowledge of his teaching and Mystery practice. Yet both in the long run evidently
accommodated his influence to older pre-Christian traditions.
It remains difficult to be sure of the exact form of the original
teaching and original practice, especially since the two documents offer such opposite emphases — one ritualistic and
sacramental, the other austerely meditational. Yet the evidence can be looked at another way, offering a further step
forward. For we have not yet examined the extent to which
the *Gospel of Philip* and the *Gospel of Thomas* agree.

In fact there are many traces in *Thomas* that its content may
have overlapped at one stage with something much more like
the *Gospel of Philip* . Moreover, despite its outright rejection of
ritual, there are even signs of a ritual structure in which the different aspects of the *Gospel's* message cohere.

For one thing, there is a curious mention of the:

> five Trees in Paradise, which do not move in summer or
> in winter, and their leaves do not fall. He who knows
> them shall not taste of death.

Does this have any relationship to the five-stage mystery
enacted in the *Gospel of Philip*, and its ritual re-entry into
Paradise? That might help explain, for example, how it is that
the 'chosen' are said to return to where they 'came forth,' that is,
to a renewed innocence. The condition of renewal in *Philip* is a
rebirth, and this is prominent in the *Gospel of Thomas* in connection with Jesus' words about 'becoming as a child.' Ideas of
innocence, childhood, and the spiritual vision are combined in a
saying such as:

His disciples said: On what day will you be revealed to
us, and on what day shall we see thee? Jesus said: When
you unclothe yourselves and are not ashamed, and take
your garments and lay them beneath your feet like little
children, and tread upon them, then shall you see the Son
of the Living One, and you shall not fear.

The repeated idea of 'shall not fear' in the *Gospel* points to an initiatory ordeal. Surely the unrobing of innocence, not shameful,
once referred to baptism and reattaining the condition of
Paradise.[29]

Other threads in the *Gospel of Thomas* familiar from the
Sayings of *Philip* include ideas about eating 'dead things' and
'living' food; there is a teaching about 'images'; above all there
are references to the 'Marriage Chamber.' In a version of the
Saying known from Matthew ('Many are called, but few are the
chosen'), Jesus says:

There are many standing outside at the door, but the
single ones are those who shall enter the Marriage
Chamber.

Evidently the moment when the initiate emerged from the
Bridal Chamber was one of special holiness, and he was
helped by the fasting and prayer of the community.[30] The
scholar F. F. Bruce may be right when he infers from the language of rebirth, and particularly the discussion of 'true' or
spiritual motherhood (as opposed to natural) in some of the
Sayings, that the underlying idea is of becoming a 'Son of the
Holy Spirit,' known already from the *Gospel of the Hebrews*. If
he is correct, that would again seem to point to Jesus' baptismal experience as the foundation of his ritual and teaching.
It would also link the *Gospel of Thomas* with those Jewish-
Christian early traditions of baptism, connected with the figure of James, the brother of the Lord, which also regard
becoming a son of the Spirit as their goal. And indeed, James
is given high praise in the *Gospel of Thomas* as he 'for whom
heaven and earth were brought into being.'[31]

The famous Saying about wonder and 'reigning' that heads

the collection of the *Gospel of Thomas* likewise points strongly to a ritual background. Baptism had been a part of the Near Eastern royal initiations.

Another passage in *Thomas* invites comparison with the Gospel of John, where Jesus tells Nicodemus that man must be reborn before he can see the Kingdom. 'How can a man be born when he is old?' Nicodemus retorts. 'Surely he cannot enter a second time into his mother's womb to be born?' Jesus speaks in reply about the birth 'from water and the spirit.' In the passage from *Thomas*, Jesus says that the 'little ones' at the breast are like those who enter the Kingdom. His disciples reply with the same kind of literal-mindedness as Nicodemus: 'If we are little, shall we enter the Kingdom?'

> Jesus said to them: When you make the two one, and
> when you make the inside as the outside, and the outside
> as the inside, and the upper as the lower: and when you
> make the male and female into a single one, that the male
> be not male and the female female; when you put an eye
> in the place of an eye, and a hand in the place of a hand, a
> foot in the place of a foot, an image in the place of an
> image — then you shall enter the Kingdom.

There is no reference here to the elements of the baptismal mystery, 'water and the spirit.' Nevertheless, being as a 'little child' is defined in non-literal terms which we recognize clearly from the themes of the *Gospel of Philip*. It is an overcoming of psychic divisions — inner/outer, male/female — and a transformation of perception. In fact, the themes are both major ones throughout the *Gospel of Thomas* as well as *Philip*.[32]

Hence, despite its austere emphasis on 'spirit and truth' as against communal and sacramental life, the *Gospel* must be classed as a 'Mystery' document with ritual practices of initiation not far away. A structure of baptismal Mystery, involving death-rebirth, illumination, enthronement and mystic marriage is still clear, and is presented emerging from the words of Jesus himself.

The similarities and contrasts of *Thomas* and *Philip* show in strong colours the diversity of early Christianity. The apostles who preserved Jesus' teaching, and took it out to the world, spent the rest of their lives meditating, practising and deepening their understanding of the Gospel. In the process, it seemed to some of them that the ritual element had been of negligible importance: what had been essential was the inner response, the 'interpretation' that had arisen in the soul and made it aware of its undying essence. Thomas, or his followers who used the *Gospel* and finalized its form, belong to this class. The result of his preaching was to create a distinct type, the Christian 'single one' or solitary (*monachos*), found wandering through Syria and deserts elsewhere in the early Christian centuries searching for an inner truth. To other apostles, on the other hand, the ritual process seemed to have been primary. Philip (or his followers) felt justified therefore in reintegrating their Christianity into the kind of elaborate sacramentalism cultivated among the baptist sects.

We need not think that Jesus practised the complex Mandaean rites. Nevertheless, the evidence is that he drew on a background similar to their Gnostic vision, as well as on Essene types of ritual practice. There can be no question of a ritual pattern being read into Jesus' words by Thomas, since he has no interest in ritual or is actively against it. The teaching on a transformation of perception, of becoming a child, baptismal rebirth and a mystery of inner unification, marriage or becoming all light, the achievement of 'kingship' or reigning (enthronement) — these elements all emerge in *Thomas* and *Philip* as connected with the 'Son of Man' and with the vision of the Kingdom in the content of Jesus' inner-circle teaching. With the benefit of these two *Gospels*, the secret *Mark*, and the modern research-discoveries of the esoteric movements of the Essenes and Gnostics, we can at last answer the question from which this book started out — the question about Jesus' esoteric teaching, and the context in which such knowledge was imparted.

It would be a mistake to suppose, however, that the new evidence is to be set against the older evidence of the New Testament documents. We have shown throughout that the background discovered is also the true background of the familiar gospels, which appear in a new light. It is striking, indeed, that the *Gospel of Thomas* is the work from the Nag Hammadi library which shows the closest, intimate relationship with the canonical gospels. That is part of the force of its testimony to the original significance of Jesus' words.

The evidence of a baptismal Mystery sheds a direct light on some of the most perplexing passages of Jesus' teaching. Many readers have wondered about the parable of the Wedding Guest. They have particularly been disturbed by the ending of the tale in Matthew's version, where the guest who lacks a wedding-garment is expelled from the feast. The whole scene acquires a sudden translucency, however, when we realize wherein the Kingdom is like a marriage: namely, in the setting of an initiatory rite. Such a happening calls man away from the round of his duties in the world — or should do. Jesus' parable notices that the great ones of the earth are not prepared to give up their possessions for spiritual enrichment. The same is true also of the moral elites, like the Pharisees. Yet the poor man can aspire to the illumination they have rejected. In fact, anyone and everyone good or bad, rich or poor, is called to the feast:

> So the servants went out into the streets and gathered all
> the people they could find, both good and bad, and the
> Marriage Chamber was filled with guests. But when the
> King came in to see the guests, he noticed a man there
> who was not wearing wedding clothes. 'Friend,' he asked,
> 'how did you get in here without wedding clothes?' The
> man was speechless. Then the King told the attendants,
> 'Tie him hand and foot, and cast him into the outer
> darkness, where there will be weeping and gnashing of
> teeth.'[33]

The point is now surely clear, and confirms the recent suggestion that the 'garment' is the white baptismal robe. The end of the parable concerns those who try to thrust their way into the spiritual domain without going through the death and rebirth of initiation; they are told that they risk the fate of their soul by doing so. The psychic dangers of improperly prepared initiatory experience have always been stressed by the guardians of Mysteries. The image of the outer darkness is a vivid warning of the psychic disruption, the moral paralysis, that may follow. The setting is thus a baptismal Mystery, and the whole passage concludes with the Mystery formula we have already quoted in the version from *Thomas*:

> For many are called, but few are the chosen.

Thomas says this concerns the 'single ones,' or those who have achieved the inner unity of the 'Marriage Chamber.'[34]

The Mystery Gospels under the names of Thomas and Philip ultimately confirm the character of the Christian Mystery. A transformation of consciousness is intimated which can transform man's vision of the earth and reveal 'the Kingdom.' Both Philip and Thomas show a tendency to slip back into Gnostic patterns deriving from older Mystery-rites. But in their metamorphosis at the hands of Jesus they acquired the new meaning of man's maturing individuality, rather than cosmic mysticism: Jesus said:

> He who knows the All but fails to know himself, lacks everything.[35]

The cosmic, mythic dimension is not lost; but it includes above all the sphere of the earthly, and history, man's finite world. A Saying in Thomas has generally been taken as a statement of pantheism:

> Jesus said: I am the light that is over them all. I am the All. The All has come forth from me, and the All has attained unto me. Cleave the wood: I am there. Raise up the stone, and you will find me there.[36]

Yet it can be read with a different emphasis. The All, the light of the world, can also be found in those rudiments of earthly life, in a piece of wood, in the lifting of a stone. The earth is no realm estranged from the divine. In the consciousness intimated by the Christian vision, the perspective of the myth does not exclude the material world: there too the divine is actively present.

The fulfilment of the Mystery was to take place on the material stage of things, in the 'place of the skull' outside Jerusalem. And now the pieces of the jigsaw begin to fall into place, both as ritual and as history. We can understand a little better how it was that Jesus spoke in anticipation of that Event of Golgotha, still using the language of baptismal Mystery. There is the occasion, for instance, when John the Baptist's disciples are puzzled at the unconventional behaviour of those of Jesus; but Jesus asks them:

> How can the sons of the Marriage Chamber mourn while the Bridegroom (*nymphios*) is with them? The time will come when the *nymphios* will be taken from them; then they will fast.

Often dismissed by commentators as a misunderstood allegory, or an invention of the Church projected back into the life of Jesus, the Saying can now be understood as a surviving indication of Jesus' ritual language. The context — discussion with John's baptized disciples — is obviously important. John's baptism of *metanoia* stands close to Hermetic Mysteries as well as to the Essenes and Mandaeans: the significance of Jesus' language would not be lost on them.[37] He refers to the disciples as initiates into the secret of his destiny, in which they too will have a share of suffering. Specifically, the *nymphios* terminology is that of a baptismal mystery (there is certainly no suggestion of any strange orgiastic goings-on). The further stage of 'fasting' reminds us again of the *Gospel of Thomas*.

This evidence can be linked with another fragment of a lost Gospel found on a leaf of ancient papyrus in 1905. Oxyrhyncus Papyrus 840 records a typical encounter of Jesus and his disciples with the Pharisaic leadership. Accused of ritual impurity whilst walking in the forecourt of the Temple, Jesus replies by contrasting the corrupt and stagnant water of the Jewish purification rites, which anyway can only 'chafe the outer skin,' with his own practice:

> But I and my disciples of whom you say that we have not immersed ourselves — we have been immersed in the

living (...) water, which comes down from ... (text
damaged)

'Living water,' that is, running water, is demanded for
Mandaean baptism. There it is regarded as water from the heavenly river, the archetypal Jordan. The Christian-Essene manual
called the *Didache* insists on 'living water' for baptism, too. The
authenticity of the fragment is supported by this and by the new
evidence, and adds to our conviction that Jesus did indeed prac-
tise a baptism of initiation.[38]

That Jesus saw baptismal initiation, however, as an intimation
of his own historical role is still more strongly apparent when,
before his triumphal entry into Jerusalem, James and John wish
to share at the deepest level in his mission and his destined
glory. Jesus tells them:

> You do not know what you ask. Can you drink the cup I
> drink, or be baptized with the baptism I must be baptized
> with?

On the basis of this passage it has been suggested in the past
that Jesus must have performed baptismal rites, possibly in the
earliest part of his career, and was here recalling that activity.[39]
But in the light of the newer evidence it is clear that we are concerned with something far more central, indeed crucial to his
ministry. Here once more are overtones of royalty and
Messianism: James and John wish to sit on the right and left of
Jesus in the heavenly Kingdom. And of course the passage'
acquires vastly more weight since in Mark's version it follows
directly upon the story of the nocturnal baptism — the initiation
into the 'Mysteries of the heavens.' Thus the threads of tradition
are closely interwoven.[40]

But Jesus replies by reinterpreting the ideal of kingship,
assigning to it a role contrasting with that of 'the rulers of the
Gentiles':

> For even the Son of Man did not come to be served, but to
> serve, and to give his life as a ransom for many. (Mark
> 10:45)

For an understanding of this deepest paradox in the heart of the Mystery we may turn to another writer, still close in time to the happenings — indeed the earliest Christian writer known to us, the vastly influential yet oddly unfamiliar Paul.

11. An Unfamiliar Paul

For Paul, the fiery personality who did more than anyone else to spread the message of Christianity, the Christian vision did nothing less than turn the whole world of values upside down. Not only did his own Damascus-experience transform him from persecutor into enthusiast: it meant the overthrow of all the old distinctions, Jew and Gentile, Pharisees and publicans, glory and degradation, 'righteous' and 'sinners.' We can sense him wrestling his way to a realignment of his ideas about the Godhead itself in its transcendence:

> Christ Jesus ... being in the form of God, did not account
> equality with God as something to be grasped, but
> poured himself out, taking the form of a servant, coming-
> to-be in the likeness of men; and being found in fashion
> as a man, he humbled himself, becoming obedient — to
> the point of death, and that a death on a cross.[1]

The very concept of God, the ultimate Being or source of reality, is turned upside down to account for a God who gave himself up to the conditions of earth. The thinking is tentative, personal, full of amazement; at the same time brilliant, full of delighted paradox and subtleties in distinction.

Reading Paul afresh, it is hard to see how he gained his reputation for dogmatism and bigotry. Perhaps all paradoxers run the risk of misunderstanding. Perhaps after all his attempt to be 'all things to all men' proved a radical mistake, causing him to be treated with resentful suspicion on all sides. At the same time, the subtleties of Pauline dialectic could easily be exploited and perverted into that legalistic exercise of entailing damnations it was designed to evade. Once out of their personal context in the struggles, disasters and successes of the mushrooming Christian communities, founded by Paul round the Mediterranean shore, the apostle's words could be given the aura of an *ipse dixit* against which there was no appeal.

It is worth realizing that some of the most famous pronouncements have the least claim to authenticity. No saying from early Christian times has caused more scandal than the celebrated *taceat mulier in ecclesia*:

> The women should keep silence in the churches. For they are not permitted to speak, but should be subordinate, as the Law says.[2]

But this passage has the air of an intrusion into the context of Paul's argument. Moreover it is extremely odd to find an appeal to the Law in the very writer who maintains with such vigour and ingenuity the overthrow of the Law in the liberty of Christ. The suspicion that it has been inserted by a later Church-disciplinarian might seem too easy, were it not for the clinching proof that the passage simply contradicts Paul's remarks earlier in the same letter, where he assumes quite naturally that a woman can speak prayers or prophecies in the course of worship in Church (1 Cor. 11:2–16).

Even allowing for the problems of authenticity, it must be said that Paul has been subjected to the strangest interpretations. A whole modern school of psychological interpretation assumes that Paul is responsible for the Western emphasis on intellect as opposed to the body and the senses, on male subjection of women, and many more dualities of a similarly unhealthy nature. But it is puzzling that a man should be accused of 'dualism' or of originating hostile attitudes to the body when he wrote in such memorable words: 'Our struggle is not against the flesh and blood' (Eph.6:12) and who believed in the 'glorification' of the physical body through Christ. It is puzzling that a man should be thought a misogynist who refers in such friendly terms to so many women who, like himself, work hard for the Lord: Priscilla, Phoebe, Tryphaena, and 'my dear friend Persis,' Mary, Tryphosa and more, crowded into the greetings at the end of his letters and sent 'a holy kiss.' Perhaps after all the psychologists are only analysing their own prejudices.

Another line of argument takes Paul to be the villain in a

process that is supposed to have transformed Christianity, or indeed to have created it in the sense of a world-religion with a missionary purpose. Paul is claimed to have turned the 'Jesus of history' into the 'Christ of the Church.' Such a reading, which tends to the view that Paul was remote from the circles around Jesus, draws strength from his own boasted independence of the Jerusalem apostles; sometimes Paul is associated by its adherents with radical Gnosticism and a 'supernatural' view of Christ. But we have seen that it is nonsense to oppose the 'simple Jesus of Nazareth' to 'Gnostic' extravagances. And still less can one oppose the simplicity of the Gospels to the 'theological' complexity of Paul: we have seen that all kinds of religious and esoteric conceptions were in the air around the figure of Jesus, and that the Gospels have richly developed backgrounds of thought. Moreover, the evidence about Paul and the Gnostics is ambiguous, to say the least. But in the end the argument founders on the matter of chronology. Paul's letters are earlier than the written Gospels. When he speaks of the world-changing, cosmic significance of Christ, this is not a 'later' development pointing to the emergence of the organized Church's theology. It expresses that overwhelming sense of change which stems from closeness to the tremendous happening Paul came to acknowledge.

An editorial judgment has undoubtedly affected Paul's reception as a Christian thinker. When his letters were collected, the long and intellectually important Letter to the Romans was given pride of place. It is a brilliant work, whose argumentation has yielded food for thought ever since he wrote it, and has virtually made Paul the patron saint of theologians. At the same time, it colours our encounter with Paul and can create a misleading impression. Like his other letters, it talks of the all-transforming event, a change of consciousness, a revelation of God in a new righteousness 'apart from the Law' that also has a cosmic dimension; but it is unusual in defending the concept of that change in terms of the legalistic mentality, exploding it from within. If we start with the personal reflections and urgent persuading of the Letter to the Galatians, our response is likely to be somewhat different. Other letters reveal still more and unfamiliar sides of a many-faceted man.[2b]

Behind all of Paul's writings stands his strong sense of the universality of the Christian transformation, taking him out of the Jewish sphere-into the wider culture of his time. That is not to say that he rejected the religious consciousness characteristic of Judaism outright. He inherited the historical awareness of Judaism, having been brought up as a Pharisee. He inherited the Jewish awareness of the inner complexity of consciousness:

> For I have the desire to do what is good, but I cannot carry it out. What I do is not the good I want to do; no, the evil I do not want to do — that I keep on doing.[3]

The struggle with inner temptation was the great theme of Judaism, and led to its ideals of freedom and inwardness. The Law came into the human situation as the expression of those ideals. It gave each individual the possibility of commitment, and a standard against which to measure his inner development. But Paul is at his most profound in recognizing that the Law brought about a division in the self: what 'I' do is the very thing 'I' see is wrong and want not to do. The second 'I' identifies itself with the ideals of the Law; but thereby the first 'I' increases in guilt and seems irredeemably cut off from the 'I' which aspires to the ideal. The Law fixes and perpetuates a struggle which is actually made irresolvable. Man measures himself against a standard of perfection outside himself, and condemns himself to a painful consciousness of guilt. Paul sees that without it, man would have been in an easier, but at the same time lower state, without his developing individuality. Nevertheless he believes that through Christianity a still higher possibility has been given to man: he can live by the Christ-ideal within himself, not by an external Law. A further step forward in history and in consciousness had become necessary. But how was it to be achieved? Not just by arguments. It was indeed necessary to understand man's situation and what was offered to him by God's grace. But the overcoming of the 'guilt' consciousness required a deeper upheaval, a more thoroughgoing tr:ansformation of the soul. Paul describes it in terms of death and rebirth, a Mystery-rite:

> Do you not know that all of us who were baptized into
> Christ Jesus were baptized into his death? We were
> therefore buried with him through baptism into death in
> order that, just as Christ was raised from the dead
> through the glory of the Father, we too may live a new
> life.[4]

Pauline baptism has generally been interpreted as a symbolic gesture of 'ritual incorporation' into the community of the Church. But there has been a growing recognition in recent times that it was really much more than that. Why then did he need the Mystery language, the 'Christ-mysticism' of union with Jesus, death and regeneration?

In the light of our other studies, especially of the several forms of Christian baptism, going back to Jesus himself, we can shed new light on Paul's ritual practice. In particular we can re-examine the evidence in that riddling document, the so-called 'Letter to the Ephesians.'

The 'Letter to the Ephesians'

The so called 'Letter to the Ephesians' has none of the characteristics of a letter, and may have nothing to do with Ephesus.

As it stands in most English translations, of course, it is addressed by Paul the apostle to the Christian adherents (or 'saints') in Ephesus; but most of the reliable manuscripts lack the words 'in Ephesus,' and we can be sure that they did not appear there in early Christian times. For the heretic Marcion thought that this was the *Letter to the Laodiceans* which Paul is known to have written, though it has never been found. He was, undoubtedly, wrong; with the best critical methods available in antiquity, Tertullian ably devoted himself to refuting the error. But the revealing fact is that when Tertullian argues that Marcion's heading 'to the Laodiceans' is inauthentic, he makes no appeal to any other heading that contradicts it, so we may fairly assume that in his time the text still bore no indication of the so-called Letter's destination.[5] Wherever it was written, and whether or not it was ever sent to Ephesus, the work does not fall into the main category of Paul's letters, those addressed to particular communities and concerned with particular problems. It lacks his familiar form of address, and indeed almost all the characteristic features of a Pauline letter.

Apart from the note appended to chapter 6 of Ephesians, recommending his friend Tychicus, there is actually nothing to suggest the style or tone of a letter at all. On the contrary, Paul's language is unusually elaborate, general and exalted, employing words rarely found in his letters and developing concepts only touched upon in the urgent contexts of his other writings. And yet the voice speaking through the language seems authentically Paul's.[6] Once one abandons the supposition of a letter, one can easily observe that the work is some kind of an address to the followers of Christ, reminding them in the grandest terms of the scope of their faith, and setting their commitment not only against the backdrop of history but also of cosmic reality. The most suitable and likely occasion for such a discourse to be read, we need hardly say, is following baptism-initiation into the Christian Mystery.

Such an interpretation is readily confirmed by the allusions to baptismal liturgy, the frequent use of Mystery terminology, and the exhortations which end the address to live the Christian life. In the letters we meet the exoteric Paul, confronting difficulties, organizing churches, clearing the way for an understanding of his vision. In this initiatory address we meet the esoteric Paul, unveiling the Mystery of man's transformation and its cosmic significance, speaking to the 'insiders' at the most solemn moment in their spiritual career.[7]

It begins with a hymn of thanksgiving, worth quoting in its entirety because it conveys the peculiar intensity and atmosphere of Paul's address to the initiated:

> The highest praise be to the Father of our Lord Jesus
> Christ. He it is who bestows on us the great fullness of
> spiritual blessings which are prepared for us through
> Christ in the heavenly worlds. In him he chose us all even
> before the world was created, so that we can stand before
> his countenance, hallowed and without blemish, in the
> stream of his love. He formed us inwardly so that we can,
> according to his will and pleasure, be of his sonship in

Jesus Christ to the praise of his gracious revelation,
bestowed on us in the One who is his Beloved.

In him we receive the redemption through his blood,
the lifting of the curse which hangs over us because of our
strayings: all flows from the riches of his grace which he
pours over us and so lavished on us all wisdom and
insight. He has granted us insight into the mystery which
lies hidden in his world-aims, into his healing intention
which he let appear in Christ, to give purpose to the
fulfilment of the cycles of time: All that is in the heavens
and on the earth shall be renewed and united into one
being in Christ.

In Christ indeed the lot has fallen to us to partake in
the heritage which has been provided for us in accordance
with the purposeful will of him who is the driving force
in all things. For it was his intention that we who have
hoped for Christ, have waited for Christ, should be the
ones in whom his light-glory is revealed. In him you also
are sheltered, you who have heard the word of truth, the
Gospel of the salvation which is intended for you.
Through your faith in him you have been sealed with the
promised Holy Spirit, which is the certain promise of our
inheritance of the spirit and of our salvation through
which he makes us his own to the enhancement of his
glory.[8]

In the original Greek this is all one long, rhetorical sentence,
undoubtedly written with just the kind of premeditation that is
utterly lacking in the letters. Other features, too, show that Paul
is accommodating himself to the demands of an occasion. The
reference to 'the Beloved' of God is unusual, not at all part of the
terminology Paul generally employs: but it falls into place in the
setting of baptism, since it calls up precisely the oracular
moment of Jesus' own baptism in the Jordan and the heavenly
voice saying: 'You are my Son, the Beloved ...' For the rest, the
concepts are essentially Pauline, although the tone stands in
such contrast with the vivid, even jerky manner of the letters
that we must say, in the words of a modern scholar, that 'the
symphony of the Pauline doctrine has been transposed as a

whole from a lower manual into a higher one: the gospel has become the Mystery.'[9]

Paul continues the address by stressing even more the 'insider' quality of what he has to say. He speaks to those, he says, who have been 'sealed' in the promise of the Holy Spirit. Sealing was a technical process in the Mysteries, perhaps involving handgestures and sacred signs, but serving above all to mark off those undertaking an initiation from the profane. As he proceeds, we find that Paul is reminding the Christian initiates of all that they have experienced. He asks them to keep it in their consciousness, stressing its overwhelming importance and its place in the cosmic mystery. The themes he evokes may by now have become familiar. There is the fundamental imagery of death and reawakening to life; there is the mention of alienation and its overcoming. There is also much about the overcoming of inner divisions, and the enlightening of the eye of the heart, that reminds us of the *Gospel of Thomas* and its version of the teaching of Jesus. According to Paul, through being united with Christ Jesus it is possible 'to transform the duality into the unity of the New Man,' so that 'out of what was twofold we have access through him to the Father, in the unity of the spirit.' In a brilliant way, *via* a clever cross-reference back to Isaiah, Paul has adapted this theme to signify not only the transcendence of human, psychological and sexual oppositions (master/slave, male/female, guilt/law, and so on), but also the special concern of his own missionary work among the pagan cities from which he himself came. In Christ the 'dividing fence' between Jew and Gentile (the metaphor so beloved of the Rabbis) has likewise been broken down.[10]

The achievement of the 'unity of the spirit,' or of 'the New Man,' is described as a birth following death, which was the condition subsisting before baptism. Indeed, the imagery of 'building up the body of Christ' might remind us of the 'redemption,' or rite of building up the embryonic form of the 'secret Adam,' the true Man hidden in each of us, and his initiatory birth into spiritual reality. The maturing of the New Man in us is rendered in Paul's address by the well-established Mystery terms 'mature,' 'perfect' or 'initiate-man,' with the punning reference to being no longer 'children,' who do not yet bear the responsibility for their existence. In the symbolism, however, 'childhood' is by no means devalued: rather it must be raised to a higher level, an innocence not born of ignorance and without responsibility, but regained on the spiritual level through knowledge and inner 'light.' Indeed, in chapter 5 we find the idea of becoming a 'child' of God, and thereby an imitator of the divine. (Here we might remember some further ideas from the *Gospel of Philip*.) The symbolism of death/rebirth is then raised to a still higher key, if we may adopt the musical analogy, with its re-expression in terms of light and darkness. Paul now looks away from the immediate drama, the violent emotions of initiation, to the enduring significance of the events in the inner life, and to their archetypes in the cosmic struggle of light and darkness: the ultimate duality to be resolved in the 'mystery of Christ.'[11]

Paul's speech to the initiated gives us a profound insight into the character and mood of the communities that the 'apostle to the Gentiles' had founded and fostered. Far from being only a symbolic gesture of inclusion, or even being comparable to the Jewish ceremonies for the welcome of proselytes (converts), the baptism of the Pauline churches was in the fullest sense an initiation, demanding a far-reaching transformation of the personality and spiritual life. Interestingly, this has been recognized by modern scholars who approach their studies, not in the light of theology, but from the investigation of ancient and archaic societies. Wayne Meeks employs anthropological concepts to examine the transformations and their social repercussions. He notes, for example, the symbolic stripping off of the old garments, associated with the former social role of the person, and the reclothing in white robes — symbolism linked to the death/rebirth complex through the idea of stripping off the body itself. The effect of the rite is that of initiatory remaking of the self. 'Nudity, symbolic death, rebirth as a child, abolition of distinctions of role and status — all are typical of the transitional or liminal phase in initiations.'[12] Liminality means 'being on the threshold.' It suggests the way the candidates were prepared for a revelation, an experience, that would overturn their previous way of looking at things. It was like crossing a threshold: afterwards, looking back, everything was seen from a different perspective, and what had been 'inside' became 'outside,' or vice versa. Or better say that the old perspective of 'outside' and 'inside' was overturned in 'the unity of the New Man.'

Once grasped as essentially an initiation, the rite of Pauline baptism takes dramatic shape. The scattered allusions in the letters, to a 'wisdom among the initiated,' to 'becoming a child,' a 'new creation,' start to make deeper sense. A pattern emerges (see Fig.8) of dynamic opposites structured round the themes of descent (into the waters, death, burial with Christ) and cosmic ascension (into heaven, resurrection, in the body of Christ). In the background once more there are echoes of the ancient kingly initiations. According to Paul's 'Ephesian' address, indeed, the initiated are 'enthroned with Christ.'[13]

Can we discern more details? We can at least infer a little more: the central Pauline idea of 'burial with Christ' surely means that, as elsewhere, initiation took place at the Easter festival. And the imagery of light and darkness suggests the nocturnal vigil, the initiatory trial of wakefulness. Pliny, a Roman governor who later had to deal with Christians, describes their chanting in the dawn light to Jesus "as to a God' and swearing initiatory oaths. That would fit the symbolism of Paul's 'Ephesian' speech. The sense that all of life before initiation has been a sleep which has now been cast off is expressed in the hymnic fragment he quotes so beautifully:

> Awake, you who are sleeping,
> arise from the dead,
> the Christ shall be your light.

In the setting of the all-night vigil and initiatory rites, the dawn of light would also be the dawning of a higher consciousness. What 'Pliny discovered the Christians of Bithynia doing at their dawn meetings ... may thus have been the practice sixty years earlier among Christians of Asia and Macedonia.'[14]

Paul's form of Christianity, it appears, was quite different from the way it has sometimes been represented, either as a 'church-political organization' or as a sort of social reform movement. We must remember that for the early period we are dealing with

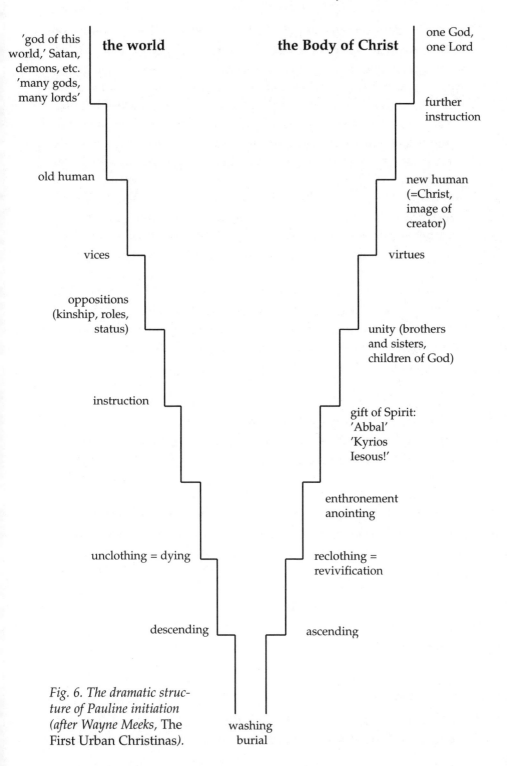

the world

the Body of Christ

'god of this world,' Satan, demons, etc. 'many gods, many lords'

one God, one Lord

further instruction

old human

new human (=Christ, image of creator)

vices

virtues

oppositions (kinship, roles, status)

unity (brothers and sisters, children of God)

instruction

gift of Spirit: 'Abba!' 'Kyrios Iesous!'

enthronement anointing

unclothing = dying

reclothing = revivification

descending

ascending

washing burial

Fig. 6. The dramatic structure of Pauline initiation (after Wayne Meeks, The First Urban Christinas).

quite small numbers of people, the Christian initiates united by the powerful experiences of being buried and rising with Christ, sharing a heightened consciousness in the 'gift of the Spirit' endowed at their baptism and anointing and enthronement. It is crucial to realize that in a Pauline community there was no 'laity,' that every member had an integral role, an active contribution to make. Everyone was still essential, nobody merely attended. It is a question to be asked, therefore, whether Paul should not rather be included with the Gnostics — with those who made of Christianity a closed, 'mystic brotherhood'. Is that not after all the meaning implied by the crossing of the threshold, leaving the world of division, darkness and the Old Man behind, to be gathered into the light and unity of the mystic Body of Christ?

Certainly the Gnostic discoveries at Nag Hammadi gave scholarship many writings that expressed Pauline ideas. For some of them Paul was '*the* Apostle,' and his sharp opposition of grace and law fitted with the cosmic dualism of the Gnostic mythology. It became clear that Paul had been championed by the Gnostic movement and that on Valentinus, say, he had been a major influence and so could be legitimately seen as a link in the chain of Gnostic-Christian development. Like the Gnostics, Paul used concepts of 'knowledge' and 'mystery,' 'pneumatic' and 'psychic,' and cosmic ascent. So then, if Gnosticism reached back to mythologies and rites of the centuries before Christ, it was only natural to assume that Paul derived from thence his fundamental ideas. He makes little or no reference to historical traditions about Jesus, of the type found in the Gospels. Behind him there seemed rather to be a highly Gnostic kind of Christianity, in which myth had completely ousted history. It is true that Paul opposed some group in the community at Corinth who were even more radically Gnostic than he was, who were prepared-actually to curse the physical Jesus in order to arrive more surely at the spiritual nature of Christ. But the argument was founded on a common network of ideas agreed by both sides, or at least sharing an agreed medium of communication.[15] The so-called 'Letter to the Ephesians' is particularly rich in suggestions of Gnostic concepts. Such features as 'the representation of Christ as the Primal Man, of the 'syzygy' (union) between Christ and the church, and of the church as the Body of Christ,' it has been argued, 'can only be understood against the background of a Christianized mythological gnosis.'[16]

And yet the whole reconstruction of 'the Gnostic Paul' is far more precarious than might at first appear. While much in the 'Letter to the Ephesians' can be paralleled in Gnosticism, for example, other scholars have urged that nearly everything in it can be derived from Essenism and the Dead Sea Scrolls from Qumran. Their efforts are just as convincing, and — if taken for a complete answer to the background of Paul's thought — just as unsatisfactory.[17] It would be hard indeed to see Paul as a Christian Essene in view of his critical attitude to the Law! What the contributions of Qumran and Gnostic scholarship really seem to suggest is that Paul's thinking inhabits precisely that dynamic middle ground, where Gnostic myth is combined with the Essene mystery of the conscious self, where the impetus of history is registered alongside the transcendent significance of a liberating, saving Event. A new kind of consciousness arose out of the breakthrough, the Christ-consciousness manifested in Jesus after his baptism and echoed among all those who are 'in Christ,' as Paul vividly puts it. Gnosticism and the Essene consciousness are absorbed and transformed in that new synthesis, and it is there too that Paul locates the source of the freedom he feels, even though he never knew Jesus, the 'Christ according to the flesh.' He had his own 'breakthrough'-experience at Damascus, which brought him his awareness of the risen Christ. The modern discoveries of Essene and Gnostic works should not therefore be used to explain Paul, one way or the other. As in the case of Jesus himself, they can be used to uncover structures of consciousness, historically existing attitudes and spiritual experiences, which are partly preserved but also partly overwhelmed in Paul's attempt to characterize the new self or 'Christ in you.'

Paul's sense of Christ as the 'Primal Man' forms a good example. Paul speaks in mysterious and mystical terms of Christ, saying that he is the 'head' and those 'in Christ' on earth are the body of a macrocosmic being. That is one obvious dimension of the 'Christ-consciousness' he describes: the sense of being greater than one's earthly self. But there is something more specific in the analogy of the 'head.' The head is the organ of our freedom, since it is the locus of our senses (whereby we look about us and evaluate our situation before we act), and its special position detaches it from the functional behaviour of the rest of our body. The limbs, the digestive and breathing systems all work to maintain bodily life, to get us from one place to another, and so forth; but without the head their activity would be undirected, even pointless in that it would not be serving the ends and purposes of our decisions and ideas, the real content of human life. It is worth noting that more archaic modes of consciousness — including some reflected in Greek philosophy — still gave no special role to the head. Indeed they often centred man's awareness in other organs and bodily regions that to us seem strangely inappropriate, such as the liver. But by Paul's time the developing individuality of man, expressed in his demand for moral freedom, has brought the special role of the head into prominence, providing the analogy to the workings of the community that we find in Ephesians:

> Let all our senses be turned to him, to Christ: he is the
> head; through him the whole body becomes harmonious,
> all members and limbs working together, each according
> to its own strength, helping each other towards proper
> growth of the body, that this body be totally built up out
> of that love which is Christ.[18]

Despite the volumes that have been written on the figure of 'cosmic Man,' pointing to oriental or Gnostic sources behind Paul's thought, the main thrust of the metaphor is surely somewhat different. The universal scope of the Christ-consciousness is one point, and that indeed is shared with the Gnostics: but Paul is also saying that the Christ-consciousness provides a pivot of freedom, out of which the separate members (the community on earth) can act. It is a source of harmony, of love, not a greater power in which the individual loses himself like the Gnostic 'Primal Man,' who gathers the scattered sparks of light back into their original oneness.

In fact Rudolf Steiner, in his extraordinarily original comparison of *The Bhagavad Gita and the Epistles of Paul*, already drew attention to the profound differences between Paul and oriental cosmic revelation. The 'Great Teacher' of an oriental masterpiece like the *Bhagavad Gita* confronts the soul of the seeker in essential privacy, and directs him through the many stages by which he will find his way back to the primal revelations, to his oneness with the All. Paul, however, the Christian apostle, speaks to the community of members as well as to the spiritual 'head.' He addresses the plurality of individuals, working 'each according to its own strength.' 'Paul writes to the Corinthians,' says Steiner, 'about the variety of talents present in a group, and of how they must be fostered in co-operation. Krishna said to Arjuna, "You must be so and so, do this or that; then step by step your soul will progress." Paul said, "One of you has this gift, another that, a third another; if these work together harmoniously like the members of a human body a spiritual wholeness results, which can then be permeated by the Christ."'[19]

Steiner's insight has been belatedly echoed by modern 'anthropological' research into Paul's communities and Pauline initiation. For there goes with it the realization that incorporation into the 'body of Christ' did not there carry the meaning of leaving the world behind, to acknowledge a higher and contrary order. The Christian initiates did indeed cross a 'threshold,' passing through a liminal stage into a 'new creation.' Yet when we consider the graph of the ritual structure, we meet the paradox that 'some liminal elements had to be placed, not at the perigee of the parabola, but high on the "reaggregation" side.' There is a continuing tension with the 'old structures' of the wider society surrounding them, 'for the Christians continue to live in the city and to interact with its institutions, and besides, they still carry some of its structures in their minds and in the houses where they meet.'[20] To put it another way: they continue to be 'members,' though their 'head' is the cosmic Christ. It will not do for them to give up their individuality, even when they have broken through to the mythic, macrocosmic dimension of the Christ-experience.

Far from taking them out of the world, therefore, the initiatory transformation intensifies their sense at once of their earthly role and of its mythic overshadowing by the vaster issues of the cosmic struggle. Sometimes the latter takes the form of imminent apocalypse. Yet the individual self has an active role in the linking of earthly and spiritual. The initiation-address concludes with the imagery of a soldier being equipped for battle — spiritual warfare, certainly, but definitely not a retreat from the world:

> Stand fast, girded about the loins with truth. Put on the breastplate of your true higher being. Shoe your feet with preparedness to spread the message of peace. In all your deeds raise high the shield of faith with which you can quench all the flaming darts of the evil one. Take into your thoughts the certainty of salvation that it protect your head as with a helmet, and grasp the sword of the Spirit which is the active word of God.[21]

It is as if the 'holy war' anticipated in the future by the Essenes had been transferred to the struggle of the spiritual now in the Christian's life on earth.

Paul's thought always includes more than the impending apocalyptic End, in fact, and the events of the Last Day he often sees being played out in the present, or forming themselves on earth for a change that will spread to the universe and bring about the Christmystery mentioned in his sublime Blessing ('All that is in heaven and on earth shall be renewed and united into one being in Christ'). In addition to the End, the force of renewal is also at work, and not only in the sphere of consciousness of the Christian. Paul approaches in his own way the insight we have expressed by saying that a change in consciousness must finally be understood to imply a change happening within reality itself. Central to Pauline Christianity, it is true, is his version of initiation. But the awakening in man of a higher consciousness is only a part, perhaps only a symptom, of a deeper process:

> For it is said, 'He has ascended to the heights, in order to put that power which holds you captive, into captivity, and so can he give his gifts to men.'

Christ died and rose: and likewise the initiate is buried, raised and enthroned with Christ. Yet the wider aspect of Christ's work has still to be mentioned:

That 'he has ascended,' is that not the same as his having
descended into the lowest regions — those of the earth?
He who has descended is the same as he who ascended
higher than all the heavens; he wanted to fill all existence
with his being.[22]

The flashing-up of the Christ-consciousness is one moment in a
process whose mythological shape is clearly expressed. It must
be seen in the context of a development in cosmic reality. Christ's
appearance in human form in Jesus, and in the consciousness of
Christians, is the initial phase in the movement whereby the
Divine takes back to itself, and fills once more, the realm of the
earthly that had fallen away.

Again, there is the sense of a background in Gnostic myth,
which interpreted the 'Fall' in such cosmic terms. The process of
the Christ-presence descending to permeate the earth, however,
is quite antithetical to the Gnostic dualism. It may remind us,
however, of those passages in the Mystery-gospels of Thomas
and Philip which spoke of a mystical presence in earthly things,
or in the physical body — an emphasis we traced to the influence
of Jesus' teaching itself.

We can understand the process Paul describes mythologically
in terms of the evolution of consciousness. It was in developing
his sense of his ego or moral individuality that man separated
himself from the world, and even came to experience it as alien.
Gnosticism pointed backward to the primal unity of developmental origins. But the Christ-consciousness of Paul looks rather
to a further extension: the moral ego is confirmed and strengthened in its freedom, yet at the same time the sense of estrangement is to be overcome and the Divine will show itself once more
in the cosmos. For the Jewish consciousness, it seemed that such
divine activity had ceased with the Creation, and continued only
in the sphere of consciousness, of human decisions and history.
In Paul, or in the Christ-consciousness of Paul, that mode of perception and experience is transcended.

How Paul and his followers conceived the relation between
what had happened in consciousness, through baptismal initiation into Christ's burial and resurrection, and the change that
would come about in man's own bodily nature and in the

material world, we shall examine shortly in connection with a writing on the resurrection addressed to a certain Rheginus. For the present, however, it remains for us to return to, and to answer, the question about the closeness of Paul to the original Christian spirit, or to Gnosticism, or to Jesus.

Far from veering off into the extreme positions of radical Gnosticism, Paul's consciousness inhabited that tense and dynamic middle ground between inwardness and myth and social reality which was the territory of the Christian vision from the beginning. There is simply no truth in the view that he distorted the original direction of Christian thought. The Gnostic elements in his vision are those which form part of the presupposition of Christianity itself, and like the Essene features are reinterpreted in the light of a new synthesis, reaching back to the archaic mythologies yet integrated with a much more 'modern' self-consciousness. All the recent evidence and discoveries only add their confirmation. Indeed, so many of the components we have found in Pauline initiation were already known from our previous chapters — death and reawakening, overcoming oppositions in the soul, becoming a child, the clothes-symbolism, light and darkness, the 'earth mysticism,' to which we may now add the designation of the mystery as 'marriage' — that we may hazard a definite conclusion. It used to be one of the main problems in the history of Christianity to explain how Paul came by his baptismal practice and the world of ideas connected with it. We now know. He received it, at the shortest possible remove through his immediate followers, from Jesus himself.[23]

Many other aspects of the problem fall into place. The close but never very clear connection of the giving of the Holy Spirit, for instance, in Paul's baptism-initiation can be seen to develop the idea of becoming a 'son of the Holy Spirit' which we found in the Jewish-Christianity of James and his followers, and which was alluded to in the *Gospel of Thomas*. This too serves not at all to distance Paul from the thought of the Christians in Jerusalem, but rather reveals his close fidelity to the primal forms of Christian practice. He was no doubt initiated by those who received him at Damascus; and withdrew into 'Arabia' (the name for the Syrian territories under Nabataean rule) to mull over the experiences he had had. Perhaps it is to that time we should attribute the 'ascension' experience he describes to the Corinthians.[24] There could have been no objection to his speedy ritual initiation in view of the extraordinary 'calling' he had received on the road.

We concluded in an earlier chapter that the centre of Jesus' esoteric teaching was the Son of Man, as that of his outer teaching was the coming of the Kingdom. It might therefore seem to be a problem, if Paul stands so close to Jesus, that the phrase 'Son of Man' never occurs in Paul's writings. But in reality the concept behind the expression does occur frequently, and contains an answer to the issue of Paul's so-called 'Gnostic' idea: the 'Primal Man,' or new Adam, or 'inner Man.' For we recall that 'Son of Man' was a Semitic expression, standing for the 'I' as part of an esoteric psychology, imprinted into man's being from his cosmic archetype. And it was as the 'Son of Man' that Jesus lived out his destiny on earth.

T. W. Manson is surely right, in identifying Paul's central idea of the 'new Adam' with Jesus' concept of the Son of Man — thus giving it an emphasis quite different to that Gnostic 'Primal Man' who contains the universe. It is a higher self, a 'no longer I, but Christ in me.' Paul was too thoroughly at home in the Greek language to adopt the more literal rendering of *bar nasha* as 'Son of Man,' so barbarous in Greek, which would more idiomatically speak of Man (*anthropos*) and qualify it in terms of 'inner' or 'outer,' or historically as the 'old' or 'new' Man. Thus it is in Jesus' own teaching that we find the basis for Paul's Christ-mysticism, according to which the suffering and glorification of the Son of Man can and must be shared by all.[25] It is worth noting, for example, that the 'new Man' passage in Ephesians contains a background allusion to Psalm 80: where in the original Hebrew there is reference to the 'Son of Man.'[26]

Of course, Paul had a highly creative mind, was deeply learned in Jewish religion and in the Hellenistic culture of Asia Minor, his native province. We need not doubt that he left his personal stamp on the Gentile Christian movement. It was he who evolved its language, finding and borrowing Greek terms for its crucial ideas. But we can see that he was also heir to the esotericism of Christianity's founder. It was in Paul, converted after his death and resurrection, that Jesus found a mind profoundly akin to the spirit in which he taught and suffered.

Rather often in history the solving of one problem raises another. The relationship of Paul to Jesus becomes clear when we recognize the Mystery-activity of Jesus as a starting-point: but then we have to account for something that seems less like Mystery than mystification. We must explain why all mention of Jesus' ritual practice came to be expelled from the tradition of the New Testament, so that a definite picture of it can only be constructed from luckily surviving fragments and apocrypha, and modern esotericism. What was being covered up?

Several sorts of answer are conceivable. Esotericism can lead to aberrations in the hands of those who do not understand it. Clement mentions that the secret *Mark* has led some to corrupt practices. There may have been a concern, therefore, to distance the Church from the possibility of scandalous misconceptions. By extension, it would also be thought safer to attribute the authority of Christian sacramental practice to the Church rather than to Jesus, since otherwise the bishops were likely to have their authority questioned by 'esoteric' Christians who looked back directly to the Master. There is perhaps some truth in both these suppositions.

Yet the real issue was undoubtedly a deeper one. It had to do with the nature of the Christian proclamation, which was not (and is not) the teaching of Jesus, however important that may be, but 'Christ — and him crucified,' in Paul's words. That does not contradict the message of Jesus. Indeed we have seen that Jesus already pointed to the necessary transitions by referring to his coming 'baptism.' He must, as 'Son of Man,' suffer the price of attaining individual existence, or separateness: that is, death. Thus he made his disciples primarily initiates into the mystery of his destiny, and that could only be fulfilled on the Cross; his words from the Cross are precisely that: 'It is fulfilled' — the word could also be translated 'initiated.' (John 19:30)

The new, historical meaning Jesus was able to give to his baptismal practice immeasurably deepens our understanding of how, conversely, his destiny took on 'initiatory' meaning. Yet we can surely understand, too, the considerable danger that the centre of gravity, so to speak, of the Christian proclamation would be displaced if it were based on the life and baptismal practice of Jesus rather than on the destiny to which they pointed. In fact, we can see precisely that problem in the very earliest Christian times, that is, in the background of Paul's mission. Those who based the pattern of baptism-initiation too closely upon Jesus' own baptismal experience, like the Gnostic baptizers of Alexandria, put all the weight on the exaltation, the Christ-consciousness of Jesus, and tended to neglect the suffering Son of Man. The Gospel of Mark, as we have seen, by no means accepted that one-sided emphasis on the divinely descending Being, but added to the grandeur of the Gnostic vision the crucifixion, as the central mystery and the path to the ultimate revelation: the empty tomb and its implications. Yet Mark hardly succeeded in redirecting all the Gnostic tendencies within Alexandrian Christianity. And elsewhere, Paul himself had encountered Christians who still gave too little attention to the historical fulfillment of Jesus' earthly destiny, notably in Corinth.

Hence we may suppose that, in order to insist the more strongly on the full transposition of the Mystery-pattern into history, including the reality of Jesus' suffering and death, the knowledge of Jesus' own activity was carefully guarded. It must have been known to the initiates: in Alexandria to those who heard the 'secret Mark' passage; in the Pauline churches to those who understood the allusion to 'the Beloved'; in Jewish Christianity to those who became 'sons of the Holy Spirit.' But heavy secrecy, especially as the Church came to distance itself from anything with a dangerous aura of Gnosticism, gradually led to the actual loss of a part of the tradition. Ironically, the history of Jesus' sufferings was preserved, but the vital knowledge of how Jesus and his disciples gave it the significance of an initiation of the 'Son of Man,' the spiritual individual, disappeared.

That loss, was not, I think necessary to maintain the central strand in the Christian proclamation. Indeed it obscured and rendered incoherent the early history of Christianity, and the proper relation of Jesus to Paul, now restored for us in some measure through modern perspectives. Paul's continuance of Jesus' baptismal rite did not lead him to underestimate the awful events following Jesus' condemnation. It remains for us to examine the all-important teaching of Paul on the central mystery, the crucifixion — and the further dimension, the resurrection.

Pauline Esotericism: the Resurrection

Luke's book of Acts of the Apostles records that Paul, on his missionary wanderings, passed through Athens. The city was naturally a stronghold of paganism, one of the old capitals of classical culture and still a centre of philosophy — though it had its synagogue too. We may detect a note of slight mockery when a group of Stoics and Epicureans bundle Paul off to a meeting on the Areopagus Hill for a kind of 'Oxford Union' debate. But Paul turns the occasion spectacularly to advantage, with his usual technique of adopting his hearers' starting-point. His message of the God 'in whom we live and move and have our being' would have been highly acceptable to the Stoics, at least. Epicureans are harder to please: their gods are beyond the upset and accident of material life. Yet for that very reason they were hardly in a position to challenge Paul's annexation of an 'unknown god,' to whom he had seen an inscription, and whom he chose to identify with the Creator of heaven and earth. The audience must have been impressed. But Paul lost nearly all of them again when he came to the latest wonder wrought by his God, namely, the 'standing up of corpses.'[27]

I render the phrase literally — too literally of course. By doing so we can put ourselves back into the position of intelligent Athenians who had never heard of such a thing, and then were not sure they wanted to. We can notice just how little of the biblical resonance of the 'resurrection of the dead' comes through in the Greek phrase, especially when it has been transplanted into a semi-philosophical discussion. It all seems a long way from the promises of Yahweh chanted in the Psalms or the Book of Job: from Paul's own language of 'glorification,' of 'ensouled' and 'pneumatic' bodies in the letters to Corinth; furthest of all from those mysterious yet palpable appearances of the risen Christ, through closed doors, recognizable and unrecognizable, tangibly wounded yet suddenly vanishing, that are told in the Gospels. Whatever the truth about them, they were anything but a walking corpse. And yet there is a further paradox. For it was precisely in the crudest, most grotesque form, as the 'standing up of corpses,' that resurrection passed into the teaching of the Church.[28]

Did Paul really use the phrase, without further explanation, or is Luke summarizing his message in the terms current rather later? We shall probably never know. But we can come to a deeper understanding of what Paul meant by 'resurrection,' if we can clear our minds of the literalism of the Fathers and the Middle Ages. Especially in the writings to Corinth, where mis-understandings had already occurred, Paul strove to make clear what was essential to his concept of resurrection, both of Christ and of the rest of mankind.

The idea of resurrection was of course familiar to Paul before his conversion to Christianity from his studies with the Pharisees. It was also taught by the Essenes. That is not to say, however, that it was an archaic biblical concept. Despite a few suggestive passages in the Old Testament, there is no evidence that the ancient Hebrews believed either in personal immortality or in the resurrection of the dead. The Sadducees, or priestly-aristocratic party in Judaism, remained close to authentic biblical faith and persistently denied resurrection right up to Christian times. The other two factions presumably evolved the idea before their own split from the less organized body of the Hasidim, known to have existed in Maccabaean times, when they formed one general group of 'the pious' (Asidaeans as the *Books of Maccabees* sometimes transcribe the word). Research has suggested that they grasped the idea under the influence of Eastern thought, again notably from Iran. Their adaptation, how-ever, took on a uniquely Jewish meaning from the biblical and historical framework into which it was transplanted.

Zoroastrianism taught of God, or Ohrmazd, as the Boundless Light, who had existed before the mingling of Light with Darkness, or Ahriman. The world was created as a result of that mixture, and the light-souls of men entered into it and resolved to fight against the Dark. Human life was thus an expression of the mythic struggle proceeding in the universe. At the end of time, the struggle would inevitably result, so it was taught, in the total purification of the world from the dark shadow of Ahriman. Primal unity would be regained: the Zoroastrians called that future state *frashkart*, at once the 'Restoration' and

'Transfiguration' of the world — including man. Certain mythical or legendary heroes were expected to be reborn alongside the Saoshyant, or Saviour, to bring about the ultimate defeat of Ahriman. The Saviour is to be joined by six other religious leaders of mankind to celebrate the Final Sacrifice, parallel to that which created the world in the first place. And in the last days, men and all creatures would become gradually less material, ceasing to require material sustenance, and eventually the world would be resolved back into pure Light. It is a grandiose vision. And sometimes it could generate expressions and hopes which sound to us very like 'resurrection.'

Close study shows, on the other hand, that Iranian thought here remains fundamentally in the realm of myth-consciousness. The myth restores the time of the beginning, the primal wholeness. That is why the bones or material substance are sometimes mentioned in this connection. It does not mean that man's bodily individuality is given a special place. It rather expresses an intuition of an original oneness, when body and soul had not separated out, a condition of pure Light. In Zoroastrian thought the wholeness is threatened by the 'mixture,' the state in which Ahriman obtrudes himself into the Light. The 'cyclical' movement of time is like that of a grand cosmic ritual — which indeed is what it becomes in the hands of the Saoshyant. The detour or cyclical movement of human time is necessary for disentangling the world from Ahriman's grip; but there is no history, no qualitative gain to be made through time, no developing relationship with God. The end lies in the beginning, as in all myth. And man is subsumed along with the earth in the ritualistic pattern which becomes finally the structure of all reality, echoing Ohrmazd and his seven Spirits who made the world and at last will be reflected in it everywhere.[29]

The Jewish Essenes and Pharisees may well have learned something from the cosmic mythology of Iran. In their writings, even the most apocalyptic, however, the sense of history asserts itself, and is bound up as we know with their different sense of the Creation. Judaic time moves consciously forward along its historical axis toward the Last Days. Then God's promises will be fulfilled indeed, and much that was lost will be restored. But there is no overturning of the conditions of history. Rather there is to be the final affirmation of all that history means — at least for all those who entered into history, the covenant with history's God.

Judaism also accepted the body as a part of man's created nature. Genesis relates that God made Adam from the earth and then breathed into him a soul or 'breath of life.' As a living being, man was felt to be a whole. The only idea of man without a body, that is, after death, was of a ghastly shade, a half-reality in Sheol the underworld, gloomier even than the Hades of the Greeks. The body was an intrinsic part of man's make-up, a view partly paralleled in Egypt, but fundamentally different from the idea in Iran, where man's essential self pre-existed the body and indeed the making of the world. For Judaism the body was an expression of man's individual existence — though the degree of individualism was limited by the emphasis on the common stock of Abraham, the collective body of Israel. When Yahweh was to affirm man's nature at the End of history, therefore, there was no question in the Jewish mind of his material body being ethereally dissolved away, as in Iranian thought. Man would be given wholeness, including his body and the individual existence that the body expresses.[30] That is the meaning of the Jewish concept of resurrection: that man will go forward into a future state and the end of historical time with his ethical and bodily individuality. Of that reality the standing up of corpses is only the crudest effort at imagination.

It would make our reconstruction convenient and schematic if we could rigidly separate the 'Jewish' from the 'mythic-cyclical' version of resurrection. But in reality these streams of thought met each other in the most diverse ways, and among the Essenes, for instance, the Last Day and the resurrection are sometimes strongly coloured by suggestions of myth and even of ritual. The Qumran community felt the presence of angels during their rites, and this meant in effect that they were already living the life of those in the 'End Time' who would be raised, and share the company of the angelic hosts. Moreover, the work of the priestly Messiah who was to help bring in the End is described as that of re-opening the barred gates of Paradise — restoring the harmony of the beginning. That was the aim, as we know, of much ritual practice in the ancient Near East.[31] Nevertheless, in Essene teaching generally, the linear historical and apocalyptic framework is upheld.

272 • *The Beginnings of Christianity*

As we might expect, it is in Gnosticism that the antihistorical elements gained the upper hand. Ritual experience and myth in Essenism have to be construed as anticipations of what will one day become actuality, whereas in Gnosticism they define a reality of their own. The Gnostic consciousness does know the experience of the created body. But that experience more than any other stands in the way of the Gnostic aspiration. The development of a Judaic sense of moral individuality, establishing the possibility of 'history,' was for the Gnostics a detour into an alien mode of being. The body-experience that was part of it felt to them like the fastening of the immortal light-spark to a 'dying animal.' Man's body was hardly something to be given an external existence at the End of time, but an incrustation to be 'put off' forever by the enlightened spirit. For the Gnostic attitude there is to be no resurrection of the body, but only a resurrection from the body.[32]

Now Paul, when he talks about resurrection, might again seem to lean toward Gnostic ideas. For him just as much as for the Gnostic, to be fixed in bodily, material life for ever cannot be the goal of man's existence. A perpetuation of man's earthly form would be a denial of his more spiritual destiny, indeed a triumph of materialism. Paul decisively rejects the vulgar desire of coming back to life 'just as you are,' in flesh and blood:

> I tell you this, my brothers: flesh and blood cannot inherit
> the Kingdom of God. For that which is perishable does not
> inherit the imperishable ...

When he characterizes the 'resurrection body' of Christ, or the bodies in which redeemed mankind will live, Paul evokes something more elusive, hinting at it by means of strong contrasts which are highly poetic but do little to define its corporeality: corruption/incorruption, shame/honour, weakness/strength. It prompts images of celestial radiance, like that of sun, moon or stars. It is a pneumatic or spiritual body, essentially different from everything that is 'of the earth, earthy.' No wonder that the Gnostics found so much in Paul that seemed to buttress their spiritualistic interpretation, and that they could refer to him as *the* Apostle!

Yet when we read the arguments and expostulations in the letters to Corinth we realize that the advocates of 'flesh and blood' are not in fact the main target of Paul's subtle mind. If flesh and blood cannot inherit imperishability, we may recall from the so-called 'Letter to the Ephesians' that neither are they the 'enemies' against whom we have to struggle as the Gnostics thought. Paul rather seems to accept that flesh-and-blood corporeality is the rightful expression of man's nature, under his present condition of life. It accords with the way God made the man of earth, the first Adam; and Paul goes to some lengths to explain that the 'ensouled,' earthly man rightly comes first. It is only when we try to project this earthly model of human existence in the apocalyptic realization of God's promise, the resurrection, that it has to be rejected. Then we must rise to the concept of a more spiritual mode of existence, and grasp the work of the 'second Adam' or 'enlivening spirit.'[33]

Paul has no time for those who would quarrel with the conditions of life, yet want to accept its gifts. Indeed, he argues, Christ's 'victory' can only be understood when we see that he took on the challenge of man's earthly nature, its mortality and perishability included. He grasps in its essence the Jewish concept of man's wholeness, without the crude imaginings which some attached to it; but his argument is actually directed against those who Gnostically assume that Christ evaded the human condition. Thus 'the dilemma with which Paul is confronted in Corinth,' writes a modern commentator, 'is not that these people denied the resurrection of Christ. What they dehied was rather the resurrection of the dead ... The key word of course is 'dead.''[34] Paul steers a difficult course between opposing perils. Rejecting a materialistic notion of mere continuance of earthly conditions, he insists against the Corinthian Gnostics that man must maintain wholeness of being. Christ did so, taking on bodily nature, even when it involved death.

Christ's resurrection is therefore not the rejection of bodily existence, but the raising of it to a new level, not the avoidance but the overcoming of death. That is why, as we have been considering Paul's teaching on the resurrection, we have all along been essentially concerned with his understanding of Christ's death — the Mystery of Golgotha.

Paul's thought on the subject of resurrection, then, is charged by the new Christian consciousness. Christ's death is the central mystery: without it, 'resurrection' would simply be a return to the ancient Mysteries. They had given an assurance of man's continuing inner vitality, despite his bodily condition, and expressed that assurance in rites and myths of ascension and cyclic rebirth. In the Jewish concept of resurrection, conversely, man's historical limitations are simply affirmed as inevitable rather than overcome, and that will not do for Paul either. For his Christian mind the historical Event of Christ's death-resurrection has the power of myth to transform man's life, lifts history to a new level while remaining absolutely historical. This principle of transformation in fact provides him with the way forward:

> We shall not all remain dead, but all be transformed ... .
> For this corruptible must clothe itself in incorruptibility,
> and this mortal clothe itself in immortality (1 Cor. 15:51–3.)

Through the Christian concept of development and evolution he arrives at the view that tile conditions of existence have themselves been changed by the Christian mystery. The change has taken place in man's consciousness first of all, but that is part of a greater change. In Ephesians he described this by saying that the wisdom of the community on earth will spread from thence to the cosmic-angelic powers (3:10–11). The resurrection of the body is the manifestation of the process whereby the change extends beyond the sphere of consciousness to man's whole being, the very conditions of spiritual and corporeal existence.

These are extraordinarily far-reaching ideas, and by no means easy to reconcile with what passes for our modern understanding of the universe. Science has been almost exclusively concerned with looking for regularities in nature, and has admitted the idea of evolution (transformation, metamorphosis) only within the strict framework of an assumed uniformity of conditions over vast (and equally hypothetical) periods of time. Yet there is now a revival of interest in a more phenomenological, close-to-experience type of science, like that advocated by Goethe, for which the idea of 'metamorphosis' is central. And it can be argued that in the life-sciences, at least, the quest for mechanical uniformities has been a dead-end. Organisms may be better understood as process, rhythm and transformation. There at least it looks as though science will have to take the principle of metamorphosis much more seriously than it does now. In the longer perspective, it will be a matter of making that readjustment in cosmological thinking — as mentioned by Professor Clark or already carried through by Rudolf Steiner.

A more immediate difficulty is that Paul stops here, and leaves it highly obscure what he thinks will actually be transformed to go forward in man's resurrection-existence. The attempt to win further enlightenment from his other letters, moreover, only leads to further uncertainty. It seems impossible to pin him down. His standpoint changes so much according to the special circumstances he was addressing.

We cannot tell even whether he expected the transformation of things to come about with great rapidity or as a slow process. Writing to the Thessalonian community, for instance, he implies that the apocalyptic events, including the *parousia*, the renewed presence of the Lord, will all take place in his own lifetime:

> For the Lord himself will come down from heaven, with a loud command, with the voice of the archangel and with the trumpet call of God, and the dead in Christ will rise first. After that, we who are still alive and are left will be caught up with them in the clouds to meet the Lord in the air. (1 Thess.4:16–17)

Paul is dealing here with 'Imaginations,' vivid spiritual pictures, though purified in their vision of ethereal corporeality from any taint of the 'standing up of corpses.' Yet it is hard to reconcile with them the prospect in the so-called 'Letter to the Ephesians' of long-drawn processes in time, of 'generation after generation.' Some scholars have concluded that Paul's ideas changed, and that Ephesians is his later view while the Letter to the Thessalonians is very early. But the theoretical chronology simply begs the question, since there are no independent criteria by which to check it. Others merely take it for granted that Paul was sometimes speculative, that he took ideas as far as they would go and then left the matter mysterious and suggestive. A completely different approach is suggested by some of the newly discovered Nag Hammadi writings, however, where Pauline ideas rather frequently appear.

These help us to see that Paul's different accounts may relate more clearly to a definite, 'esoteric' conception than at first appears. When he says to the Corinthians, 'See, I am speaking of a mystery ...' he does not after all mean that he is about to launch into 'speculation'; he was referring to a part of his 'wisdom among the initiated.' His vision was not based on speculative notions, but on what he saw on the way to Damascus. It was rooted in the actuality, the 'primary phenomenon' of the resurrection of Christ.

We can refer in particular to a section in the *Gospel of Philip*. That is not a document from one of Paul's communities, of course, but an expression of Christianity based on apostolic traditions, and on Gnostic-Mystery ideas which Philip and his followers came to emphasize rather strongly. We recognized in it, however, the distinct influence of the teaching of Jesus, and the still preserved knowledge of his Mystery-activity. But it was composed at Antioch: and since Antioch served as the base for much of Paul's mission in Syria and Asia Minor, it would be surprising if the *Gospel* did not show signs of interest in Pauline ideas. There are in fact a number of allusions to Paul's thought, showing that although his version of Christianity did not become the dominant one in Syria, he made his presence felt in Christian circles there. The interest of the Philip-Christians was a sympathetic one. Quite in line with its modified Mystery-teachings, the *Gospel of Philip* wants to take in the ideas of Paul, notably on the resurrection.

Saying 23 tackles the subject. The patterning of ideas, not to mention the well-known quotation, shows that it came of the mainstream of Pauline thought on the issues of the resurrection: it begins with the familiar rejection of those who want to come back 'just as they are now' and feel that without the material body of flesh and blood they would be incomplete:

> Some are afraid lest they rise naked. Because of this they
> wish to rise in this flesh, and they do not know that those
> who wear the flesh are naked; those who (prepare to)

unclothe themselves are not naked. 'Flesh and blood shall not inherit the Kingdom of God.' What is this which will not inherit? This which we have.

The resurrection-body is not the material flesh and blood. Behind the expressions used are the important Pauline concepts of the 'old' and 'new' Man or Adam: after all it was Adam and Eve who fell from grace, and realized that they were naked in their fleshly bodies. The idea of 'unclothing' suggests the 'putting off' of the body, the context being clearly baptism where we share in the death and resurrection of Christ. All this is thoroughly Pauline.

Despite the rejection of 'the standing up of corpses,' and despite the Gnostic background of parts of the *Gospel of Philip*, however, there is no concession to the Gnostic view that the body has to be abandoned. Rather there are parallels with Jewish writings which mention the fear of rising 'naked' — presumably showing the background of Paul's own thought on one aspect of resurrection. Bodily wholeness, the retaining of the spiritual essence of the body experience, is insisted on in what follows:

> But what is it which will inherit? That which belongs to Jesus with his blood. Because of this he said, 'He who shall not eat of my flesh and drink of my blood has no life in him.' What does this mean? His flesh is the *logos*, and his blood is the Holy Spirit. He who has received these has food and drink and clothing.

The resurrection is now centred directly on Christ and the archetypal, historic event. It is not the material flesh and blood that have been united with Christ. They are treated as outward expressions of man's being. In the case of fallen man, his bodily nature expressed itself outwardly in corruptible flesh; but now even in the outer expression of his body man reveals the Word (*logos*). The lifeblood of fallen man was the vehicle of his egotism, his self-centred consciousness; now it is to become the expression of his spiritual awareness, the Holy Spirit.

The idea of the Word as the essence, the supersensory truth of a thing, was to be found in much ancient philosophy. Yet there is also something much more specific in the allusion to it here, which is elaborated in the last part of the statement. On the basis of the 'essential' flesh and blood, rather than their material 'fallen' manifestations, the writer has decisively rejected the Gnostic view, and now goes on to define more closely what he regards as the actual essence of the body:

> For myself, I find fault with the others who say that it will not rise. Then both of these are at fault. You say that the flesh will not rise. But tell me what will rise, that we may do you honour. You say, 'The spirit in the flesh, which is also this light in the flesh.' But this too is a *logos* which is in the flesh, and whatever thou shalt say thou sayest nothing outside the flesh. It is necessary to rise in this flesh, in which everything exists.

Paul's ideas still provide the frame of reference. He had spoken of a 'spiritual body,' of the baptized person becoming 'light.' But now the 'logos which is in the flesh' is advanced as the solution to the whole question. *Logos* seems to have a very specific meaning here. Can we discover what it is?

The term *logos* was current among the Stoic natural philosophers, or scientists as we should nowadays call them. To understand their concept of *logos*, we need to add to our consideration of the Jewish background of body-awareness a brief examination of ideas that had been developing in the Greek world. For, rather later than might be expected, Greek thought too arrived at a notion of physicality, or in the most general terms, of body. *Logos* was in fact used to denote the characteristic form or physical structure of a thing. Unlike Plato or Aristotle, for whom the form of something was really an 'Idea' in the mind, the Stoics, who especially used the term, thought that the form of an object could be described in physical, or better in mathematical terms (as extension and cohesion in space). When reading the older Greek philosophers it is difficult, but important, to realize how far they stand from modern assumptions. The distinction of subjective and objective, for example, of 'mind' and 'world-out-there' was only clearly made by these Stoic philosophers in the last century or two before Christ. The classical philosophers' dichotomy of 'form' and 'matter' by no means coincides with, but rather cuts right across our modern division. Hence the supposition of material bodies in the modern sense only really goes back to the Stoics with what we may call their proto-scientific attitude.

For the Stoics, the mathematical structure of an object was its *logos*, which Latin-speaking philosophers translated by *ratio*, a set of fixed proportions as in the present mathematical usage of the word. The human body could be described in this way, by the Stoic writer Seneca for instance — and it is notable that already in ancient times the names of Paul and Seneca were often linked. Despite many differences in actual size and weight, he observed, human beings are built upon a fairly regular set of proportions. Indeed, every individual changes in physical make-up through growth, ageing, and so on; yet he retains a certain structural regularity independent of the changing materials of his body. This was his *logos*. If Paul required a 'scientific' description corresponding to the Jewish sense of the body, therefore, not just as matter but as essential form, it was certainly in the Stoic *logos* that he could have found it.[35]

The concept of *logos* enables the writer of Saying 23 to present Paul's resurrection teaching with great precision and coherence. The essence of corporeality is not the material substance, the literal flesh and blood. Or putting the argument for a moment in present-day terms, flesh and blood should really be defined by their function in the living being: the chemical substances in them are continually changing. But by their workings in the organism, they express the living spirit. It is with 'flesh and blood' in this sense that Christ and the Holy Spirit have been united, according to our author, so that man's flesh has become the expression of Christ, and his lifeblood of the spiritual Self. What is important for the working of these elements of human nature is not the substances presently contained in the body, but the functional reality of the human form, its continuing 'ratio' or *logos*. The teaching on resurrection emerges with striking clarity. When man rises to a higher level of existence he will no longer be material: but he will still be a living being, even a bodily being, since the '*logos* which is in the flesh' will be the expression of his Christ-pervaded life.

Was the *logos*-teaching the 'mystery' to which Paul referred in the Letter to the Corinthians? The obvious possibility that it was is rendered a certainty, I believe, by two things.

One is the startling exactness with which the doctrine matches Rudolf Steiner's account of the esoteric conception behind the statements in the Corinthian letters. Steiner referred to the immaterial form-principle of the physical body as the *Phantom*. The German word can mean an anatomical model — though it has given wrong connotations to the idea in English translations, perhaps, where it may strike the reader as having inappropriately sinister colorations! A related word, also conveying the sense of the essential features of a human form, is *Phantombild* — an identikit picture. Steiner and his followers have been able to define the living, functioning reality of the body in much more exact scientific terms than was possible, of course, in antiquity. They have extended the idea of form (*Gestalt*) developed by German thinkers since Goethe, and in many ways been in the vanguard of developments in recent 'holistic' science. Biologists such as C. H. Waddington have likewise noted the trend of science toward the understanding of complex systems and structures which are not directly dependent on the materials which make them up. The materialist's classic question 'what is it made of?' has come to seem increasingly irrelevant, he asserts, particularly in the case of organisms, although it is obvious that organic systems make use of chemical and other properties in order to establish structure. Rudolf Steiner was able to integrate his *Gestalt*-conception of the body with his wider idea of evolution. But he also claimed that the essential points of the *Phantom*-conception were grasped, and taught, in esoteric Pauline Christianity. Such an idea renders fully intelligible Paul's distinction between body and the material constituents of bodily life — and is strikingly confirmed by the discovery of the *Gospel of Philip* with its resurrection teaching influenced by Paul. Combined with evolutionary perspective, it gives us a unique opportunity actually to understand the possibility of the extension of man's bodily existence. In modern terms Steiner offers such a perspective: and so in more rudimentary terms does a document which furnishes the second confirmation of Paul's 'mystery'-doctrine.[36]

The *Letter to Rheginus* is another writing found in the Nag

Hammadi collection, and is sometimes known from its content by the alternative title of *De Resurrectione*. It is a short letter by an unknown and unnamed writer to the equally unknown Rheginus. It attempts to clear up certain problems of under-standing the Christian teaching on the nature of resurrection, and when the Nag Hammadi documents were first put before the world as a 'Gnostic library' it was suggested by some that the work was that of a Valentinian Gnostic, or even of the great heretic Valentinus himself. We have noted, however, that the Gnostics responsible for the library in fact possessed several books which were not themselves Gnostic in origin. The *Gospel of Thomas*, though highly 'spiritual,' did not deny the resurrection of the body — until the Gnostics cut out the reference to it. In the case of the *Letter to Rheginus*, scholars gradually noticed that there was really just one short passage which spoke in technical Valentinian terms, and that had all the appearance of an interpolation. They were struck for the rest by the 'fundamentally Christian nature' of the views expressed. On the resurrection, they had to admit that it advanced a surprisingly 'faithful inter-pretation of the Pauline view — more faithful, in fact, than that of many of the heresiologists of early Christendom!'[37]

The idea that the *Letter* is Valentinian still lingers on: but there are decisive arguments against it. For example, the basic Christian attitude of mind is described, not in terms of *gnosis* but of *pistis*, 'faith,' as in Paul. Valentinus had a doctrine strictly relat-ing salvation to *gnosis* alone. Then, Christ is several times referred to in the *Letter* as 'the Lord.' But one of the things we know about the Valentinians is that they did not wish to call Christ by that title, probably because it associated him with the 'Lord' of the Old Testament. A survey of Valentinian literature shows that they did in practice avoid it except in quotations or passages of exegesis where it was unavoidable.[38] It is in the Pauline churches that the affirmation 'Jesus is Lord' had its home. So the evidence points strongly to the *Letter* having been written by a follower of Paul; and, as we shall see, the underly-ing attitudes of the writer's thought are not Gnostic but Pauline Christian ones. All of which makes the esoteric character of the work the more significant. Indeed, it promises that a little more of the Pauline 'Mystery' will be unveiled.

Certainly on the resurrection of the body its teaching confirms that of the Pauline extract in the *Gospel of Philip*, and develops its ideas against a similar background. The gross flesh and blood belong to the part of man's nature, the writer explains, which is inherently subject to 'the law of death.' As material substance, they can be described as 'dead' even while they belong to the living organism. What is alive is not the visible substance of man's members, but the 'living members' — the vital form which the *Gospel* described as a '*logos* in the flesh,' the human 'ratio' or *Phantom* of Steiner's esoteric Christianity. And it is these living members or invisible form of which the *Letter* speaks in the context of resurrection:

> Let no-one be given cause to doubt concerning this ... indeed, the visible members which are dead shall not be saved — only the living members which exist within them are to be resurrected.[39]

And to avoid the least hint of confusion with some sort of Gnostic idea, on the lines of man's higher members being raised *from* the physical body, the writer goes on to insist that these 'living members' in the body are always and always will be clothed in a 'flesh.'

It is true that he may conceive of a pre-existent state in which man had not yet 'received flesh':

> But if you did not exist in flesh, you received flesh when you entered this world. Why, then will you not receive flesh when you ascend into the Aeon?[40]

Man's bodily existence expresses itself outwardly in a 'flesh' that is added to his nature of soul and spirit. When he ascends into the eternal, imperishable world through resurrection, he will still remain a bodily being. His 'flesh,' however, will be suitable to the reality of the 'living members' which have been exalted above the perishable substance that now clothes them. The *Gospel of Philip* also spoke of a 'flesh in which everything exists,' whether on a lower (material) or higher level. In fact, the teaching on the resurrection-body is essentially identical in both accounts.

Fig. 7. *The structure of time as seen by the* Letter to Rheginus *(after M.L.Peel).*

(a) The 'Beginning.' *The pre-existent state of perfection of the Pleroma. In this state were the 'All,' the Saviour, emanations, and the potential 'cosmos.' From this point the time line dips downward, denoting a fall into an inferior state.*

(b) Creation. *The coming into existence of the 'cosmos.' Note that creation corresponds with the beginning of cosmic time.*

(c) The Christ Event. *The decisive descent into cosmic time of the Saviour and his defeat — within cosmic time — of death. This event decisively affects everything that follows: thus the double black line.*

(d) Birth. *The beginning of the individual's 'life' within the cosmic sphere. The individual pre-existed in the 'All,' but became an identifiable person in the flesh only within the cosmic sphere of death and corruption.*
   We intersect the time line of the individual to indicate the point of present existence, i.e. the point from which our author views things. Note that the intersection is made at a point nearer the individual's death than to his birth, thus representing the 'already/not yet' tension of the Letter's eschatology, but emphasizing the importance of the 'already.'

(e) Death. *The cessation of the individual's life and the beginning of his ascension.*

(f) Escape. *The point of departure of the Elect from the cosmic plane of existence through his resurrection-ascension.*

(g) The 'Restoration.' *The final goal toward which the time line of salvation moves. The parabola permits us to indicate that the 'Restoration' ends with the restored Pleroma and thus essentially on the same plane as the 'Beginning.' Nevertheless, the 'Restoration' differs from the 'Beginning' in that in the former the Elect have identifiable resurrection bodies which they did not have before; furthermore, the 'cosmos' is excluded, whereas it was included at the 'Beginning.'*

(Explanatory notes from M. L. Peel, The Epistle to Rhegmus.)

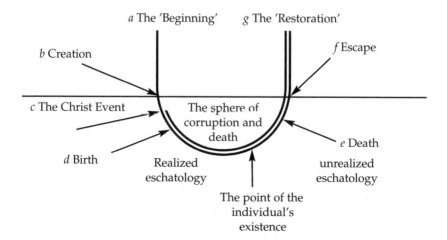

The *Letter to Rheginus* has the distinguishing feature, however, of being a short yet full treatment of the topic of resurrection, whereas in *Philip* we have only a short inserted fragment of teaching. The *Letter* reveals much more of the broader Christian framework of ideas. The time dimension is especially interesting, since the structure of time envisaged by the *Letter* is quite different from the typical Gnostic 'return to the beginning.' Rather, through emerging from his primitive spiritual pre-existence and descending into incarnation, man has evidently gained something — has evolved to a new level, and the bodily mode of existence he has acquired goes forward with him in his further evolution. The pattern is forward-looking and irreversible, not the Gnostic-mythical detour, as can be seen in the diagram devised by Malcolm Peel, who has worked extensively on the text (see Fig. 9). And for that matter, the view also transcends the Jewish resurrection-concept, according to which God affirms and perfects man's historical condition. For Judaism the body — and the creation generally — is a direct manifestation of the primal act of the creator. For the Christian thinker, the created form is provisional, and must in the course of things be spiritualized and purified of its earthly substance. A radically new concept of 'transformation,' of metamorphosis, emerges. Indeed it becomes the central statement of the document:

> The resurrection is a revelation of that which exists, and
> the transformation of things, and a transition unto
> newness. For imperishability descends upon the
> perishable ... (48:34–49:2)

At this crucial juncture it is to be noted that all the fundamental ideas and terms are Paul's. It is he who said 'in a mystery' that we shall all be transformed, it is he who spoke of the transition into 'newness,' he who posed the dilemma of the perishable flesh and blood against the imperishable-glory of the 'spiritual body.'

The doctrine of bodily resurrection in the *Letter to Rheginus*, then, is this: the invisible, living members of man, hidden in the visible flesh, are to be rescued from the law of death and to be revealed as man is transformed. The 'new Man' will not only retain his existential wholeness, but take his whole nature to a further stage of evolution. There is much that remains in the highest sense a 'mystery'; but there is a clear underlying conception, closely linked with Paul's central ideas, and which is not the invention of the *Letter*'s author, though the expressions may be his. For an identical concept was described in different words by the writer of the Pauline fragment in the *Gospel of Philip*. The best explanation for all this is that the idea was not a later 'speculative' development from Paul, but that it goes back to the apostle himself. If either the *Letter to Rheginus* or the *Gospel of Philip* had invented the idea, and influenced the other, we should expect to find exact correspondence of terms and copying of thoughts. Instead, we have the impression that both are explaining from their point of view an older teaching.

Yet both are somewhat later than Paul. It remains to be shown that the concepts found in the *Letter* can be pushed back to Paul's own time or nearer it. But that we can do: significantly, we can do so by attending to the larger frame of ideas.

The *Letter to Rheginus* does not mention only a bodily resurrection. It discusses alongside it a psychic or 'soul' resurrection, inwardly experienced, and a pneumatic or 'spiritual' resurrection. The basis is the threefold anthropology of Paul with its main terms, body, soul, spirit.

Since the general background of the whole work is Paul's sense of the Christian's dying and rising with Christ, the writer not unnaturally has to confront the issue of what happens when a man comes to the end of life: in other words, dies. Of course, he believes that man's spirit lives on after the death of the body. He points out that some philosophers have also come to that conclusion. Nevertheless he asserts that this is not essentially a matter for intellectual argument: 'It is the place of faith, my son, and not of persuasion. He who is dead shall arise.' The philosophical idea of 'immortality,' we may object, is hardly that of 'arising,' that is, resurrection; but that is not what the author is saying. He sees that Christ's 'victory over death' means that the situation of man in the life after earthly death must itself have been transformed.

Jewish Christians expressed their version of this insight in the Imagination of Christ's 'descent into Hell' and appearance to the dead patriarchs: but that would have made less sense to Paul's

Gentile followers. Nevertheless, the author of the *Letter to Rheginus* describes in his own way the transformed situation of those who have died in Christ, since the Mystery of Golgotha. For that is the matter of faith in the sense of the transformation wrought by Christ. The writer believes that those 'who have known the Son of Man' and 'believed' in him undergo a drawing heavenward after death. Paul's characterization of the baptized as 'light' underlies the analogy:

> For we are his beams. And we are enwrapped by him until our setting, that is to say, our death in this life. (Then) we are drawn to heaven by him like the beams of the sun, not being restrained by anything. This is the spiritual resurrection which swallows up the psychic along with the other fleshly.(45:31–46:2)

Whatever juncture we have reached in the evolution of our bodily, external life, or of our inner, soul life, at death we are caught up to a higher sphere. The doctrine is rather different from the teaching of the medieval Church, which combined Greek philosophical notions of immortality very unsatisfactorily with a far from evolutionary notion of 'the standing up of corpses' at the Last Day!

Perhaps still more interesting than the spiritual resurrection — the working of Christ into the sphere of after-death — is the *Letter*'s insistence that in the soul the power of resurrection is already working now. The attitude of soul of the Christian is already touched by the Christ-Event, and the baptized soul is aware of having died and risen. At least in inward awareness, death has been faced and overcome:

> For if he who will die knows himself that he will die —
> even if he spends many years in this life it comes to this:
> Why do you not consider yourself as risen (already)?
> (49:16–23)

This is the 'psychic resurrection,' and in the sphere of soul-life it has already taken place, unlike either the future transformation of the body or the spiritual life after death.

The *Letter to Rheginus* shows that early Christian concepts of resurrection, among Paul's followers at least, were far more subtle and intelligent than the bizarre doctrine of the standing corpses of the later church. The passage on the 'psychic resurrection' is also historically significant. For the idea that 'the resurrection has already taken place' is one we meet in the New Testament, and in a letter attributed to Paul. Two factors complicate the issue, however. Firstly, the reference is a vehement denial of the doctrine; secondly, the letter in which it occurs belongs to a group of letters where we have the strongest evidence that it is not really Paul's.

The Second Letter to Timothy purports to be written by Paul, indeed a personal communication. In contrast to the social and community interests of the other letters, it shows the apostle much concerned about those who, like Phygelus and Hermogenes, have 'deserted me,' that is, those who have diverged from his teaching. It includes a reference to:

> Hymenaeus and Philetus, who have wandered away from the truth. They say that the resurrection has already taken place, and they destroy the faith of some.[41]

Thus the teaching we find in the *Letter to Rheginus* about the psychic resurrection was known at the time of the Second Letter to Timothy, and associated with the names of two teachers, Hymenaeus and Philetus.

By the time of the Second Letter, if not earlier, that teaching was leading to misunderstandings among Christians, or so it seemed to some. Of course, we cannot be sure that Hymenaeus and Philetus taught all the other doctrines expounded to Rheginus. However, since they were both pupils of Paul (before they 'wandered from the truth'), their starting-point would likewise have been the apostle's teaching on resurrection.

The *Letter to Rheginus* shows how the idea of the 'already risen' experience can arise out of a thoroughly Pauline pattern, and coexists with an expectation of a bodily, as well as a spiritual resurrection. It is certainly wrong, therefore, to assume that Hymenaeus and Philetus had abandoned the other aspects of Paul's resurrection teachings. Given their original background before they swerved (if they really did), it is highly unlikely.

The question of their Pauline orthodoxy is crucial to the writer of the Second Letter to Timothy. And indeed the consistent concern with orthodoxy is one of the features which gives away the different standpoint of the author. He is not Paul, pioneering new paths and communities, but a consolidator, as we may call him, of the next generation, or the next. Most scholars agree that he also wrote the First Letter to Timothy and the Letter to Titus, perhaps around the end of the first century, some sixty years after Paul. The little group is sometimes given the name of 'Pastoral Epistles,' and was rejected as spurious by some Christians from the beginning.[42] However, the difficulty concerning the frame of mind in which a pious churchman could forge letters in the name of the apostle Paul has continued to be an obstacle for some in the way of admitting the forgery. Yet the evidence of language and the consolidator-mentality of the writer seem decisive. Moreover, our new *Letter to Rheginus* may provide some answers to these problems too.

Consider for instance the assurance by the consolidator: 'Here is a saying — and a trustworthy one'; consider the references to those who have deserted Paul, or wandered from his teaching. It is evident that a situation of tension, if not crisis, had come about in the Pauline churches. There was uncertainty, faith had been 'destroyed.' The consolidator writes on behalf of a highly ecclesiastical or church-orientated position, trying to establish an orthodoxy based on Paul's teaching. Yet it is most significant that the crisis is evidently an internal one. There is no mention of outsiders, no going off after false gods, no going back to ancient or off after Gnostic teachings. The consolidator has to admit that his opponents are following on from figures known to be closely connected with Paul himself. He cannot play the heresy-hunter's trump-card, which is to claim that the 'false' teachings are a new innovation, to be contrasted with the pure, original orthodoxy. Hence he has only one real alternative: he has to admit that the teachings go back to the time of Paul, but claim that the apostle even then struggled against and condemned them.

The end of the first century, then, may have witnessed one of the many internal crises of the expanding Church. Perhaps already the complex, intelligent, esoteric teachings 'among the initiated' were too subtle for some of the rank-and-file Christians; or certain elements of them could be and were being taken one-sidedly and misunderstood. A strong movement towards Church authority emerged, and found all too soon that the real enemies were within the fold. Nevertheless, those enemies were only carrying on the inner teachings of the apostle Paul and his followers such as Hymenaeus and Philetus. The pressure to commit a 'pious fraud' and condemn them out of the mouth of the apostle must have been very great. And we can see from the Pastoral Epistles that someone yielded to the temptation. We must add that the trick worked. Despite the doubts of some, they were included in the New Testament canon. We thus have the only real explanation for the forgery of letters in Paul's own name. It was done, from the consolidator's point of view, to save the Pauline tradition from itself. The argument only works, only makes sense, if the position to be combatted was indeed internal to the tradition: on any other assumption the forgery appears too monstrously improbable. The *Letter to Rheginus* fits the evidence concerning the Pauline tradition before it was purged and ecclesiasticized, that is, as it was taught for instance by Hymenaeus, Philetus and their followers. And they, as even the consolidator admits, originally had the 'truth' from Paul himself.

The best way of regarding the *Letter to Rheginus,* for all these reasons, is to see it as based upon resurrection ideas taught esoterically by Paul. With its sensitivity to the working of the Christ impulse in the soul, in the life-after-death, and in the future evolution of man, it casts a notable light on the seeming contradictions of Paul's own letters — as when he seems sometimes to speak as if the resurrection were already beginning to happen, or would do so in his lifetime, leading to a changed consciousness (the vision of Christ 'in the clouds of heaven'), while at other times he envisages a long succession of coming ages, culminating in a thoroughgoing bodily transformation of man. These differing views do not point to a change of mind; they reveal different aspects of a teaching that remained in part esoteric, different sections of a wheel whose hub remained hidden. Or at least, it was hidden until the threefold resurrection-teaching preserved in the *Letter to Rheginus* began to reveal the profundity and scientific scope of the apostle's mind. The teaching on resurrection expresses the deepest convictions of Christianity, demanding a cosmic and 'evolutionary' vision of man and world. That cosmic vision is presented from still further points of view in the other great personal expression of the gospel — by the writer known as 'John.' At the same time, it is central to their thinking that the fulcrum of cosmic vision is the maturing of man's free individuality. There is no better way to make the transition from the one to the other than to examine the core of the message common to Paul and John alike. For both of them the Christian proclamation is a cosmic vision, but also essentially human in significance: it is the Gospel of Love.

The Gospel of Love

Although he never wrote a book or dictated a document with the name of 'Gospel,' we may speak of a Pauline Gospel which the apostle proclaimed through his letters and addresses. He used the word in its original sense of a royal proclamation, specifically about a new accession of the Emperor or King. It is the announcement of a happy change, or a new era. For the old barriers between God and man can be overturned, he declares, because of the deed of Christ.

The Law had its historical justification, nurturing man's sense of moral individuality; but the Law as the framework of a religious consciousness had resulted in irresolvable contradictions. In the new world and for the new consciousness, all things are permitted. Guilt and condemnation under the categories of the Law no longer existed for the followers of Christ Jesus. They were 'acquitted,' in the technical sense that the case against them was dropped since the Law was recognized as an inappropriate instrument. That is Paul's brilliant legal argument in the Letter to the Romans. The moral self is seen to have outgrown the apparatus that enabled it to take its first steps. And our studies have confirmed the Christian transformation of the self, making it the means of divine revelation, endowing it with the awareness of autonomy that goes with the knowledge of its own infinity. To it all things are permitted.[43]

Is the Gospel then libertinism? No, because that is still not to judge by categories any deeper than the Law. But the power by which the Christ-self orders its thoughts and acts is love.

Paul is convinced that man's new self-awareness, through sharing in the 'burial and resurrection' of Christ, a selfless offering, can enable him to overcome the tendency to selfish egotism. Man can help his fellow men, not because he ought to do right by the Law, but because of the love that flows from his own deepest self. And in that sense man is acting at the same time out of the God within him. The external absolute of moral behaviour held up by the Law inevitably left imperfect man in guilty shortcomings, and his guilt was a sense of his otherness from God. Acting out of love, however, to whatever extent man could achieve it, he was acting in unity with his sense of the God, the 'Christ in me.' Hence when Paul addresses his famous 'hymn' to love, contrasting love with the legalistic mentality that keeps a list of wrongs, with the spiritual gifts that have value only if offered in love to others, he is expressing the essence of the Christian Gospel:

> Love is patient, love is kind. It does not envy, it does not boast, it is not proud. It is not rude, it is not self-seeking, it is not easily angered, it keeps no record of wrongs. Love does not delight in evil but rejoices with the truth. It always protects, always trusts, always hopes, always preserves.
>
> Love never fails. But where there are prophecies, they will cease; where there are tongues, they will be stilled; where there is knowledge, it will pass away. For we know in part and we prophesy in part, but when perfection comes, the imperfect disappears.
>
> When I was a child, I talked like a child, I thought like a child, I reasoned like a child. When I became a man, I put childish ways behind me. Now we see but a poor reflection; then we shall see face to face. Now I know in part; then I shall know fully, even as I am fully known.
> (1 Cor.13:4–12)

Above all the Gospel of Love is not a shallow cry of 'Why can't people be nice to one another?' On the contrary, it is the message of an extraordinarily demanding vision of the self, its power to determine its destiny and its world. In its deeper ramifications it leads directly to the 'maturing' of childish humanity through initiation, as the end of Paul's statement shows. The self must offer itself to die, and trust to its rebirth through love. It is the message of the utter freedom of that self; and of the effort of consciousness required to judge every situation, not by a stereotype, but by loving comprehension of individual circumstances. It is a determination to think and act out of the deepest resources of that self, and the conviction that to do so is to act out of Christ, and thus out of God. It was in this deepest sense, too, that John (or whichever of his pupils wrote the First Letter of John on the basis of his teaching) said, 'God is love.' Not that God commands love, nor even that he bestows it. But absolutely — 'seeing face to face' — 'God is love.'[44]

It would be idle to pretend that we have got very far, over the centuries of Christendom, with the attempt to live out of a Christ-consciousness of love. The fabric of society is still based largely on the obligations of law, and in personal relations love is still limited by factors of family bonds, self-interest, authority, and so on, as much as it ever was. Indeed we seem hardly to have started considering any other possibility. This is something to which we shall return in our final chapter, in a context which may make the sense of 'just beginning' more understandable.

Certainly in antiquity the message was strikingly novel. Jesus and the apostles formed a unique and unprecedented 'community of love.' And the Christians used the term for love, *agape*, in extended senses that had no earlier parallel. The Pythagorean fraternities had a bond of 'brotherhood,' but were hardly organized on the same principle, and the similarities to the Christian 'communion' are mostly external. The Greeks had developed a concept of love as self-realization, giving it a cosmic rather than a personal scope. It is love, according to Aristotle, which makes imperfect things change and grow, since they love and desire the 'form' which is as yet only partially revealed in them. Man's love for what is higher likewise makes him wish to be better. But love here is essentially 'desire' (*erōs*), albeit for higher things. It is the attempt of all things to lift themselves heavenward. The gesture of turning to help those further behind, however, the gesture of

Jesus when he said that the Son of Man came to serve, or when he washed the disciples' feet, is lacking from the classical spirit. It is not love but 'friendship' — the mutual support and affirmation of two nobly independent (male) beings — that earns the moral approval of the ancient philosophers. The Mysteries shared the attitude in the divine realm. 'To those ascending the gods hold out a hand,' it was said. But the descending, or retrospective, love for those left below was new to Christianity. [45]

Christian love, with its unlimited scope, corresponded to the discovery of the Christian self-consciousness. Its teaching is rooted in the being and presence of Jesus as portrayed in all the traditions. We shall see that it refers in a special way in John's Christianity to 'the disciple whom Jesus loved,' who recorded 'the commandment of love' which was to replace the Law. The 'commandment' expresses the type of paradox typically found in Paul, rather than John. For of course no one can be commanded to love. That is just the point. And yet this commandment is the only one which can stand in the new world that opened up for the Christian consciousness. In John as in Paul, individual development and cosmic events stand in extraordinary close relation. The Fourth Gospel tells in its own terms of the 'turning-point of the world'; but the starting-off point for a grasp of cosmic evolution is the new power, and the new demands made on man's own self. Conversely, it would be an error to suppose we had comprehended the Johannine doctrine of love without understanding its cosmic import. The form of the Fourth Gospel itself is a brilliant encapsulation of personal and cosmic in one unfathomable meditation. But to understand that, we must first consider its origin and context in the early Christian world.

12. The Gospel of John

The 'disciple whom Jesus loved': that is how 'John' — the writer of the Fourth Gospel — speaks of one whose experience catches the essence of his relationship to Christ, one whose experience he describes so directly and intimately that it is hard not to suppose that he means himself.

I say 'the writer of the Fourth Gospel,' 'John' and 'the disciple Jesus loved' in this rather cautious and explanatory fashion because it is important to realize just how little we know about the author except from the internal patterns and references of the Gospel itself. True, the Fathers of the Church generally supposed that 'John' was John the son of Zebedee, and brother of James. But that notion is entirely secondary. It has no evidence to recommend it historically and involves a large number of implausibilities. Various other John's have been proposed by scholars in an effort to escape these problems, but it may be as well to admit that we really have no independent knowledge about who wrote the Gospel.[1] Rather than running through every John in the early Christian world, we might look to the results of Steiner's spiritual researches, which point in a completely different direction. It is one, however, which turns out to be amply confirmed by the internal evidence of the Fourth Gospel, and by a remarkable parallel in the secret *Mark*. As for the writer's identity with 'the disciple Jesus loved,' that is supported above all by the fundamental tone of the Gospel, which as deeply as the urgent message of Paul proclaims 'the Gospel of Love.'

Anyone reading through the four canonical Gospels, that is, those that have come down in the New Testament, must be struck immediately by the different approach adopted in the Fourth from the other three. Matthew and Luke go back before Jesus' life and teaching to present his ancestry and birth; Luke even goes back to Adam, the Son of God: but John takes us at once into the mysteries of God before the world began. His Jesus later speaks, moreover, with a direct awareness of his cosmic significance — 'I am the light of the world,' he says at one point — and expounds his own nature and meaning in astonishing discourses quite unlike the tradition of the *mashal*, the forceful saying, the picture or parable we know from Jesus' teaching elsewhere. It is impossible to miss the highly reflective, meditative quality of the work, or the way in which the material, familiar and unfamiliar from the other Gospels, has been arranged to bring out the inner significance of the events. We must not jump to the conclusion that it therefore distorts history, or is unreliable on matters of fact, though it used to be widely accused of being so. The modern trend of research has been to find John increasingly reliable on the level of factual tradition as well as for spiritual insight. It belongs to our whole interpretation of Christianity that the essential Christian spirit puts value on both inward and material truth, and even identifies them and regards them as inseparable.

In that sense the Gospel of John is a centrally Christian statement, and we may discount all attempts to portray it as in some way marginal, 'Gnostic' or otherwise. Despite its unusual features of style, it has certain points of contact with the other canonical Gospels which were accepted by the Church. (And indeed, we now know that the other Gospels were somewhat modified when taken up for orthodox use.) The use of the term 'remember,' with the specially charged meaning we noted from the Gospel of Luke, for instance, draws our attention directly to the way the events of Christ's life and death are the bearers of his message. Likewise the idea of 'remaining in my words' evokes the 'ministry of the word' underlying Luke's recreation of the Gospel in literary form. Yet in John the effect is not so much to call up vivid 'Imaginations,' the 'autoptic' images of the Christian prophets and apostles. The overwhelming quality of the Fourth Gospel is that of the immediate presence of Christ, more resembling the experience of the *epopteia* in Mystery terminology. Christ's real presence is felt, for example, in the way the writer is able to move from the citing of Jesus' words to his own meditative comment without sharp transition. Thus in the account given by Oscar Cullmann it becomes clear that 'on the ground of his conviction that he is being guided by the Paraclete in this remembrance, the evangelist can allow himself to develop the discourses beyond what the incarnate Jesus said ... The risen Christ speaks through the evangelist. Through him the Christ continues the teaching which he gave during his incarnation.'[2] The phenomenon is deepened and intensified far beyond the point to which it is taken by Luke, so that we can indeed express the distinction by saying that Luke is primarily the autoptic, but John the epoptic Gospel.

The analogy with Luke prompts a first tentative step toward clarifying the background of the Fourth Gospel. Affinity with the Lucan 'remembering' suggests an origin outside the mainstream of Judaism (compare Chapter 7 above), under Hellenistic or oriental influence. The Fourth Gospel's manner of referring to 'the Jews' confirms its outsideness, though it need not mean that 'the Church' was a well-established organization by the time of its author, to be set alongside 'the Synagogue.' Adherents of the esoteric baptizing sects, for instance, could well refer to the Jewish mainstream parties in some such way as 'the Jews.' Further hints as to the Gospel's background come from its evident connections with the Gospel of Mark, especially now that the secret *Mark* has brought to light further Johannine materials from the original Alexandrian Gospel. Those features of the Gospel of John which have tempted many to describe it as 'Gnostic' might fall into place if it shared the spiritual environment of Mark, which Rudolf Steiner had already characterized as a backdrop of Gnostic ideas. Setting aside the vexed issue of whether the author of John knew Mark's Gospel and used it as a source, some sort of spiritual proximity is obvious when the two are compared — though again there are definite differences. The Gospel of John is sometimes also strikingly akin to the Hermetic writings, or pagan Gnosis of Alexandria.[3] Yet on the whole the scriptures of the Mandaeans furnish still closer parallels, pointing us back to Syria or Palestine. The *Gospel of Philip*'s evidence of a sacramental Christianity close to Mandaeism adds a further clue, and sheds some light on the Fourth Gospel's allusions to ritual and sacrament, again rather telling against an Alexandrian origin. On the whole, we may be fairly sure that the links between John and Mark lie farther back, in the Gnostic tendencies of the baptizing sects. It was actually from Syria that Gnostic thought and the teaching of *metanoia* came to Alexandria. Contrary to the view once prevalent, the evidence of language and the history of ideas shows that the Gospel of John might well have come from esoteric circles in Palestine itself, and in the lifetime of a follower of Jesus.[4]

The language of the Gospel, for instance, is hardly Alexandrian literary Greek. It is an odd though effective Greek that often uses the idioms of Aramaic. Scholars have sometimes supposed that its author must have thought in Aramaic but written in Greek; others conclude that the basic document behind our Gospel text was actually composed in Aramaic. It is even possible that the editorial notes, written in the plural form 'we,' at the end of chapter 21 in the Gospel, come from those who translated it into Greek, adding their testimony as to who wrote the original.

What is certain is that the Gospel of John, with its unique 'difference' from the other Gospels, its spiritual qualities and sense of immediate presence, could be accepted by the organized Church only with great difficulty. To many, no doubt, it seemed a threat to the authority of the traditions stemming from the twelve disciples. There it palpably did not belong, although the needs of the Church authorities later overrode all other considerations and gave it a pedigree that attached it to John son of Zebedee. Yet its spirituality based on immediate relationship to Christ clearly undercut the structure of the Church hierarchy, and the evidence survives of the campaign to discredit it, notably around the time when the visionary followers of Montanus were proving somewhat intractable to Church discipline (second century). A campaign was launched suggesting its attribution to the Gnostic Cerinthus, and some rather tasteless stories about the supposed conflict of 'John' with Cerinthus in a bath-house in Asia Minor were circulated. Those Christians who held to the specifically Johannine teaching, we saw in an earlier chapter, were manoeuvred out of the Church into the tactical company of Gnostics and 'heretics' when the official synthesis of orthodox traditions became mandatory.[5] Hence it is that several features of Johannine Christianity can now be found in the company of Gnostic doctrines, for instance, in the *Secret Book of*

John. It remains a matter of credit to the early Christians, however, that the profundity and directness of the Fourth Gospel guaranteed its survival and the spreading of its message, the Gospel of Love.

The 'Beloved Disciple'

Modern research into the language and thought of the Gospel of John, then, shows that it is compatible with the Gospel's sense of closeness to Christ. We are historically justified in taking the internal evidence of the Gospel as a reliable guide to its writer, in preference to the late Church tradition that 'John' was John the brother of James (the sons of Zebedee). And the Gospel contains evidence of a most striking kind.

The evidence is mainly to be found in chapter 21; but because of the special nature of that chapter, we must briefly examine its connection with the rest of the Gospel.

At first sight, it appears an excrescence, since the Gospel comes to an obvious conclusion immediately before the chapter begins. Moreover, it has quite obviously been added by the editors who inserted the note 'We know that his testimony is true' — presumably because they had been the evangelist's close disciples. On the other hand, the editors must equally have added it because they felt it was vital to the meaning of tite Gospel, especially in clearing up the identity of the writer and his relationship to Jesus. No manuscript of the Gospel has come down without it. Before we jump on the bandwagon of those scholars who analyze the Gospel as the work of successive ecclesiastical editors or redactors — a late weaving together of secondary traditions, therefore — we should perhaps consider what reasons might underlie the publication of the Gospel with its problematic additional chapter.

As soon as we consider the question of literary origins and development of the Gospel in this way, however, we encounter a serious problem in the evidence. There is a basic contradiction between the Gospel's sense of closeness to Christ and the lateness of its appearance in Christian history. The lack of any sign of it until after AD 100 led most historians to conclude that it was written considerably later than the other Gospels. And then, it is another century still before Church tradition claims it for John, son of Zebedee. The facts take on quite another significance, however, in the light of B. Rigaux's recent argument that the Gospel was addressed to initiated Christians only. It was never intended to be the kind of book that would win over the masses, as indeed we could infer from its whole character and meditative depth. Accordingly its absence from outer history must be seen, not as evidence that it had not yet appeared, but of its restriction to circles of initiated Christians.[6] The Gospel presumably was taught in the form of oral tradition. Only later was the decision made to publish the Gospel and to circulate it more widely.

The decision was taken, in fact, only after the evangelist's death. At least, such is the most obvious reading of the internal evidence. For in chapter 21 the editors are at pains to disavow the vulgar misinterpretation of Jesus' prophetic words, which some had thought meant the evangelist would never die. (Strangely, the stories that accumulated around the 'undying' John are in singularly bad taste, for instance, the notion that if you listen at his tomb in Ephesus you can still hear him snoring.) That was never the meaning of the words, imply the editors, so the evangelist's death in no way detracts from the truth. The fact that no version of the Gospel appears to have existed without chapter 21 confirms that it was then published for the first time. We shall see that the final chapter is actually an integral part of the structure of the whole. It may seem odd to commence our discussion at the end of the Gospel: but by its very unusual nature, the end will be found to cast a much-needed light on the middle and the beginning.

So why was the decision taken? Why did the Gospel not remain in the esoteric circles for which it was intended? The answer surely lies in the direction taken by the developing Church. The trend which progressively isolated those Christians who had taken a Johannine path and was to push them out of the Church, into the company of Gnostics and the Jewish-Christian 'Ebionites,' began to make itself felt in the second century. The esotericists who used the Fourth Gospel were gradually faced with a choice. They could give up any attempt to influence broader Christian society and accept ever increas-

ing isolation; or, they could publish their esoteric Gospel, establish its authority and closeness to Christ, and so hope to keep
alive the more spiritual dimension of Christianity in the Church.
They chose the latter path. And indeed their gamble paid off.
Although the full esoteric tradition soon came to be unacceptable in Church circles, the Gospel itself was taken up and preserved. There was strenuous resistance, but the price finally
paid was relatively small. The reference to Jesus' ritual activity
(baptism) had to be explained away by the addition of a contradictory note saying simply that he did not do it, for example.
And the Gospel had to be given an authority from the circle of
the Twelve. But that is a small price to pay for the historic decision which saved us from losing the Fourth Gospel. Otherwise
we might never have known it: or we might have been dependent upon an accident of history like that which unexpectedly
restored to us the *Gospels* of *Philip* and *Thomas*.

The period of difficult decision-making perhaps also affected
the Fourth Gospel in one or two marginal ways. Oscar Cullman
has thrown great light on the setting of the 'Johannine circle' in
the stormy time after the fall of Jerusalem to the Roman armies
in AD 70. It was in that time that the esotericists were trying to
make contact with wider groups, notably with the more esoteric
elements among the Jewish Christians, successors of the Essenes
and the *Ebionim*. The task of establishing the direction and leadership of Christianity must never have seemed more desperate.
Many Christians fled from Judea across the river into the
Transjordan, and it is there that Cullman posits a contact
between the Johannine circle and the Jewish-Christians. In this
way we can best explain how Essene-derived ideas crop up in
the Fourth Gospel, though it is far removed in spirit and origin
from the transformed legalism of the 'Ebionite' Christians.[7]
Probably it was at that same stage that the Gospel acquired the
story of the 'woman taken in adultery,' which originally
belonged to the *Gospel of the Hebrews* or Jewish-Christian prototype of the Gospel of Matthew. The special link with the
Samaritans that shines through other parts of the Gospel may
also go back to the restless period after the Jewish-Roman war.

Yet for the most part the Gospel is clearly the product of a single author, close in time and space to Jesus. Similarities gener-

ally with the esotericism of Jewish, Gnostic or Alexandrian Christianity point rather to the common matrix out of which they emerged, as Cullman again stressed. The editors, when they finally decided to publish the Gospel, did so with only minor adjustments of their own. Thus the problem of the concluding chapter comes more sharply into focus. Perhaps there was at one stage the serious possibility that the work would be published in a form ending with chapter 20. But even so it would be quite wrong to suppose that the materials deriving orally from the evangelist could not already have existed in a highly organized state, as we know from the history of Jewish oral tradition and the oral traditions behind *Thomas* or the other Gospels. And so it would be quite wrong also to think of the material of chapter 21 as 'floating' tradition, captured and anchored to the end of the Gospel by the editors. It certainly corresponded to a part of the exposition of the evangelist to his disciples. Papias, who may have been a 'hearer' of the evangelist, expressed his relatively disparaging view of written texts in comparison with 'the living and enduring voice,' remembered as the apostle himself urged.[8] The oral Gospel will have possessed a 'living and enduring' structure, long before it was written down. However, an oral stage may at the same time help account for the apparent 'misplacing' of some episodes by literary standards, interrupting the development of ideas.

Chapter 21 was a significant part of it, despite the fact that the Gospel story as such was complete with chapter 20; for it was the part in which the author of the Gospel revealed to his hearers his own identity in terms of that story. Hence to have published the Gospel without it would have been to deprive it of its spiritual grounding, of the source of its astonishing power. The Gospel never was published without it because, as Rudolf Steiner understood, and was able to confirm spiritually, it reveals that the writer of the Gospel was Lazarus.

We must take care to follow the steps which lead to his assertion. We must start again with chapter 21. There the 'beloved disciple' is actually mentioned twice. Firstly, he is in the boat on Lake Tiberias, and experiences a recognition of the risen Christ. It is he who says to the other disciples, who have not yet recognized the figure on the shore, not even Peter, 'It is the Lord!'

Then, later in the chapter, he is following Peter. The latter turns and asks Jesus about him. Jesus replies with the famous prophetic but riddling words:

> If I wish him to remain until I come back again, what is that to you? But do you follow me.

To which the editors append their note that he did not mean the disciple would never die. Further, they tell us that they had received the contents of the Gospel from that 'beloved disciple.' The assertion that he 'wrote them down' need not, perhaps, be taken in too strong a sense: most likely we have to do with 'memory-jogging' notes of the type which underlay the Gospel of Mark. Then, they tell us that the 'beloved disciple' was 'the one who had reclined next to Jesus at the supper and had said, 'Lord, who is going to betray you?'

'This information enables us to make a reconstruction with far-reaching consequences, if we follow it through clearly in our minds. The editors received the key to their deeper understanding from the author, who at the end of his exposition of the Gospel revealed to them that he had himself been the 'disciple whom Jesus loved.' I do not mean they thought, as a result, that the author could vouch for everything he described. That is not strictly true, for the 'beloved disciple' only appears in the second half of the Gospel, so that they (and we) would still have to assume that all the information about Jesus' life and ministry was derived from tradition. For later events, the 'beloved disciple' indeed figures as a witness. At the last supper he reclines next to Jesus and asks about his betrayal; and he is almost certainly the anonymous disciple who, after Jesus' arrest, takes Peter into the palace.[9]

But that is only a fraction of the significance given to the Gospel by his self-identification, revealed by the evangelist at the very end of his exposition. The pupil now realized that the voice narrating the events of Jesus' life and teaching came from an intimate disciple. But the impact of the revelation was infinitely greater than that. For in the light of it the pupil of the evangelist was compelled to re-examine the whole fabric of what he had learnt. One may rightly claim for the Fourth Gospel an *avant-garde* literary method. It has to be read first for the second time. And the full extent of its meaning is only unleashed by the chapter which stands at the very centre of the Gospel, chapter 11. It is the chapter of the so-called 'raising of Lazarus.'

The opening of the story is familiar, yet it contains an element we may previously have overlooked:

> Now a man named Lazarus was sick. He was from
> Bethany, the village of Mary and her sister Martha. This
> Mary, whose brother Lazarus now lay sick, was the same
> one who poured perfume on the Lord and wiped his feet
> with her hair. So the sisters sent word to Jesus: 'Lord, the
> one you love is sick.'

There can be no doubt of his identity. The phrasing of the last sentence is sufficient to identify him to Jesus — and to us. 'This same expression "whom the Lord loved,"' Rudolf Steiner pointed out, 'is always used later in the Gospel in connection with John, or perhaps we should say in connection with the writer of the Gospel, for the name "John" is not employed.'[10] The 'beloved disciple' we know from the editors to have been the authority of the Gospel. Looking back through the Gospel we find that confirmed by his special role. And there is a startling further discovery. At the same time he is Lazarus.

The allusion to the one whom Jesus loved is made two more times in chapter 11: but we need not emphasize the point. For any pupil of the Fourth Gospel the revelation that the author of the Gospel is Lazarus now extends far beyond the question of eyewitness and authority. The Gospel comes from one who through the intervention of the Christ has experienced directly the mysteries of life and death:

> Jesus heard that Lazarus was sick, yet he stayed where he
> was two more days. Then he said to his disciples, 'Let us
> go back to Judea.' ... He went on to tell them, 'Our friend
> Lazarus has fallen asleep, but I am going there to wake
> him!' ... Jesus had been speaking of his death, but his
> disciples thought he meant natural sleep. So he told them
> plainly, 'Lazarus is dead, and for your sake I am glad I

was not there, so that you may believe. But let us go to
him.' Then Thomas (called Didymus) said to the rest of
the disciples, 'Let us also go, that we may die with him.'
On his arrival, Jesus found that Lazarus had already been
in the tomb for four days ...

Jesus, once more deeply moved, came to the tomb. It
was a cave with a stone laid across the entrance. 'Take
away the stone,' he said ... So they took away the stone.
Then Jesus looked up and said, 'Father, I thank you that
you have heard me. I knew that you always heard me,
but this I said for the sake of the people standing here,
that they may believe that you sent me.' When he had
said this, Jesus called in a loud voice, 'Lazarus, come out!'

The dead man came out, his hands and feet wrapped
with strips of linen, and a cloth around his face.

Much remains for the moment mysterious about Lazarus'
death, as about the 'miracle' of his resurrection. But now the
power of this event inevitably communicates itself to the whole
of the Gospel, making it a profoundly personal document in a
way we could not before have envisaged; though it is also far
more than that, in the universal, archetypal quality of the event
at its heart. On another level, we can quite understand the genesis of that common rumour about the 'beloved disciple': how
those who were standing by the way, who see and yet do not
see, who hear and do not understand, could spread the rumour
that henceforth this disciple was immortal.

The identification is so definite, so unambiguous, that one
may wonder why it remained unapprehended before Steiner's
researches into the Gospel and before modern scholars such as
F. Filson unravelled the clues.[11] Such was the haze of confusion
thrown up by the Church tradition about John, son of Zebedee
and the hunt for other John's when it was found he would not
do, coupled with the erroneous result of nineteenth-century
philology which declared that the Gospel came from Hellenistic
Judaism and so could not possibly have had any direct connection with Palestine or the circle round Jesus. Modern research
into the Gospel's language and ideas has freed us from the latter misconception. Freeing ourselves from the former, it seems

that we find ourselves — after so many centuries! — for the first time able to read the Gospel on its own terms.

The reading of the Gospel in the terms established by the identification of Lazarus is so potent, so brilliant, that we must point out that it suffers from an unfortunate, indeed a fatal flaw. The identification depends on a supposition: namely, that only one person is designated as the man whom Jesus loved in this special sense. If the phrase could refer to more than one person, the ground of the whole edifice crumbles away. And in chapter 10 of the Gospel of Mark, in quite a different context, we encounter a rich young man, of whom it is said that Jesus 'loved him.'

The young man sounds absolutely different, from the dramatic incident when he appears:

> As Jesus started on his way, a man ran up to him and fell on his knees before him. 'Good teacher,' he asked, 'what must I do to inherit eternal life?'

to the sad face he makes when he learns he must give up everything, his great wealth included. He has nothing in common with the Lazarus of the Fourth Gospel, and that is the last we see of him. All we know otherwise is that Jesus 'loved him.'

Of course, the passage in Mark does not prove that the one 'whom Jesus loved' could not be Lazarus — only, there is no reason to suppose that he must be. Rudolf Steiner's and Filson's idea would only have convincing force if it could be shown that every 'beloved' disciple reference applied to one and the same man, or in other words, that the rich young man in Mark actually was the figure known under the name Lazarus in John. And before 1958 that looked a highly implausible line of argument. Not least among the revelations of 1958, however, came the confirmation that, after all, Steiner's astounding results of spiritual investigation could be applied with the strictest accuracy.

That year the fragment of the secret *Mark* turned up, giving us for the first time the original, longer version of a part of the text. By an amazing turn of events, the additional material comes from chapter 10 of the Gospel. In a most astonishing way, the figure of the rich young man is further described. We have already, in an earlier chapter, cited the account from the secret *Mark* for the ritual Jesus performed, and the young man in his white baptismal cloth. It was not then the moment to quote in full detail what goes before the ritual. That time has now come. The new fragment dovetails into canonical Mark, chapter 10 after verse 34. Following verse 22, the crestfallen disappearance of the young man, Jesus gives the *mashal* of the camel passing through the eye of the needle — a fantastic impossibility, yet 'easier than for a rich man to enter the kingdom of God!' He talks then of renouncing possessions and relations, and of his own coming rejection and condemnation, which the disciples do not yet fully understand, any more than the allusions to his resurrection. Then events take a further turn. The 'secret' section begins:

> They reached Bethany. And a woman, whose brother had died, was there. And she came and prostrated herself before Jesus, and said to him, 'Son of David, have mercy upon me.' The disciples rebuked her; but Jesus was angry (with them), and went with her into the garden where the tomb was. And immediately a great cry was heard from the tomb. And going near, Jesus rolled the stone away from the door of the tomb. And immediately he went in, and there was the youth. He stretched forth his hand and raised him, seizing his hand. But the youth looked at him, loved him, and began to beseech him that he might be with him.
>
> And leaving the tomb, they went into the house owned by the youth, for he was rich. And after six days Jesus instructed him and in the evening the youth came to him, wearing a linen cloth over his naked body. And he remained with him that night, for Jesus taught him the Mystery of the kingdom of God.
>
> And thence, arising, he returned to the other side of the Jordan. Then James and John, the sons of Zebedee, came to him ...

And so the text returned to canonical Mark (with slight variations a little further on). The passage about James and John is the one where Jesus asks them 'Can you drink the cup I drink, or be baptized with the baptism I am baptized with?'

There can be no doubt on two scores. Firstly, the 'youth' who is rich is the same youth we met earlier in the chapter. Jesus effectually said he must 'die' to the world to attain the kingdom, and it transpires that he has done so. Secondly, the story related about him is identical with the story of — Lazarus.[12]

It is possible to shed great light on the Gospel traditions through a detailed comparison of the secret *Mark* and the Fourth Gospel. The confirmation of the Lazarus story in the original Mark not only proves decisively Steiner's interpretation of the authorship of 'John.' It confirms the powerfully structured form of the Fourth Gospel itself, centred spiritually on the chapter of Lazarus' own appearance. It is no accident that the raising of Lazarus stands in chapter 11, preceded by the ten chapters of the life and teaching of Jesus, and followed by the ten chapters of the Last Supper and the Passion-Resurrection. The first chapter, containing the cosmic Prologue, to some extent stands apart from the first ten chapters, just as the last chapter, with the vision of the risen Christ and the 'testimony,' stands out after the natural 'end' of chapter 20:

(1)	(2–10)	(11)	(12–20)	(21)
Prologue	Jesus' Life and Teaching	Lazarus	Jesus' Passion and Resurrection	Supplement

The centrality of Lazarus' own experience is indeed the key to the esoteric meaning and relationship of the various parts of the Gospel, and sheds light on every aspect of its meaning and composition.[13]

The parallel structure of *Mark* and the Fourth Gospel further shows that we are dealing with early and deeply-rooted elements in the Christian handing-down of the 'word.' The connection made in John between Lazarus' sisters, Mary and Martha, and the episode of the anointing with perfume, demonstrates the underlying factor of the concern with wealth, with worldly and spiritual 'riches.' That was raised when Mary poured expensive perfume on Jesus: the money might have been spent on the poor and needy; it was raised by Lazarus himself in the Gospel of Mark, that is, by the 'rich young man.' In both cases the issue is resolved in a very interesting way, through a freedom from the power of money (possessions), enabling the spiritual to be put first. Only then can material wealth in fact be used rightly. Even seemingly good causes may otherwise only increase spiritual blindness, limiting the perspective to material concerns and missing the ultimate meaning of things.

Even more importantly, the narrative of the 'secret' text throws into relief the initiatory character of the whole episode — again something foreseen by Steiner in his treatment of the Gospel of John. And that in turn explains the most important aspect of the new interpretation, the way the central experience, the death and regeneration of Lazarus, extends itself over the whole Gospel. It draws upon the life and teaching of Jesus, reported before the central chapter, culminating in the death to the world of the disciple who followed his teaching. It also means that the events of Christ's passion, which follow in the second half of the Gospel, are experienced by Lazarus in a heightened, initiatory state of consciousness. They form the content of his awakened spiritual vision, and Lazarus' initiation really continues to the end of the Gospel, when the full meaning of the events is revealed. Hence it is that the whole sequence of chapters from 12 to the end can be described in terms of an initiation in process, leading over from the old baptism rooted in the Mysteries to a Christ-initiation that takes its significance from the historical death and resurrection of Jesus.

The initiates of the 'Johannine circle,' we may imagine, were led to ever deeper awareness of the Christian Mystery through their instruction in the Gospel. The realization that the authority of the Gospel was none other than Lazarus (chapter 21) would send them back to the central Mystery of chapter 11. But the entire Gospel then needed to be read anew, working both forwards and backwards from Lazarus, immeasurably deepening the impact of the Christ-Mystery following, and tracing back into Christ's earthly presence the origins of the power over life and death manifested in the heart of the work. The 'rhythms' and 'correspondences' between the two halves of the Gospel, which meditative study has discovered, therefore, are not clever and abstract attempts to create pattern out of the traditional materials of the Christian story. They emerge out of the very nature of the events described at first hand, and the 'mystery of interpretation' that has to be fathomed as those events are understood. They are the 'Way' of the Gospel, pointing the direction from the 'signs' or parable-realities which were done and spoken on earth to the inner reality of the 'kingdom of heaven.' The method of Christ himself is given its profoundest expression in the initiatory and 'interpretative' form of the Gospel.

The allusions to initiation in the Lazarus-chapter also make sense for the first time of the reaction from Jesus' disciples. Thomas says, 'Let us also go, that we may die with him.' This is not a personal, hysterical answer, as might first appear, but a desire to be deeply initiated into the Christ-Mystery, like Lazarus. There is a close parallel in the Markan version, where it is James and John who, knowing of Lazarus' death and regeneration, also wish to 'drink the cup and be baptized' with the baptism of Jesus himself, that is, to participate in the coming Mystery of his death and resurrection as Lazarus will do with his heightened initiatory consciousness.

They, however, have not quite reached a sufficient level of awareness. The disciples of Jesus, according to the 'Unknown Gospel' fragment, had been baptized in 'living water.' The initiation of Lazarus, though it too culminates in a ritual-baptismal act, was clearly something higher. Indeed it must surely be regarded as the highest initiation, conferred by Christ in his earthly ministry.

Nevertheless, it is an extension of the ritual practice related to Jesus' own baptism, with which Clement's tradition in the Alexandrian church strongly linked it. When in the Gospel of John we encounter many references to the initiatory background, we need no longer regard them as projections back in time from the 'Hellenistic church' with its sacraments. Modern discoveries have now confirmed Jesus' own use of baptism-initiation. The Fourth Gospel repeatedly mentions that Jesus baptized (despite the received text adding a contradictory note). It reproduces a discussion with the disciples of John the Baptist, very like the one we discussed earlier from the Gospel of

Matthew. The terminology is that of the *nymphios* (bridegroom) and the initiate who is united with him, recalling. the pagan and Mandaean mysteries of purification with water — and of course Jesus' own mystery of the 'Marriage Chamber' expressed in parable and rite, still known in the Gospels of *Thomas* and *Philip*. The Fourth Gospel places the discussion with John the Baptist's disciples immediately after the episode of Nicodemus.[14]

To Nicodemus Jesus reveals the mystery of rebirth through water and spirit. We mentioned this passage in our former discussions, remarking that it is close in content to a short dialogue in the *Gospel of Thomas*. There, however, Jesus addresses a group of unnamed disciples. Their question corresponds almost *verbatim* to Nicodemus' words. And the context — rebirth, or becoming a child — is identical. In *Thomas*, Jesus characterizes rebirth as a change in perception, and as the overcoming of divisions in the soul. In the Gospel of John it is rebirth, and a reorganization of inner experience, a transposition to the place of the 'spirit':

> Now there was a man of the Pharisees named
> Nicodemus, a ruler of the Jews. He came to Jesus by night
> and said, 'Rabbi, we know you are a teacher who has
> come from God. For no-one could perform such signs as
> you are doing if God were not with him.'
>   In reply Jesus declared, 'I tell you the truth: unless a
> man is born again, he cannot see the kingdom of God.'
>   'How can a man be born when he is old?' Nicodemus
> asked. 'Surely he cannot enter a second time into his
> mother's womb and be born?' Jesus answered, 'I tell you
> the truth: unless a man is born of water and the spirit, he
> cannot enter the kingdom of God. Flesh gives birth to
> flesh, but the spirit gives birth to spirit. You should not be
> surprised at my saying 'You must be born again.' The
> wind blows wherever it pleases, you hear its sound, but
> you cannot tell where it comes from or where it is going.
> So it is with everyone born of the spirit.'[15]

The Gospel of John thus adds strong evidence that the 'change in consciousness' taught by Jesus in the *Gospel of Thomas* was rooted originally in a ritual process.[16]

Other phrases in John's account suggest a ritual setting such as we know from the other 'Mystery-gospel' under the name of *Philip*. That 'the flesh gives birth to the flesh, but the spirit to spirit' recalls several Sayings in *Philip* on rebirth.[17] And the fact that Nicodemus comes to Jesus by night is also significant. It points to the time when we know Jesus performed his initiation-rite, exactly as in the secret *Mark*, and in the nocturnal practice continued by Paul. In accordance with the deeply-rooted symbolism of night and darkness, it would also represent the 'unenlightened' condition of the candidate's soul. He comes to be initiated into the light — the light of a higher consciousness that will dawn in him. The *Gospel of Philip* says:

> If someone becomes a child of the Marriage Chamber, he will receive the light ... and it is revealed to him alone, not hidden in the darkness and the night, but hidden in a perfect day and holy light.[18]

It is the most intimate experience of union. The whole scene with Nicodemus thus takes on significant reality. The old notion that a dithering Pharisee came to Jesus in a false beard under cover of darkness gives way to a profounder reading. He comes at night because he is prepared for the nocturnal initiation. He was not an 'interested' outsider, either. From the parallel passage in the *Gospel of Thomas* we may infer that he was one of several 'disciples,' though from a circle not that of the Twelve. And he receives from Jesus Mystery-instruction concerning regeneration through a ritual process (in *Thomas*, inner transformation). It is typical of John's style that he never completes the story, but next follows through the ideas and symbols of Christ's discourse. We may certainly assume, however, that after his instruction Nicodemus was duly initiated.

The initiation of Lazarus, then, takes its place in the Gospel of John against the background of Jesus' initiatory activity, of which it represents the furthest, most dramatic extension. In it we see that Jesus himself made the spiritual link between ritual events and his own earthly destiny of suffering. Lazarus was the one who entered into that destiny most deeply. For although we must insist that the 'death' and 'raising' of Lazarus are not literal, but spiritual and initiatory, the reality of what was experienced must not be underplayed. To provide a perspective, we may cite two initiation-texts, one from ancient Babylonia, and the other, from Judea in the first century BC. In both the suffering of 'detachment from the world' leads through anxieties, through mental and physical stress, before the crisis is finally resolved.

The first is called 'I will praise the Lord of wisdom,' a poem written by an initiate of Bel Marduk, the great god of Babylon who slew the chaos-monster and gave order to the world.[19] The poem will finish in the famous temple in Babylon and tell how the god Marduk rescued his initiate from death and the 'underworld.' On the way lies acute mental disjunction. For to 'die to the world' means to lose all those outside props of the personality, to feel that the world is turning hostile and will no longer give the troubled spirit space to breathe. The agonizing symptoms are described:

> I, who used to walk like a proud man, have learned to slip
> by unnoticed.
> Though I was a respectable man, I have become a slave.
> If I walk the street, fingers are pointed at me;
> If I enter the palace, eyes blink.
> My own town looks on me as an enemy;
> Even my land is savage and hostile.
> My friend has become a stranger,
> My companion has become an evil person and a demon.
> In his rage my comrade denounces me,
> Constantly my associate prepares his weapons.
> My close friend has brought my life into danger;
> My slave has publicly cursed me in the assembly.

The hostility, of course, is in his own mind, with its 'panic and fear.' He feels that every one is looking at him and condemning him — an anxiety all too familiar from the stress-conditions of modern life! He continues the recital of his difficulties, hoping still that his crisis would soon be over:

I survived to the next year; the appointed time passed.
I turn around, but it is bad, very bad;
My ill luck increases and I cannot find what is right.
I called to my god, but he did not show his face,
I prayed to my goddess, but she did not raise her head.
Even the diviner with his divination could not make
a prediction,
And the interpreter of dreams with his libation could
not elucidate my case.

Everything in his psyche that is dependent on the outside world must be purged away before the rebirth, the reorganization of the soul on a higher level, can begin. The destructive power that seems to haunt him becomes a source of physical oppression:

(All the ills joined in) and came on me together.
They struck my head, they enveloped my skull;
My face is gloomy, my eyes flow.
They have wrenched my neck muscles and made my neck
limp ...
My upright stance they knocked down like a wall ...
My eyes stare straight ahead, but cannot see,
My ears are open, but cannot hear.
Feebleness has overcome my whole body,
An attack of illness has fallen upon my flesh.
Stiffness has taken over my arms,
Weakness has come upon my knees,
My feet forget their motion ...
Death has approached and has covered my face.

He cannot even reply to the question of those around him. He is indeed living in the world of death.

The text is so personal and vivid that it is hard for us to remember that a ritual pattern lies behind the suffering, and the conclusion in the temple is foreseen. For the god Marduk himself was once trapped in death and suffering, in the underworld, but ascended once more to victory and heaven. His initiates share in his death — and his liberation. As in the case of Lazarus, then, the presence of a ritual form does not mean that it was all mummery and playacting. Lazarus' 'death' must no doubt have been a psychosomatic crisis as real as that described by the initiate of Marduk long before.

His main purpose in writing the Gospel, of course, was not to characterize his own soul, but to point to the greater reality of Christ which underlies his experience. Hence the different emphasis. But we can certainly show that these kinds of initiatory ordeals were undergone in Palestine shortly before the time of Christ, namely among the Essenes. The Gospel of John, in my view, shows no very close relation to Essenism in particular among the esoteric sects — much more, for instance, to the Mandaeans — but we must remember that Jesus has spent some time at the Essene centres.

The Essene 'Teacher of Righteousness' employed the same imagery of initiation in his Hymns, found in the Dead Sea Scrolls at Qumran. He had known the same agonies and the experience of regeneration:

> I was as a man forsaken in ... (text damaged)
> no refuge had I.
> For that which I had planted
> was turned into wormwood.
> Grievous was my pain, and could not be stayed.
> My soul was overwhelmed,
> like them that go down to Sheol, the land of shades,
> and my spirit was sunken low amid the dead.
> My life had reached the Pit,
> and my soul waxed faint day and night without rest.
> There burst forth, as it were a blazing fire,
> held in my bones,
> the flame whereof devoured unto the nethermost seas
> exhausting my strength every moment,
> consuming my flesh every minute.
> Disasters hovered about me,
> And my soul was utterly bowed down.
> For all my strength had ceased from my body,
> and my heart was poured out like water,
> and my flesh melted like wax,
> and the strength of my loins was turned to confusion,

and my arm was wrenched from the shoulder.
I could not move my hand,
and my foot was caught in a shackle,
and my knees were dissolved like water.
I could take neither pace nor step;
heaviness replaced my fleetness of foot;
my steps were trammelled.
My tongue was tied and protruded.
I could not lift my voice
in any articulate speech.[20]

The Hymns are full of such terrible experiences, and the personal voice of the Teacher is unmistakable. Yet they are basically ritual texts; and indeed they are hymns of Thanksgiving, for the agonies are all a prelude to the initiatory awakening: to the 'new word' of God that is given to the unworthy creature and makes him new. Once more, the crisis is real and even physical: but it is healed in the overall form and culminates in the ritual of remaking, rebirth.

Lazarus' experience is understandable when placed against the initiatory background. At the same time, the context in the secret *Mark* especially makes it clear that Jesus initiated his beloved disciple into the Mystery of his own coming passion. The underlying myth was no longer that of the primordial creation, but of an impending historical Event. He tried to explain that on the way to Bethany to the other disciples, and to James and John afterwards. Already, the beloved disciple was 'waiting' for the fulfilment of the earthly Mystery — as it seems later Christ speaks of him 'waiting' for the fulfilment of the heavenly. Heavenly and earthly Mysteries are woven together, and both will only find completion through the events of the Gospel. The secret *Mark* passage tells us of the ritual of baptism by night which healed and restored his spirit on the higher spiritual level, that of the 'kingdom of the heavens.' Did the initiated Lazarus, like so many initiates, receive a new name? The original form of John is Yohannan — 'God has been gracious.' It would be appropriate for one whose suffering had not been mere death, but had revealed the glory of God in Christ through his Christ-initiation.

We can, I believe, enter yet more deeply into the ritual baptism and especially its cosmic significance. But first we must approach the Gospel from a different angle, by turning to the celebrated 'Prologue' of chapter 1.

The Mystery of the 'Prologue'

In the beginning was the Word,
And the Word was with God,
And the Word was God.
He was in the beginning with God.

Through him everything entered into existence,
And without him nothing entered into existence,
What existed was Life in him.
And the Life was the Light of mankind.
And the Light shines in the Darkness,
but the Darkness has not taken hold of it.

There entered into existence a man sent out from God.
His name was John. He came as a witness,
To bear witness to the Light,
So that everyone might believe through him.
He was not the Light, but should bear witness to the Light.
The true Light, which enlightens every human being,
Was coming into the world.
He was in the world.
Through him the world entered into existence,
And the world was not aware of him.
He came into his own, and those who were his own did
                                        not receive him.
To all who accepted him he gave authority
For their existence as children of God.
To those who believe in his name, their birth
Was not by blood, nor by the will of the flesh,
Nor of the masculine, fathering will,
but of God

The Word entered into fleshly existence,
And pitched his tent among us.
And we beheld the Glory of his revelation,
Glory revealed as of the sole offspring from his Father,
Full of grace and truth.

John bears witness to him, and has cried out:
This was the one of whom I spoke,
The one who, coming after me, has existed before me;
Because he preceded me.
Out of his Fullness we have all received grace upon grace,
Because the Law was given through Moses,
But grace and truth entered into existence through Jesus
                                                    Christ.

No-one has ever had sight of God.
The only-born Son
Who is within the being of the Father,
He is the interpreter.[21]

The opening of the Fourth Gospel is strikingly unlike that of any other gospel, canonical or otherwise. With its resonant, condensed and mysterious language, and simultaneously its directness and forceful expression, it holds in a single frame of consciousness vast cosmic realities (the primal Word, worlds of Life and Light) and events of recent history (the ministry of the Baptist). It connects remote universal origins with inner changes now happening in the souls of some few among mankind: those to whom the Light came as 'his own.' Luke had extended his autoptic vision back to Adam, the 'Son of God.' The Johannine *epopteia* draws back the veil from huger perspectives still, for which the natural creation and emergence of life and consciousness are mere episodes.

At one or two points in the translation I have allowed the strangeness of the language to come through, for the purposes of study; more so, indeed, than a straightforward translator of the Gospel could risk. We can sense the hieroglyphic, esoteric quality of the Prologue more readily by so doing. We can see too that behind the Greek stand nuances of meaning that yield themselves only in the light of an underlying Semitic (Aramaic?)

text. Thus the odd turn of phrase 'He pitched his tent among us,' for instance, uses the Greek word for 'tent' (*skene*) as a verb. One can think of several reasons for this highly unconventional turn of phrase. There are suggestions, appropriately enough, of a short sojourn on earth; hints, too, of the Tent or 'tabernacle' carried through the wilderness by the ancient Israelites, in which God was felt to be present. But much more arresting to those with an ear attuned to Semitic tongues would be the emergence of the sound-pattern that spells God's 'Glory,' *shekinah*. The Glory was often conceived almost in terms of a separate divine being, God's personified 'Presence,' and associated mystically with the Temple or true place of the worship of God. The strange phraseology of the Prologue would suggest to the deeper student of Jewish spirituality that Jesus was the revelation of the *shekinah* upon earth.[22]

Many other subtleties are concealed in this extraordinary section of the Gospel; they stand out once we can place them in their rightful context. The difficulty, is however, that finding the correct background to the Prologue in particular has proved bafflingly difficult, despite all the efforts of modern scholarship. Certainly it is in early, Jewish-esoteric and not in later Hellenistic-Churchly circles as used to be thought. But the actual nature of the thought-world behind the Prologue is hard to elucidate, simply because there are no real parallels to its kind of language and expression anywhere in ancient literature. Various discoveries — the Dead Sea Scrolls, the books of the Samaritans, the Mandaean poems — made whole generations of scholars thrill with excitement and promise to elucidate the Fourth Gospel. But the next generation has invariably noted the way parallels had to be over-stretched to mean what they had to mean, and the analogies of thought usually turned out to be illuminating in a somewhat secondary manner. That cannot be the case, however, with the work I am about to mention. For in it, for the first time ever, were located phrases almost verbally identical to some in the Prologue. And the nature of the work is at once sufficiently unlike the Gospel in form and structure to be obviously independent and apparently uninfluenced by the Gospel-tradition, yet sufficiently analogous in important respects to shed a great deal of light on their common background. This work is called the *Trimorphic Protennoia*. It turned up in the Nag Hammadi library, and is usually described as a 'Gnostic revelation discourse.'

The neat Greek title — *Trimorphic Protennoia* — could be expanded into clumsy English somewhat as follows: 'On the Threefold Form of the Manifestation of the Primal Divine Thought.' And it is indeed a threefold revelation. Each of three revelations to an unnamed visionary is itself threefold. The Primal Thought shows itself (or should I say herself?) in various aspects of spiritual and cosmic life. The one which especially concerns us is the revelation as Word, which occurs mainly in the third large division of the tractate. Enough has been said to suggest that this sequence of visionary appearances does not have the look of a work consciously imitating the Fourth Gospel. Yet if we give the main outlines of the third revelation, we shall soon discern more than a passing resemblance. To begin with, the Word is closely linked with the creation; the 'Mother' mentioned here probably refers to the Spirit of God, known from the Bible and being of feminine gender in Hebrew. The following material will bear strict comparison with the content of the Prologue. I give the most striking passages only, but in their actual order:

> I am the Word ... . I dwell in undefiled Light. And a
> Thought revealed itself perceptibly through the great Sound
> of the Mother ... And the Sound exists from the
> beginning in the foundations of the All.

> (The Word) is a hidden Light, bearing a fruit of Life,
> pouring forth living waters from the invisible, unpolluted,
> immeasurable spring — the unreproducible Voice of the
> Glory ... the Glory of the offspring of God.

> And a third time I revealed myself to them in their tents
> as the Word, and I revealed myself in the likeness of their
> shape. And I wore everyone's garment and I hid myself
> within them. And they did not know the one who
> empowers me.

And I hid myself within them until I revealed myself to
my brethren. And none of them knew me, although it is I
who work in them (the Powers of the world).

I am the Light that illumines the All. I am the Light that
rejoices in my brethren. For I came down to the world of
mortals on account of the spirit that remains in what had
descended ... from the guileless Sophia.

I hid myself within them until I revealed myself among my
members, which are mine. And I taught them about the
ineffable ordinances ... These are the glories that are
higher than every glory, that is, the Five Seals ... He
who possesses the Five Seals of these particular names has
stripped off the garments of ignorance and put on a
shining Light.

And I proclaimed to them the ineffable Five Seals in order
that I might abide in them and they also might abide in
me. I put on Jesus. I bore him from the cursed wood and
established him in the dwelling-place of his Father.[23]

The reference to Jesus at the end has something of the appearance of an interpolation, like the other occasional references to
Christ. It is not there that we are to seek the connection with
Christianity. Rather it is in the profound ideas about the Word,
manifesting as Light and Life, to be discovered in the universe
and in the 'hidden' depth of the soul, which form the background of one particular form of early Christianity, namely that
of the Gospel of John.

That the *Trimorphic Protennoia*, although in its final form it is a
Gnostic revelation, stands close to the sources of Christianity
and Jewish esotericism can further be seen from the use of 'tent,'
corresponding exactly to its use in the Prologue. The translator
(into Greek, from which the Coptic version we possess is
derived) grasped the fact that it was a reference to 'revelation,'
that is, the revelation of the *shekinah*, which is identified with the
divine Word. The 'revelation in the tents' is odd for the same
reason as 'he pitched his tent among us,' namely that it presup-

poses a sensitivity to hidden meanings in a Semitic tongue.

Many other features in the text evoke the language and thought of the Fourth Gospel. When the Word is described 'pouring forth living waters from the invisible, unpolluted, immeasurable spring,' bearing 'the fruit of Life,' our minds are cast forward from the Prologue to the fourth chapter of the Gospel, Jesus there promises the Samaritan woman 'living water,' and says: 'Whoever drinks the water I give him will never thirst. Indeed, the water I give him will become in him a spring welling up to eternal Life.' We recognize the 'living water' as that of initiation, and Life therefore as the fruit of an inner rebirth. The *Trimorphic Protennoia* and the Prologue alike point towards the cosmic meaning and origin of the Mystery. In the former, the 'spring' is said to be the 'unreproducible Voice of the Glory ... the Glory of the offspring of God' — tying the 'water' imagery back into the world of the Prologue's 'Glory of his revelation, Glory revealed as of the sole offspring from his Father.'

The theme next emerges of the hidden Word or Light, who was not grasped by men although he was concealed within them, waiting for them to recognize him. He was hidden too from the Powers of the world, although he is the Light that illumines the All. He does reveal himself, however, to those who are his 'members' or his 'brethren' or simply those 'which are mine' — 'his own' according to the Gospel. We can see many allusions here to the Christian initiation-practices known independently from Paul, which he developed directly, as we have argued, from those of Jesus. In Paul too we meet the idea of being 'members' of Christ, who thus figures in Ephesians as a Cosmic Man. The notion in the *Trimorphic Protennoia* that the Word 'wore everyone's garment' further coincides with Pauline symbolism of the body as a garment. Those initiated by the Word in the Gnostic discourse are likewise said to have 'stripped off the garments of ignorance and put on a shining Light' — just as Paul spoke of the baptized becoming 'Light.' We may notice, therefore, that the uncovering of the secret background of early Christianity helps to show the underlying unity of the several developing streams; and in fact, some sections of *Trimorphic Protennoia* (notably the second revelation) shed striking light on the thought of Paul in the Letters to Corinth as this does on the Gospel of John. The tone of the Gnostic work, on the other hand, is more pervasively Johannine. Hence it would appear that Pauline and Johannine circles continued to employ the same esoteric practices and symbolism, though doubtless with some variation. The final reference to the coming of the Word, 'that I might abide in them and they also might abide in me' has a strongly Johannine mood.

With the extract on 'I am the Light that illumines the All' (compare the Johannine 'I am the Light of the world'), we move explicitly into the realm of cosmology — the cosmic events which underlie the human drama of regeneration. In *Trimorphic Protennoia* there is the great Gnostic myth of Sophia, the Wisdom of God which descended into the maelstrom of matter and is scattered there, like so many myriad sparks, in the souls of men. If fanned into life, the 'spark' of Sophia in us can give birth to the higher Man, who thereby becomes an object of knowledge (*gnosis*). Did some such myth underlie the thought of the Prologue? Is that why the mother of Christ is never named in the Gospel, but mysteriously hinted at — to suggest that his real, his heavenly mother is the 'guileless Sophia'?[24] In the Jewish-Christian Gospels Jesus called himself a 'Son of the Holy Spirit': certainly the three female hypostases, the Mother-Spirit, the *shekinah*, and the Gnostic Sophia seem somehow involved in the divine world of preparation for the Mystery revealed in our sources.

Rudolf Steiner interpreted the opening verses of the Fourth Gospel in precisely the way now suggested by the *Trimorphic Protennoia*. For him Word, Life and Light were pre-existent worlds preceding the material creation. It is worth glancing back to our reconstruction of the 'Ophite Diagram,' which gives the Gnostic version of an ancient cosmogony. Surely some version of its worldsystem is hinted at in the Gospel of John, and in the *Trimorphic Protennoia* that comes from a similar background. That, in fact, is the way the Prologue was interpreted in the two earliest commentaries on the Gospel of John, by Ptolemaeus and Heracleon, both of them second-century Gnostics, followers of Valentinus. Their exegesis admittedly involves a certain amount of special pleading for the specifically Valentinian cosmological system; but we can now see that fundamentally they preserved authentic sources on the meaning of the Prologue. Heracleon indeed has an elaborate theology of Word, Voice and Echo to describe the way the divine Thought becomes outwardly manifest in sound, corresponding in reverse order to a path of discipleship that ascends through Echo (the outer shell of the sound) to Voice and up to the Word. He plainly knew a teaching very like the statements in *Trimorphic Protennoia*, where the Word evolves from Thought to reveal itself perceptibly in the Sound of the Mother-Spirit, and is grasped by the initiate as the 'unreproducible Voice.' This process is a history of primordial events, the successive 'aeons' of cosmic evolution leading to the emergence of the present earth. But Heracleon also relates it to Hebrew prophecy and John the Baptist. Note, in this context, that in John it is the Baptist who reproduces the words of the *Protennoia*: 'I am the Voice.'[25]

We shall shortly try to make sense of these cosmological ideas, or at least some of them, in a little more detail. But it is worth stressing immediately that they are not in any sense 'speculations.' If they do not agree with modern speculations about the origins of the cosmos, that is because we are comparing incommensurables. 'Cosmology' emerges from the Prologue and the *Trimorphic Protennoia* as a way of describing, perhaps a way of rendering intelligible to the initiate himself, experiences he has undergone through initiation. They are an attempt, on the basis of such experiences, to express the relation between the physical and the spiritual worlds — not, like modern science, to extrapolate from present conditions of the universe the material laws which must have brought it into being. Initiatory cosmology tackles issues which must remain outside the domain of physical science, which lacks the experiences on which it is built. Some scientists certainly would not want them. Many others, however, are aware that such experiences occur and are feeling the need to gesture towards a larger picture that will include them. And we have said repeatedly that in the long run a complete history of consciousness and a history of the 'objective' world must obviously turn out to be two aspects of the same whole.

For the moment, then, we will remain with the 'initiatory significance' of the cosmic teaching. For from the *Trimorphic Protennoia* we can actually discover considerably more about the esoteric processes underlying it.

For the revelations do not come out of nowhere. They are attained in the framework of a ritual. Maddalena Scopello has reconstructed the outlines of the rite, and from the phase which constitutes its final stage and goal we may call it the 'Rite of Glorification.' Its recovery from these ancient texts may turn out to be the most important aspect of the whole Nag Hammadi find. She analyses it in five basic stages:

> Instruction in the Mysteries;
> Investiture;
> Ablution or ritual purification in 'living water';
> Enthronement;
> Glorification.

It is tempting to identify these stages with the 'Five Seals' mentioned in the text, the 'ineffable ordinances' of the Mysteries. But I am inclined to think that would be an error. More likely the 'Seals' are five separate sacraments, of which this is only one. Evidently we are close here to the traditions affecting the *Gospel of Thomas* and the *Gospel of Philip*, where five sacraments are mentioned, or for that matter to the Mandaeans, yet the incorporation of the ritual in a fivefold canon is most probably a secondary development, and tells us more about the group which adopted the rite and transmitted it to the Gnostics in the form underlying the *Trimorphic Protennoia* than it does about the original setting. The Gnostic users were closely related to those esoteric baptizing groups who took up Thomas-Christianity and Philip-Christianity in their several ways. The users of *Trimorphic Protennoia* likewise took up Christianity at a late stage, as is evidenced in the rather occasional additions referring to Jesus. The rite itself, however, must certainly go back before these secondary developments.[26]

So let us examine the course of the rite behind the Light-theology and Word-theology of the *Trimorphic Protennoia*.

It requires, firstly, a period of extensive instruction. Otherwise the experiences, so unlike those of ordinary life, will hardly be grasped or understood. The Light would shine uncomprehended in the Darkness.

Then follows an investiture. We know from the text that there was a 'stripping off' of the old garments of ignorance, of the former identity. The candidate is being prepared for baptism, and must come naked except for the white cloth, symbolic of renewal and innocence and light: that is his investiture, and corresponded spiritually no doubt to the appearance of the 'crown of light,' the aura or glory around his head. Hence the old royal and priestly language that was still used.

Then comes the baptism itself, a purifying plunge in the 'living' or flowing water of a river. That in turn leads to an enthronement: again pointing back to the original kingly initiations of the ancient Near East, and to the inner 'kingship' which was later its spiritual counterpart. From the analogous practice of Paul we know that this continued to be a central symbol of initiation.

And lastly comes the glorification, corresponding no doubt to Paul's idea of the initiate becoming Light, here identified with the 'glory' of the heavenly lights. For the initiate's consciousness is now open to the revelation of the cosmic prehistory of Word, Life and Light. And 'glorification' is, of course, a charged word in the Gospel of John, where however it refers to the Mystery of Golgotha and the deepest meaning of Christianity for mankind and the earth. How these cosmic and earthly meanings are related, we shall endeavour to understand shortly. But first let us consider the general shape of the rite.

Where have we met such a ritual process in the course of our studies? It corresponds exactly to the rite performed by Jesus with the youth in the fragment of secret *Mark*. And we know too that the youth is none other than Lazarus, the author of the Fourth Gospel! In short we can hardly avoid a momentous conclusion: the origin of the Prologue is no longer in doubt, but derives straight from the initiation of the beloved disciple into the Mysteries of the heavens by Jesus himself.

Here, then, is further stupendous confirmation of the initiatory structure of the Gospel. The earthly event of Lazarus' death and reawakening occupies the centre of the narrative. The initiation rite that followed and completed it furnishes the content of the cosmic Prologue, placing the coming of Christ and Lazarus' experience in an eternal and universal frame.

All this serves to show how tremendously deep was Rudolf Steiner's insight into the nature of the Fourth, Gospel. And some further comments add still more illumination. He connects the rite of Lazarus' initiation very closely with John the Baptist. That is another, still deeper reason why the initiated Lazarus took the name of John, explains Steiner: from that time onward he was in some sense a new John whose vision completed that of the old. And that is why the content of the Prologue is interwoven with references to the Baptist. In this respect at least Steiner's researches concurred with those of Rudolf Bultmann, who also regarded the content of the Prologue as stemming from the sphere of the Baptist — though he was not yet in a position to recover the underlying 'Rite of Glorification.'[27] Now if the rite performed by Jesus originates in the circle around the Baptist, not only do its affinities with the esoteric baptizing sects (including some of those indirect ones with the Essenes) fall into place; but yet once more we are referred back to Jesus' own spiritual experience at his own baptism by John. Steiner likened that experience to what had occurred in earlier Mysteries, whose aim was to unite man with the macrocosm, the forces of the spiritual universe. 'For if we contemplate the soul which was in Christ Jesus after the baptism in the Jordan,' he says, 'we find the same thing ... So long as men should think of this soul as confined 'in one human body, they would be victims of illusion. In reality this soul pervades all space, and exercises its influence from-the whole of space, though for the mind held captive by the sense-world it seems to work through the body of Jesus of Nazareth. After the baptism by John we have to see the cosmos as a whole through the body of Jesus.' That was clearly also very much the experience of Lazarus at what the Fourth Gospel repeatedly describes as his 'glorification,' reflected in the cosmic Prologue.[28]

We have seen in our earlier studies that the 'Marriage Chamber' rite of baptism undergone by Jesus' disciples reflected the great happening in the Jordan too in many ways, and was the basis of Pauline and other baptismal initiations. We suspected that the 'higher initiation' performed for Lazarus was an extension or further elaboration of the rite, which we can now term that of Glorification. That view seems to be confirmed. In this single case, Jesus performed the highest rite of initiation stemming from the circles of the Baptist, the one which provided in essence the sum of the Baptist's prophetic knowledge and the foundation of his message. Thereafter Lazarus was himself a kind of new John. But Jesus also related the death and rebirth of his own impending fate, to the suffering Son of Man. His 'glorification,' described precisely so by the Gospel of John, was his crucifixion and death.

Thus, by a strange paradox, he made the very type of initiation he performed for Lazarus, the highest form of baptismal rite, henceforward fundamentally outmoded. The spiritual insight it contained could afterwards be obtained through an understanding of the Mystery of the Cross, an historical reality full of spiritual meaning, or myth made fact. 'The old form of initiation must end, but a transition had to be made from the old to the new age and to make this transition, someone had once more to be initiated in the old way, but initiated into Christian esotericism. This only Christ Jesus himself could perform, and the neophyte was the one who is called Lazarus.'[29]

The transition was not immediate. We know that the tradition of the secret *Mark* in the Fourth Gospel long influenced baptismal initiation at Alexandria. But there was a decisive shift, already made in the Fourth Gospel itself. We shall see how the transition is effected in the Gospel narrative. But we must first attempt to grasp more exactly the 'cosmic' meaning of the knowledge the beloved disciple has to convey, and for this a particular term must be investigated in greater detail.

The Mystery of 'Pleroma'

'Out of his Fullness we have all received grace upon grace,' says the Prologue.

The word for 'Fullness' in the original Greek is *pleroma*, another of those terms which seem to be charged with special resonances of meaning in the context of the Gospel, and indeed elsewhere in early Christian thought. Translators and commentators have rarely succeeded in bringing this out. The usual impression is that it refers vaguely to the overwhelming abundance of God's being or love; there is rarely any suggestion that it is meant to evoke any very exact idea. Rudolf Steiner, on the other hand, insisted strongly that the Prologue 'can only be understood by someone who knows that in the ancient Mysteries *pleroma* (or fullness) referred to something quite definite.'[30]

We should not be mistaken, as a preliminary to ascertaining what that meaning is, if we were to note the association in biblical tradition of Fullness with the events of creation. Thus Psalm 24:

> The earth is Yahweh's, and the fullness thereof;
> The world, and they that dwell therein.
> For he hath founded it upon the seas,
> And established it upon the floods ...

And in Jeremiah 23:24 we have ' 'Do I not fill the heaven and the earth?' declares Yahweh.' The Prologue picks up the link with the myth of creation, then, in harmony with its evocation of the 'beginning,' the primordial reality of the Word, and echoes it also in its use of *pleroma*. But before we try to elucidate the meaning and development of the idea, however, we can take advantage of a parallel line of enquiry, based on the Prologue in conjunction with the Gospels of Luke and Mark. For the Gospel of John itself tells us what it is that we have received from the 'Fullness' of the divine Word:

> To all who accepted him he gave *exousia*
> For their existence as children of God.

It is the concept of *exousia* which will permit us to deeper understanding of the 'Fullness.'

The standard reference-works on New Testament words translate *exousia*, quite correctly, by 'authority.' Certainly the verb from which it is derived conveys the meaning of 'it is authorized, permitted.' It is the word used by Paul to characterize the 'free' Christian consciousness, to which 'all is permitted' without referral to an outside criterion of morality. But in Greek it also has the sense of 'it is possible, in (my) power': so that we might equally well translate 'he gave the potential for their existence as children of God.' But that does not exhaust the range of the term either. For the suggestion of spiritual 'power' in the concept of *exousia* is much more far-reaching, as we can see if we examine the way it is employed in the Gospel of Luke. And this in turn will show up the inadequacy of the reference-book rendering 'authority,' which has usually been compared to the kind of arbitration in religious matters performed by a rabbi. In fact, the analogues lie more in the field of ancient magic. And behind both can be discerned vastly older, Near Eastern perceptions of religious 'power.'

J.M. Hull, in a fascinating monograph on the Gospels and magic, noted the close association in the magical texts of late antiquity of *exousia* and sister-concepts of (magical) force, *dynamis* and grace, *charis*.[31] Rather different as the context may be, in the Prologue, too, the giving of *charis* ('grace upon grace') is somehow joined with the receiving of *exousia*. He then studied the use of *exousia* in the Gospel of Luke, where it is mentioned several times. The 'authority' with which Jesus proclaimed his message caused amazement, sometimes hostility, among the people who saw and heard him. Hull points out that it is impossible to square the people's reaction with the interpretation of Jesus' *exousia* as a quasi-rabbinic authorization to preach. How could that have caused so much disquiet? Nor do the settings of the stories suggest any argument with religious authorities who might object to Jesus' purloining their privileges. Rather the *exousia* almost always manifests itself in the setting of casting out demons. It is frequently joined in Luke, as in the magical texts, by the mention of *dynamis*: both referring to a supernatural 'power' working through Jesus, sometimes under his control but sometimes manifesting without his will. This 'power,' says Hull, 'is particularly effective in exorcism and is often associated there with *exousia* as in Luke 4:36 ... . The power is elsewhere described as being the 'power of the Lord,' the Lord here probably being God, the Highest ...' Later in the same Gospel it is characterized as the 'power from the Heights.'[32]

We gain our closest insight into the working of the power from the well-known episode in Luke of the woman with the haemorrhage:

And there was a woman who had been subject to
bleeding for twelve years, and no-one could heal her. She
came up behind Jesus and touched the edge of his cloak,
and immediately her bleeding stopped.

'Who touched me?' Jesus asked.

Everyone denied it, and Peter said, 'Master, the people
are jostling and pressing against you.'

But Jesus said, 'Someone touched me; I know that
dynamis has gone out from me.'

Then the woman, seeing that she could not go
unnoticed, came trembling and fell at his feet. In the
presence of all the people, she told why she had touched
him and how she had been instantly healed. Then he said
to her, 'Daughter, your faith has healed you. Go in peace.'

The description here stands closest to the experience of the magician. The going-out of the power is involuntary, though Jesus is
its agent. Also 'magical' is the way the power passes over as a
'charge' of energy into the garments he wears. It goes out only to
the touch of faith, however; the rest of the jostling crowd does
not tap the energy, the *dynamis*. Jesus emphasizes this in his
words to the woman: 'Your faith has healed you.' Again it is
tempting to compare the Prologue: the ones who can receive
exousia are 'those who accepted him,' 'who believe in his name.'
At any rate we are certainly right, with Hull, in regarding the
transference of power as one manifestation of Jesus' *exousia*.

The picture is basically similar when we consider the Gospel
of Mark. Drawing this time on the research of earlier investigators, he again challenges the general interpretation of *exousia* as
'rabbinic' authority, showing that for Mark's readers it meant 'a
mysterious superhuman force whereby demons were controlled
and afflictions healed.'[33]

Does the sign-working power then designate Jesus a
Hellenistic magician? Hardly. Rather, behind both stands an oriental apprehension of divine power at work through a representative figure, such as initiate-king. Hull refers to the
Egyptian ideas bound up with the god Amon-Re, adored as the
Hidden-and-Manifest. The god was conceived as a source of
vital energy, filling the universe. His power floods into every-

thing which will receive it. But in the highest degree it charges the King, who is the living portrait of the god. And by extension it flows into things connected with the King and his form, such as his garments and regalia. The source of energy in the god is infinite. Hence we must see in the background of the Gospels another influence, comparable to the many examples touched on earlier, from the Mystery-sphere of ancient 'divine kingship.' 'Christ is like a divine king; he will suffer no permanent depletion of his energy because he is directly sustained by the divine Father of all.'[34] Indeed, he is a heightened realization of the initiate-king ideal (as the magician is its debased representative). But here at any rate lies the origin of the 'authority' of Jesus: it is the authority of the spiritual king who rules by cosmic power, who is in touch with the creative, life-giving energy of the Father and banishes the forces of evil, death and disease.

The Egyptian analogy also gives us a vivid picture of the meaning, in the context of 'bestowing *exousia*,' connected with the 'Fullness' from which it flows. It points to the infinite reservoir of vital energy filling the universe, which the Egyptians felt to be the god Amon-Re, visible as the sun but invisible as the ethereal, flooding power extending everywhere beyond it. The earth and the Fullness, hymned by the Psalmist praising Yahweh's creation, suggest in Hebrew terms a comparable image: the physical world, and the infinite reservoir of creative energy filling the universe around it. The Prologue to the Gospel of John identifies this Fullness with the creative power of the Word, which appeared in Jesus and which is the source of his *exousia*, in turn bestowed upon us as children of God.

How close to the language of the Prologue such Egyptian ideas could come may be seen from a statement in later Hermetic literature. The 'reservoir' of vital energy is there described as an influence flowing down from the stars into the 'womb' of the earthly elements. In the earthly world, the pure forces mingle with evil in most of the 'offspring' that resulted. Sometimes however:

> It may come to pass that among the offspring produced is
> a being compounded of the pure parts of those elemental
> stuffs without (any of) the impure parts of them, and that

Fig 8. The Pharoah as "living portrait" of a god. Here the divine king is shown as a youthful god, the son of the royal sun-divinity Horus of Edfu and the sky-goddess Hathor. His divine birth or initiation was portrayed in the temples or in a special "birth-house". Here he is shown being acknowledged by the other gods before his mother Hathor.

> this being is so composed as to have a perfect
> temperament; so that through this being God personified
> himself in the world.[35]

The being in whom the vital forces dominate completely would be a 'living portrait,' a 'divine King' or a Jesus who likewise possesses *exousia*. (The Hermetic passage of course does not imply that there is any unique incarnation which 'personifies' God in the world.)

But it would be unwise to limit the consideration of these ideas too closely to Egypt. Initiate-kingship was widespread through the ancient East, including early Israel. We saw the image of the Fullness in a Jewish psalm; and the Jewish woman who touches Jesus' cloak seems to take for granted a popular understanding of the supernatural, or at least has been fitted into it in the imagination of Luke. The sense of God as power and the earthly representative as 'personification' was rather one of those concepts which fostered constructive meetings between the minds of different spiritual traditions — such as the Hermetists, indeed, when they made contact with the Jewish esoteric baptizers, from whom they learned about *metanoia*, baptism, and so on. The mention of Fullness in the Johannine Prologue most likely does not derive from Hermetism, but from a parallel development in esoteric Judaism. Jesus' *exousia* may not be like the rabbi's 'authority' in mainstream Judaism; but the Jewish esotericism of the baptist sects included 'Mystery' ideas, as we have repeatedly seen, derived from the East or from older notions preserved in Palestine itself. These were often analogous to what we found in Egyptian Hermetism. In fact, the scholar David Flusser has pointed out the survival of older Semitic ideas about a 'Power of God' and his earthly vehicle which fit our case very well. There seem to have been underground survivals particularly of solar images and ideas within the basic lunar orientation of Judaism. They surfaced, for instance, in Essenism — and in other areas close to Christian beginnings.

Flusser's investigation centres on another key term, *doxa* ('glory'). And again the Gospel of Luke shows interesting traces of the deeper significance behind such conceptions. We have it in the Johannine Prologue, too:

And we beheld the Glory of his revelation,
Glory revealed as of the sole offspring from his Father.

Flusser was concerned with an extraordinary passage in the Gospel of Luke about the 'countenance' of Jesus, about calling down fire from heaven, and Jesus' reception by the Samaritans. He detects behind it an old theological conception of the 'countenance' as the revelation of the 'glory' of a god: another instance of a representative figure revealing a universal divinity, as the Glory in the Prologue reveals the relationship of the Christ to his Father. (The word 'person,' which we used to render the Hermetic idea, originally meant 'mask,' or the face worn in a play.) In the old, pre-Jewish religion of the Semites in Palestine, the goddess Tanit (or more properly Tinnit) is described by the title 'Countenance of Baal.' The title implies that she reveals the splendour of the great divinity, Baal, making his universality accessible to his worshippers on earth. And still in New Testament contexts, 'countenance,' 'image' and 'radiance' or 'glory' are vitally interrelated concepts.

Flusser extends his considerations then to an apocryphal gospel, of which an important fragment survives, and in which he notices similar elements of the 'representative' theology. It is the *Gospel of Peter,* which is very early and comes once more from Syria. It contains, in fact, our earliest non-canonical account of Christ's passion, and it just may be an independent witness to traditions about his death, though some think its author may have known the canonical versions too. Its importance here, however, lies in its use of a term to express the divine presence in Jesus — a term which enables us to close the circle of our investigations into these ideas. That term is *exousia*. If Flusser is right, therefore, we do not need to look abroad to Egypt for the underlying ideas about Jesus' Power or *exousia*. The Egyptian version remains invaluable, because from Egyptian sources we can build up a full picture of the workings of the Power, whereas from the old Semitic religion we have very little information; but such older Mystery-ideas were widespread in Syria and Palestine, exerting a subterranean and esoteric influence on Jewish thought.

There are in fact traces in early Christianity of a continuing comprehension that Jesus was the vessel of such a Power. Clement of Alexandria wrote a grand, descriptive-theological treatise called the *Outlines*, and although it is lost we have a few quotations from it in later writers. One of them cites a fascinating passage where Clement insists on a distinction between the divine Word in its eternal nature and what appeared in Jesus. The divinity which sustains the order of the universe, he points out, did not suspend his eternal activity to be present in the earthly body. It was not the Eternal Word as such 'which became flesh ... but a Power of God, a sort of emanation from his Word.'[36]

A fairly clear if largely unfamiliar picture emerges, then, from the range of sources, canonical and apocryphal gospels, and some later echoes. What we have not managed to clarify for the moment is the form these teachings took in Judaism: to which problem we now turn.

Judaism differed, of course, from all the religions we have mentioned, in that tor the Jewish mind there could be no direct 'personification' of God in the world. God maintained his distance from the world. Earlier in this book we suggested that man gained his freedom, and the possibility of deeper inwardness, through stepping out of the mythological world-vision, where the gods had been present in everything. For Judaism, the world certainly manifested the nature of God, for he had created it; but since the beginning God had not shown himself in that way. He had moved rather toward more inward revelation, in the moral self and in history which expresses the meaning of man's actions and relationships. As a result, it was impossible for the Jewish mind to conceive of a physical man, even one of 'perfect temperament' who could 'personify' God. That would violate the gap between God and world essential to the Jewish consciousness. Ideas related to *exousia*, Power, and so on, could therefore function with the Jewish spiritual world-vision only in two ways: first in connection with the creation itself, the one event where God was active in the domain of matter; and secondly, in relation to those beings who populated the gap between God and world, and bridged over the otherwise incommunicable vacuum, namely the 'messengers,' the angels.

That is precisely where we find them. Virtually all the terms and concepts we have discussed turn up in Judaism in the form of angels. Thus the Power (*Dynamis*) for instance, is spoken of in Jewish tradition as an angel before God. The great mystical scholar Gershom Scholem has pointed out that it is authentic Jewish tradition when it is said that Jesus will ascend 'to sit at the right hand of the *Dynamis*.' Angelic beings receive the titles 'Countenance,' and even 'the lesser Yahweh' — a 'representative' trend which continued and reached its greatest expression in the kabbalah, the mysticism of mediaeval Jewry. The 'glory' (*kavod*) and even the *shekinah* have epiphanies in angelic form. And, most importantly, when we meet the term *exousia*, it is again to refer to angels: specifically, the angels who created the world. If the objection rises up that surely it was God who made the world, that is to forget that it is just here that the old notions of 'representation' apply, in the creation: God 'personified himself' in these seven angels or Exousiai, who are identified with the plural Elohim (literally 'gods') described in the opening chapter of Genesis.[37]

We thus arrive, by yet another route, at the Prologue and its new version of 'in the beginning,' which is where these ideas all have their home within esoteric Jewish thought. And more precisely, we return to it in the setting of an esoteric angelology.

It would be fascinating, at least for some, to trace the emergence of these cosmological visions from the mystical or esoteric interpretation of 'the work of creation' in Judaism. The creation, along with the chariot-vision of Ezekiel, was a designated 'esoteric' topic, to be discussed only among those 'with knowledge.' And even mentioning the angels could be dangerous. The seven Exousiai are clearly related to the seven days of creation, on each of which God revealed himself in a different aspect. For each aspect, as we shall see, he might have a different name, and, since the days of the week go back in Babylonian thought to the seven planets, they would collectively reveal the totality of God's cosmic nature — in other words, the Fullness. That is, in fact, how we find the term Fullness (*pleroma*) used in Gnostic and other early Christian writings which delve into cosmology. And that is how the term Fullness was explained by Rudolf Steiner in his discussion of the Gospel of John.[38] With the help of modern research and discoveries, it has been possible to uncover its background, and show why it takes the form it does in esoteric Judaism, including presumably the circle of John the Baptist.

Through one of these discoveries we can further recover the form which the teaching assumed in the esoteric circle which used the Gospel of John, at least with some probability. For in the *Secret Book of John* we have a Gnostic revelation, evidently incorporating some genuine traditions in the name of John. They came in at a secondary stage, for fundamentally it is a book of pure Gnostic teaching. They came in at a time after the Gospel of John had been accepted, with reservations, by the Church: for he is here supposed to be the son of Zebedee. As a result of these mixings, the *Secret Book* as we have it attributes to John, son of Zebedee, a highly Gnostic revelation, but overlays it with teachings that actually reflect Johannine teachings from the same source as the Fourth Gospel. A complex situation! And of course, it is not always possible to know exactly what came from where, or how it has been affected by its new setting. But one feature of it almost certainly existed in a Jewish context, with a meaning rather different from its present Gnostic one. Presumably it arrived in the *Secret Book* with the other Johannine elements.

There is a list of names for the 'rulers' of the seven planets. They are not the usual astrological planet-names, however, but strange esoteric ones:

Moon	Athoth	= ?
Mercury	Eloaios	= Elohim
Venus	Astanfeus	= Lucifer
Sun	Iao	= Yahweh
Mars	Sabaoth	= Zevaot, (God) of Hosts
Jupiter	Adoni	= Adonai, (Lord)
Saturn	Sabbataios	= Shabbatai

The curious name Athoth remains baffling, but the table shows that all the other names for the rulers are actually Jewish divine names which appear in the Bible and rabbinic literature. Eloaios is a transcription of Elohim (literally Gods), Iao of Yahweh, the holiest divine name and that connected here with the source of light reflected by the other bodies. Sabaoth or Zevaot, meaning 'of hosts,' is a further title much used to refer to God in the Bible, and Shabbatai reproduces 'the Seventh,' that is, the God of the seventh planet or of the Sabbath (seventh day). Notice too that Satan-Lucifer appears as a member of the heavenly entourage, exactly as in the Book of Job in the Old Testament and in accordance with older Jewish ideas.[39]

The seven planets, in other words, are taken to reveal the several aspects under which God has shown himself to men. That was not an acceptable message to the Gnostics. For them the planets were the agents of cosmic repression, the signs of natural Necessity which opposed the spirit of man. The Gnostic teaching therefore makes these beings into wicked demons. That, however, was hardly the original import of the scheme. The fact that it included the aspect of Accuser, Satan, under which God arraigned man for his sins shows that it fundamentally expressed the idea that sin was an element in the essentially good universe — not that the universe was intrinsically bad in contrast to the spirit. It constitutes a sort of early kabbalistic system, where the divine names are assigned to the spheres (Greek, *sphaira* kabbalistic Hebrew *sefirah*).

Moreover, we learn from the *Secret Book* something extremely important about the system, namely that the Sun stood in a special relation to the rest of the powers. It included the essence of them all in itself, as the light reflected back from all the planets is actually the light of the Sun. Now the name for the Sun in the system is Yahweh, and behind this correlation is an understanding of that moment in the Book of Genesis when, at the end of the first chapter, the divine name Elohim which has been used thus far gives way to the composite Yahweh-Elohim — implying that thenceforward Yahweh contains in himself the creative totality, or is its divine centre and ground. If we want a term with which to describe this, it must certainly be Fullness, *pleroma*. And by implying that in Christ is revealed the Fullness, John is declaring his conviction that it was not just some one creative aspect of the cosmic Godhead that was present in him: it was the meaning of the whole for subsequent history. The moment of Christ is equal in significance to the wholeness and spiritual impetus of the creation.

It is interesting that *pleroma* survives in Gnostic literature itself with a positive meaning. Behind both the Jewish and Gnostic usage we must ultimately see another contact with the Mysteries of Iran. For it is in Zoroastrian cosmology that we find the archetypal image of Ohrmazd and his six fellow 'Bounteous Immortals' or Creator Spirits. And in the Zoroastrian texts it is also said that Ohrmazd is one of the Creator Spirits, yet at the same time he is the Totality. We have the rare opportunity of making use of visual evidence from early Christian times at this juncture. Set among the mosaics of the great Basilica of St Mark, Venice, can be found a representation of the events in Genesis. Each 'Day' of creation appears as an angelic being, and at the end of the sequence we see God in a purely Iranian position at the centre with three angels on either side of him. We know that the image comes from a Christianity much earlier than thirteenth-century Venice; for J.B. Trapp points out that the series 'is an astonishingly close translation into mosaic of the illustrations in a literary and very early version — the Cotton *Genesis*. This is one of our earliest fully illustrated Old Testament manuscripts; a fifth- or sixth-century codex, perhaps made in Alexandria.'[40] The ideas contained in it go back even further.

The concept of 'Fullness,' then, was realized in Jewish-esoteric and in Johannine circles in connection with an angelology, and with the 'work of creation.' How did the figure of the Christ fit into it all?

The Prologue, together with the statement from Clement of Alexandria in the *Outlines*, shows that Jesus was regarded as an embodiment of the Fullness. It was not in its cosmic reality, as the eternal divine Word, that the creative Fullness was present in him on earth. But it was as the *exousia*, the angelic 'Power of God' or emanation of the Word in which the sevenfold whole was mirrored. The Fullness had been reflected to the Jews formerly through Yahweh and his work of creation. Now the angelic 'personification' of God was realized in Jesus. The 'angelic' understanding of Christ was in fact deeply rooted in the earliest Christianity, emerging out of the esoteric Jewish background and — as we have seen — giving rise to a comprehensive and highly articulate theology. God personified himself in the angelic Exousiai, and in turn in Jesus after the baptism by John.

The *Ebionim*, the Essene-derived Jewish-Christians, still preserved this knowledge. They taught, as recorded by one of the Church Fathers:

> that Jesus was begotten of human seed, and chosen, and thus called by election Son of God, Christ having come upon him from on high in the form of a dove (that is, at *the baptism*). They say that he was not begotten by God the Father, but that he was created, like the archangels, but greater than they.[41]

The Church Father who reports on them searcely understands their ideas any more. The reference to angels like the seven archangels, but greater or higher up the hierarchical ranks, certainly points to the Exousiai. It does not in the least deny the reality of the incarnation of God, but points to intermediate stages of 'personification.' Indeed some Christians taught that the Christ personified himself successively in the ladder of the descending angelic order, at last reaching the condition of man.

As a footnote we may mention other traces of the Power theology: for example in those amazing and labyrinthine visions of an early Christian prophet called *The Shepherd of Hermas*, where much of the symbolism concerns seven angels, whose activity seems to include both creation and redemption, building the visible earth and the invisible order of the Church; and in a 'very early' and rather esoteric tract *On the Threefold Fruits of Christian Life*, where God makes seven angels from the heavenly fire and appoints one of them (presumably the Sun-angel) to represent, or simply to 'be,' his Son. Here again God is personifying himself in an angelic being or Exousia. That is not to deny that it is God who is present, but 'only' an angel — just the reverse! The treatise seems also to assert the eternal existence of the Son even before the 'election' of one of the angels. Its ideas have been compared to a Christian inscription of Miletus mentioning seven 'Archangel-Aeons.' In the *Threefold Fruits* similarly Christ is represented as an Aeon, a heavenly potency: 'he is the whole and equally one of the seven parts.'[42]

The 'Beloved Disciple' and his cosmic experience have introduced us to a largely unfamiliar world of cosmological thought. If nowadays it seems necessarily obscure and remote, we must remember that it was a way of talking about certain actual experiences, not a speculative indulgence. And that it expresses the dynamics of spiritual experience between the earthly world and the divine in concrete and detailed ways of which the later dogma of the incarnation is a stereotyped and even rigidified formula. It can take us back into the experiences of those who felt 'cosmic events' and changes happening around the presence of Christ.

That is perhaps the crucial point. For the Jewish consciousness, divine spiritual-material activity had ceased with the creation. The world as it existed since the creation was only product, leaving the stage free for man's history to be enacted. But the creation-imagery and creation-angelology of the Prologue states a stark new truth: that God is once more active in the material world. This is not a reversion to mythological consciousness, however, but a further step forward. God is present in a definitive historical being and a unique set of events. This rediscovery of God's spiritual activity within the world of matter, in effect a 'new creation,' was in one sense the Christian discovery. In Paul it opened the vista of man's future evolution and the metamorphosis of the resurrection-body into a vehicle of glory. How the author of the Fourth Gospel fuses his cosmic vision and ritual initiation with the events of that unique history, tragic in its human intensity but creative in its cosmic implications, must be the subject of our final sections.

The Mystery of Golgotha

Each of the Gospels has its own perspective on the trial and passion of Jesus. Each of them has its own implicit theology, and we look in vain for any recital of the 'bare facts.' More than any other part of Christ's life, the happenings of passion-week are charged with unfathomable meaning in the mind of all Christians from the very earliest stage of the tradition. It is important to remember, too, that the isolating of the 'mere facts' would itself be an interpretation, and a peculiarly limited one. 'Facts' are themselves abstractions from the world of human social and spiritual experience. And modern philosophers have suggested that pure objectivity, rather than being an ideal of knowledge, would be a vanishing-point: to characterize a matter from no point of view at all, that is, without interpretation, is in effect to say nothing about it.

The Fourth Gospel presents an especially rich interpretation of this, the central Mystery, and rather than trying to cut our way through to the mirage of 'what really happened,' we will do better to enter as deeply as we may into its vision. For after all, it is the historical experience of one close to and intimately involved in the events themselves. More even than the other Gospels, the Fourth Gospel intensifies the historical reality into something of mythic power, while we may be 'sure at {he same time that its author acknowledged a supreme obligation to historical accuracy. Without fidelity to what happened in history, the 'truth' he proclaims could not exist — though of course it transcends the limits of time and place under which the truth was manifested.

On the profoundest level, this obligation coincides with the obedience of Christ to his Father, the God of history. It is the obedience which prevented the mythic dimension of the Christ-Event from cutting-free, dissociating itself from history and so being simply a return to the ancient Mysteries. It is the supreme obedience to the conditions of historical actuality, namely to death.

The Beloved Disciple experiences the events of the Last Supper, the arrest, trial and crucifixion of Jesus with overwhelming intensity — with a heightened consciousness, we proposed, through his initiation. The cosmic content of his initiation, the 'mystery of the kingdom of the heavens,' he embodied in the Prologue, framing the tradition of Jesus' life up to the point where the Disciple himself had his life-and-death encounter: the raising of Lazarus. His initiation was not fulfilled, however, in the cosmic vision. The 'old initiation' was given its redirection by Jesus through its association) with his own destiny, that of the suffering Son of Man on earth. The Disciple finds the reality of his cosmic, mythic experience in what is recounted in the second half of his Gospel.

Hence arises the famous 'Johannine irony.' For the Disciple sees on two levels: he sees the events taking place, and the motives and viewpoints of those perpetrating them; but he also sees how they are caught up in the fulfilment of a pattern, a reality, which they themselves do not grasp. When the High Priest proposes that one man should be sacrificed for the sake of the people, he means that the political situation can be restored to calm by getting rid of Jesus. But John sees that the one man is indeed going to his death for the sake of the people, in a much higher sense than the High Priest can imagine. Much of the power of the writing of the Gospel, and so of its power to affect and transform us, springs from this 'initiatory' perspective of the double significance or irony of earthly happenings. In the other literature that has come down to us with the name John, such as the *Acts of John* or the *Secret Book*, the two levels often fall apart. The *Acts of John*, for example, tells how while the crucifixion took place, John saw a vision of Christ in glory in the spiritual world: the Jews and Romans are mocked because they suffer from the illusion that a divine being could be killed by nailing him on a cross. We see how teachings that originated in the Johannine sphere have been drawn towards a fundamental Gnostic dualism. But in the authentic Johannine vision this is not the case. When in the Fourth Gospel Jesus says 'The world does not see me, but you (the disciples) see me,' he does not mean that he exists on a spiritual plane and that all else is illusion. There is only irony, in the visionary Johannine sense, because the truth actually is being enacted in the world — and yet the world does not see it. The irony presupposes, in fact, the identity of earthly happenings and eternal significance.

Hence it is that, as C.H. Dodd noticed, things that were commonly imagined to follow from or to be the spiritual consequence of the passion-events, in John's vision actually fuse with them. The language he uses about the death and resurrection is that used elsewhere in early Christianity of the ascension and second coming. The crucifixion is not *followed* by the happenings of the Last Days; between them in John is a 'vanishing distinction.' 'Christ's death on the cross *is* His ascent to the right hand of the Father; and His return to His disciples after death, which is closely associated, if not identified, with the coming of the Holy Spirit, *is* His second advent.'[43] This points to the initiatory character of John's historical experience. His initiation achieves its real meaning at the point of 'vanishing' discrepincy between the heavenly and earthly truth.

Dodd extends his interpretation of the later half of the Gospel, connecting it directly with initiation. Beginning with the 'Farewell Discourses,' he sees a close analogy with the Hermetic Mystery-dialogues. That does not mean, as we now know, Hermetic influence — but rather that the Hermetists drew their inspiration from the same Jewish-Iranian *gnosis* and baptismal rites, and so shared that background of the Gospel. Jesus' own esoteric practice was of course the immediate setting: 'the Farewell Discourses may be regarded as growing out of the tradition represented by the esoteric teaching ... of the Synoptic Gospels; in another aspect they are analogous to Hellenistic documents of the class of the *Poimandres* and the *De Regeneratione*. That is to say, they are a dialogue on initiation into eternal life through the knowledge of God, ending with a prayer or hymn which is itself the final stage of initiation.' The scene of the washing of the disciples' feet by Jesus is explicitly a purification, recalling for Dodd the descent of the heavenly Man in *Poimandres*: 'The *Poimandres* indeed speaks of a 'fall,' John of an act of condescension, but there is a real analogy of ideas ...' The difference indicates the radical change in the attitude toward historical events! But the analogy is confirmed by the similar effects and the formulae of purification in the tractate *On Rebirth*. Above all, the climactic words from the cross 'It is initiated' provide Dodd with the meaning of the whole. He notes the use of the term, ironically misunderstood by the bystanders to mean 'It is at an end,' as a technical word in the Mysteries. 'Thus in the Hermetic *De Regeneratione*, the newly initiated Tat gives thanks for his regeneration ... so here (Christ's) death is declared to be the completion of the sacrifice, regarded as the means of man's regeneration, or initiation into eternal life.'[44]

Once again, however, the most remarkable insight into the initiatory meaning of the Gospel comes from Rudolf Steiner, and it can be brought together with the discoveries, since Dodd, of the secret *Mark* and *Trimorphic Protennoia*, in striking detail.

Steiner likewise referred to the experiences of initiation underlying the pictures that come before us in the second half of the Gospel. He stressed that the pictures were not the important thing: after all, it is very easy to induce comparable visions by suggestion or other psychological pressures. The images are valuable only when they arise as the expression of inner experiences, and in a sequence pointing to the process of transformation taking place in the neophyte. And then indeed, says Steiner, the Christian initiate sees in visions what reappears in the Gospel of John on the plane of history. He goes on to characterize seven phases of the initiatory experience and the images that express them:

1   *The Washing of the Feet.* The fundamental note here is humility. Christ himself performs an act of condescension in the Gospel — the Christian equivalent of what had formerly been felt in the Mysteries as a 'fall.' The neophyte recognizes that he is dependent for all his higher development on the 'lower' beings around him: for his nourishment by plant and animal substances, on the earth itself for the ground to stand on. When in Christian initiation the feeling had been cultivated so strongly as to manifest itself in a perceptual 'symptom,' Steiner says, the candidate actually felt as though water were lapping round his feet.

2.   *Scourging.* The second stage concerns awareness of suffering and pain. 'Picture how it would be if all the suffering and sorrow possible in the world came upon you, if you were exposed to the piling up of all conceivable hindrances: you must develop the feeling of standing erect though all the adversity of the world is bearing down upon you!' The perception resulting from intense cultivation of the second stage is 'the feeling of being beaten from all sides,' and the vision of the scourging.

3.   *Crown of Thorns.* The neophyte had next to be subjected to 'jeers and gibes.' Reviled and mocked, he experienced both the burning away of his lower egotism, and a strength of his convictions that was not fostered from outside but from his own deeper self. 'When he had accustomed himself to this, he felt something like pricking upon his head, and he experienced the Crown of Thorns.'

4.   *Crucifixion.* Further exercises induced a critical experience. The neophyte came to feel his body as foreign, an inert exter-

nal object like a stick of wood. 'He no longer connected his ego with his body.' (Compare Saying 56 in the *Gospel of Thomas*: 'He who has known the world has found a corpse, and he who has found a corpse, the world is not worthy of him.'). The vision of the 'dead' body deepens into the image of the crucifixion; and as a physical 'symptom' the stigmata.

5. *Mystical Death*. The candidate 'feels as though, in an instant, a black curtain were drawn before the whole physical, visible world and as though everything had disappeared.' It can be described as a 'Descent into Hell,' to the sources of evil, pain and affliction. 'After this has been experienced, it is as though the black curtain had been rent asunder, and he looks into the spiritual world.'

6. *Resurrection*. Having been, in inner experience, buried in the dark earth, the neophyte's experience gradually changes. His consciousness expands into a cosmic form, uniting him with the whole body of the earth. 'His life has been extended into a planetary existence.'

7. *Ascension*. 'The seventh experience cannot be described in words ... It is called the Ascension, or the complete absorption into the spiritual world.'[45]

Steiner's descriptions smack of authentic initiatory processes, and in part reflect scenarios known from the Mysteries. They help us to understand many aspects of initiation, for instance, why rites were formed around water-purifications (1); and why they sometimes involved physical ordeals and tortures (2, 3), though here we have rather the psychological ordeal of 'death to the world.' We know from Mysteries such as those of Eleusis that the stage of mockery (3) was often enacted, even publicly. Experiences of the inert, soul-less body and descent into the underworld were vividly especially portrayed in the Near Eastern Mystery-rites (4, 5), where the aim was the kind of 'cosmic consciousness' and spiritual vision Steiner hints at (6, 7). At the same time, Steiner's account corresponds closely to the events of the Fourth Gospel in the passion-chapters: the terrible sufferings of betrayal, arrest (scourging and mockery, the Crown of Thorns), crucifixion, death, resurrection and the sense of Christ's pervasive presence which returned to the disciples, culminating in the enigma of the ascension. These events had an initiatory meaning for the Beloved Disciple. What is so striking, in the light of modern discoveries, is the way Steiner's characterization of the underlying spiritual process corresponds to the elements we now know from the Rite of Glorification — from secret *Mark* and the *Trimorphic Protennoia*.

There are certain differences too. And these in turn have their significance.

I do not mean simply that there are seven stages rather than five. In fact we must add an eighth preliminary stage, namely 'Instruction in the Mysteries,' which in the Gospel constitutes the Farewell Discourses. Besides likening their setting at the Last Supper to a Hellenistic initiation, C.H. Dodd noted that the content of these Discourses is fundamentally that of the 'esoteric teaching' in the other Gospels, given apart or in private to the disciples.

The ablution or washing follows, echoing the second stage of the rite undergone by the Beloved Disciple. Here in the Gospel of John, chapter 13, it is not ritual but a personal gesture. Nevertheless in the consciousness of the evangelist it gains the equivalent significance, and he invests the event with ritual atmosphere, even in the choice of the significant details:

> So Jesus rose from the meal, undressed and wrapped a
> linen cloth around his waist. Then he poured water into a
> basin, and began to wash his disciples' feet ...

The image comes straight from the world of baptismal initiation. And its meaning is identical to that of Pauline baptism: participation in Christ. 'Unless I wash you,' says this baptizer-Jesus, 'you have no part with me.'

The initiatory pattern is beginning to be enacted, then, in actual events. Jesus announced the fact himself, once we have learned to understand the language. 'Now is the Son of Man glorified,' he says as he goes out from this scene into the night, to his arrest and crucifixion. He had taught that initiation for his disciples meant initiation into the mystery of his destiny. In the heightened consciousness of the Beloved Disciple, his teaching is now fulfilled.

The stages to the 'glorification' itself, however, are still several. Steiner recognized in the ordeals of Jesus' scourging and mockery after his arrest the further experiences of the neophyte. The candidate for initiation must have undergone those sensations of suffering and revilement. Steiner took care to point out that what we witness here is not Jesus being initiated — but the revelation of a process of initiation, which as historical fact would have significance for all mankind afterwards.[46] What we can also notice about the Gospel's telling of the ordeals is that they point 'ironically' to a royal initiation. After his scourging, Jesus is given a purple robe and a 'crown' of thorns. The irony again points to John's higher consciousness: through being able to hold himself spiritually erect under suffering and mockery, Jesus has indeed earned the royal attributes. The most terrible aspect of the whole episode is that none of those involved see the reality of what they are doing. A spiritual reality is being actualized for all to see, yet they are still blind. Only in the spiritual sight of the evangelist, there is taking place a true investiture.

The Gospel accounts of the crucifixion notably avoid many of the distasteful emphases known from later Christian piety. Originally we find no stress on the physical sufferings of Jesus, horrific though it is plain they must have been. The mood rather transcends the personal. If we are inclined to use the term 'tragic,' it is because we feel in the Gospels this sense of greater, supra-personal forces. There is a higher necessity: but not, as in Greek tragedy, acting in opposition to the wills of the protagonists. It is accepted totally by Jesus in obedience to his Father, the power of history itself. Through the heightened consciousness of the evangelist, the Fourth Gospel brings material and spiritual necessity together, in the 'vanishing distinction' which makes the climactic Event of Golgotha a spiritual truth taking place on earth. An event of 'mythic' resonance becomes a wellspring of history. In the mind of the evangelist the event is the actualization of his initiatory experience. From the many references already scattered through earlier parts of the Gospel, we know that this crucifixion is none other than the Glorification: the 'exaltation' of the Son of Man as it is elsewhere called, employing the term for a star or planet at the height of its influence. The cosmic revelation of Christ's glory, on the other hand, fuses entirely with the happening on earth.

What then of the resurrection and ascension? According to Steiner's indication, these signify the transformation of consciousness, its 'planetarization.' And we know those experiences from the Mysteries of the ancient Near East, especially the cosmic initiation of the ruler. At his enthronement, the initiate-king ascended the levels of cosmic reality in seven steps,'receiving the planetary symbols of universal power, before reaching his throne. We have met cosmic enthronement not only in the traditions of Philip, but in Paul, in Ephesians where the initiated are 'enthroned with Christ,' a phrase to which we gave a 'heavenly' interpretation. These final stages of the Christ-Mystery we may likewise call, in the deepest sense, an 'enthronement' or establishing of Christ's cosmic rule.

The events of the Gospel, together with Steiner's indication of their import, point indeed to the elements of the Beloved Disciple's initiation. But it is crucial to note exactly what has happened. The earthly events have not simply mirrored a transcendent pattern, become absorbed into a non-earthly paradigm. The old Mystery rite of Glorification placed the investiture before the baptismal purification. And the transformation of consciousness of 'enthronement' originally led the neophyte into cosmic spheres, where he was then 'glorified' by partaking of celestial radiance. But in the Gospel of John, earthly happenings retain their own validity, and impose a change in the sequence. Investiture now follows the lustration in water. And now it is the earthly glorification on the cross which assumes priority; man no longer has to ascend into cosmic heights to find the sources of spiritual light, but encounters them in the Mystery of Golgotha. The Mystery-rite is turned inside-out.

One might see in the change of emphasis a shift that will playa part in the further development of Christian spiritual life, namely one away from the baptismal rites toward the sacrament of Christ's presence in matter, the eucharist. There is still a cosmic dimension. But in the Gospel, that now follows from the significance of the Event on earth — just as for Paul a change in consciousness began in the earthly, human world and spread from thence to the cosmic rulers of the universe.

Incarnation and Glorification

To put it another way, what we see happening — through the spiritual eyes of the evangelist — is a process of incarnation. A heavenly Mystery, even up to the point of the crucifixion, is entering more and more into earthly conditions. The trajectory established by the Prologue is not contradicted by the remainder of the Gospel. It is not falsified by a saviour who turns out to be an apparition, as the Gnostics said. An incarnational perspective (though of course long preceding the elaborate later theologies of the Incarnation) turns out to be strongly implied by the 'representative' tendency. Esoteric Judaism had envisaged this tendency reaching as far as the angelic world, but John breaks the bounds of the Judaic consciousness and extends the active presence of the divine *exousia* into earthly existence. That in turn does not contradict the initiationperspective. The idea that initiation and incarnation are incompatible is an unfortunate misconception of the Church, and not one shared by the Fourth Gospel.

The idea of incarnation we find here is not the literal-minded one of the orthodox Fathers, the view which rightly earned the gibe of Nestorius, 'God is not a baby three days old.' The Gospel message is not that God chose to be born, grew up in certain small villages and then announced himself to a startled and unbelieving world, as some have asked us to suppose. What we have in John is an apprehension of the process whereby earthly events are given spiritual meaning. The process extends not just up to the point of Jesus' birth, but through the events of Jesus' life and ministry, to that point of 'vanishing distinction' where the crucifixion is at the same time and in its inmost essence the Glorification, where spiritual and earthly are absolutely one. It is the theological importance of the work of Emil Bock to have described Christ's life from this point of view, taking his departure from certain ideas of Rudolf Steiner.[47] In such a process as he apprehends we have a profound and intelligible, and authentically biblical, doctrine of the Incarnation.

It is indeed from the Gospel of John that he takes his cue.[48] But he draws on the other gospels too, and we may briefly go on to consider material pointing to the wider tradition, of which the Fourth Gospel represents a special case. The words of Jesus from the cross are treated differently in the different Gospels, but we can compare with the Gospel of John the statements to be found in those of Matthew, Mark and *Peter*. The words of Christ which they give are equivalent in meaning, as I understand them, to the Johannine 'It is finished/It is initiated.'

Mark may be the most historically exact, for he gives Christ's words in Aramaic, no doubt the language in which they were spoken:

> And at the ninth hour Jesus cried out in a loud voice,
> *'Eloi, Eloi, lama sabachthani?'* — which means, 'My God,
> my God, why have you forsaken me?'

Matthew, with his special concern for the fulfilment of Old Testament prophecies, hears in the words the note sounded by Psalm 22, and gives it in his Gospel with the proper Hebrew form, *'Eli, Eli,'* but otherwise his testimony is identical. The sense of desertion given by Jesus' words has always been a problem for Christians, as on the surface it does not fit the conventional idea of an incarnate God. But we can approach its meaning once more with the help of Rudolf Steiner.

Long before the modern discovery at Nag Hammadi of the *Trimorphic Protennoia* restored to us the Rite of Glorification, he was able to catch the echo in Jesus' words of an older formula. 'At the crucifixion,' Steiner explained, 'the spiritual forsakes the physical body and therewith also the divine forces that had been taken over into it. The writer of the Matthaean Gospel directs his gaze to the separation of the inner nature of Christ Jesus from this divine element in his physical constitution. The words that always rang out in the ancient Mysteries when the spiritual nature of a man emerged from the physical body in order to have vision in the spiritual world, were 'My God, my God, how have you glorified me!' The writer of the Gospel of Matthew, his attention fixed on the physical body, changes these words to 'My God, my God, why have you forsaken me?'[49] It is important to realize here exactly what Steiner is *not* saying. He is not saying that Jesus, dying, identified himself with the mortal remains on the cross and lamented that his divinity had abandoned him. Just the opposite. With his last consciousness, Steiner's Jesus sees that the divine power that has worked through him, performing the 'signs,' healings and exorcisms, has now united itself wholly with the physical body. It is his 'spiritual' part, his consciousness, which is separated by death and speaks of being forsaken. He dies, but leaves behind him in the physical world the reality of the Glorification. What used to be attained 'spiritually,' that is, outside of the body, has now been achieved in that physical-historical event of his death, in the body on the cross.

Steiner's teaching reproduces exactly what we have discovered in the 'vanishing distinction' of the Gospel of John: namely that the death on the cross is the last point of the trajectory of incarnation. The divine glory there enters entirely into the physical event, the bodily death. And this, in the new terms of the Christian vision, is the very Glorification once obtained through out-of-the-body experience in initiation. There is a Johannine kind of irony in the way the words reach the outside world. Those around the cross hear a cry of desertion, equivalent to 'It is all at an end'; but those who catch the echo of the Mysteries know that this means the completion of the initiatory process which has become an event on earth. 'It is initiated.' The divine reality is now to be found in the physical world.

Interesting confirmation comes also from the *Gospel of Peter*, our earliest apocryphal passion-gospel. It shows that the words were understood as a reference by Jesus to the angelic being he 'personified' on earth. Whether or not it is an independent testimony to the passion, it shows how the earliest Christianity understood the divine presence in Jesus, invoked by him on the cross. David Flusser points out that the conception is therefore not in itself heretical.[50] *The Gospel of Peter* gives the words in the following form:

> And the Lord called out and cried, 'My Power, Power,
> you have forsaken me!'

The address *'Eloi'* was taken to invoke one of the *elohim,* or the Powers or the angelic Authorities who are the Spirits of

Creation. They were the Fullness from which Jesus received his power or 'grace.' One can quite rightly speak of an 'incarnation' of this power, though it is not the concept of incarnation known from the later Church.

There is in the *Gospel of Peter* no sense that Christ somehow avoided the crucifixion and left the body of Jesus to die. We have to do with the working into Jesus of a divine-angelic Power. We have learned from Rudolf Steiner and from the Gospel of John that the death on the cross was not the end but the full achievement of that incarnation-process. We must learn to hear through 'It is ended' the Mystery-word 'It is initiated'; and, through the terrible cry of the forsaken, 'How have you glorified me!'

Epilogue

Return of the Youth in the Linen Cloth

If I wish him to remain until I come back again, what is that to you?

The Johannine I AM

If I have managed to convey anything of the scope and organizing power of the Johannine Gospel, it will be evident that it achieves on an imaginatively unsurpassable level a particular fusion: a fusion of personal destiny with cosmic vision. With its pivotal centre in the initiation of the beloved disciple, it is framed by the perspective of cosmic Prologue and the resurrection-vision of the Final Chapter. Its mystery of death and rebirth is at once universal history, the unique event of Golgotha in its earthly immediacy, and the transforming spiritual experience of the writer himself. Each aspect achieves its own authenticity, yet at the same time coalesces fundamentally into a single revelation. It is the same fusion which is also implied, or intimated, or groped for, in much other early Christian literature, however. Its elements are those which in greater or lesser tension have entered into all the Christian texts we have discussed in this book, apocryphal or otherwise, Gospels or pseudepigraphic revelations. Its privileged position of closeness to Christ is a difference of degree, not of kind, from other insights in early Christianity.

From Jesus, around whom the apocalyptic metamorphosis began to become fact, to Paul, for whom the events of the resurrection were partly 'present' through initiation (baptism), the spiritual reality felt as impending apocalypse or End of the

World with the coming of the Son of Man entered, for the early Christian, into the sphere of present consciousness. A follower of Paul, expounding the Master in his *Letter on Resurrection*, felt the transformation in the domain of the soul — the psychic resurrection which had happened already as a matter of consciousness. Yet for him, the spiritual resurrection was still in the 'beyond': man entered upon it only after quitting this life and this cosmos. For John, on the other hand, the 'vanishing distinction' between earthly and spiritual means that the deepest unveiling or apocalypse, the ultimate meaning of things, is found directly within the sphere of the conscious self on earth. When Philip asks for the vision of God — of ultimate reality — Jesus says to him, according to John:

> Have I been with you all for such a long time, and you have not recognized me, Philip? He who has seen me has seen the Father.

The disciples do not understand this yet: only the death and resurrection will make it fully actual.

And when the Johannine Christ tells the disciples about his significance, it is with that extraordinary 'absolute' use of the words I AM. Such a formula outwardly resembles that in a pagan aretalogy (the announcement by a god of his divine powers and deeds). But there is nothing in the pagan world to compare with those sayings where I AM seems to be itself the subject of the sentence. The spiritual value placed on the 'holy man,' the spiritual individuality in early Christianity finds already in the Fourth Gospel its apotheosis. The Gospel is a revelation of the divine in the sphere of the ego, the spiritual self, the appearance of God as a divine I AM. By his initiation, John in his conscious self becomes the bearer of the revelation.

Steiner's understanding of the evolution of consciousness enables us to place the Johannine contribution to Christianity in historical perspective, and so to recognize in it the climax of a process that had long been coming about. That is also the perspective of the Prologue itself. The initiation underlying the Gospel epitomizes the gradually achieved shift from the old cosmic Mysteries, when man's life was determined by patterns of rhythm and order in the macrocosm and mediated through an initiate king, to a Mystery that has moved fully into the sphere of the individual I AM. It has moved into the sphere of freedom: but in doing so the self has discovered that it cannot continue in the manner of the ancient initiate-King, who was a wise ruler of his people and their centre of consciousness. It must adopt the role of a servant. Individualized man is liable to egotism in a way that could not infect archaic humanity. Individual existence brings with it temptations and the possibility of greater moral error as well as new positive achievement. And the energy by means of which it must overthrow its self-centredness is love. Love is the revelation of God to the individualized, self-conscious man, just as power and wise order were the revelation of God to ancient, pre-self-conscious humanity.

The initiatory transformation — the work of the Mysteries — has itself been transformed through history. History thus had to become an intrinsic part of the picture, in contrast to the old Mysteries with their timeless myths.

Christianity may therefore be seen as the spiritual expression of an evolution that we can trace over the millennia since the great theocratic cultures of the ancient East. The concept of that evolution may thus be seen as our modern version of the doctrine, so often misunderstood, of the pre-existence and Incarnation of the divine Word. It is the story of how man's consciousness, his relation to the natural and spiritual worlds, evolved, and the cosmic determining patterns of ancient man entered into the new organization of Christian self-consciousness. Christianity is uniquely valuable among the world-religions, because it is the religion whose message is that that history of individualization itself has a spiritual meaning. It is the cosmic Word, the Logos, becoming human. That need not by any means make us suppose that no other kinds of religious experience were (or are) true and valuable. Indeed they may remind us of aspects of religious truth pushed into the background by the historical necessities of orthodox Christianity. I have argued that originally Christianity was broader and overlapped with religious tendencies of both East and West. But the cosmic religions of the East cannot shed light on the Christian process, as I may call it, which has been the driving power of 'self-development' among Western humanity in the very broadest sense over the last several thousand years, including indeed its influence back upon the Eastern cultures in turn. Only Christianity can offer a spiritual understanding of modern man's intense life of consciousness and his quest for power to change his world. And so only Christianity can offer a cogent alternative to the secular, atheistic interpretation of modern consciousness which is so loudly and vociferously proclaimed, even within some of the Churches.

If the Christian process which I have described is as I have described it, it is clear that its importance is not thereby limited to Western humanity — nor even to humanity at all. It is important to the whole nature of the world we live in. Profound implications for a more far-seeing ecology open up here — hinted at by the *Gospel of Philip* when it says that we can go beyond treating things as 'works' of our labour, making them 'children' to which we commit a part of our own being. The teaching, found in Christianity in many forms, implies that what is first grasped as a shift in our consciousness is ultimately to be seen as a change in the nature of the world. To understand it we need that transformational or 'metamorphic' kind of thinking which goes beyond the mere looking for fixities and regular laws, which would reveal the Christian process as a facet of a greater reality, of which we and our consciously experienced world — and perhaps other worlds — are a part. The Mysteries and the early Christians expressed themselves here through the cosmologies of gods and angels, the Fullness and the divine 'personification' of creative *exousia*. We need to learn, to understand their strange language, and to express it in more scientifically exact modern ways.

The Johannine vision includes the quality of that irony resulting from the simultaneous perception of spiritual and natural. One such irony bulks so large in the history of early Christianity that it must now be mentioned. It is the unexpected conversion, after only a few centuries, of primitive Christianity into an imperial cult. After all that had been taught about the Christ-consciousness, it is indeed ironic that the religion should so rapidly accept the Byzantine emperor as Christ's vicar on earth, as the source of power descending hierarchically through his courtiers, reflected in heaven by the intercessory ranks of saints! The story behind the change is a complex and distressing one — and it is not the subject of this book. Yet it would be misleading not to point out the enormity of the deviation from the primal Christian spirit we have explored, since it would falsify our present-day relation to the Christian consciousness and the Christian tradition.

It is by no means the case that everything in early Christianity was lost in the transition to mediaeval Christendom. Many of the new Christian values still shone through: but the close interrelation of individual maturing and cosmic vision disappeared, so undermining the framework and coherence of the new consciousness. With the barbarian invasions there was a widespread return to feudal hierarchy, submission to an overlord, a loss of the dynamic of the self. Yet one can say that a Christian resonance persists in the mediaeval mind. It is necessary simply to dissent from the notion that the 'ages of faith' were the definitive expression of Christianity. That they certainly were not. To find the essence of Christianity we must return to the primal phenomenon. New discoveries and spiritual insights enable us, in some measure, to do so now: and then we can recognize the many historical expressions of Christianity for what they are, without being bound by the contingencies of the historical tradition. It would be wrong to dismiss the Middle Ages as a perversion of Christianity, but still more wrong to confuse them with the expression of the spirit we find in Christ and his disciples.

Important stages in the transition from early Christianity to mediaeval Christendom may be briefly indicated:

1. *The struggle against the Gnostics.* The need to centre the Christian vision on the conscious I AM, instead of including the cosmic vision in its new configuration, soon led many churchmen to exclude the cosmic vision altogether, for fear that in the hands of radical Gnostics it would itself exclude the earthly and historical aspect of the self. Panic measures never have much to recommend them. This struggle of the first centuries, which could have led to a rethinking of cosmology as a response to the Gnostic challenge, brought in a heavy return to the Judaic 'creation' doctrine and the Old Testament. Crucial shifts of attitude began to occur. The older acceptance of doctrinal variety waned.

Whereas early Christians had tolerated differences where there was a common sense of the importance of Christ, after the 'Gnostic crisis' many churchmen were only prepared to approve a sense of the importance of Christ if it fitted into their own set of ideas. A turning point was no doubt the attempt of the dualistic theologian Marcion, around 140 AD, to found his own separatist church. Though not a Gnostic, he had many similar ideas to theirs. In the face of this threat, the church clammed up. There was a highly important structural change. Early Christianity included some Gnostic elements, broadly defineable in the sense that man could 'ascend' to knowledge of the spirit through inner growth and development. The 'orthodox' church threw out Gnosticism: and it was left with a one-sided descending structure of authority percolating down from an absolute at the top through the levels of the community. (Equally, one can say that extreme Gnosticism suffered from the problem that it valued the experience gained by an inner ascent, but could never ground itself in the history, which means the shared experience, of the society around.)

2. *The barbarian invasions.* The history of society in which Christianity spread over the first few centuries was itself shaken severely by the changes resulting from large numbers of tribes such as Goths, Vandals and Visigoths who swept over the civilized Roman world. It has been well said that these barbarian waves were really something between an invasion and a gold-rush. Battles were fought; but the invaders were provincials from the outskirts of the Empire who really wanted a better deal and grabbed at the centres of power — including Rome itself, which fell to the Goths in AD 410. They then made their own attempt at being Romans and running the Empire in their turn. They were also enthusiastic in taking up Christianity, in their own way. Thus the character of the Empire changed, and the character of Christianity changed. The masses of people who accepted the Christian faith in the ensuing centuries did not originate from the Mediterranean civilizations with millennia of spiritual evolution behind them. They came straight out of prehistory, in the strict sense that they came from oral cultures based on tribal divisions. They had nothing of the developed consciousness able to experience the coming of the Christ-con-

sciousness as integral 'salvation,' the desperately needed articu-
lation for the self which had reached the brink of a new inner
life. They interpreted the Gospel accordingly. Lucifer became a
bad feudal baron who had not obeyed his overlord, and was
punished according to their laws. Christ became a good feudal-
ist who taught obedience, loyalty and contentment with one's
lot. Medieval Christianity arose as these tribal inheritors of the
Roman world grew up into a distinctive culture. It is important
to realize that the presuppositions on which it grew were
extraordinarily remote from the world in which Jesus lived.

We today are the inheritors of Europe from our medieval
ancestors. Much has happened since; but in a strange way
Christianity has somehow not kept pace with modern history.
At least, I think that is the underlying impression many people
have of Christian thought, especially in the most recent times. It
has tried to swallow without digesting much that comes from
the modern scientific world-view, and fit itself around what it
finds there. The theologian today hardly feels that he can challenge the materialist 'truth' of the scientist, but must simply
accept it. He may have things to say in addition, but hardly an
integral world-view. Rudolf Steiner's spiritual rethinking of science forms one of the few real exceptions. This could be a
depressing prospect. But I would like to present it another way.

We have the opportunity, in a way that was impossible for the
leaders of the Reformation, to rediscover the world and spiritual
meaning of Christian beginnings, in contradistinction to our
medieval legacy. I would like to bring that together with the
sense mentioned earlier, that in the matter of the 'Gospel of
Love' we stand still at the very beginning. For it may be that,
after the long period after the barbarian invasions, our culture
can again begin to approach the stage of self-development, of
inner awakening, to which Christianity addressed itself in the
earliest phase of its history. It has taken us many centuries —
and no doubt we have added much to our collective experience
in the process. Perhaps it would have been too much to expect
to take so great a leap with one run! But this may help to explain
the extraordinary relevance we feel in the earliest Christianity to
the modern human situation. Rudolf Steiner pointed to the kinship of our age with the first Christian centuries. The challenge

of materialism today could be the source of a new apocalyptic, to which Steiner responded with a Christian and 'Michaelic' message. He also declared what I believe to be the implication of the recent discoveries and the picture they unfold, speaking to us so much more directly than the mediaeval heritage: namely, that we stand at the very beginning of Christianity, not near its end.

The Youth in the Linen Cloth Returns

John in his conscious self became the bearer of the revelation. So, in a less archetypal and complete fashion, did other Christian prophets and 'ministers of the word.' Yet without infringing the uniqueness of our own relationship to the Christ-consciousness, the Beloved Disciple must always hold a special place at the heart of the workings of the Christian spirit. As the 'youth in the linen cloth' he is the focus of the energy that was working through Christ, and, as an Imagination, he has a continuing relevance to the further manifestations of that energy — the completing of the Christian process which I have suggested still lies essentially ahead of us.

Let us briefly reassemble what we have learnt about him through our several studies in the Gospels of Mark and John, in the *Shepherd* visions of Hermas, and from Rudolf Steiner.

We met him first at the scene of Jesus' arrest. A mysterious, almost an impalpable figure, a naked youth in a linen cloth slips away from the scene of Jesus' earthly condemnation and death. What has seemed to many an inexplicable, meaningless detail in the story became intelligible, we found, through Rudolf Steiner's indication that the youth actually appears again in Mark's Gospel. At the tomb, when the stone has been rolled away, the women looking for Jesus' body see to their amazement a youth with a white robe round him.

Steiner's explanation is to the meaning of the youth turns out to be part of a closely woven set of related ideas in the Gospels. It hangs together with his astonishingly accurate account of the origins of the Gospel of Mark, for example. That in turn confirms in detail his approach to the Gospel of John and the raising of Lazarus. But what makes Steiner's contribution all the more significant is the fact that the modern discoveries confirm his observations by going beyond them, in some instances making clear what he still left somewhat tentative or obscure. Things which might seem strained when Steiner presented them to his audience early this century actually became more lucid. One might well, for instance, have questioned the identity of the two 'youths' in Mark. And what to make of Steiner's idea that he represents the 'cosmic impulse' of the Christ? It is only in the light of texts such as the secret Mark and *Trimorphic Protennoia* from early esoteric Christianity that his view becomes fully articulate and so all the more convincing.

If the youth represents the 'cosmic impulse' of Christ, for example, we had to admit that Steiner left it completely unclear why the Imagination of the 'impulse' should take the form of a white-robed youth. A certain confirmation was derived from the reappearance of the youth in the *Shepherd* where he leads Hermas into the world of cosmic visions and expounds their meaning. But the real key to the mystery which Steiner had half unveiled only came with the discovery of the secret *Mark* — the suppressed esoteric part of the original Gospel. For there we met the youth whom Jesus initiated into the secrets of the kingdom of the heavens. And he came to Jesus at night wearing only a linen cloth, to be baptized into cosmic consciousness. He received the cosmic vision of Christ working through Jesus, we concluded. That came together with the evidence from Hermas, where the youth was even called the 'angel of *metanoia*,' of the initiatory 'transformation of mind.' And it explained fully at last why the cosmic Imagination took the shape of a baptizand, a naked figure in a white robe receiving knowledge of the heavenly secrets.

Our last chapter has enabled us to take the identification a stage further. For we recognized the story of the youth to be that of Lazarus. He was the rich youth who 'died' to the world and was reawakened, reborn through the presence of Jesus: he was also the 'Beloved Disciple,' the author of the Fourth Gospel, and the content of his cosmic initiation we discovered to be expressed in the famous Prologue, speaking of the pre-existent Christ-Word in the aeons of Life and Light, and of the Word taking flesh in earthly history. As Lazarus-John he is the conscious bearer of the cosmic revelation, and the interpreter of its earthly meaning. Through him, indeed, Christ was glorified.

So it is the Beloved Disciple, in his spiritual significance, who forms the basis of the cosmic Imagination. That must not, of course, be confused with his presence at certain parts of the story in his physical personality. It was his cosmic initiation by Jesus himself which created a new Imagination of Christ's spiritual energy: an Imagination that has appeared to Christian seers and prophets such as Mark and Hermas. And surely we have here the real meaning of that other mystery about the Beloved Disciple. Surely this is the spiritual truth behind the clumsy rumour that 'this disciple would never die.'

What Jesus actually said was:

> If I wish him to remain until I come back again, what is that to you?

The words are a reply to Peter, the leading figure among the Twelve. They occur in the visionary last scene of the Fourth Gospel. Outwardly it is a fishing expedition and a miracle, an impossible physical event. But the experience really has the quality of a dream-vision, and waking-up within the dream. The sea on which the disciples embark in the night seems to be the dark ocean into which the waking self abandons itself in sleep: the fishing miracle is the raising of unconscious secrets into the half-light of dream-consciousness. The 'significant number' 153 may have symbolic or cosmological meanings, and at any rate indicates the discovery of hidden knowledge. Jesus' appearance 'on the shore' and "as light was dawning' is extremely important. It indicates a change from the appearance 'on the water' described in the other Gospels. He now appears shining into sleep from the waking world.

The vision includes several disciples. The odd repetitions of the question-and-answer between Jesus and Peter still suggests dreamlike states (does this somehow counterbalance Peter's threefold betrayal?). The charge to Peter 'Shepherd my little sheep' confirms him as the guardian of the community. The additional presence of the Beloved Disciple, however, points to a parallel stream of Christianity, less a concern of the community than of individual vision; indeed the youth in the linen cloth, as we know, appears to those who through the crisis of their own inner development attain to spiritual awareness.

Such a Christianity cannot be organized, cannot be taken in hand by the guardians of the community. But nor does it, in the manner of radical Gnosticism, stand in contradiction to the community and its history. It is there, waiting for those who reach the necessary stage of spiritual individualization.

The Imagination of the youth in the linen cloth has made a remarkable reappearance through the insights of Rudolf Steiner. In his work the realization of the 'Johannine' individual, and above all, the nature of the community he needs and which he enriches, have been central themes. It is indeed ironic that Steiner has sometimes been branded an asocial, 'Gnostic' thinker. No one more strongly recognized the social value of individual insights, or saw more clearly that awakening to community does not contradict the transcendent spiritual value of the self. The 'Johannine' Imagination is a further development out of, but not away from, the community. It has indeed been 'waiting,' and it asks a question of us. It asks whether a certain stage of development has been reached in the development of mankind, making possible the selfconscious spiritual vision the Imagination represents. Even the recognition of its possibility is itself a beginning, in accordance with the Joannine formula 'The hour is coming and now is ...' The Imagination makes the link between human individualization and cosmic, universal process. That is, I believe, the central question for the Christianity of our time and the future.

Notes

Chapter 1

1 By Dibelius. Attention was first drawn to the theme of the 'Messianic secret' in Mark by W. Wrede. Recent commentators have become rather more open to the esoteric implications, notably in the case of W.R. Telford, *The Theology of the Gospel of Mark* Cambridge 1999, who makes the exciting proposal that the 'secret' of the Kingdom is none other than that Jesus is the Son of God. It was not possible to make this idea directly intelligible to ordinary readers, he says, and therefore it was necessary that 'Mark had to present his epiphany Christology as a secret for the initiated' (p.203).

2 E. Käsemann, *The Testament of Jesus*, London 1968, p. 6. The idea of a Gnostic background to the Gospel of John was also important to Rudolf Bultmann. A more recent scholar who finds the Gospel so different from mainstream Christianity that he speaks of a distinctive 'Johannine sect' is Wayne Meeks; cf. his 'The Man from Heaven in Johannine Sectarianism,' in J. Ashton, *The Interpretation of John* (London and Philadelphia 1986).

3 See in particular Oscar Cullmann, *The Johannine Circle*, London 1976, pp. 80ff, 89ff and the emphasis on 'the esoteric element in Late Judaism and early Christianity' in J. Jeremias, *The Eucharistic Words of Jesus* (London 1966) pp.125-137;

Jeremias' approach to the priestly secrets of the liturgy has even been rather sweepingly extended by M. Barker, *The Great High Priest*, London 2003.

4 Matthew 11:27; Luke's version is at Luke 10:22. Other passages in the Synoptics important for 'esoteric' teaching are: Matthew 9:35–10:40; Mark 6:7–11; 8:31–3; 9:30–50; 10:32–45; 13:5–23, 26–7; 14:18–21, 26–31; Luke 9:1–6; 10:1–16; 12:2–12.

5 W. Schmithals, *Gnosticism in Corinth*, New York 1971, pp. 151–2.

6 2 Corinthians 12:2–4. In the Pauline literature 'Mystery' terminology occurs strikingly e.g. at: Ephesians 1:13; 6:19; Colossians 1:28; 4:3.

7 *Mishnah Hagigah* ii:1. A detailed study of the 'Heavenly Mysteries' and the esoteric tradition in Rabbinic Judaism is C. Rowland, *The Open Heaven*, London 1982.

8 I. Gruenwald, *Apocalyptic and Merkavah Mysticism*, Leiden 1980, pp. 86ff.

9 Plutarch, *Life of Alexander*, trans. I. Scott-Kilvert in *The Age of Alexander*, Harmondsworth 1973, p. 259.

10 Apuleius, *Metamorphoses or The Golden Ass* XI:23. See the interesting discussion of these experiences in Rudolf Steiner, *Mysteries of the East and Christianity*, London 1972. A very useful anthology of evidences from the ancient cults is presented now (with illuminating comments) by

M.W. Meyer, *The Ancient Mysteries. A Sourcebook,* San Francisco 1987. For some insight into the inner reality of the experiences of the initiates, see now Steiner's wide-ranging descriptions in Welburn (ed.), *The Mysteries. Rudolf Steiner's Writings on Spiritual Initiation,* Edinburgh 1997.

An objection used to be brought against the idea of Mystery-influence on early Christianity, namely that the pagan Mysteries, oracles, and so on, were in decline at the very period they would have needed to exert vigorous influence (cf. Plutarch's *Decline of the Oracles* and other works). Now however it has been shown that the first two Christian centuries saw also an upsurge of pagan religious activity: R. Lane Fox, *Pagans and Christians,* Harmondsworth 1986, pp. 27–261. There is much valuable information in Walter Burkert, *Ancient Mystery Cults,* Harvard and London 1987.

Chapter 2

1 1 QS XI,5-9 in G. Vermes, *The Complete Dead Sea Scrolls in English,* Harmondsworth 1998. The standard system of references is based on a 'Q' number, i.e. that of the particular cave at the site where a document was found (here Cave 1), and a letter which is an abbreviation of its Hebrew title (here 'S' = *Serek,* 'Rule'); this is followed by page or other division (such as columns), and line numbers. A very few texts are in Aramaic, indicated by 'Ar.' Vermes' translation is still good overall, and the latest edition finally fills out the collection of recently recov-

ered texts. In the last decades discoveries, publications and decipherments of previously unreadable material continue to be made, although the process of making them available to wider scholarship has often seemed to be bogged down. Many of the more recent, with text and translation, were usefully presented in R. Eisenman and M. Wise, *The Dead Sea Scrolls Uncovered,* Shaftesbury, Rockport and Brisbane 1992. A broader presentation of Essenism, with full commentary especially on the crucial personal and poetic texts ascribed to the leader of the Essenes, or Teacher of Righteousness, is made in my *Gnosis. The Mysteries and Christianity: An Anthology of Essene, Gnostic and Christian Writings,* Edinburgh 1994, pp.43-117; for more on this passage see there, pp.46-7. A major event is the publication of the 'Essene Bible': or more properly M. Abegg, P. Flint and C. Ulrich (ed. and trans.), *The Dea Sea Scrolls Bible,* Edinburgh 1999. For various front-line views on the background and understanding of the Qumran discovery, see L.H. Schiffman (ed.), *Archaeology and History of the Dead Sea Scrolls,* Sheffield 1990.

It is quite legitimate to refer to the content of Essenism as a *gnosis,* a divine knowledge. On the role played by such knowledge in Essene thought, see the comments of Devorah Dimant in M.E. Stone (ed.), *Jewish Writings of the Second Temple Period,* Assen and Philadelphia 1984, p. 538 – and generally pp. 483ff for an introduction to the Qumran writings. *Gnosis* is understood by the Essenes, however, against the background of biblical tradition; *gnosis* becomes Gnosticism when it assumes absolutely central place in the religious mind, overturning or radically revaluing former traditions.

2 The change in perspective was completed by the impressive work of Martin Hengel, *Judaism and Hellenism*, London 1974, which shows in massively documented detail the extent of the penetration of Greek and Graeco-Oriental thought and mysticism into the Judaism of the time between the Old and New Testaments, of which Essenism (I, pp. 218–247) is a significant part.

3 The entire set of codices is translated and published, ed. J.M. Robinson, *The Nag Hammadi Library*, Leiden, New York, Copenhagen and Cologne 1996. Several of them have also been included with the New Testament apocrypha, see n9 below. In addition many of the Nag Hammadi texts, with other Gnostic materials, are published albeit in a sometimes tendentious form in Bentley Layton, *The Gnostic Scriptures*, London 1987. (As an example of what I mean by tendentious, the term 'Scriptures' in the title will suggest to many people that in Gnostic circles these writings formed the heretical equivalent to the Bible or New Testament; yet there is no evidence at all that they ever formed the Scripture of any group or groups in this way. In the early stages, Christianity had not yet decided on the canon of sacred books; later on, when heretical groups of Gnostic type tried to asert their claim against the 'Great Church,' it was by giving an eso-

teric interpretation e.g. of the authoritative letters of Paul, or the Gospels such as the Gospel of Luke.)

The best introduction to Gnosticism, and to the Nag Hammadi Library discovery in particular is probably still Kurt Rudolph, *Gnosticism*, Edinburgh 1984; interesting wider perspectives and clear presentation also in G. Filoramo, *A History of Gnosticism*, Oxford and Massachusetts 1990. Still exciting and crammed with fascinating information is the book by the scholar on-the-spot when the codex was found: Jean Doresse, *Secret Books of the Egyptian Gnostics*, New York 1960. From the numerous more up-to-date contributions, especially the many of them devoted to understanding the relevance of the codices to the major religious and historical issues of early Christianity, we may perhaps single out: C.M. Tuckett, *Nag Hammadi and the Gospel Tradition*, Edinburgh 1986; Majella Franzmannn, *Jesus in the Nag Hammadi Writings*, Edinburgh 1996; A.H.B. Logan, *Gnostic Truth and Christian Heresy*, Edinburgh 1996.

4 Helmut Koester, in *The Nag Hammadi Library* p.125; and see now Koester's extended consideration of the Gospel and its 'esoteric theology' in his *Ancient Christian Gospels*, London and Philadelphia 1990, pp.84-128. Koester's whole book is in general an exciting attempt to integrate our knowledge of the apocryphal and orthodox traditions, even though it sometimes creates a tangle of historical and hypothetical, discussing newly discovered real documents

alongside the products of scholarly guesswork such 'proto-Mark' or the famous made-up source-document 'Q.' Nowadays there are a number of useful guides to *Thomas* in particular, such as S. Davies, *The Gospel of Thomas*. Annotated and Explained, London 2002; still useful and informative in many details is R.M. Grant and D.N. Freedman, *The Secret Sayings of Jesus*, London 1960. The *Gospel* together with other apocrypha is included in the helpful paperback collection ed. R. Cameron, *The Other Gospels, Introductions and Translations*, Philadelphia 1982. The case for the independent witness to Jesus' sayings in the *Secret Book of James* has been made in depth by Ron Cameron. It is used to provide support for Koester's similar conclusion, drawing connections especially to the Fourth Gospel, that 'its sayings are not drawn from several written gospels ... but represent an earlier stage of the development of the sayings tradition' — a stage which must be "presupposed for the composition and writing of the dialogues and discourses of the Gospel of John': *Ancient Christian Gospels*, p.200 (and generally pp.187ff).

5 Steiner, *Building Stones for an Understanding of the Mystery of Golgotha*, London 1972, p. 18.

6 *Gospel of Thomas* Saying 13. Different editions of the *Gospel* have numbered the Sayings (*logoi*) in different ways; we follow the system in *The Nag Hammadi Library in English*. The teaching in question was probably an esoteric exposition of Isaiah 28:10: see Grant and Freedman, *Secret Sayings of Jesus* p. 127.

7 The older edition of these works by R.H. Charles has now been definitively replaced by the two volumes ed. J.H. Charlesworth, *The Old Testament, Pseudepigrapha*. Vol I, *Apocalyptic Literature and Testaments*, London 1983; Vol II, *Expansions of the Old Testament, Wisdom, Philosophical and Poetic Literature*, London 1985.

An important commentary on many of the apocrypha and pseudepigrapha is to be found in M.E. Stone et al., *Jewish Writings of the Second Temple Period* (vol. II of the series *Compendia Rerum Iudaicarum ad Novum Testamentum*, Section 2), Assen and Philadelphia 1984.

8 C.H. Dodd, *The Interpretation of the Fourth Gospel*, Cambridge 1953, p. 449.

9 See Grant and Freedman, *Secret Sayings of Jesus* pp. 25–7.

The indispensable larger collection of New Testament apocrypha, including many from Nag Hammadi, with detailed studies of their bearing and the tradition behind them, is W. Schneemelcher (ed.), *New Testament Apocrypha*. vol. I: *Gospels and Related Writings*, London 1991; vol.II: *Writings Related to the Apostles*, London 1992. It might be said that, despite the inclusion of new materials and revised introductions and commentary, the volumes nevertheless now represent a rather conservative viewpoint on the history and development of early Christianity.

10 Clement, *Outlines*, in Hennecke-Schneemelcher, *New Testament Apocrypha* vol II (1965 ed.) pp.80, 82. And cf. the remarks in Rudolf Steiner, *The Fifth Gospel*, London 1978, pp.158-60.

11 Steiner, *Christianity as Mystical Fact*, London 1972, p. 131.

12 See Walter Bauer, *Orthodoxy and Heresy in Earliest Christianity*, London 1972. This has recently been confirmed, e.g. by Helmut Koester, *Introduction to the New Testament*, Berlin and New York 1982, II, p. 94: the 'expansion of Christianity in the first years and decades after the death of Jesus was a phenomenon that utterly lacked unity. On the contrary, great variety resulted from these early missions.' Cf. pp. 164ff. The diversity of approaches and 'titles' of Jesus in the formative period is decisive evidence against the notion, recently popularized by Sheehan, that after his death Jesus was systematically propagandized as the Son of God and made into something he had never claimed. If that had been the case, we would expect one or two definite concepts of Jesus' divinity to have been at the root of all further development. But that we do not find at all. Rather there was a widespread sense of the overwhelming, 'divine' manifestation through Jesus and the events of his life and death, even of their 'cosmic' significance, but no clear single basis for understanding them until very much later.

13 See M. Hornschuh, 'The Apostles as Bearers of the Tradition', in Hennecke-Schneemelcher, *New Testament Apocrypha*, II, pp. 78–87. Also very valuable is J. Daniélou, 'Les traditions secrètes des Apôtres', in *Eranos Jahrbuch* 31 (1962), pp. 199–215.

14 Colin Wilson, *Rudolf Steiner. The Man and his Vision*, Wellingborough 1985, pp. 114–6. It is unfortunate that Wilson wants to put the accuracy of Steiner's claims to the test using material relating to Arthur and Tintagel. He rejects Steiner's view in favour of what 'in fact' happened there. However, versions of the 'historical' Arthur and his links with specific places command no common agreement among historians.

Good introductions to Steiner are still regrettably few, at least in English. Still very valuable is A.P. Shepherd, *A Scientist of the Invisible. Introduction to the Life and Work of Rudolf Steiner* (repr. Edinburgh 1983); or more recently, Rudi Lissau, *Rudolf Steiner. Life, Work, Inner Path and Social Initiatives*, Stroud 1987. An excellent introductory anthology is R.A. McDermott (ed.), *The Essential Steiner*, New York 1984.

Steiner's main books and lecture-cycles on Christianity will be referred to below. Courses on many aspects of his work are provided by the Anthroposophical Society, which has branches in most countries.

15 The view represented e.g. by the *Pelican History of Christianity*. Even stranger and more completely unfounded accounts of Steiner's philosophy are encountered in standard reference-works, even those whose general standard is high. The *Oxford Companion to German Literature* shows that in Steiner's case Professor Garland was unable to maintain the common level of bibliographical competence! Nor does there seem to be in his article even the wish to be precise and factual. A curious circular situation means that nearly all serious accounts of Steiner are by 'insiders'; but one can hardly be criticised for referring only to

these when 'outside' accounts are so badly informed, crude and lacking in intellectual courtesy. The situation is less vicious than sad. How does it come about, for instance, that a profound student of religion like Mircea Eliade declines to attach any importance to Anthroposophy, contrasting it with the 'initiatory' form of Freemasonry, which he supposes to be the only modern initiation-knowledge to achieve 'social reality'? The network of social Freemasonry is indeed wide. But the quiet, generally unobtrusive work of Anthroposophy in education, medicine, agriculture and other fields shows a social awareness that penetrates far deeper and, at least in the present century, has been productive of much more far-reaching results.

16 Steiner, *Building Stones for an Understanding of the Mystery of Golgotha* p. 19.

17 Owen Barfield, *Saving the Appearances. A Study in Idolatry*, New York 1965, is a very demanding but comparably rewarding sketch of a radical new approach to meaning, science and the history of consciousness. Nor does it lack a treatment of the explicitly theological dimension (pp. 156ff).

Theological and historical work on Christianity undertaken by Steiner's followers will also be mentioned in notes to the present book. Many come from the circles of The Christian Community, a Movement for Religious Renewal which looked to Steiner from its foundation in 1922 by Friedrich Rittelmeyer. The Christian Community now has churches or communities in many countries.

Chapter 3

1 A. Caquot, 'Pour une étude de l'initiation dans l'ancien Israel,' in C.J. Bleeker (ed.), *Initiation*, Leiden 1965, p. 121.

See in general: I. Engnell, *Studies in Divine Kingship in the Ancient Near East*, Uppsala 1943; H. Frankfort, *Kingship and the Gods*, Chicago 1948; A.R. Johnson, *Sacral Kingship in Ancient Israel*, Cardiff 1955; detailed studies in several languages by many scholars are assembled in *La Regalità Sacra/The Sacral Kingship*, published as a supplement to the journal *Numen*, Leiden 1959.

2 Cited by F.H. Borsch, *The Son of Man in Myth and History*, London 1967, pp. 97–8.

3 F.H. Borsch, op. cit. p. 110. The fullest study of the Psalms from this point of view is that of S. Mowinckel, *The Psalms in Israel's Worship*, 2 vols., Oxford 1962.

4 Cf. the interesting study of J. Morgenstern, 'The King-God among the Western Semites,' in the journal *Vetus Testamentum* 10 (1960), 138ff; Rudolf Steiner, *Die Tempellegende und die Goldene Legende* Dornach 1979.

5 See, for a general perspective: R. Steiner, *The Evolution of Consciousness*, London 1966 and *World History*, London 1977; also Owen Barfield, *Saving the Appearances*, New York 1965.

6 Jeremiah 1:4. On the nature of the *nabiim* of Israel, see Steiner, *Gospel of Mark*, New York and London 1986, pp.25ff.

7 Steiner, *Ancient Myths and their Connection with Evolution*, Toronto 1971, p. 33. Steiner adopts a view of the Old Testament closer to that of the Jewish tradition, with its empha-

sis on *torah*, than the more radical (modern) view of it as salvation-history. For a strong criticism of the modern approach, see G. Fohrer, *Theologische Grundstrukturen des Alten Testaments*, Berlin 1972 pp. 42ff.

8 See Steiner, *The Gospel of Mark* pp. 44ff.

9 *Testament of Levi* 8:3–10.

10 The Essenes, and the Jewish 'Hasidim' in general, certainly supported the Maccabees at the time of the revolt against the Seleucids and their supporters in Israel. Some scholars believe, however, that the Essenes quickly turned against the Hasmonaeans, basing their conclusions on an interpretation of the date of the Teacher of Righteousness and the 'Wicked Priest' at around 150 BC. The presence of the *Testament of Levi* at Qumran in this situation, however, becomes virtually impossible to explain. The results of Steiner's spiritual-scientific researches, on the other hand, favour a date nearer 100 BC for the Teacher of Righteousness. If the Essenes continued to support the Hasmonaean priest-kings for some considerable time, down to the period of Alexander Jannaeus (103–76 BC), the discovery of the *Testaments* at Qumran is natural and points to the connection.

Steiner referred to the activity of a great Essene teacher around 100 BC. In view of the increasing support for this as the date of the Teacher of Righteousness referred to in the 'Scrolls,' of course, the Essene writings come into much closer proximity with Christian origins than on the previously popular 'Maccabaean' view: on the whole question, covering historical sources and the statements of Rudolf Steiner, see further my *Gnosis. The Mysteries and Christianity* pp.52–58. In particular, Steiner said that the content of the Teacher's ideas was written down in the form of a description of the rituals contained in the ancient Mystery-scripts (Steiner, *Esoteric Christianity*. 13 lectures given 1911–12, London 1984, p114). This description is, I take it, now extant thanks to the Qumran discovery. It is the *Community Rule*, dated by Vermes to around 100 BC. J.T. Milik proposes that the oldest form of the document goes back to the Teacher of Righteousness; others such as D.C. Allison think that only one or some few parts of it go back to him. In its surviving form it contains: a description of the process of initiation into the Essene sect (I–IV); the "Rule" of the community proper (V–IX); further material including the Hymn (X–XI) which was recited by the initiates. See D. Dimant, in Stone et al., *Jewish Literature of the Second Temple Period*, pp.497–502, esp. p.501 n86 and p.502 n92. See also Vermes, pp.61–80.

11 'Iamblichus,' *De Mysteriis* III, 7. (The author's identity with the Neoplatonic philosopher Iamblichus is highly uncertain.)

For the Essenes, see T.H. Gaster, *The Scriptures of the Dead Sea Sect*, London 1957 pp. 30–31. On the Mandaeans, see Lady E.S. Drower, *The Mandaeans of Iraq and Iran*, Oxford 1937. At the time I write, it must unfortunately be said that most remaining Mandaeans may have vanished, casualties of persecution in Iran and the Iran-Iraq war. The central Mandaean mystery-text is presented in Welburn, *Gnosis. The Mysteries and Christianity* pp.31-41.

For the rise of the baptizing sects, see J. Thomas, *Le mouvement baptiste en Palestine et Syrie*, Gembloux 1935; Borsch, *Son of Man in Myth and History* pp. 199ff.

12 The view of such scholars as Böhlig, Widengren, Rudolph, and so on. Cf. Steiner, *The Gospel of Matthew*, London 1965.

13 Lindsay, *The Origins of Alchemy*, London 1970. The ancient references to legends of Zoroaster and his reappearances, from Greek and Latin writers (with an important section on Syriac legends) were collected by J. Bidez and F. Cumont, *Les Mages Hellénisés*, Paris 1937–8; repr. 1973.

See further my article, 'Iranian Prophetology and the Birth of the Messiah: the *Apocalypse of Adam*' inW. Haase and H. Temporini (eds.), *Aufstieg und Niedergang der römischen Welt*, Part II, vol.25.4, Berlin and New York 1988, pp.4752–4794.

14 A. Böhlig, 'Jüdisches und Iranisches in der Adamapokalypse des Codex V von Nag Hammadi,' in his *Mysterion und Wahrheit*, Leiden 1968. For full details and identification of the traditions behind each of the incarnations, see now Welburn, *The Book with Fourteen Seals. The Prophet Zarathustra and the Christ-Revelation*, London 1991; shorter commentary on the *Apocalypse of Adam* in: Welburn, *Gnosis. The Mysteries and Christianity* pp.211-233.

15 The theory advanced by R.C. Zaehner, *Zurvan, A Zoroastrian Dilemma*, Oxford 1955, about the place of Zurvan in Iranian religious history remains controversial. Zervanite teachings are admitted to be present from the sixth century BC onward however by all researchers. Cf. Steiner, *Gospel of Matthew* pp. 35ff. He seems to regard Zervanism as an 'esoteric' teaching within Zoroastrianism, rather than as an alternative church. Some such view is held, for instance by R.N. Frye and by M. Boyce.

16 1 QS III,13-14,1. To some scholars it looks as though the connection must be one of literal familiarity with at least one of the Zoroastrians' sacred texts, their liturgy or *Yasna* which incorporates words of Zarathustra himself. 'There are so many parallels that this Iranian-Zoroastrian writing, which is very much older, must have served as the foundation for the Qumran text:' so writes H. Burgmann, *Die essenischen Gemeinden von Qumran und Damaskus*, Frankfurt-am-Main 1988, p.22. In general terms, the connection with Iranian teaching was first made by K.G. Kuhn, and has been generally accepted: see in particular the remarks of Hengel, *Judaism and Hellenism* I, pp. 228ff; D.S. Russell, *The Method and Message of Jewish Apocalyptic*, London 1964 pp. 257ff.

Chapter 4

1 Rudolf Steiner on Jesus and the Essene order: see his *The Fifth Gospel*, London 1968 pp. 75–6. His admiration for Hillel, id. pp. 85ff; the story about Hillel

recounted there is to be found in the *Talmud, tractate Shabbat* 30b.

Jesus' hymn of thanksgiving: Matthew 11:25; Luke 10:21. Discussed by David Flusser in M.E. Stone (ed.), *Jewish Writings of the Second Temple Period*, Assen and Philadelphia 1984, pp. 566–7.

2 C.H.H. Scobie, 'John the Baptist,' in Matthew Black (ed.), *The Scrolls and Christianity*, London 1969, p. 58.

3 Steiner, *The Fifth Gospel* p. 77.

4 *Epistle of Barnabas* 18, in *Early Christian Writings* trans. M. Staniforth, Harmondsworth 1972 p. 217; cf. *Didache* 1 (p. 227). The impact of the Essenes on the earliest Christianity was brought out by Jean Daniélou in his *The Theology of Jewish Christianity*, London 1964.

5 R.M. Grant, *Gnosticism and Early Christianity*, New York 1966, p. 39. For those who know Grant's book, it might be added that my account of Gnosticism has somewhat more in common with his than might at first appear. The main difference is that I see a gradual process of separation and division based on developing, polarizing spiritual attitudes, whereas Grant views the split as a response to a single catastrophic event, namely the destruction of Jerusalem by the Romans.

6 See especially Steiner's lecture on *The Gospel of Matthew*, London and, for the distinction between Gnosticism and 'esoteric Christianity,' his *The Apocalypse of John*, London 1985, pp.25-6.

7 Synesius of Cyrene, cited by J. Doresse, *Secret Books of the Egyptian Gnostics*, New York 1960 pp. 298–9. Doresse supports the identification with Qumran; see also Hans Jonas, *The Gnostic Religion*, Boston 1963 pp. 307–8. The archaeological evidence on Qumran was published under the catchpenny title *The Search for Sodom and Gomorrah*, Kansas 1962.

8 Borsch, *The Son of Man in Myth and History* p. 99. See the study by G. Widengren, *The King and the Tree of Life in Ancient Near Eastern Religion*, Uppsala 1951. For the legend of Seth, see E.C. Quinn, *The Quest of Seth for the Oil of Life*, Chicago 1967.

9 1QS XI,7-9.

10 *Sacred Book of the Invisible Great Spirit* in the Nag Hammadi Library, Codex III 60:9–18 and 55:10–12. It should be noted that the *Sacred Book* bears an alternative title, *Gospel of the Egyptians*. It is not, however, the famous apocryphal Egyptian gospel, the fragments of which were occasionally mentioned by Rudolf Steiner.

11 The suggestion of C.J. Bleeker, 'The Egyptian Background of Gnosticism,' in U. Bianchi (ed.), *Le Origini dello Gnosticismo*, Leiden 1967 p. 235. Ptolemy II, called Philadelphus, reigned from 282 to 246 BC. The actual Hermetic texts we possess date from a time nearer the turn of the epoch, and many of them after it. Behind them, however, lies a complex process of 'translation,' both verbal and in terms of updated ideas, resulting in the writings of the *Corpus Hermeticum*: see now G. Fowden, *The Egyptian Hermes*, Cambridge 1986, pp. 45ff. For a reliable and well-annotated translation of the *Corpus Hermeticum*, and the Latin *Asclepius* or 'Initiatory Discourse,' see now B.

Copenhaver, *Hermetica*, Cambridge 1992.

The genuine Egyptian background of Hermetism has been increasingly established, notably by Fowden, Quispel and on the literary level above all by J.-P. Mahé, *Hermès en Haute-Égypte*, 2 vols, Quebec 1982 (e.g. locating the central passage of the *Asclepius* in the tradition of Egyptian prophecy: vol. II pp.68ff). There is at the same time a generally admitted overlay of Greek philosophy and features deriving strongly from Jewish liturgical poetry, as well as Jewish-Iranian apocalypticism and similar developments. For some earlier Egyptian Hermetica, that is, sacred books attributed to Thoth (not yet identified with Hermes in Greek terms), see E.A.E. Reymond, *From Ancient Egyptian Hermetic Writings*, Vienna 1977 — these are texts in demotic from the second and first centuries BC. I incline to the view given above, that from the time of Ptolemy II there were efforts made to develop Hermetic teaching in a new form, where Miss Reymond advances an alternative theory that there was a 'leak' from the secret archives of the Egyptian temples which led to the publication of Hermetica and their rendering into Greek. Reasons against this also have a bearing on Hermetism and Christianity: no trace of knowledge of the Hermetica appears in Philo or in Clement of Alexandria, indicating that the Hermetic writings remained restricted to closed circles of the initiated throughout the first and second centuries AD, being inaccessible even to those Jewish and Christian writers who would have been basically sympathetic to them. Later, the Hermetica became known exoterically, and were hailed as Christian prophecies from ancient Egypt, for instance, by Lactantius. The only earlier exception seems to be the more esoteric Christian tradition connected with Thomas and his *Gospel*, which shows the activity of the Hermetic Mysteries in an early form of Christian esotericism. See further chapter 10 below.

'New' Hermetic writings, that is, old ones long thought lost, were recently discovered in an Armenian translation. They are published with commentary by Mahé in Clement Salman *et al.*, *The Way of Hermes. The Corpus Hermeticum and the Definitions of Hermes*, London 1999, pp.101-124.

12 See *On the Eighth and Ninth*, in *The Nag Hammadi Library in English* pp. 292–7: discussed by Fowden, *The Egyptian Hermes* pp. 97ff; and fully by L.S. Keizer, *The Eighth Reveals the Ninth: a New Hermetic Initiation Discourse*, Seaside, California 1974. Closest to the new discourse among the traditional Hermetic writings is *Corpus Hermeticum* XIII, called *On Rebirth (De Regeneratione)*. For the call to *metanoia* in Hermetism, see *Corpus Hermeticum* I:28. The baptism is described in *Corpus Hermeticum* IV.
One tradition or stream in early Christianity which can be illumined by Hermetism is that of the Gospel of John – not because the Gospel was influenced by Hermetism (as the *Gospel of Thomas* seems to be), but because it is rooted in the esoteric-baptismal practices which the

Hermetists likewise adopted. For similarities, see C.H. Dodd, *The Interpretation of the Fourth Gospel*, Cambridge 1953 pp. 10–53.

13 *Corpus Hermeticum* I:15.

14 Daniélou, cited by S.J. Isser, *The Dositheans*, Leiden 1976, p. 198. The Samaritans accept the books of Moses, but not the rest of the Old Testament, nor did they admit the authenticity of the Temple in Jerusalem but worshipped God on Mount Gerizim in Samaria. A small number are still to be found today; at the time of Christ they still outnumbered the Jews, and when the Romans turned Palestine into a province of the Empire it was natural that their administrative centre should be in Samaria, rather than in the small and troublesome Temple-state of Judea to the south. Dosietheus and Simon introduced Gnostic ideas into Samaritanism, and when in later times numbers dwindled, orthodox and Gnostic Samarians pooled their resources, creating the odd mixture of Old Testament and Gnostic ideas which makes up present-day Samaritan teaching. See John Bowman, *The Samaritan Problem*, Pittsburgh 1975.

15 Simon of Gitta, *Great Annunciation* in Welburn, *Gnosis. The Mysteries and Christianity*, Edinburgh 1994, p.177.

16 The Diagram is described by Origen in his *Reply to Celsus (Contra Celsum)*, Book VI:24–38. For a reconstruction, see my article 'Reconstructing the Ophite Diagram' in the journal *Novum Testamentum* 23 (1981) 3:261–287.

17 See W. Schmithals, *Gnosticism in Corinth*, New York 1971. As an important trade-centre with sea and land links, Corinth was no doubt open to many new religious ideas coming from the East.

In my commentary on Simon, I have stressed that his scheme does not contain the idea of an incarnate Redeemer-figure or unique, historical Saviour as in Christianity. Human beings are saved *from* the world by the knowledge of which Simon is the mouthpiece. Although Schmithals' is right to speak of a 'Messiah-' or 'Christ-Gnosticism' — see his Introduction, pp.36ff, we still do not have to do with a conception of the Messiah taking on of the material condition, but rather of a revelatory dynamic in which he unites with those who can awaken in response to his prophet's 'annuciation' of his eternal being (hence the formula 'which stood, stands, and will stand'). The underlying was universalistic and cyclical in the oriental manner. Human beings take part in a cosmic drama — the very same cosmic drama, it seems, which Christianity sees transposed into earthly history. See further: *Gnosis. The Mysteries and Christianity* pp.149ff.

Chapter 5

1 Rudolf Steiner, *The Gospel of Matthew* pp. 81–2; *Babylonian Talmud*, tractate *Shabbat* 116a–b.

2 See C.U. Wolf, 'The Gospel of the Essenes,' in the journal *Biblical Research* 3 (1958), 28ff. H. Burgmann, *Die essenischen Gemeinden*, has concluded that the evangelist Matthew must have been a former Essene — and see further below. Recent scholars have wondered whether Matthew's community was already really separate from the

Jewish community, or rather just comprised those of them who accepted Jesus' messianic claim: D. Sim, *The Gospel of Matthew and Christian Judaism*, Edinburgh 1998.

3 1 QS V,24–VI,1.

4 Matthew 5:43-5; cf. 1 QS I,9-10. For detailed similarities e.g. in the techniques of biblical interpretation between Matthew and Qumran, see Krister Stendahl, *The School of St. Matthew*, Uppsala 1968 especially pp. 35ff. Helmut Koester, *Introduction to the New Testament*, II, Berlin and New York 1987 p. 175 agrees that one must speak of a school and that 'Matthew is not isolated in this learned activity.' Awareness of such elaborate literary background lends new weight, I think, to the studies investigating the structure and rhythms of the gospel: see in particular Christoph Rau, *Das Matthäusevangelium*, Stuttgart 1976. For Steiner on the Essene background, see *The Gospel of Matthew* pp. 93ff.

5 4Q MessAr; cf. Martin Hengel *Judaism and Hellenism*, I, pp. 237–8: 'One of the most valuable "products" of ancient astrology,' comments Hengel, 'was the horoscope of a wise "world ruler" expected in the future.' The horoscope of the royal Messiah was drawn up, it appears, in the late first century BC.

For Steiner's remarks on the early chapters of Matthew, see *The Gospel of Matthew* p. 111. For the background of the *Genesis Apocryphon* in the Essene books *Jubilees and I Enoch*, with the views of J.A. Fitzmyer on the relation to Matthew, see G.W.E. Nickelsburg in M.E. Stone, *Jewish*

Writings of the Second Temple Period pp. 93–4.

6 Jerome, *On Famous Men* 3. Papias is quoted in Eusebius, *History of the Church* III, 39:16. Papias also solves the problem of the famous insertion into the Gospel of John, the story of the woman taken in adultery (following John 7:52). It is almost certainly Papias' story 'concerning the woman accused of many sins before the Lord, which is contained in the *Gospel of the Hebrews*' (III, 39:17). Following the suggestion of H. Waitz, we may place it in the original Hebrew Matthew between the verses 22:22 and 23 as they stand in our present Greek version.

The other evidence in the Fathers relating to the *Gospel of the Hebrews* may be found in Hennecke-Schneemelcher, *New Testament Apocrypha* vol. I, pp. 134-178, with the discussion by Vielhauer now revised by the noted expert on Jewish-Christianity, Georg Strecker, who still concludes however that 'it is not yet possible to fit these J(ewish-Christian) G(ospels) into place in the history of Jewish Christianity' (p.152). The evidence is extraordinarily hard to evaluate, but I cannot go along with Vielhauer's general approach. His attempt to distinguish three separate Jewish-Christian gospels can hardly be regarded as successful. Rather, we probably have to do with successive versions of the same original, one of whose descendants is of course our canonical Matthew. By the fourth century AD, it seems that some Jewish Christians had gone over to a Greek text, referred to by

Epiphanius, but that this Greek edition still contained esoteric matter not in our canonical Matthew. Vielhauer's attempt to separate off the esoteric ('syncretistic,' 'heterodox') material from the work which was closely related to Matthew serves an obvious tendentious purpose, but expressly contradicts the evidence, for instance, of Jerome in the passage we have cited. If Strecker throws up his hands, Koester decides to dodge the issue altogether, and simply says he is omitting to deal with what he admits are 'such important writings as the Jewish-Christian Gospels,' for once accepting uncritically the older view that they are a patchwork from orthodox sources, the kind of approach which he elsewhere so vehemently challenges: *Ancient Christian Gospels* p.xxxi.

However difficult the problems, we should critically follow those who have tried to grapple with them, from which there have certainly been interesting results. Jerome's account of Matthew's approach to the Hebrew Old Testament was supported by R.H. Gundry, *The Use of the Old Testament in St. Matthew's Gospel*, Leiden 1967 who argues that the citations 'can be traced back ultimately to the Apostle Matthew who was his own targumist and drew on his knowledge of Hebrew, Aramaic and Greek textual traditions of the Old Testament.' *Targum* = 'a translation of the Hebrew Bible into the Aramaic language for liturgical use in the synagogue.' Such considerations already led P. Gaechter, *Die literarische Kunst im Matthäusevangelium*, Stuttgart

1965 to the conclusion that the Gospel was written by the apostle in Hebrew.

7 For Steiner's remark, see his *From Jesus to Christ*, London 1973, p. 76; Jerome, *Dialogue against Pelagius*, 2 (where the implication seems rather to be that the Gospel *was* written in Aramaic!). On the Hebrew of the original Gospel, see the article by D. Flusser and M. Lowe in the journal *New Testament Studies* 29 (1983) 1, 25–47.

For the text from *Even Bohan* ('The Touchstone'), see G. Howard, *The Gospel of Matthew according to a Primitive Hebrew Text*, Macon, Georgia 1987, which includes a complete translation of the Hebrew and introductory discussion. Other aspects of the text are discussed in his article "A Primitive Hebrew Gospel of Matthew,' again in *New Testament Studies* 34 (1988) 1, 60–70 (e.g. the two forms of the name Jesus).

See note 1 above for the story of Gamaliel and his Gospel citation.

8 Matthew 4:1; *Gospel of the Hebrews* cited by Origen, Commentary on the Gospel of John II,12 (and see Schneemelcher, vol.I p.177.) For the 'ecstasy' cf. Ezekiel 8:3; Bel and the Dragon (= an apocryphal part of the Book of Daniel) 36.

9 Matthew 7:7 and 11:28–9; *Gospel of the Hebrews* cited by Clement of Alexandria, *Miscellanies* V, 14:96; cf. II, 9:45; *Gospel of Thomas* 2: see Schneemelcher, vol. I loc cit. Helmut Koester emphasises this quality in the received sayings and parables of Jesus about the 'Kingdom' (cf. 'reign'): 'In understanding all these parables

it is important to detect the particular element of surprise. This element appears especially in those features that do not correspond to the normal experiences of life. What sort of farmer does nothing at all during the entire growing season, or simply lets the weeds grow with the wheat? Or what kind of dignified father would run down the street joyfully to meet his misfit son ... The miracle, mystery, and incalculability of the coming of God's rule — these are the topics of the parables.' (*Introduction to the New Testament*, II, Berlin and New York 1987 p. 80.)

See further Chapter 10 below.

10 Steiner, *From Jesus to Christ*, p. 76.

11 Klijn, *Seth in Jewish, Christian and Gnostic Literature*, Leiden 1977 p. 28.

12 Widengren, *Iranisch-semitische Kulturbegegnung in parthischer Zeit*, Köln-Opladen 1960 pp. 62ff.

13 *Sacred Book of the Invisible Great Spirit*, in *The Nag Hammadi Library* p.218. The legends of the Magi as they were written down in later Christian circles were studied by G. Messina, who concluded the fundamentals were already present as the background of Matthew's Gospel and its view of Jesus' miraculous origin. 'He sees the possible origins of the whole idea' — including the virgin birth — 'in the doctrine of the Avesta concerning the expectation of the Saošyant, a son to be born after Zoroaster's death ... This salvific figure was to raise the dead and crush the forces of evil. However,' objects R.E. Brown in his comprehensive study of the Gospel infancy stories *The Birth of the Messiah* (London and New York 1978) pp.168–9, 'there is no

evidence that Christians in Matthew's time knew of this expectation.' That is no longer true, or at least the early dating of the *Apocalypse of Adam* is now increasingly accepted: the influential scholar H.M. Schenke, for example, originally sceptical, is now inclined to accept its pre-Christian origins. I have pointed to further connections between its contents and the Gospel of Matthew in *The Book with Fourteen Seals* pp.166ff.

14 *Gospel of the Hebrews* cited by Sedulius Scotus, *Commentary* on the *Gospel of Matthew*: in Hennecke-Schneemelcher, vol. I p.163.

15 On Mithraism, see now R. Merkelback, *Mithras*, Königstein 1984. Also Steiner, *Building Stones for an Understanding of the Mystery of Golgotha*, London 1972 pp. 188ff.

Important in this connection are the specific Mithraic elements in the *Apocalypse of Adam* pointed out by Böhlig. See also the brilliant article by G. Widengren, 'The Sacral Kingship of Iran' in *La Regalità Sacra*, a supplement to the journal *Numen*, Leiden 1959. More generally on the resemblances and connections between Mithraism and the baptizing groups of Syria-Palestine, cf. Borsch, *Son of Man in Myth and History* pp. 81ff. And see chapter 10 below.

Connections between the Gospel of Matthew and Mithraism/Zoroastrianism are noted by R.E. Osborne, 'The Provenance of Matthew's Gospel' in the journal *Studies in Religion* 3 (1973), pp. 22–25.

16 Steiner, *From Jesus to Christ* p. 78.

17 Epistle of James 2:5; cf. Matthew 5:3.

18 Epiphanius, *Refutation of All Heresies* XXX, 16; XXX, 3.

19 Daniélou, *The Theology of Jewish Christianity* p. 57.

20 Cullmann, *The Christology of the New Testament*, London 1975 p. 40.

21 *Gospel of the Hebrews* cited by Jerome, *Commentary on Isaiah*, IV. The passage must have followed upon our present Matthew 3:17.

22 The fact that, as Cullmann points out, the understanding of Christ's work in terms of prophethood was abandoned by later Christianity means neither that it is not present in New Testament writings nor that its consequences are necessarily heretical, to be set in contrast to an 'incarnational' theology. A view of Jesus the Prophet is contained, for example, in the Gospel of John. See Cullmann, *Christology of the New Testament* pp. 13–50.

23 A. Bentzen, *King and Messiah*, London 1955 p. 79.

24 Mary Boyce, *Zoroastrians*, London 1980 p. 99.

Chapter 6

1 *Didache*, in *Early Christian Writings* pp. 230–31. The Mandaeans and many other Gnostic and esoteric groups demanded 'living' water, which also features significantly in the Gospel of John.

2 The Essene initiates with their baptismal rites already felt that they received from God the gift of his Holy Spirit: indeed God has set each one apart as by leading him into the Community through special ritual and inner processes, 'purifying him with a Spirit of Holiness from all deeds of evil. And He will sprinkle upon him a Spirit of Truth like waters of purification' (1 QS 4,20-21); and many times the Teacher of Righteousness speaks of the grace of receiving God's Holy Spirit. Such ideas seem to continue in early Christianity, and particularly as we now know in writings that speak with special reverence of James, the 'brother of the Lord' (for a comprehensive study emphasising the Jewish background and Dead Sea Scrolls material, see: R. Eisenman, *James*, London 2002). The *Secret Book of James* from Nag Hammadi talks of becoming a 'son of the Holy Spirit' through baptism: see *The Nag Hammadi Library* p.32. This writing came from circles which regarded James as guardian of their secret tradition, and which preserved as part of it a tradition of Jesus' sayings in an independent form, with a radical interpretation stressing the difference between the earthly and the spiritual (post-resurrection) understandings of Christ. See above, Ch.2 n4.

3 *Dialogue of the Saviour* — in *The Nag Hammadi Library*: 'Truly, fear is the power (of darkness) ... So if you are going to be afraid of what is about to come upon you, it will swallow you up. ... For the place of crossing-over is fearful before you. But you with single mind, pass it by!' (p.247). For the laying-on of hands and cosmic visions, p.250.

4 *Paraphrase of Shem* in *The Nag Hammadi Library* pp.354-5. Such an experience of the 'swirling waters' is also mentioned among the Mandaeans. Are initiation experiences at the basis of the comparable scenes in the Gospels where Jesus passes

382 • *The Beginnings of Christianity*

undisturbed through raging storm, or 'walks on the water'? For an approach to the possibility of experiences in a changed state of consciousness, see now B. Malina, 'Assessing the Historicity of Jesus' Walking on Water,' in B. Chilton and C.A. Evans, *Autheticating the Activities of Jesus*, Leiden 1999, pp.351–371.

5 The Peratae, as reported by Hippolytus, *Refutation of Heresies* V, 17:6.

6 My remarks may seem unduly critical of a method which, like statistics in the physical sciences, holds many highly intelligent minds in thrall. Essentially a product of the nineteenth century's discovery of philology and an exaggerated confidence in its methods, the 'Synoptic Theory' has been endlessly refined to paper over the contradictions. Recently, it is pleasant to record, scholars have started to show greater awareness that different constructions can be put upon the literary relations studied by the theory. I do not intend to enter into argument with the theorists; I shall merely cite here the recognition by J.A. Fitzmyer, one of its acknowledge experts, that the 'synoptic problem' treated as a literary puzzle remains 'practically insoluble ... the data for its solution are scarcely adequate or available to us.' Fitzmyer, in *Jesus and Man's Hope*, Pittsburgh 1970 p. 132.

Since the synoptic theory cannot actually demonstrate the relationships it purports to deduce, it is time to adopt more historical criteria, and the new discoveries may at last be allowing us to see the Gospels in a realistic setting. Important historical changes in perspective that have come about in recent years include the re-evaluation of the Gospels' literary genre, which used to be held irrelevant to the self-contained 'synoptic' debate. See now R.A. Burridge, *What are the Gospels? A Comparison with Graeco-Roman Biography*, Cambridge 1992. Many have come to think that failure to understand the literary approach behind the Gospels led to the once almost universal dismissal of the earliest evidence about them, now once again understood as relevant. Papias of Hierapolis characterised Mark as employing *chreiae*, lit. 'things as needed' but in literary terminology really meaning short scenes or stories to make a significant point (often more or less 'anecdote'), and his criticism that the events were not told 'in order' can now be grasped as a literary comment about their lack of proper arrangement rather than a rejection of Mark's chronology. The original work on these 'rhetorical' terms by J. Kürzinger has flowered in many new commentaries, such as Ben Witherington III, *The Gospel of Mark. A Socio-Rhetorical Commentary*, Grand Rapids and Cambridge 2001, pp.9ff; C. Bryan, *A Preface to Mark. Notes on the Gospel in its Literary and Cultural Settings*, New York and Oxford 1993, pp.22ff. Questioning the usual scholarly account of the way the Gospels were composed, M. Goulder has argued with growing support in recent years that Luke knew Matthew's Gospel; see his technical and detailed *Luke: A New Paradigm*, Sheffield 1989. At the same time this approach removes Mark from its place as the supposed authoritative version for both later synoptic Gospels, and those such as myself wonder whether one should not simply see in Mark and Matthew two different developments from a body of oral tradition that already had some shape? One version went more in a gentile-Christian, the other in a Jewish-Christian direction.

7 Steiner, *Gospel of Mark* pp.188ff.

8 Cf. Bauer, *Orthodoxy and Heresy* pp. 44ff. The view is adopted to explain early Egyptian Christianity also by H. Koester, *Introduction to the New Testament*, II, pp. 219–39. Eusebius does give the 'information' that Mark became the first bishop of Alexandria, which cannot be true since the Alexandrian Church was ruled not by a bishop but a council of Elders until much later; and even then there is nothing to prompt Steiner's suggestion that Mark went there to write the Gospel. It is generally accepted that Eusebius had, as Harnack had put it, 'virtually nothing' from his sources about primitive Christianity in Alexandria. For what can be conjectured, see now the presentation by B.A. Pearson and E. Goehring (eds.), *The Roots of Egyptian Christianity*, Philadelphia 1986. The only traditional evidence which seems to link the Gospel with Alexandria comes from John Chrysostom, and that is virtually four hundred years too late. The early Church on the contrary made strenuous efforts to associate the composition of the Gospel, via the authority of Peter, with Rome. On that condition it was evidently accepted into the wider church. Clifton Black has shown in a richly documented

study how the picture of Mark was shaped by the demands for an 'apostolic' author in his *Mark: Images of an Apostolic Interpreter*, Edinburgh 2001.

9 The genuineness of the letter as coming from Clement of Alexandria has been widely accepted and established by the usual analytical techniques. The letter's claim to be preserving an original text of Mark, prior to that edited by the Church for the New Testament canon has provoked more resistance, but is also gaining ground. Thus M.W. Meyer admits: 'Recent studies of the Secret Gospel of Mark suggest that this edition ... in fact may antedate the edition received into the New Testament canon': Meyer, *The Ancient Mysteries*, New York 1987 p. 232; and see the studies cited there. Support for the primary character of the passage has also come from investigations by such careful scholars as R.H. Fuller, H. Koester, J.D. Crossan and others. For the text of the Gospel passage, see Welburn, *Gnosis: The Mysteries and Christianity* p.317 and restored to its original context, pp.327-333. The section from Clement's *Letter to Theodore* which includes the Gospel quotations but not the account of its authorship is given in Schneemelcher, *New Testament Apocrypha* vol.I pp.106-9; (there is moreover an important error in frag.1 v.10 where Jesus is said to teach the youth 'mysteries', whereas the text uses the more technical singular, 'the mystery'.) The letter is given, including the 'secret Gospel' extract in: M. Meyer, *The Ancient Mysteries. A Sourcebook*, San Francisco 1987, pp.232-4. See also Meyer's recent

Secret Gospels. Essays on Thomas and the Secret Gospel of Mark, Harrisburg 2003. As for its discoverer Morton Smith's extraordinary views, I have not tried to deal with them here, but rather to interpret the document from a different perspective.

One point deserves clarification, however, since it probably does conform to wider opinion. Smith (p. 142) takes the mention of a 'former book' to mean our canonical Mark, the original version, to which esoteric material was added in Alexandria. Yet it is clear from Clement that this 'book' consisted only of *notes* (literally 'memory-joggers'), presumably to help Mark in his oral preaching of the gospel message he learnt from Peter; Peter himself had evidently used similar notes. It is easier to suppose that Mark worked his earlier material up into a Gospel from such notes in Alexandria: (a) from the character of the Gospel, as we shall see below; and (b) because Smith has tortuously to argue that although the esoteric elements are authentic, and go back to a stage prior to our existing texts of both Mark and John (his chapter 7), they have actually been reintroduced from the original tradition into a Gospel identical with our canonical Mark, which thus occupies an improbably intermediate position, purged of esoteric elements between the primary esoteric tradition and the later esoteric 'expansion'. There is, finally, no real reason to invent an Aramaic original (Smith p. 142), since the language of Jews and Christians in Alexandria would almost certainly be Greek and the literary character of the Gospel of Mark is best seen in Greek terms; Alexandria in fact is the least probable place for pockets of devoted Aramaic speakers to flourish!

An over-complex theory of the relations between the supposed several versions of Mark still mars the otherwise fruitful approach, I feel, of Koester, *Ancient Christian Gospels* pp.293ff.

10 Richardson, cited in M. Smith, *The Secret Gospel*, Clearlake California 1982, p.64.

11 Basilides, reported by Hippolytus, *Refutation of Heresies* VII, 26:8. Cf. Steiner, *The Gospel of Mark* pp.17ff.

12 On the small vestiges of Egyptian-Christian writings, see Bauer, *Orthodoxy and Heresy* pp. 47–8; Koester, *Introduction* pp. 233ff.

13 Acts of the Apostles 18:24–19:7. Codex D adds the confirmatory information that Apollos had learnt his Christianity in his native land, that is, Alexandria. A detailed interpretation along our lines was developed by A. Ehrhardt, *The Acts of the Apostles*, Manchester 1969. He identifies the disciples of ch. 19 as Alexandrian Christians.

14 E.g. John 4:2.

15 Steiner, *Gospel of Mark* pp.175-6.

16 Steiner op. cit. p.174.

17 *Shepherd of Hermas: Visions* III, 10. On the Jewish-Christian nature of the work, see Daniélou, *Theology of Jewish Christianity* pp. 36–9. Essene elements are also recently stressed by L.W. Nijendijk, *Die Christologie des Hirten des Hermas*, esp. pp. 53–66. This need not rule out the possibility of Hermetic influence, originally suggested by Reitzenstein. Indeed, the *Shepherd* had been swayed by

several sources of visionary wisdom, notably the literature of the Sybils, as well. This might well suggest a connection to Jewish circles in Greek-speaking Egypt (near Alexandria), since that was where one layer of the Sibylline oracular literature (collected as Books III and V) originated: see J.J. Collins, *The Sibylline Oracles of Egyptian Judaism*, Missoula 1974.

18 Smith, *The Secret Gospel* pp. 16–17. I wonder whether Rudolf Steiner did not already develop his own ideas along these lines more fully in private, since his early pupil, the orientalist scholar H. Beckh remarkably extends the conception in Steiner of John the Baptist being important at the outset, adding that by the end we have not a John-mystery but a Lazarus-mystery: Beckh, *Der kosmische Rhythmus im Markusevangelium*, Stuttgart 1960 (orig. 1928) pp.49-52.

19 Smith, *The Secret Gospel* p. 108.

20 The good manuscripts of Mark end the Gospel (rightly) at 16:8. On the Gnostic fragmentation, see the brilliant essay on 'Gnosis and Time' by H.C. Puech, in J. Campbell (ed.), *Man and Time*, London and New York 1957.

21 From the Mandaean Gnostic book called *Treasure (Ginza)*, cited with discussion by Jonas, *The Gnostic Religion* p. 75.

22 Wolfgang Schenk, 'Die gnostisierende Deutung des Todes Jesu und ihre kritische Interpretation durch den Evangelisten Markus' in K.-W. Tröger (ed.), *Gnosis und Neues Testament*, Berlin 1973 pp. 231–243.

An interesting interpretation of Mark as a Gnostic document is also to be found in the article by J. Schreiber, 'Die Christologie des Markus-evangliums' in the journal *Zeitschrift für Theologie und Kirche* 58 (1961), pp. 154ff; but Schreiber uncritically assumes that Mark is simply reproducing a myth taken from pre-Christian Gnosticism.

Chapter 7

1 The best introductions to the period in general are: Tarn and Griffith, *Hellenistic Civilisation*, London 1966, and the stimulating: John Onians, *Art and Thought in the Hellenistic Age*, London 1979 also M. Hadas, *Hellenistic Culture*, New York 1972. For the religious situation, see the unusually sympathetic approach in: Luther H. Martin, *Hellenistic Religions*, Oxford 1987; Welburn (ed.), *The Mysteries. Rudolf Steiner's Writings on Spiritual Initiation*, Edinburgh 1997, pp.89ff.

2 *Gospel of Thomas* 13. Elaine Pagels, *The Gnostic Gospels*, London 1980 p. xxi.

3 See Günther Bornkamm, *Mythos und Legende in den Thomasakten*, Göttingen 1933; for the birth legends, see the very extensive presentation of parallels in Z.P. Thundy, *Buddha and Christ. Nativity Stories and Indian Traditions*, Leiden, New York and Cologne 1993, pp.75ff On the value of the stories concerning Jesus' childhood, see Emil Bock, *Kindheit und Jugend Jesu*, Stuttgart 1956.

4 Ashvaghosha, *Buddhacarita* ('Acts of the Buddha'), in Conze (ed.), *Buddhist Scriptures*, Harmondsworth 1969 pp. 35–6.

5 *Protevangelium* ('first gospel' or perhaps 'the gospel of Jesus' life') in Schneemelcher, *New*

386 • *The Beginnings of Christianity*

Testament Apocrypha, vol. I,
pp.421-439; discussion also in H.
Koester, *Ancient Christian
Gospels*, London and
Philadelphia 1990, pp.308-311.
The work goes back in essence to
around the year AD 150 and
apparently combines use of the
canonical narratives with oral
tradition, leading to the conclusion (so Cullmann in
Schneemelcher, p.423).

6 Oscar Cullmann in
Schneemelcher, op. cit. vol. I,
p.442. *The Infancy Gospel of
Thomas* (= pp.444–451) probably
goes back to the second century.
See also Koester, *Ancient
Christian Gospels* pp.311-314;
Thundy, pp.120-121.

7 Luke 22:61–2; contrast Mark
14:72; Matthew 26:74–5.

8 Vision in the Temple: Luke 1:11;
appearance to Mary, 1:28; vision
of Ananias, Acts of the Apostles
9:10–16; the three tellings of
Paul's vision on the way to
Damascus, 9:3–9; 22:6–13;
26:12–20. On 'seeing the gods' in
the Hellenistic and later period,
R. Lane Fox, *Pagans and
Christians*, Harmondsworth,
1986, esp. pp. 117ff.

9 P. Vielhauer in: Hennecke-
Schneemelcher, *New Testament
Apocrypha* vol. II (1965 ed.) p.606.
A striking example of the way
the process of 'remembering'the
tradition could deepen into clairvoyant experience is to be found
in the opening scene of the *Secret
Book of James*: 'The twelve disciples were all sitting together and
remembering what the Saviour
had said to each one of them,
whether in secret or openly, and
putting it into books. But while
I was writing that which was in
my book, behold, the Saviour
appeared .....': in Robinson (ed.),

The Nag Hammadi Library p.30.
The dialogue which follows contains materials like those of the
'farewell discourses' in the
Gospel of John, where the speaking presence of the Saviour may
well have been experienced in
the same visionary way.

The addressees of the *Secret
Book of James* who remember the
Saviour's words and see visions
are characterised as 'ministers of
salvation' (loc. cit.); Luke himself
uses the term 'minister'
(*hypéretés*) in various contexts in
his other book, the Acts, but specially notable is his reference to
John Mark (in Church tradition
assimilated to the future evangelist Mark) as such in Acts 13,5.
'In an oft-cited article ... B.T.
Holmes argued that the term
probably entailed the function of
looking after documents ...
R.O.P. Taylor proposed that
hypéretés in Acts 13:5 was func-
tionally equivalent to the
chazzan, the priestly assistant in
the cult of Palestinian and later
rabbinic Judaism' (cf. Luke 4,20)
so that he would have had
responsibility for 'teaching the
actual wording of the sacred
records, the exact and precise
statements of the facts and dicta
on which their religion was
based.' We may note also that
he appears as 'minister' in interesting company: 'Gathered at
Antioch, worshipping and fasting, are various prophets (*prophé-
tai*) and teachers (*didaskaloi*):
Barnabas etc.' (Acts 13,1-3) even
if John Mark is not specifically
numbered among them: Clifton
Black, *Mark* (Edinburgh 2001)
pp.31–2.

10 Hermes Trismegistus, fragment
of a discourse cited by Stobaeus,
Excerpt VI in Scott, *Hermetica*,

vol. I, p. 419. The 'images' in question are the so-called 'decans,' star-divinities which indeed held a place in the imagination of artists for many centuries, cf. Frances Yates, *Giordano Bruno and the Hermetic Tradition* London 1964 p. 45f. and the many references to 'decans' in the index.

On *autoptes and epoptes*, see Michael Psellus, *Exposition of the Chaldaean Oracles* in Migne, *Patrologia Graeca*, vol. CXXII, p. 1135 (no translation available). For the meaning of *autoptes*, cf. Rudolf Steiner, *The Gospel of Luke*, London 1964 pp. 25ff. The usage survived among the later Fathers in the term *autoptotheia*, the 'personal vision of God' granted to a saint.

11 C.H. Talbert, *Luke and the Gnostics*, Nashville and New York 1966, argued that Luke is responding to Gnostic currents; also important are the related views of C.K. Barrett. It has occasionally been suggested that Marcion's version of the Gospel of Luke is prior to our 'ecclesiastical' text — but this seems rather unlikely. For Valentinus and the Gospel of Luke, see Irenaeus, *Against Heresies* III, 14:3ff; the remark of Origen, in his *Homilies on Luke*, XVI.

12 *Buddhacarita*, in *Buddhist Scriptures* pp. 36–7. Steiner, *The Gospel of Luke* pp. 54–5; *Christianity as Mystical Fact*, London 1972, pp. 87–8. Z.P. Thundy, *Buddha and Christ* pp.115-6.

13 Conze, 'Buddhism and Gnosis' in U. Bianchi (ed.), *Le Origini dello Gnosticismo*, Leiden 1967, pp. 651–57. Cf. Steiner, *The Gospel of Luke* pp. 73ff. Edward Conze refers specifically to the version of the teaching found in Manichaeism, but the doctrine is already fully present in the Valentinian Gnosticism of Ptolemaeus, reported by Irenaeus, *Against Heresies* I, 7, 1–2 and in Clement, *Excerpts from Theodotus* (another pupil of Valentinus) 58–60.

14 C.H. Talbert, 'An Anti-Gnostic Tendency in Lucan Christology' in the journal *New Testament Studies* 14 (1967–8) pp. 270f argues that Luke is combatting in certain passages the Gnostic idea that Jesus suffered only in an illusory body.

15 Rudolf Steiner, *Christianity as Mystical Fact* p. 89. For the Transfiguration, see Luke 9:28–36; cf. Mark 9:2–8; Matthew 17:1–8. Matthew uses the expression 'bright cloud' as in the *Protevangelium*.

Chapter 8

1 Zechariah (or Zacharias) in the Temple: Luke 1:5ff; the disciples in the Temple: 24:52–3; infant Jesus in the Temple: 2:21–39; *bar mitzvah*: 2:41–51; teaching in the Temple: 19:45–7; 21:37–8; cf. 22:53.

2 Oscar Cullmann, *Christology of the New Testament*, London 1963, p. 85; and see generally pp. 83–107, including substantial discussion of the Letter to the Hebrews. Cf. Steiner, *Gospel of Luke* pp. 88ff.

3 See Steiner, *The Gospel of Luke* pp. 132–3. This reading of the best texts is rejected or put in the margin by most editions of the Bible because of theological prejudices. It is a coherent citation of the kingship oracle from psalm 2:7 and is quoted in that form by early Church Fathers. For the

version in the *Gospel of the Hebrews*, see Jerome, Commentary on Isaiah, iv (Schneemelcher, *New Testament Apocrypha* vol. I p.177.)

4 Cf. Steiner, *The Gospel of Luke* pp. 90–91.

5 *Testament of Simeon* 7:2–3. A translation of the *Testaments* is to be found in J.H. Charlesworth (ed.), *The Old Testament Pseudepigrapha*, I, London 1983, pp. 77ff. Crucial extracts on the Messiahs from the *Testaments of Levi* and *Judah* are presented with commentary in Welburn, *Gnosis. The Mysteries and Christianity*, pp.119–147.

6 *Testament of Naphtali* 5:3–5.

7 *Testament of Levi* 18:2–5 and 9–11. For the royal Messiah, see *Testament of Judah* 24:1–6.

8 Excellently summed up by Vermes, *The Dead Sea Scrolls*, Cleveland, Ohio 1978, pp. 184ff. See also K.G. Kuhn, 'The Two Messiahs of Aaron and Israel' in K. Stendhal (ed.), *The Scrolls and the New Testament*, London 1957; and the interesting if sometimes strained discussion by G. Friedrich, 'Beobachtungen zur messianischen Hohepriestererwartung in den Synoptikern' in the journal *Zeitschrift für Theologie und Kirche* 53(1956), pp. 265ff. The latter made the attempt to see the Messianic expectations of the Gospels against the background of the new discoveries.

9 Hippolytus, *Benedictions*: the relevant texts from this obscure work are reconstructed and discussed in L. Mariès, 'Le Messie issue de Levi chez Hippolyte de Rome' in the journal *Recherches de Science Religieuse* (1951), pp. 381ff.

10 From the Zoroastrian book *Denkart*, in Zaehner, *Teachings of the Magi*, London 1975, pp. 95–6. The full development of these ideas belonged to the time of the post-Christian Sassanian rulers of Iran; but they must no doubt have been worked out in the period of tension between the pan-Aryan religion of the kings and the reform-religion of Zarathustra in the earlier Achaemenid period.

11 Cf. Steiner, *The Gospel of Matthew* pp. 124ff; *From Jesus to Christ*, London 1973, pp. 133ff.

12 *Gospel of the Egyptians* in Schneemelcher, *New Testament Apocrypha* vol.I p.211. Discussion in Steiner, *The Gospel of Matthew* pp.115-6.

13 Reitzenstein, *Die hellenistischen Mysterienreligionen*, Leipzig 1920, p. 60. For the *Book of Baruch* by Justin, or what survives of it, see Welburn, *Gnosis. The Mysteries and Christianity*, pp.235-257. There is now an important study of the work in M. Marcovich, *Studies in Graeco-Roman Religions and Gnosticism*, Leiden 1988: he recognises the Iranian basis of the ideas (p.95) as well as the Jewish-esoteric material studied by Widengren and G. Scholem. I am also inclined to accept the special significance of references to Mysteries of Isis, placing the work in Egypt though in touch with the traditions behind the *Apocalypse of Adam*.

14 In Welburn, *Gnosis* p.253.

15 In Welburn, *Gnosis p.127* (in a slightly different Greek text); an Aramaic version of the passage has now been recovered from Qumran, see R. Eisenman and M. Wise, *The Dead Sea Scrolls Uncovered*, Shaftesbury, Rockport and Brisbane 1992, p.140 where the locale is identified as Abel Mayin.

16 So close is the connection between the traditions of Thomas and Luke here that several 'synopses' of the New Testament text have begun to include *Infancy Thomas'* version as a witness to the primary form of the story alongside the customary Gospel line. J.K. Elliott characterises *Thomas* as 'a fresh, independent version' even though it is not clear whether it is really free from dependency on Luke: in *The Oxford Bible Commentary*, Oxford 2001, p.1320.

17 *Pistis Sophia* 61.

Chapter 9

1 Mark 15:2ff; John 18:33ff.

2 Oscar Cullmann, *The Christology of the New Testament*, London 1959, p. 89.

3 Mark 1:12–13. There are parallel and at the same time more elaborate versions in Matthew 4:1–11 and Luke 4:1–13. For much fascinating discussion of the Temptation, see now J. Marcus, *The Way of the Lord*, Edinburgh 1992, which uses the 'wilderness tradition' reflected in this enigmatic episode as a veritable key to the gospel message (pp.23ff). The Old Testament, and Isaiah in particular provide the backdrop — but the re-emergence of wider aspects of the theme (e.g. being with the animals) might also relate to other mythological resonances, from Egypt, Babylonia, or Iran: on the latter parallels cf. Steiner, *Background to the Gospel of Mark*, London 1968, pp.88ff.

4 For an excellent account of the emergence of Greek consciousness from this perspective see Barfield, *Saving the Appearances* pp. 96ff. Also, H. and H.A. Frankfort, *Before Philosophy: The Intellectual Adventure of Ancient Man*, Harmondsworth 1949, pp. 248ff on the transition from mythology to rational consciousness.

5 Steiner, *The Gospel of Matthew* p. 146. I am aware that making the Temptation-episode so decisive, even taking Jesus 'beyond Judaism' I may seem to be giving it excessive importance or even an unrealistic, 'theological' significance that really depends on a later, Christian perspective. Could it truly have been experienced by Jesus in such a way? And yet: other scholars such as Marcus have come to regard it as a 'watershed' in Jesus' attitude. Marcus concludes that the themes of the exorcisms and related controversies show a fundamental shift, occurring in Jesus at the point of the baptism-temptation, from a futuristic to a present eschatology — from an earlier, Jewish and apocalyptic vision of a world still subject to the power of Beelzeboul-Satan and the daemons until a future time, giving way to one in which the grip of the dark powers over the world has essentially been loosened and individuals are set free: see J. Marcus, 'The Beelzeboul Controversies and the Eschatologies of Jesus,' in B. Chilton and C.A. Evans, *Authenticating the Activities of Jesus*, Leiden 1999. Are we right to find such a change? Scholars who believe that it is methodologically impermissible to read into Jesus' teaching a 'development' of any sort (cf. n14 below) perhaps need to be reminded that a methodological assumption that Jesus did not change is just as unfounded in the evidence.

6 See Rudolf Bultmann, *The Theology of the New Testament*,

London 1952, vol. I, pp. 4ff.

7 See especially the work of F.H. Borsch, *The Son of Man in Myth and History*, London 1967; C.H. Kraeling, *Anthropos and Son of Man*, New York 1927; Cullmann, *Christology of the New Testament*, ch. 6. The complexities of the 'Son of Man problem' are such that no single answer to all the questions seems to be available. Without undertaking a full exposition of a very large subject, we shall try to suggest that the phrase had a rich series of connotations, certain of which could be exploited to enable Jesus to express what was in fact the essence of his teaching and the central idea of his self-consciousness. The main references to the 'Son of Man' in the New Testament are; Matthew 5:11; 8:20; 10:23; 10:32, 11:19; 12:32; 12:40; 13:37; 13:41; 19:28; 22:44; 24:27; 24:28; 24:30; 24:37; 25:31; Mark 2:10; 2:28; 8:31; 8:38; 9:9; 9:12; 9:31; 10:33; 10:45; 13:26; 14:21; 14:41; 14:62; Luke 6:22; 7:34; 9:58; 11:30; 12:8; 12:10; 12:40; 17:22; 17:24; 17:26; 17:30; 18:8; 19:10; 21:36; 22:48; 22:69; John 1:51; 3:14; 5:27; 6:27; 6:53; 6:62; 9:35; 12:23; 12:34; 13:31.

8 Steiner, *The Gospel of John*, New York 1962, pp. 104–5.

9 Borsch, *The Christian and Gnostic Son of Man*, London 1970, pp. 110ff.

10 Hippolytus, *Refutation of Heresies* V, 7:33.

11 See the passages from the *Gospel of Philip* etc. discussed in Borsch, *Christian and Gnostic Son of Man* pp. 78ff.

12 In bringing the 'Son of Man' into connection with the 'Messianic Secret' I follow the line of research opened up by Erik Sjöberg, *Der verborgene Menschensohn in den Evangelien*, Lund 1955. Sjöberg's extensive conclusions linking the Enochian Son of Man with the gospels have sometimes been found questionable; yet they remain a valuable starting-point and one that is in accord with the views developed here. I would stress, however, that in fulfilling the Jewish eschatological expectations of the glorified Son of Man, Jesus had then to develop something qualitatively new on that foundation, going beyond the limits of Judaism in the realization of a new consciousness. To this extent Sjöberg's emphasis on *Enoch* suffers from the tendency of scholars to overestimate the importance of a single approach.
  On the other hand, the Enochian Son of Man passages, now that they have been confirmed by the evidence of Qumran, have recently been stressed once more by J.H. Charlesworth, *Jesus within Judaism*, London 1988, pp. 39ff; and there is the provocative new work of Margaret Barker, *The Older Testament*, London 1987, esp. pp. 8–80.

13 Cullmann, *Christology of the New Testament* p. 156.

14 T.W. Manson, *The Teaching of Jesus*, Cambridge 1963, pp. 214ff. Manson's version of the 'development' of the teaching after Peter's confession has been criticized; nevertheless it seems substantially valid, and agrees with Steiner's view of the 'esoteric' character of what occurred at that point: Steiner, *The Gospel of Mark* pp. 131ff.

15 Violet MacDermot, *The Cult of the Seer in the Ancient Middle East*, London 1971, p. 67.

16 Cf. E.R. Dodds, *Pagan and*

Christian in an Age of Anxiety, London and New York 1970, esp. pp. 8ff.

17 Paul, Letter to the Galatians 4:3.

18 Peter Brown, *The World of Late Antiquity*, London 1971, p. 102.

19 Cf. the conclusions of K.V. Thomas from his study *Man and the Natural World*, Harmondsworth 1984, pp. 300–301. There are some highly pertinent reflections on the problem of 'causation' in relation to changes in consciousness in Barfield, *Saving the Appearances* p. 97, and generally pp. 65ff.

20 Stephen R.L. Clark, *From Athens to Jerusalem: Philosophy and the Care of the Soul*, Oxford 1984, p. 123.

21 For an exposition of Steiner's main philosophical ideas, see Steiner-Barfield, *The Case for Anthroposophy*, London 1970; Rudolf Steiner, T*he Philosophy of Freedom: The Basis for a Modern World-Conception*, London 1970; and for a recent evaluation, A.J. Welburn, *Rudolf Steiner's Philosophy and the Crisis of Contemporary Thought*, Edinburgh 2004.

Chapter 10

1 The correspondence was noted as early as 1952. The fragments are translated in Schneemelcher, *New Testament Apocrypha* vol. I p.118, and for the other Greek fragments, pp.117, 121-3 being printed in parallel to the Nag Hammadi version, which is now presented in a fully annotated form, pp.110-133; also in B. Layton, *The Gnostic Scriptures*, London 1987, pp.376-399. Generally on the *Gospel of Thomas* in relation to the Gospel

traditions we know, see H. Koester, *Ancient Christian Gospels* pp.75ff and the literature there referred to.

2 Acts of the Apostles 11,26. The *Gospel of Philip* is presented with commentary in Welburn, *Gnosis. The Mysteries and Christianity* pp.259-315; an annotated and up-dated version also in Schneemelcher, *New Testament Apocrypha* vol. I pp.179–208. I prefer these renderings to those of B. Layton, *Gnostic Scriptures* pp.325-353 and of W. Isenberg in *The Nag Hammadi Library* pp.139-160. The former two both use the convenient numbering of the 'Sayings' by H.M. Schenke. The term 'Sayings' has been attacked by Layton and others, perhaps with some justification although Layton's assertion that the materials are mere 'excerpts' assembled from a variety of sources does not ring true. The sense of a tradition and of liturgical use (cf. *Gnosis* p.263), and the clear relation to the training of catechumens suggests that passages would have been read out, so the literary term 'paragraphs' may not be entirely appropriate either.
     On 'becoming a Christian' see Sayings 6 (cf.1), 46, 59, 95.

3 *Gospel of Philip* Saying 109; cf. Sayings 90, 57, 59.

4 *Gospel of Philip* Saying 101; Sayings 67, 69, 82, 86.

5 R. Steiner, *The Easter Festival in Relation to the Mysteries*, London 1968, pp. 9ff. On the Mystery-Gnostic background of the *Gospel of Philip*, see now my introduction and commentary in *Gnosis*; a very similar perspective in M. Meyer, *The Ancient Mysteries: A Sourcebook*, San Francisco 1987, who presents

extracts from the Gospel under the rubric of 'The Mysteries within Judaism and Christianity': pp. 235–242 .

6 On the ritual reattainment of Paradise, cosmic ascension, etc. in the *Gospel*, cf. the important study by H.G. Gaffron, *Studien zum koptischen Philippusevangelium*, Bonn 1969. On being 'raised up above the world,' see Saying 10; on Paradise, Sayings 83, 84, 92, and on the mistake which 'when he said: Eat this, do not eat this, it became the beginning of death,' Saying 94. Spiritual freedom: Saying 110 (again with reference to cosmic ascension). For the Plant of Life or Tree in Paradise, see Sayings 84, 92; the Plant as the Cross, Saying 91 which strengthens the Easter context of the Mystery. For these Mesopotamian images, see the interesting work by Widengren, *The King and the Tree of Life in Ancient Near Eastern Religions*, Uppsala 1951. For Gilgamesh, see *The Epic of Gilgamesh*, Harmondsworth 1960; the myth of Adapa ('The Man') in *Poems of Heaven and Hell from Ancient Mesopotamia*, Harmondsworth 1971, pp. 167ff.

7 Steiner, *The Easter Festival in Relation to the Mysteries*, p. 40; 'spiritual chemistry', p. 41. See *Gospel of Philip* Sayings 15, 31, 84, and especially Saying 93. On 'chemical' transformation, Sayings 35, 36, 43, 51, 54, 66, 115.

8 For the difference between the lower grades and the higher, cf. Saying 98, which mentions 'the bread and the cup and the oil — though there is something more exalted than these.' The meaning of the eucharist for the Philip-Christians is indicated in the Sayings 14, 15, 50, 53, 100, 108.
   On the Marriage Chamber initiation, see Sayings 60, 66, 67, 73, 76, 77, 121, 122, 124, 125, 126, 127. The paradisal unity of the sexes and the restoration of unity in Christ: Sayings 71, 78, 79, etc. The cosmic nature of the Marriage Chamber is expounded in Saying 82.

9 The experience of one's own image: Sayings 75, 105; cf. Sayings 44, 113. For 'penetrating through the image into the truth,' Saying 67 and with reference to 'angelic' counterparts, Saying 26. The transformation of the world into a 'child' is described in Saying 99, cf. the distinction of works, images, children in Saying 86.

10 See Sayings 108, 127.

11 Saying 120. The Son of Man figures also in Sayings 54, 43, 102, cf. Borsch, *The Christian and Gnostic Son of Man*, London 1970, pp. 78–82.

12 Especially valuable is the *Mystery-Instruction* of Cyril of Jerusalem, available as *Lectures on the Christian Sacraments*, ed. F.L. Cross, (with a translation by R.W. Church) London 1951. Parallels with Syrian Christianity are discussed in my article on 'The Ancient Near Eastern Background' (note 5 above).

13 *Gospel of Philip* Saying 10; *The Thousand and Twelve Questions* (Alf Trisar Šuialia) ed. and trans. E.S. Drower, Berlin 1960, no. 95. The Mandaean work does not form part of their regular liturgy, but is a 'secret scroll' for priests only. The best account of the Mandaean secret wisdom is E.S. Drower, *The Secret Adam*, Oxford 1960.

14 Drower, *The Secret Adam* pp. 74–80. The *consolamentum* is

described by S. Runciman, *The Medieval Manichee*, Cambridge 1947, pp. 154–7, who notes the affinity with Christian ritual though of course the *Gospel of Philip* was not available to him.

15 Mithraic analogies are discussed in some detail in my article on 'The Ancient Near Eastern Background.' The rites are well described in M.J. Vermaseren, *Mithras. The Secret God*, London 1963, pp. 141ff. For the rite of the *Nymphus*, p. 143: 'It is probable,' writes Vermaseren, 'that immediately after the initiation of the *Nymphus*, the Mithraeum was flooded with a powerful light.' Cf. Sayings 66, 75, 77, 113, 126, 127. For Mithras as the god in the Tree, Vermaseren p. 74; the Mithraic 'right hand,' p. 136.

16 Modern Mithraic research has recognized both a core of Iranian ideas and practice, and the adoption of many extraneous elements in pagan Mithraism. The Iranian core is emphasised anew by R. Merkelbach, *Mithras*, Königstein 1984 (with many valuable illustrations). In the end the Hellenistic features tended to swamp everything else, though just under the surface older elements of the Mystery were often preserved, as in the symbolism of the Grades and their cosmic correspondences.

Reconstruction of its history is difficult, but basically Mithraism must be seen as a further phenomenon of the East-West encounter rather than as a simple continuation of archaic Mithra worship. The Iranian elements involved in its expansion westward are strikingly similar to those which made contact with the Essenes and Gnostics, and so already working in the background of Christianity.

The spiritual experiences connected with the different stages of Mithraic initiation are described by Rudolf Steiner: see in particular Welburn (ed.), *The Mysteries. Rudolf Steiner's Writings on Spiritual Initiation*, Edinburgh 1997, pp.94ff and especially the additional materials collected in the Notes, pp.174ff.

17 See for example the timeless, mythic conception of Christ's work in Sayings 9, 81.

18 In the notes of his edition, *L'Évangile selon Thomas*, Leiden 1975, J. Ménard refers 149 times to Matthew, as against 53 times to Mark, 118 times to Luke, and 85 times to John. Thus it appears that in his perspective Thomas stands somewhere between Matthew and Luke, though considerably closer to Matthew. The relationship does not mean, however, that Thomas knew the canonical texts: rather we have an independent, parallel tradition of equal importance, a view confirmed by the important studies of the *Gospel of Thomas* in J.D. Crossan, *Four Other Gospels: Shadows on the Contour of Canon*, Minneapolis, Chicago and New York 1985.

19 *Gospel of Thomas* Saying 106, 108. For other uses of the 'Son of Man' see Saying 86 and cf. Saying 61.

20 Saying 9: cf. Matthew 13:3–8; Mark 4:3–8; Luke 8:5–8. Saying 20: cf. Matthew 13:31–2; Mark 4:30–32; Luke 13:18–19. Saying 63: cf. Luke 12:16–21. Saying 64: cf. Matthew 22:1–14; Luke 14:16–24. Saying 65: cf. Mathew 21:33–39; Mark 12:1–8; Luke 20:9–15. Saying 76: cf. Matthew 13:45–6. See also Luke 12:33.

Saying 96: cf. Matthew 13:33; Luke 13:20–21.

Saying 107: cf. Matthew 18:12–13; Luke 15:3–7.

Saying 109: cf. Matthew 13:44.

21 Of the Sayings in *Thomas*, Koester comments that many 'are preserved in a form which is older than the forms of their parallels in the Synoptic Gospels. This is especially the case for the parables.' H. Koester, *Introduction to the New Testament*, II, Berlin and New York 1982, p. 154.

22 T.W. Manson, *The Teaching of Jesus*, Cambridge 1963, pp. 59ff. The account of the Fig-Tree in Mark 11:11–14 and its relation to the parable in Luke 13:6–7 is discussed in Steiner, *Christianity as Mystical Fact*, London 1972, pp. 96–7.

23 Mark 4:11. Compare the passage in the *Gospel of Philip* Saying 16(b):

Truth, which is from the beginning, is sown everywhere, and many see it being sown. But few who see it reap it.

The Saying characterizes very exactly the experience of the parables!

24 Saying 49; cf. Sayings 18, 50, 70.

25 Saying 113; cf. Sayings 2, 3, 5, 17, 24.

26 Saying 111. Note how the apocalyptic vision, the upfurling of the heavens like a scroll, is balanced by the achievement of self-knowledge and so a firm point of inner equilibrium. Cf. Matthew 24:6 (Mark 13:7, Luke 21:9) on the Elect in the times of tribulation to come before the End.

27 Christopher Rowland, *The Open Heaven. A Study of Apocalyptic in Judaism and Early Christianity*, London 1982, p. 358.

28 G. Quispel, article 'The *Gospel of Thomas* revisited' in B. Barc (ed.), *Colloque international sur les textes de Nag Hammadi*, Quebec 1981. Hermetism in Edessa is discussed in G. Fowden, *The Egyptian Hermes*, Cambridge 1986, pp. 203–4. Hermes came to be regarded as a 'prophet of Christ' in certain Christian circles, as we know from the writings of Lactantius and his representation as such, for instance on the pavement of Siena Cathedral where he keeps company with the equally prophetic Sybils. Hermetic influences on the development of Christian esotericism are discernible too in the Syrian writings under the authority of Dionysius the Areopagite, cf. R. Roques, *L'univers dionysien*, Paris 1954, pp. 240ff. The importance of Hermetic Mysteries for the Grail mysticism of the Middle Ages is shown by H. and R. Kahane, *The Krater and the Grail*, Urbana 1965.

29 *Gospel of Thomas* Sayings 19, 37.

30 Eating dead things: *Gospel of Thomas* Sayings 11, 60; cf. 7. Images: Sayings 22, 50, 83, 84. Marriage Chamber: Sayings 75 and 64, 104. For the context of 'Many are called ...' see further below. On Jesus as 'Bridegroom', cf. Matthew 9:15 (Mark 2:19–20; Luke 5:34–5).

31 F.F. Bruce, *Jesus and Christian Origins outside the New Testament*, London 1974, pp. 150–51, on Saying 105. For James the Just, Saying 12.

32 Gospel of John 3:3–13; *Gospel of Thomas* Saying 22. Overcoming of divisions: *Gospel of Thomas* 11, 23, 48, 49, 72, 75, 106, 114.

33 Matthew 22:1–14. Cf. Luke 14:15–24; *Gospel of Thomas* Sayings 64, 75. The disparities between the versions are reveal-

ing, and one may connect the suppression of the reference to baptism and the 'marriage garment' with the anti-ritualism of *Thomas*. In Luke the knowledge of Jesus' ritual activity has also disappeared, since he belongs to Pauline and 'ecclesiastical' circles.

34 The formula was widespread in the Mysteries. Another version of it figures as Saying 74 in the *Gospel of Thomas* and was in this guise used by the Ophite Gnostics. Plato quotes the Greek form of it as 'The thyrsus-bearers are many, but the initiates are few.' (Thyrsus = a ritual wand.)

35 *Gospel of Thomas* Saying 67.

36 *Gospel of Thomas* Saying 77; cf. Matthew 18:20 and *Gospel of Thomas* Saying 30 which in the Greek fragments is joined to the material of Saying 77.

37 Matthew 9:15 (for parallels see note 30 above).

38 Oxyrhynchus Papyrus 840, translated in Hennecke-Schneemelcher, *New Testament Apocrypha*, I, 1963 pp. 92–4.

By the time of Christianity's beginnings,' points out Wayne Meeks, 'Pharisaic sages seem already to have invented the *mikveh*, an immersion pool deemed pure if it had adequate dimensions and the prescribed construction even though its water was still.' See his *The First Urban Christians*, Yale 1983, p. 151, and also p. 153. The lost-Gospel fragment thus deals with an important issue of Jesus' time, and sheds considerable light on the reasons for the constant confrontation with the Pharisees described in all the Gospels: it was a disagreement on the central Pharisaic notion of purity before God. Jesus insists that man can only be raised into

the presence of God by a very different kind of 'immersion' experience. J. Jeremias argues (in Hennecke-Schneemelcher, I, p. 93) that the several objections made to the language and content of the fragment can be discounted. 'On the contrary it is excellently informed, exhibits numerous Semitisms ... and in substance ranks as high as the Synoptic account.'

39 G.R. Beasley-Murray, *Baptism in the New Testament*, London and New York 1962, p. 70 (and see generally pp. 67ff).

40 Mark 10:35–40; 10:43–5. The 'secret Mark' passage falls between verses 34 and 35 of canonical Mark 10: see *Gnosis. The Mysteries and Christianity* pp.327–333. Cf. Matthew 20,20–27; Jesus uses similar language in Luke 12:50.

Chapter 11

1 Philippians 2:6–8. Several scholars take the unevenness of tone here, not to mean that Paul is 'feeling his way' but that he is quoting a hymn about the pre-existent Christ, and they even discover metre and verse-divisions. Confidence in the reconstruction is shaken, however, by the totally different 'verses' that they offer. It is hard to take the passage, as it stands, to be poetry, though Paul may well be citing phrases from such a hymn and weaving his argument round them. The thought proceeds by paraphrases ('in the form of God ... equality with God'; 'poured himself out ... taking the form ... coming-to-be'; 'humbled himself ... becoming obedient'; 'death ... death on a cross') as if Paul takes a phrase, then paraphrases it to

bring out its meaning, exploring
its implications, then sometimes
paraphrasing it again definitively
before moving on.

2 Corinthians 1 14:33–4. Cf. John
Ruef, *Paul's First Letter to Corinth*,
Harmondsworth 1971, pp. 154–5.
On the 'full participation of
women in the church offices and
in worship' among the Pauline
communities, see H. Koester,
Introduction to the New Testament,
II, Berlin and New York 1982,
pp. 124–5.

2b This insight not only liberates us
to read Paul's other writings
without the sense of subordina-
tion, but has in turn formed a
new point of departure for J.D.G.
Dunn's fine study of *Romans*, 2
vols., Dallas 1988. That letter too
needs to be seen in the living
context of Paul's arguments with
the Jewish community at Rome,
not as a monolithic statement.

3 Romans 7:15. The whole passage
brilliantly analyses the psychic
'split' necessitated by the Law,
the real agony of self-division
that must be lived with. Equally
remarkable is Paul's historical
awareness that the Law was a
necessary stage, at least for part
of humanity. This marks him off
from any Gnostic condemnation
of the Law as such, or of the
Lawgiver: thus he maintains
essential unity too in his apprehension of the divine.

4 Romans 6:3–4. Recognition of the
Mystery-character of Pauline
'death and new life' through baptism is by no means new – see e.g.
Angus, *Mystery Religions and
Christianity* (1925; repr. New York
1966) pp. 295–6 discussing the
theories of Kennedy and
Macchioro. Their evidence was,
however, limited (the statement
that the initiate 'becomes like

Christ, but never Christ' – p. 296 –
is now contradicted in the *Gospel
of Philip*, for instance) and they
were unable to clarify the background of Paul's mysticism, as we
can now do, but only refer nebu-
lously to ideas that were 'in the
air.' The alternative notion that
Paul had direct contact with
pagan Mysteries was too far-
fetched. It is only in recent times
that the intermediary world of the
esoteric Jewish and semi-Jewish
sects has come to light. In-depth
studies of Paul have confirmed
the depth of the Jewish background, and the many different
strands, esoteric and otherwise,
making it up: E.P. Sanders, *Paul
and Palestinian Judaism: A
Comparison of Patterns of Religion*,
Philadelphia 1977; W.D. Davies,
Paul and Rabbinic Judaism,
Philadelphia 1980; a robust
reassertion of extra-Jewish features in H. Maccoby, *Paul and
Hellenism*, London and
Philadelphia 1991. For a more
general introduction, see G.
Bornkamm, *Paul*, New York 1971;
a view shaped by Rudolf
Steiner's ideas in E. Bock, *Saint
Paul*, Edinburgh 1993.

5 See Kümmel, *Introduction to the
New Testament*, London 1975, pp.
353–4.

6 A matter of judgment, of course,
which has been called in question from the time of Erasmus.
The so-called 'Letter to the
Ephesians' is somehow closely
bound up with the Letter to the
Colossians, which in turn is
closely related to the Letter to
Philemon. The last is undoubtedly Paul's, and Colossians
therefore is probably genuine:
see J.L. Houlden, *Paul's Letters
from Prison*, Harmondsworth
1977, pp. 124ff, 138. 'Ephesians'

overlaps in its material with Colossians, tempting many scholars to suppose that the longer letter is worked up by a later follower of Paul using material from Colossians and elsewhere. It is important to stress, however, that any statement going beyond an analysis of the literary facts must be guesswork. We have no independent historical evidence. It would be easier to envisage circumstances under which Paul would employ material from a document on which he was working in another letter when it seemed appropriate. A grammatical oddity in Colossians 2:19 is very hard to explain in terms of an original writing, but falls into place if Paul was adapting slightly material he was using in Ephesians 4:15–16. On the whole, there is nothing in Ephesians which *could* not be by Paul, given the variety of styles he adopts in the uncontested letters. The literary case against its authenticity remains unproved. As for the content, I shall suggest that it fits well with what we know about Jesus' own ritual activity and that of his earliest followers.

7 A 'postbaptismal Mystery address': this view has been developed especially by J.C. Kirby, *Ephesians, Baptism and Pentecost*, London 1968; and see the article by G. Schille in the journal *Theologische Literaturzeitung* (1957), pp. 326ff.

8 Quoted in the translation by Jon and Louise Madsen, which conveys the atmosphere and tone of the address with unprecedented sensitivity: in *Galatians, Ephesians, Philippians, Colossians. The Letters of Paul*, ed. Stanley

Drake, Edinburgh 1984, pp. 45–6. Ephesians 1:3–14. The address initially takes the form of a *berakah*, a form of blessing known from Jewish liturgy and probably standard in Christian initiatory lectures as here, whether or not Paul is composing an original example or adapting a given outline.

9 L. Cerfaux, 'En faveur de l'authenticité des Épîtres de la Captivité' in *Littérature et théologie Pauliniennes. Recherches Bibliques* 5(1960), pp. 60ff (68).

10 Sealing: 1:13; 4:30. The ritual seems also to have involved anointing, as we gather from the passage in 2 Corinthians 1:21: see Wayne Meeks, *The First Urban Christians*, New Haven and London 1983, p. 151. The term *mysterion* is applied at 1:9. Death and reawakening to life is a theme announced at 2:5. The cosmic aspect will only fully emerge at 6:12. The idea of overcoming divisions, another baptismal theme, is adapted to Paul's special purpose, the Gentile-Jewish union in the Christian *ekklesia*, with the help of Isaiah 57:19 ('Peace, peace to those far, and to those near, says Yahweh, and I shall heal them'). The rabbinic 'fence' was a moral barrier around the Law, but had already received a cosmological interpretation.

11 Birth of the 'new man': 3:16. The technical terminology of 'perfect man'/immature: 4:13–14. Rebirth as 'becoming a child' of God: 5:1. Light and darkness symbolism becomes dominant with 5:8. *Mysterion* again: 5:32.

12 Wayne Meeks, *The First Urban Christians* p. 157. For nudity and the 'stripping off' of the body, see Ephesians 4:22, and the same

398 • *The Beginnings of Christianity*

terminology used explicitly of baptism in Colossians 3:9–10 and Galatians 3:27; Meeks, p. 155. On the remaking of the self through the agency of the Spirit, cf. the remarks of Houlden, *Paul's Letters from Prison*, pp. 318–19. Meeks, like earlier authors (note 4 above), brings out the parallels with Mystery-rites in the Greek, Hellenistic Egyptian and Jewish religions: pp. 152–3 and p. 238 note 62 (the rabbinic school of Hillel says, 'He that separates himself from his uncircumcision' – a process involving a baptism – 'is as one that separates himself from a grave').

13 Ephesians 2:6; cf. Colossians 1:5; 1:12; 2:12; 2:20; 3:1–4. Meeks, p. 155.

14 Meeks, p. 152. Most commentators take the 'oath' to refer to baptism, although it is not specified as such.

15 W. Schmithals, *Gnosticism in Corinth. An Investigation of the Letters to the Corinthians*, New York 1971, is a detailed and often specialist examination of Gnostic ideas among Paul's opponents, and the most successful of Schmithals' attempts to pin down Gnostic ideas in Paul's environment. Cf. also his article, 'Zur Herkunft der gnostischen Elemente in der Sprache des Paulus' in Barbara Aland (ed.), *Gnosis. Festschrift für Hans Jonas*, Göttingen 1978, pp. 385ff.

16 Kümmel, *Introduction to the New Testament*, p. 365. Ephesians was interpreted in a thoroughgoing way from this perspective, with often fascinating insights, by P. Pokorny, *Der Epheserbrief und die Gnosis*, Berlin 1965. For Christ as primal Man see 1:4 and 1:22; 2:15ff; 4:13ff; 5:22ff. For 'marriage' as a *mysterion* imaging the syzygy of Christ and the *ekklesia* 5:22ff. ('Syzygy' is a Gnostic term for the spiritual union of beings in the supersensory world, especially of the Aeons emanated from the Godhead.)

17 The passage on the children of Light and children of Darkness at 5:7ff, for example, could be taken straight from an Essene text (cf. Houlden, *Paul's Letters from Prison* p. 326) though that does not mean that it was! On the other hand the evidence for a connection between Ephesians and early tendencies toward Catholicism is not hard to seek (Kümmel, p. 365). And its use is quite justified: but the view implied is really that these different streams at one stage had much in common.

18 Ephesians 4:15–16. Paul introduces the concept with reference to 'the initiated man' and the measure 'of his maturity according to how much the fullness of Christ's being is in him' (4:13).

19 Steiner, *The Bhagavad Gita and the Epistles of Paul*, New York 1971, p. 83. On the seeker in relation to Krishna or oriental Teacher (Revealer), p. 82.

20 Meeks, *The First Urban Christians*, p. 157.

21 Ephesians 6:14–17. There are more echoes of Isaiah here, from a passage close to the one already cited. Isaiah 59:17: 'He put on righteousness as his breastplate, and the helmet of salvation on his head ...' Cf. the *War Rule* from Qumran for this kind of imagery.

22 Ephesians 4:8–10. The proper rendering of 'the lowest regions, those of the earth' without which the passage is unintelligible was already seen by Calvin, long before it was urged by Rudolf

Bultmann. In the latter part of the passage one should avoid the implication that Christ burst out of earthly limitations and went on to fill the universe. The exact opposite is the meaning. The raising of Christ is the work of God, and the whole movement of descent-reascent is directed toward the 'fallen' world. Cosmological ideas about the Fullness are involved here which will become clearer through their exposition in the Gospel of John in the next chapter.

23 'Marriage' as the final revelation of the *mysterion* at 5:22 is thus Paul's development of the original rite, expressing now in post-resurrection terms Christ's relation to his community.

24 2 Corinthians 12:2–4.

25 T.W. Manson, *The Teaching of Jesus*, Cambridge 1963, p. 234: 'If this interpretation is correct, we have in the Pauline teaching the same conception of the Son of Man as in the teaching of Jesus, with just that difference of orientation which arises from the historic facts of the death of Jesus and the resurrection. In the interval ... the Son of Man has been incarnated in the person of Jesus. The Son of Man is no longer a mere religious ideal: it has been realized to the full in Jesus, the head of the new humanity: and men are now called to become "the man" by union with him. As we study the life of Jesus we seem to see him become the Son of Man ... by a process of elimination; when we turn to the teaching of Paul, we find the same idea being carried further ... by a process of inclusion. The road to the cross is a road of ever-increasing loneliness: and at the

end of it Jesus is absolutely alone. From that point onwards, if we read Paul aright, there is ever-increasing fellowship of the sufferings of Christ. The prophecy of Jesus is fulfilled: "The cup that I drink ye shall drink: and with the baptism that I am baptized withal shall ye be baptized". This word could not be fulfilled in his lifetime; it is fulfilled after and through his death and resurrection.'

26 Ephesians 2:14–15: with an allusion to Psalm 80:17 which mentions 'the Man at your right hand, the Son of Man you have raised up for yourself.' Houlden, *Paul's Letters from Prison* pp. 290–91.

27 Acts of the Apostles 17:16–32. The term *nekros* means "corpse": Greek thought had no concept of integral survival after death.

28 See R.M. Grant, 'The Resurrection of the Body' in the *Journal of Religion* 28(1948), pp. 124ff, 188ff.

29 Cf. the fascinating discussion of many of these ideas in H. Corbin, *Terre céleste et Corps de Résurrection*, Paris 1960.

30 The concepts of 'body,' parts of the body, and aspects of man's being as they were felt and employed in the ancient world cannot be easily summarized or fully understood. For the ancient Hebrews, cf. the detailed studies of H.W. Wolff, *Anthropology of the Old Testament*, London 1974, especially pp. 26ff, 59ff. One should not hastily generalize the biblical use of 'body' on the assumption that it always 'means' the whole person: cf. the study (with special stress on the background to Paul) by R. Gundry, *Soma (Body) in Biblical Theology*, Cambridge 1976.

However, it is certainly possible to contrast the essential attitudes to man's nature including 'body' in Judaism with the consciousness of the Iranian or Greek thinkers. We have here a sensitive indicator for the history of consciousness. I have pointed out above that Judaism generated its own intense inwardness, which in its own way eroded the older Semitic 'whole person.' And of course there were points of contact with 'dualistic' anthropology from Greece and the East, for instance among the Essenes. The main point here, on the other hand, is that the biblical commitment to wholeness in man's being held in check the tendency to extremes, and exerted itself in Christian resurrection teaching, while being itself transformed and extended.

31 Cf. the treatment of the *Gospel of Philip* in the preceding chapter for the ritual attainment of Paradise. For the Essene prophecy, *Testament of Levi* 18:10–11:

And he shall open the gates of Paradise;

he shall remove the sword that has threatened since Adam,

and he will grant to the saints to eat of the Tree of Life.

The spirit of holiness shall be upon them.

32 The 'dying animal' (memorably used in modern times in poetry by Yeats) is a Hermetic figure, and it reappears in Thomas-Christianity. But the attitude is general in Gnosticism.

33 1 Corinthians 15:50; 15:35–49. The principle that 'God gives it a body as he has chosen' (38) is applied strictly throughout, and will apply equally to the future state of transfigured humanity under the 'second Adam.'

34 J. Ruef, *Paul's First Letter to Corinth* p. xxiv. Cf. *Gospel of Philip* Saying 90 which may represent the kind of view Paul is striving to correct.

35 Seneca, *Questions on Natural Subjects* III, 29:2 argues that 'the *ratio* of the future man is included already in the seed' and even before birth contains the 'law' which will produce the mature beard, etc. The whole body and its acts are present as lineaments 'in an occult manner' or 'in little,' that is, as proportions though not yet actualized in the full-scale man.

36 The fullest account by Steiner of the *Phantom* is that in *From Jesus to Christ*, London 1973, pp. 99ff. Thomas Weihs, *Embryogenesis*, Edinburgh 1986, developed ideas on the distinction between the genetic component in man's make-up and the general human form which cannot be regarded as genetically determined. In a final section of the book he already pointed to Christian implications (pp. 127ff) A specifically Pauline application of the same biological view is made by Ormond Edwards, connecting evolutionary time with *The Time of Christ*, Edinburgh 1986, pp. 176ff.

Steiner was emphatically opposed to the modern notion that the understanding of nature should be left to physical science, and that theology should confine itself to what science leaves over. He would not have accepted, either, the vacuous contention by the authors of *The Myth of God Incarnate* that a positive interest in the physical world is something Christianity shares with Judaism and therefore cannot be of special importance, for instance, for the idea of the Incarnation. He upbraided the modern intellectual world with its failure to consider formulations of science which furnished the possibility of understanding the spirit in matter. He was thinking primarily of the Goethean method (more phenomenological and less speculative than conventional scientific theory) which is interested in metamorphosis as much as in regularities in nature: see *Building Stones for an Understanding of the Mystery of Golgotha*, London 1972, e.g. pp. 74ff. If we allow a science to develop which methodically isolates material from spiritual, we can hardly be surprised that the result will not bear the moral and spiritual significance we need to attribute to it in Christianity; and nor can Christianity survive in the interstices of the materialist's world-view.

Steiner's holistic and phenomenological type of approach has won many adherents, even outside the sphere of his actual influence, in recent times. Waddington's popular presentation of *Tools for Thought*, St. Albans 1977, shows the wide range of more imaginative approaches that have become necessary in the sciences. For structures and systems, see pp. 48ff.

37 Malcolm I.. Peel, *The Epistle to Rheginos*, London 1969, p. 149. The short Valentinian insertion in the document comes at 47:35. The text is also included in B, Layton, *The Gnostic Scriptures*, pp.316-324. Layton holds to the idea of a Gnostic, specifically Valentinian work. But he is forced to concede that though a

small amount of 'Valentinian jargon is introduced,' it is 'without any direct explanation or definition,' and has to argue that the work must be guilefully addressed to ordinary Christians to tempt them to ask further after the Valentinian philosophical 'higher truth' thus hinted at. How does this square with the rather forceful argumentation and immediacy of the writer? Certainly he draws on a certain amount of philosophical orientation, but is that enough to divorce him from a Christian milieu except for specifically Valentinian circles?

38 Irenaeus, *Refutation of Heresies* I 1:3.

39 *Letter to Rheginus*, 47:36–48:3; cf. 1 Corinthians 15:50.

40 *Letter to Rheginus* 47:4–8. The Iranian background of the *Letter* is discussed in J. Ménard, 'La Notion de Résurrection dans l'Epître à Rheginos' in G. Widengren (ed.), *Proceedings of the International Colloquium on Gnosticism*, Stockholm 1977, especially pp. 126–8, though he does not give enough weight to the new orientation present in the *Letter* through its teaching of transformation.

41 2 Tim. 2:17. Decisive arguments against the Pauline authorship of the letters addressed to Timothy and Titus in J.L. Houlden, *The Pastoral Epistles*, Harmondsworth 1976, pp. 18ff; Kümmel, *Introduction to the New Testament*, pp. 370ff.

42 E. Pagels, *The Gnostic Paul*, Philadelphia 1975, p. 5.

43 1 Corinthians 6:12. The most brilliant modern account of Paul's attack on the Law is that of Rudolf Bultmann, *The Theology of the New Testament*, I,

London 1952, pp. 270ff.

44 The 'new commandment of love' is the formulation of the Johannine tradition: Gospel of John 13:34. 'God is love': 1 John 4:8.

45 All attempts to explain Christian love by deriving it from earlier forms have failed to account for its intrinsic features and new role. It was essentially a new force. It was not — and is not — 'idealistic,' in the sense of requiring the assumption that human nature is better than it generally is. 'Love is patient, love is kind ... it is not rude' means in effect that human nature is exasperating, frustrating, and often offensive. The point about love was precisely that it was a force capable of surviving these things.

Chapter 12

1 On the lack of real evidence in the tradition concerning John son of Zebedee as the author of the Gospel, cf. Kümmel, *Introduction to the New Testament* pp. 239ff; Cullman, *The Johannine Circle*, London 1976, pp. 69ff. No trace of the tradition is to be found before the end of the second century, in Irenaeus and Eusebius (c. 180 or 190) probably a century after the Fourth Gospel was written. The need to base conclusions about the writer on internal evidence was recently stressed by Vernard Eller in his quaintly written *The Beloved Disciple*, Grand Rapids, Michigan 1987. His Sherlock Holmesian procedures arrive at good results. Exactly the opposite method was needed, however, for his tendentious second part of the book, on the Beloved Disciple's thought. There it is

important to set the Gospel in the world of its contemporaries: otherwise the temptation to read one's own emphases into the Gospel cannot be resisted, as when Eller's Beloved Disciple turns out to have been an American-style protestant, opposed to sacraments, and close to Kierkegaard's existentialism. On the implausibilities of John son of Zebedee, Eller pp. 44ff.

2 Cullman, *The Johannine circle* p. 18.

3 See Kümmel, *Introduction* p. 217–228 for a summary of the Gnostic and other backgrounds attributed to the Fourth Gospel. Alexandrian materials (Hermetic writings, the Greek Old Testament, and the Jewish scripture-interpretations of the mystical Philo Judaeus) were examined in depth by C.H. Dodd, *The Fourth Gospel*, Cambridge 1953; cf. Steiner *Christianity as Mystical Fact*, London 1972, pp. 137ff.

4 Dodd, *The Fourth Gospel* pp. 115ff; Kümmel, pp. 221ff. Many recent scholars, whilst admitting the parallels between the Gospel and the Mandaean Gnostic writings, point out that the latter in their present form are later than the Gospel, and propose that the Fourth Gospel was rather a step on the way towards Gnosticism than a reflection of its influence on Christianity: W. Meeks, 'The Man from Heaven' in J. Ashton (ed.), *The Interpretation of John*, Philadelphia and London 1986, p. 142. There is undoubtedly some truth here. The Gnostic element is not a systematic Gnosticism 'outside' Christianity, but still an element held in the synthesis of

Johannine thought, which in Christian Gnosticism will break loose in a one-sided way. However, it is difficult to argue from this that a Mandaean gnosis did not already exist in some form: indeed, Mandaeism (unlike Christian Gnosticism) is the one tradition most resistant to such an argument. It evolved as a non-Christian, Jewish-Iranian gnosis, and not on the basis of a post-Johannine myth about Christ, who appears in it only as a minor figure and clearly came in at a time of encounter with hostile churchly Christianity. It remains most likely that the primary layers of Mandaean tradition are good evidence about the background of the Fourth Gospel; we may then certainly admit the Gospel's importance for the way this background of Christianity was shaped and sifted, leading later to Christian-Gnostic heresies. But in the Gospel, it leads to a distinctive and profound Christianity.

Syria as the place of origin for the Gospel is supported by H. Koester, *Introduction to the New Testament*, II, p. 178 (with discussion of Gnostic analogies); for the historical knowledge and the language of the Gospel writer, see Cullmann, The Johannine Circle pp. 20ff, 26ff; also E.R. Goodenough, 'John a Primitive Gospel' in the *Journal of Biblical Literature* 54 (1945), pp. 145–83.

5 Koester, *Introduction*, II, p. 198; Hennecke-Schneemelcher, *New Testament Apocrypha*, I, p. 33 (citing the conclusions of Walter Bauer and others); II, p. 54.

6 B. Rigaux, 'Les destinataires du quatrième évangile' in the journal *Revue théologique de Louvain* 1

(1970), pp. 289ff (especially pp. 318–9); more tentative but pointing in a similar direction, Cullmann, *The Johannine Circle*, pp. 81–2.

7 Cullmann, pp. 59ff. On the internal evidence of the Gospel, the Beloved Disciple was a disciple of John the Baptist: but the Baptist's links with Qumran and the Essenes, as we have seen in an earlier chapter, were not the direct source of his teaching. He can hardly be the connection with Essenism some have looked for. On Essene ideas in the Gospel and the excessive significance sometimes attached to them, see Kümmel pp. 218–221.

8 Papias, in Eusebius, *History of the Church* III, 39:3 together with the information in Irenaeus, *Against Heresies* V, 33, 4. There is likely to be a core of truth here, as the expression accords so well with the Johannine emphasis on 'remembering' in a special sense, but there are problems about the precise interpretation of the passage (Kümmel, pp. 241–2).

The importance of oral tradition for understanding the origins of the Fourth Gospel had been brilliantly brought out by B. Noack, *Zur johanneischen Tradition*, Copenhagen 1954.

9 Cullmann, pp. 71ff; cf. Eller, *The Beloved Disciple* pp. 43ff.

10 Steiner, *The Gospel of John*, New York 1962, p. 64; the general argument, p. 60ff; cf. Eller, pp. 53ff.

11 F.V. Filson, 'Who was the Beloved Disciple?' in the *Journal of Biblical Literature* 68 (1949), pp. 83ff. Several variants of the theory try to introduce literary intermediaries (as is indeed necessary) and to tie them up with a 'John' from ecclesiastical tradition (which is probably misguided): thus J.N.

Sanders, 'Those whom Jesus Loved' in the journal *New Testament Studies* 1 (1954–5), pp. 29ff, bringing in John Mark (known elsewhere from N.T. writings thought not as a gospel writer) to transmit the memoirs of Lazarus; Eller, pp. 43–4 bringing in John the Elder. More speculative are those who try to make the 'Beloved Disciple' an 'ideal' figure, and give the real responsibility to the secondary writer, or to a 'redactor' at even a further stage removed. H.M. Schenke thinks he is modelled on Thomas as he appears in the Thomas-traditions: see his 'The Function and Background of the Beloved Disciple in the Gospel of John' in C.W. Hedrick and R. Hodgson (eds.), *Nag Hammadi, Gnosticism and Early Christianity*, Peabody, Massachusetts 1986, pp. 111ff, especially pp. 122–5. However, Schenke himself notes that in this type of reconstruction 'the extent of the material ascribed to the redactor is increasing to such an extent that the evangelist is about to disappear' (p. 117). In other words, we are pushed in the end towards deciding that it is either a total fiction, or is substantially from the Beloved Disciple and transmitted with only a minimum literary mediation. The latter is preferable, on the ground of the new philological recognition of the authentic language and historical position of the Gospel. (The fact too that a sceptic such as R. Lane Fox is convinced by the evidence of a historical link to Jesus' circle should add to our conviction independent of the tempting theological rewards that might sway others.) For a largely convincing attempt to put the special character of this

figure into the history of the New Testament, see R.E. Brown, *The Community of the Beloved Disciple*, New York 1979.

Oscar Cullmann seems to come to the very brink of accepting that the author is Lazarus, but for no clear reason refuses a definite conclusion and prefers an 'anonymous' disciple: p. 77. He is aware of Rudolf Steiner's view (p. 117). Steiner was probably aware of the theory that Lazarus-Beloved Disciple was the author of the Gospel in the version held by Kreyenbühl and published in a work of 1900. We need not enter into his not very clear ideas on the matter, also mentioned by Cullmann, p. 117.

12 See Morton Smith, *The Secret Gospel*, pp. 45-62, which sets out the parallels in full. Cf. also Eller, pp. 62-3.

13 Further ideas about the structure of the Gospel in the light of Steiner's thought in C. Rau, *Struktur und Rhythmus im Johannes-Evangelium*, Stuttgart 1972.

14 John 3:26–29; cf. Matthew 9:15.

15 John 3:1–8; cf. *Gospel of Thomas* 22. Further witness to Jesus' saying is found in Justin Martyr (who did not know the Fourth Gospel), who cites it from a baptismal liturgy: Justin, *Apology* I, 61:4–5. Further parallels to Thomas in the Fourth Gospel are discussed in Koester, *Introduction*, II, p. 180. He compares the following:
John 6:33 — *Thomas* Saying 28;
John 7:33-4 — *Thomas* Saying 38;
John 7:38 — *Thomas* Saying 108;
John 8:12 — *Thomas* Saying 77;
John 8:52 — *Thomas* Saying 1.

16 The Fourth Gospel also seems to give a primary form of the tradition, compared with the de-ritu-

alised *Thomas*. This does not bear out Schenke's idea that Thomas-tradition influenced the Fourth Gospel (in *Nag Hammadi, Gnosticism and Early Christianity* p. 125), but is rather a development of early tradition in two forms.

17 Cf. Steiner, *The Gospel of John* pp. 90ff. On 'flesh gives birth to flesh' (John 3:6) cf. *Gospel of Philip* Sayings 1, 60, 102, and especially 113 and 121.

18 *Gospel of Philip* Saying 127.

19 This Babylonian text is available in J.B. Pritchard, *The Ancient Near East. A New Anthology of Texts and Pictures*, II, Princeton 1975, p. 148–160. A good discussion of this work in the context of the background to Christianity is to be found in F.H. Borsch, *The Son of Man in Myth and History*, London 1967, pp. 177ff.

20 IQH VIII 30–36, in T.H. Gaster, *The Scriptures of the Dead Sea Sect*, London 1957, pp. 166–7. Many similar passages occur in other of the Hymns.

21 John 1:1–18. I use, with some variations because of my immediate purpose and the different format-requirements, the recent translation by Kalmia Bittleston, *The Gospel of John*, Edinburgh 1984, which remarkably captures the strange power and movement of the original.

22 First perceived by H.H. Schaeder, in Reitzenstein-Schaeder, *Studien zum antiken Synkretismus aus Iran und Griechenland*, Leipzig and Berlin 1926, p. 318. The concept of the *shekinah* was originally closely tied to the 'presence' of God in the Temple. The term already among the Mandaeans, however, had cut loose: it refers there to the 'heavenly abode' of a being

in the spiritual world. In later Jewish mysticism, the *shekinah* embodies the feminine aspect of God's nature, suffering with mankind until the redemption.

23 *Trimorphic Protennoia*, section III = Codex III 46:5–11; 46:16–21; 47:13–19; 47:22–25; 47:28–34; 49:20–32 (trans. by John D. Turner in: *The Nag Hammadi Library* pp.519-521. There is a full edition in French by Yvonne Janssens, *La Protennoia Trimorphe*, Quebec 1978. The realization of the 'stupendous parallels' (as Colpe has called them) with the Johannine Prologue was made by the members of the so-called Berlin Study Group (*Berliner Arbeitskreis*), some of whose publications will be referred to below. Their view is that, though in present form the *Trimorphic Protennoia* is a Gnostic revelation, its 'text ... attests to an older tradition, sufficiently ancient to have influenced the Prologue': J.M. Robinson, 'Sethians and Johannine Thought. The Trimorphic Protennoia and the Prologue to the Gospel of John' in B. Layton (ed.), *The Rediscovery of Gnosticism*, II, Leiden 1981, pp. 643ff (p. 663). A fuller list of parallels, p. 658. Janssens interestingly refers to a parallel in the three descents of the Redeemer in the *Secret Book of John* in Codex II 30:11–31:25 (*The Nag Hammadi Library* pp. 115–6), once more showing that authentic Johannine materials are embedded in that work. On the relationship with the Prologue, see G. Schenke (for the *Berliner Arbeitskreis*), 'Die Dreigestaltige Protennoia — Eine gnostische Offenbargunsrede,' in the journal *Theologische Literaturzeitung* 99 (1974), pp. 731ff; C.A. Evans, 'On

the Prologue of John and the
Trimorphic Protennoia' in the jour-
nal *New Testament Studies*
27(1980–81), pp. 395ff; Y.
Janssens, 'The *Trimorphic
Protennoia* and the Fourth
Gospel' in A.H. Logan and A.J.
Wedderburn (eds.), *The New
Testament and Gnosis*, Edinburgh
1983, pp. 229ff (especially pp.
235–42).

24 Cf. Steiner, *The Gospel of John* pp.
180–81.

25 Gospel of John 1:23; *Trimorphic
Protennoia* XIII 42:4: pointed out
by Janssens, '*Trimorphic Protennoia*
and the Fourth Gospel,' p. 231.
For the commentaries of
Ptolemaeus and Heracleon on
John, see W. Foerster, *Gnosis*, I,
Oxford 1972, pp. 144f and 162ff.
See especially Heracleon, fr. 5
(pp. 162–3). Steiner, *The Gospel of
John*, pp. 34ff.

26 M. Scopello, 'Un rituel idéal d'in-
tronisation dans trois textes
gnostiques de Nag Hammadi', in
R.McL. Wilson (ed.). She compares the rites suggested by Nag
Hammadi documents to those in
the *Books of Enoch*, etc. It is, of
course, not possible to restore the
rite fully from purely literary evidence: we would need to know
much more precisely what was
done as well as said. However,
much can be gathered from the
'ritual passage' which comes in
between the verses we quoted
for their parallelism to John. The
Revealer says (*Trimorphic
Protennoia* XIII 48 15–35):

   'I delivered him to those who
give robes — (the angelic beings)
Yammon, Elasso, Amenai — and
they covered him with a robe
from the robes of the Light. And
I delivered him to the baptizers
and they baptized him —
Michev, Michar, Mnesinous —

and they immersed him in the
spring of the (Water) of Life.
And I delivered him to those
who enthrone — Bariel,
Nouthan, Sabenai — and they
enthroned him from the throne
of glory. And I delivered him to
those who glorify — Ariom,
Elien, Phariel — and they glorified him with the glory of the
Fatherhood ... And it was
granted him to partake of the
(mystery) of knowledge, and (he
became a Light) in Light.'

   For a 'glorification' in the
pagan Mysteries, see Apuleius,
Metamorphoses, or The Golden Ass
XI 24. The origins of the rite are
ascribed by Reitzenstein, in a
passage which already brings
together pagan, Mandaean and
other evidence, and discussion
of the *shekinah*, to Syria: *Die hellenistischen Mysterienreligionen*,
Leipzig 1927, pp. 228–9.

27 Steiner, *The Gospel of John* pp.
64ff; Bultmann, 'The History-of-
Religious Background of the
Prologue to the Gospel of John'
in Ashton (ed), *The Interpretation
of John*, pp. 18ff (p. 33). Literary-
critical efforts have been made to
weed out the references in the
Prologue of John the Baptist as
'insertions,' but on maturer consideration H.M. Schenke for
instance would now revert to the
view of Bultmann: Schenke, 'The
Functions and Background of
the Beloved Disciple,' p. 113
(heading 3).

28 Steiner, *Wonders of the World,
Ordeals of the Soul, Revelations of
the Spirit*, London 1963, pp. 86–7.
Cf. Apuleius' account, and the
symbolism (noted by
Reitzenstein) of the supreme Sky-
God of the Syrian Mysteries, to
whom the initiate seems to be
assimilated. The 'raising' or

'awakening' of Lazarus is repeatedly described in the Fourth Gospel as a 'glorification': Gospel of John 11:4; 11:40. Cf. 12:23; 12:28.

29 Steiner, *The Gospel of John* p. 64. See also *Christianity as Mystical Fact* pp. 108ff.

30 Steiner, *The Gospel of John* p. 74.

31 J.M. Hull, *Hellenistic Magic and the Synoptic Tradition*, London 1974, p. 164 n50.

32 Hull, op. cit. p. 106; and see generally pp. 106–8, which includes mention of similarities in Acts of the Apostles, as well as the passage in the Gospel of Luke 8:43–48, discussed below.

33 Hull, op. cit. p. 164 n52.

34 Hull, op. cit. pp. 110–111; cf. Steiner, *Background to the Gospel of Mark*, London 1968, pp. 99–102. On the relation of 'power' and 'faith' in the story from Luke and elsewhere, Steiner, *Building Stones for an Understanding of the Mystery of Golgotha*, London 1972, pp. 56ff. Hull drew on the earlier research of F. Preisigke, *Die Gotteskraft der früchristlichen Zeit*, Berlin and Leipzig 1922.

35 Hermetic teaching preserved by al-Shahrastani (twelfth century), in Scott, *Hermetica*, vol. IV, Oxford 1936, pp. 259–60.

36 Clement, preserved in Photius, *The Library* 2 80: cited by D. Flusser 'Lukas 9:51–56 — ein hebräisches Fragment,' in Weinreich (ed.), *The New Testament Age*, Macon, Georgia 1984, pp. 165–179 (175–6). The *Gospel of Peter* is traced back by such scholars as S. Pines to Syria; cf. Koester, *Introduction*, II, pp. 162–4. The surviving fragments of the Gospel are given in Schneemelcher, *New Testament Apocrypha* vol I. pp.216ff. There is an increasing tendency among some scholars, notably Koester and J.D. Crossan, to see here an early form of the passion-tradition — perhaps even something from which we can discover the original 'passion-gospel': Koester, *Ancient Christian Gospels* pp.216ff; Crossan, *The Cross that Spoke: The Origins of the Passion-Narrative*, San Francisco 1988; problems with Crossan's over-emphasis on literary forms in the early period, Koester pp.219–220.

37 Steiner, *Genesis*, London 1959, pp. 54ff. Steiner appeals to the angelology of the tradition under the name of Dionysius the Areopagite (pseudo-Dionysius), which in turn looks back to Paul, notably Ephesians 1:21 and Colossians 1:16. That his system reproduces Jewish esoteric angelology is confirmed by the discovery, embedded in the so-called 'Testament of Adam,' of 'The Hierarchy': the Exousiai are there rightly connected with the moon, sun and planets (stars), i.e. with the cosmic creation. The system is precisely that preserved by pseudo-Dionysius. See S.E. Robinson's edition in J.H. Charlesworth (ed.), *Old Testament Pseudepigrapha*, I, pp. 989ff, especially 995. The work is originally Jewish, and was perhaps 'a midrash on the creation story' (p. 991).

38 Steiner, *The Gospel of John* pp. 52ff, 74–5. Steiner refers also to the Pauline form of the teaching, presumably thinking particularly of Colossians. There we hear much about the 'elemental spirits of the universe' (2:20 RSV) and of 'the entire *pleroma* of the Deity' which 'dwells bodily in Christ' (2:9; cf. 1:19). Paul's exposition is complicated by allusion to the

misinterpretation of these matters by a group of opponents in
Colossae. Modern scholars disen-
tangle the matter differently. The
crux of the problem, I take it, is
that the Colossian opponents
accepted Jewish angel-doctrine,
but interpreted Christ simply as
one of the Elemental Spirits, not
as the Fullness of them all. Paul
must persuade them to leave
behind their teaching of the
seven spirits, because these are
present in new unity in Christ.
The 'Head' analogy, I further
take it, is Paul's contributed solution (cf. pp. 375ff above), not
something taken over from the
opponents as often claimed.

The importance (and sad neglect) of angel-Christology has
been recently stated by C.
Rowland, *The Open Heaven*,
London 1982, p. 112; and on
angelology, pp. 78ff. However,
he does not make the necessary
link with Creation. See in addition therefore the introduction to
creation-angelology in J.
Daniélou, *Theology of Jewish
Christianity*, London 1964, pp.
107ff and pp. 166ff. Challenging
as always is the more recent
study by M. Barker, *The Great
Angel*, London 1992. Whilst
undoubtedly bringing out the
huge importance of 'angelic'
conceptions, her rewriting of the
history of Judaism to include
them is perhaps too drastic. She
takes the Gnostic sources, for
example, seriously: but the effect
may be to show just how different one must assume early
Judaism would really have to
have been to generate later
Gnostic ideas! If on the other
hand one sees Gnosticism in
terms of an encounter between
Jewish and other streams — then
it may seem possible to find
more plausible models e.g. in the
cosmic myths still central in
Babylonia and Iran, which inter-
acted with native developments
in angelology. For the seven
angels in a 'Gnostic version,' cf.
the account given in the name of
Simon Magus. pp.121ff above.

For what we may now recognize as a Gnostic version of this
teaching, see the account of
Simon Magus, pp. 121ff above.

39 See my article 'The Identity of
the Archons in the *Apocryphon
Johannis*,' in the journal *Vigiliae
Christianae* 32 (1978), pp. 241–54,
especially pp. 243–7; and
'Reconstructing the Ophite
Diagram' in the journal *Novum
Testamentum* 23 (1981) 3, pp.
261ff (263).

40 J.B. Trapp, in J. Broadbent (ed.),
John Milton: Introductions,
Cambridge 1973, p. 166.

41 Epiphanius, *Panarion XX*, 16.

42 Reitzenstein, 'Eine frühchristliche
Schrift von der dreierlei Früchten
des christlichen Lebens' in the
journal *Zeitschrift für die neutesta-
mentliche Wissenschaft* 15 (1914),
pp.60ff. More on this esoteric text
(under its Latin name) in J.
Daniélou, *The Origins of Early
Latin Christianity*, London and
Philadelphia 1977, pp.63ff. He
finds evidence of 'very early' origins and Jewish-Christian ideas,
rather than appealing as did
Reitzenstein to Gnostic influence.
For the Christian inscription
from Miletus see Deissmann,
Licht vom Osten, Tübingen 1908,
p. 328.

43 C.H. Dodd, *The Fourth Gospel*
p.395.

44 Dodd, op. cit. pp. 401–2; cf. p.
421, 428.

45 Steiner, *The Gospel of John* pp.
170–173.

46 See Steiner, *Man in the Light of Occultism, Theosophy and Philosophy*, London 1964, pp. 155–6 — evidently correcting wrong impressions of his teaching about the 'initiation' stages in the Gospels.

47 Emil Bock, *The Three Years*, Edinburgh 1980, pp. 76ff and *passim*.

48 Bock, op. cit. pp. 46ff.

49 Steiner, *The Gospel of Matthew*, London 1965, pp. 219–20. See Gospel of Matthew 27:46; Mark 15:34.

50 Flusser, art. cit. p. 176. For the passage in the *Gospel of Peter*, see Schneemelcher, *New Testament Apocrypha* vol I p.224.

Bibliography

Many books, articles and commentaries are referred to in the Notes to this book. The following suggestions are limited to making accessible the main sources on which all study of Christian beginnings is based.

Firstly, a note on the Bible. The *New International Version* may be generally recommended among the available translations, not least because it takes cognizance of the older readings and versions now known from the 'Dead Sea Scrolls,' which include biblical texts far earlier than those formerly extant. Quotations in this book often make use of it, though for the purposes of bringing out a particular aspect I have also used other renderings.

The aim of biblical scholars is to get back to the most original form e.g. of the prophets or the historical books. Exciting in itself, however, is the fact that we can now read the greater part of the Hebrew Bible in the form known to the Essenes at the time of Jesus: see *The Dead Sea Scrolls Bible* ed. and trans. by M. Abegg, P. Flint and C. Ulrich; for the non-biblical Scrolls, or spiritual writings of the Essenes themselves, there is: Geza Vermes, *The Complete Dead Sea Scrolls in English*, Harmondsworth 1998. Some of the most important texts, especially those going back to the 'Teacher of Righteousness' are presented with introduction and commentary in Welburn, *Gnosis. The Mysteries and Christianity*, Edinburgh 1994.

The fullest presentation of the other non-biblical texts connected with the background of Christianity is: J.H. Charlesworth, *The Old Testament Pseudepigrapha* 2 volumes, with introductions and commentaries (London 1983, 1985). A smaller selection is: H.F.D. Sparks, *The Apocryphal Old Testament* (Oxford 1985).

For the writings discovered at Nag Hammadi, including the 'Cnew' Gospels, the full edition is: J .M. Robinson, *The Nag Hammadi Library* (Leiden 1988). Important texts belonging to Gnosticism, as it relates both to the Christian and pagan-

412 • *The Beginnings of Christianity*

Hermetic traditions, are again included in Welburn, *Gnosis. The Mysteries and Christianity* (details as above). More texts, especially from the later sectarian groups can be found in the selection by B. Layton, *The Gnostic Scriptures*, London 1987.

All the major Christian apocryphal texts are published in W. Schneemelcher, *New Testament Apocrypha*, vol. I, *Gospels and Related Writings*, London 1991; vol. II, *Writings Related to the Apostles*, London 1992.

A smaller selection, including the 'Secret Mark' fragment, is: R. Cameron, *The Other Gospels, Introductions and translations* (Philadelphia 1982).

A selection of the Essene, Gnostic and early Christian writings discussed in this book is found with a commentary in A.Welburn, *Gnosis the Mysteries and Christianity* (Edinburgh 1994).

The 'Secret Mark' and selections from the *Gospel of Philip* are illuminatingly presented against the backdrop of the older religious Mysteries in M. Meyer. *The Ancient Mysteries: A Source-Book*, San Francisco 1987.

Index of Biblical and Related References

C. Qumran Writings ("Dead Sea Scrolls")

D. Rabbinic Writings

E. New Testament

F. New Testament Apocrypha

G. Nag Hammadi and other Gnostic Writings

H. Early Church Literature

Index of Modern Authors

Sjöberg, E. 390
Smith, A. 142, 384, 404
Steiner, R. 9f, 39, 49, 53f, 59, 63, 66,
    70, 74, 80, 83ff, 105, 108ff, 116, 122,
    125, 133ff, 156ff, 174, 188ff, 193f,
    200, 208f, 211, 216, 218f, 233, 260ff,
    275, 280f, 295f, 302ff, 323, 327,
    337, 345ff, 361ff, 367f, 370ff, 400ff.
Stendahl, K. 378
Stone, M.E. 368, 370, 373, 375, 378

Talbert, C.H. 387
Tarn, W. 385
Thomas, J. 374
Thomas, K.V. 391
Trapp, J.B. 340, 408
Tröger, K.W. 385

Vermaseren, M. 393
Vermes, G. 368, 373, 388, 411

Vielhauer, P. 378, 379, 386

Waddington, C.H. 280, 401
Waitz, H. 378
Weihs, T. 400
Wedderburn, A.J. 406
Welburn, A.J. 368, 374, 377, 383,
    385, 388, 391, 393, 411f
Widengren, G. 118, 374f, 380f, 388,
    392, 401
Wilde, O. 27
Wilson, C. 371
Wilson, R.McL. 406
Wolf, C.U. 377
Wolff, H.W. 399
Wrede, W. 367

Yates, F. 387

Zaehner, R.C. 374, 388

Index of Subjects